Beyond Groupthink

Beyond Groupthink

Political Group Dynamics
and Foreign Policy-making

Edited by Paul 't Hart,
Eric K. Stern, and Bengt Sundelius

Ann Arbor

THE UNIVERSITY OF MICHIGAN PRESS

2004   2003   4   3

A CIP catalog record for this book is available from the British Library

Library of Congress Cataloging-in-Publication Data

Beyond groupthink : political group dynamics and foreign policy-making
   / edited by Paul 't Hart, Eric K. Stern, and Bengt Sundelius.
       p.   cm.
   Includes bibliographical references and index.
   ISBN 0-472-09653-2. — ISBN 0-472-06653-6 (pbk.)
   I. International relations—Decision-making.   2. Social groups.
   I. Hart, Paul 't.   II. Stern, Eric K.   III. Sundelius, Bengt.
   JX1391.B459   1997
   302.3—dc21   97-3410
                                                            CIP

Contents

Acknowledgments

The *Small Group Initiative* (SGI) was launched in 1993 as an international network of scholars interested in studying the dynamics of political decision making in small, high-level groups. The three editors of this volume founded SGI, but its momentum has since been maintained through the active participation of many colleagues across three continents. Numerous SGI workshops, conference panels, and other forms of interaction have been organized in the past three years. This volume is the first major collaborative product of this network, and we hope it will be followed by others, with other SGI colleagues at the helm.

We would like to acknowledge the contributors to this volume, who, in discussing one another's work during several sessions in preparation of this volume, have been most helpful. In addition, many other SGI members repeatedly have provided us and the authors with constructive criticism. Rick Guzzo, Dick Moreland, and Steve Walker deserve special mention for their thorough review of a previous version of the introductory chapter. Berndt Brehmer and Walter Carlsnaes of Uppsala University proved to be exemplary outside commentators on all of the chapters during an authors' workshop in Stockholm. Marieke Kleiboer from Leiden University gave the first and last chapters an extraordinarily perceptive reading. Charles F. Hermann and the students in his 1996 graduate seminar at Texas A&M University provided valuable, eleventh-hour feedback on the manuscript.

Peg Hermann and Bob Billings, coleaders of the National Science Foundation's Research and Training Group on Cognition and Collective Political Decision Making, have been a constant source of inspiration, encouragement, and assistance in the development of SGI. During the final stages of this project, Charles Parker of the Swedish Institute for International Affairs and Michelle Ariga of Stockholm University proved to be skillful and diligent copy editors, correcting many of our omissions and lapses. Donald Lavery of Stockholm University helped us out with conversions and other software queries. Finally, thanks are due to Uriel Rosenthal and other members of the Leiden-Rotterdam Crisis Research Center for taking care of business in Paul's absence during a particularly hectic semester.

Financial support came from several sources. First of all, the Stockholm Center for Organizational Research (SCORE) provided a major grant. Among others, this enabled Paul 't Hart to spend the spring of 1995 at the University of Stockholm to complete the editing of this book. Additional financial support for this extended research visit came from the Netherlands' Institute of Government, the national school for research in public administration in the Netherlands. The Swedish Council for Research in the Humanities and Social Sciences (HSFR) funded the authors' workshop in Stockholm in November 1994. Peg Hermann and the RTG (National Science Foundation Grant DIR-9113599) provided repeated financial support to RTG members involved in this project. The workshop program of the International Studies Association awarded a grant to Paul 't Hart and Steve Walker for a SGI workshop in Chicago in 1995, where parts of the book were discussed. Similar meetings took place at the 1994 Annual Meeting of the International Society for Political Psychology and the 1995 Joint Sessions of Workshops of the European Consortium of Political Research. During the formative years of SGI and this volume, Paul 't Hart was supported by an extended fellowship from the Royal Dutch Academy of Sciences. The support of all these organizations is gratefully acknowledged.

In many ways, the process of making this book resembles the object of study. Like most of the groups examined in the chapters to come, we as editors accept individual responsibility for any parts worthy of praise, while we shall refer our critics to the responsibility of the group as a whole for any errors or shortcomings. It goes without saying that the group process leading toward the completion of this book was characterized by vigilance. Although the editors operated as a highly cohesive team, we like to think that symptoms of groupthink were conspicuously absent. There might have been the odd bit of manipulation and perhaps a bit of entrapment here and there, but no doubt all of that has been to the benefit of the project. It is now up to our readers to assess the relationship between process and product.

Part 1
Groupthink and Beyond

CHAPTER 1

Foreign Policy-making at the Top: Political Group Dynamics

Paul 't Hart, Eric K. Stern, and Bengt Sundelius

Small Groups and Foreign Policy-making

Thursday, November 19, 1992, was a hectic day in Stockholm as well as in the international money markets around the world.[1] Just two months before, several European currencies were under pressure from waves of speculation. The British pound, the Italian lira, the Spanish peseta, and the Finnish mark all suffered heavily. The Swedish crown had escaped virtually unscathed, mostly due to the Bank of Sweden's decision to raise the overnight lending rate to 500 percent for a few days. This policy had received wide support from the conservative-led coalition government and the social democratic opposition.

Speculation was up again, and the Swedish crown was one of the main targets. The governing board of the Bank of Sweden met twice that day. First, during one of its weekly Thursday 7:30 A.M. sessions, this body of politically appointed officials decided to intervene heavily in the market through large purchases. This proved insufficient to stop the major outflow of currency during the rest of the morning. It appeared that in the last 72 hours, some 158 billion Swedish crowns worth of foreign currency (USD 29 billion) had left the country, depleting at an alarming rate the national hard currency reserve of some 177 billion.

The board reconvened in an emergency atmosphere at 2:00 P.M. Its ten members were fully aware that this time, the crisis could not be resolved by "the 500% solution" that had been used in September. The decision was made to let the currency float immediately as the huge New York money markets opened for business. At 2:15, the Head of the National Bank, Bengt Dennis, informed the conservative Prime Minister Carl Bildt of the board's decision, which was sure to have major political repercussions. Bildt asked for a short delay to enable him to confer with Ingvar Carlsson, the social democratic opposition leader. The Bank made its decision public at 2:28. The Swedish currency market closed at 3:00. By that time, the crown had dropped 10 percent in value, while the stock market had gained 4 percent (and another 9 percent the day after). Under pressure by the Swedish devaluation, the Spanish and Portuguese currencies were depreciated by 6 percent on Sunday and the Norwegian currency followed the Swedish float on December 10. The outcome of the crisis greatly embarrassed the government, which had been committed to a fixed rate policy, as a financial symbol for Swedish economic credibility abroad.

Although the crucial decision had been made by the independent Bank board, the cabinet had played a role in the drama, too. In the days before "Black Thursday," intensive negotiations had been conducted between a small group of representatives from the government with their opposition counterparts. The aim was to produce a bipartisan austerity budget package that would strengthen international confidence in the Swedish economy. This had been vital to the successful management of the September crisis. On Wednesday, November 18, the group, composed of the same people who had produced the September compromise, met several times. By 10:00 P.M., the government negotiators hand-delivered a draft agreement to the prime negotiator for the Social Democratic Party. This was backed up by a phone call slightly before midnight from Prime Minister Bildt to opposition leader Carlsson, who told Bildt that the executive committee of his party could not meet to discuss the proposals until the next morning. Before that, no firm decision could be made.

The government's negotiating team faxed through a definitive set of austerity proposals by 2:30 A.M. and waited eagerly for the opposition's response. At 5:00 A.M., the minister of finance became anxious and called the opposition's headquarters for a response, but none was yet available. She got the same message an hour later when she called her counterpart in the Social Democratic Party, former finance minister Allan Larsson. She then conferred with Bengt Dennis, the head of the National Bank.

Feeling the pressure of yet another day of uncontrollable currency trading, the conservative minority coalition cabinet had to go out on a limb and presented its own budget package at an 8:30 A.M. press conference on November 19. The social democratic executive met and announced by 11:20 that it would not support the proposed austerity package. The news that in this currency crisis there was no bipartisan support spread quickly. It was in this feverish atmosphere that the governors of the National Bank met again, and decided to present the cabinet with their fateful "fait accompli." The Swedish currency at 2:28 floated for the first time since 1933.

This example illustrates something about the nature of foreign policy-making well-known to insiders but often overlooked by observers and scholars: many important decisions and developments in foreign policy are shaped in relatively small groups and informal face-to-face interaction. As the Swedish case shows, these groups may take a range of forms. Policy in this case evolved from the interplay between the cabinet, a bipartisan negotiation team, a major opposition party's executive committee, and the governing board of the National Bank. Each of these groups had a distinct profile in terms of its composition, durability, prerogatives, and interaction rules, among other differences. Each of them played an essential role in the crisis. At the time, their behavior could not be easily predicted, not even by insiders. To explain why they acted as they did, it is necessary to study their internal dynamics more closely.

The case of the Swedish monetary crisis does not stand out on its own. There are many more examples where crucial episodes in a country's foreign policy are shaped by relatively small elite groups. In the postwar period alone, for example, the British cabinet has been the site of some fateful foreign policy decisions, including the decolonization of India, the Suez invasion, the EEC application, the devaluation of the pound sterling, and to a certain extent the Falklands war. In its time, the Soviet Politburo was crucially important. It made the crucial decisions to intervene in Hungary and Czechoslovakia, and the ill-fated choice to invade Afghanistan. The groups involved may also be less conspicuous and more informal: President Kennedy's ExCom during the Cuban missile crisis, the six "wise men" that were occasionally consulted by U.S. presidents, President Mitterrand's inner circle of advisers for foreign and security affairs, or an interdepartmental committee preparing a member state's negotiating posture for a new EU intergovernmental conference.

Despite this apparent variety and incomparability, each of these groups are small-scale social units where political leaders, officials, experts, and perhaps representatives from political parties and interest groups meet, enact their respective roles, exchange information, argue, exert and experience influence, and somehow arrive at shared understandings and decisions. The central idea underlying this book and related works on the role of small groups in the policy-making process is that many aspects of foreign policy are shaped by small groups such as cabinets, committees, commissions, and cliques. Furthermore, it is argued that in many crucial cases, the resulting policies cannot be predicted by parsimonious models of rational choice, nor can the behavior and outcomes of these policy-making groups be fully explained by meso-level decision-making models, such as Allison's paradigms of organizational process and bureaucratic politics.

Therefore, it is important to study the dynamics of these groups in their own right. Instead of assuming that what goes on in these groups is a mere reflection or artifact of the larger organizational, political, and even international system structure of which they are a part, the small group perspective suggests that they form the scene of rather complex and relatively unpredictable social-psychological dynamics. These group-level interactions may have a profound impact on the process and outcomes of foreign policy-making. Small groups, in other words, often serve as a bridge between impersonal and institutional forces on the one hand, and concrete decisions and actions by political leaders on the other (Vertzberger 1990). Hence it is important for foreign policy analysts to study such group-level factors as composition (who is in, who remains out of the decisional loop?), interpersonal dynamics (who has the ear of the leader, who does not?), and leadership (has the leader made up her mind or does she want to hear all possible options?).

The Small Group Approach to Foreign Policy Analysis

This volume seeks to increase our awareness of the political group dynamics of foreign policy-making. Its authors present a variety of analytical tools for gaining a better understanding of the forces inside and around high-level policy groups that determine their impact on policies and actions. The kinds of small group analysis presented here are part of the decision-making approach to foreign policy analysis, as pioneered by Snyder, Bruck, and Sapin (1962).[2] A key premise of this approach is that to understand foreign policy choices, one needs to study the process by which they are made. This encompasses the ways in which issues come to be perceived as problems, alternative courses of action are articulated and considered, and specific courses of action eventually become dominant (Mintzberg, Raisinghani, and Theoret 1976; Burnstein and Berbaum 1983; Anderson 1983, 1987). To do so, decision-making theorists argue, one needs to study the behavior of policymakers as individuals, in groups, and in the context of organizations. It is crucial to understand how policymakers construct and maintain worldviews, how they arrive at definitions of the situation they are facing at particular critical junctures, and how they argue, negotiate, and fight over what ought to be done and how (Ripley 1993).

A decision-making analysis is not particularly parsimonious in explaining or predicting foreign policy behavior. Instead, however, it aims at a more in-depth, comprehensive explanation of how major foreign policy developments come about. This becomes particularly important if one sees it as the responsibility of scholars to produce policy-relevant theories of foreign policy, for example, theories that identify crucial variables that can actually be manipulated by actors in the foreign policy process (George 1993; Hill and Besthoff 1994). Decision-making analysis is almost by definition multi-disciplinary. It draws upon cognitive and social psychology, organization theory, sociology, anthropology, and political science (Neack, Hay, and Haney 1995).

Once regarded as anathema to the scientific study of foreign policy, the decision-making approach has by now gained an established position as an indispensable counterweight and complement to more general, abstract, and parsimonious theories of international relations and foreign policy (Voss and Dorsey 1992). It is specifically geared toward explaining policies that are at odds with predictions based upon system-level, rational-choice, or other input-output models of international politics, or where the high level of generality and abstraction of such theories make them underdeterminate (Lebow 1981; Khong 1992; Ripley 1993). Furthermore, it extends and complements the logic of the school of comparative foreign policy analysis, which was also premised on the idea that the organization and procedures of policy-making made an important difference in shaping the foreign policy behavior of states (Rosenau 1966, 1967, 1974; East, Salmore, and Hermann 1978). It has been especially prolific in analyses of state behavior during international crises (Hermann 1972; Holsti 1972; Holsti and George 1975; Brecher 1980, 1993; Lebow 1981; Roberts 1988; Lebow and Stein 1994; Richardson 1994).

In the present volume, we seek to enhance the analytical repertoire of the decision-making approach by concentrating upon the role of small groups in the foreign policy process. So far, the policy-making of advisory groups has received less attention than the behavior of individual leaders, whose personalities, belief systems, problem definitions, decisional conflicts, and information-processing styles have been amply documented (Rosati 1995). Likewise, interest in group dynamics pales in comparison with the volume of work on the role of bureaucratic organizations, whose routines, structural features, culture, internal politics, and interrelationships have received equally exhaustive attention (Wilensky 1967; Allison 1971; Halperin 1974; Steinbruner 1974).

In contrast, attention for the small group as a unit of decision in foreign policy has mainly been guided by Irving Janis's highly influential work on groupthink (Janis 1972, 1982). As will be explained further below and in chapters 2 and 3, however, Janis has concentrated his efforts on a rather specific feature of small group behavior in foreign policy. As a consequence, many other aspects of small groups investigated by social psychologists and management theorists and initially recognized as important by political scientists have received relatively little attention in foreign policy analysis (Verba 1962; Golembiewski 1962; yet see Hermann 1978; George 1980; Minix 1982; Vertzberger 1990; and Gaenslen 1992).

Core Assumptions

Before going into the substance of small group behavior in foreign policy, it may be useful to specify two basic, interrelated premises of the small group perspective. First, *small group factors have a distinct, and significant, poten-*

tial explanatory power in the analysis of foreign policy. Small groups are far
more significant entities in the foreign policy-making process than is generally
recognized. They are in fact ubiquitous. Analysts and practitioners of foreign
policy-making will be the first to recognize the pivotal role played by certain
committees, negotiation platforms, study groups, inner circles, and informal
cliques, yet they seldom view them as comparable units of collective decision
making (e.g., as small groups) that may exhibit certain recurrent features and
behavioral patterns that can be studied systematically. The small group perspective assumes that given this ubiquity of committees, teams, and the like,
doing just that is worth the effort.

Two broad classes of situations are particularly germane to small group
analysis. First, small group analysis is of course most pertinent in instances
where a single small group is at the apex of the policy-making process. The
small group is the ultimate decision unit, and as such its dynamics are as close
to the dependent variable (the decisions) as they can be. Secondly, however,
small group analysis is also extremely important when policies arise from the
interplay between a number of interlocking small groups. The locus of initiative and decision here is less clearly definable, but the sequence of events
suggests that it is at least plausible to assume that the dynamics *within* as well
as the relations *between* the participating groups are among the significant
forces shaping the substance of policy.

The second major assumption is that *the purpose of small group analysis
is to help us explain better the crucial, formative policy decisions that shape
significant parts of a country's foreign policy.* In other words, small group
analysis is particularly pertinent to describe and analyze the origins of those
watershed policy episodes that are sufficiently consequential, controversial, or
precedent-setting to generate an intrinsic interest as to how they came about. It
is these kinds of decisions that we study to learn more about the core values
and operating logic of the system as whole, and the quality of those who are in
charge of it at a particular juncture in history.

We mentioned earlier that small group analysis is not a parsimonious
undertaking. In fact, it raises a number of crucial methodological challenges,
and it is not conducive to producing sweeping generalizations (see Gaenslen
1992, 172–76). The small group approach produces instead an analytical tool
kit suitable to fine-grained reconstruction and explanation of why certain
major, puzzling, often controversial policy initiatives occurred. It also forms
the basis for systematic counterfactual analysis of where these initiatives
could plausibly have taken a different turn. In both cases, small group analysis
can form the basis for policy recommendations that may help policymakers
organize and manage the decision-making process in ways that prevent them
from making avoidable errors of judgment.

Toward a Contingent Approach
to Small Group Analysis

The key assumptions mentioned above suggest that small group analysis in foreign policy is most productive in particular types of situations. At present, we do not possess an empirically grounded set of contingency rules specifying in a more operational sense when small group prominence is most likely to occur in the foreign policy process. It is doubtful, moreover, if there could ever be one: structures of decision making are highly variable across political systems, policy domains, and incumbent governments (Blondel 1982). One way to handle this problem is to try to trace the locus of initiative in foreign policy on a case-by-case basis, taking into account the specifics of the institutional context (Hermann 1978; Hermann and Hermann 1982, 1989). This is a time-consuming affair. An acceptable compromise would be to adopt a few rules of thumb about which types of issues are most likely to generate small group prominence (and thus to warrant small group analysis). Two such rules may be mentioned here.

First, small group analysis is imperative for foreign policy issues that generate small group dominance as a matter of standard operating procedures. These include routine, low and medium politics issues just complex and important enough to warrant collective decision making rather than handling by individual officials, yet not controversial enough to arouse a larger number of stakeholders and forums. The groups in question here are typically standing committees or task forces, and the decisions taken are at least formally subject to high-level political and bureaucratic clearance. As long as the group proposals are judged to be relatively well-programmed or inconsequential by senior-level policymakers, they will not interfere (Rosati 1981).

Second, small group analysis should also include issues that are deemed crucially important by major stakeholders in the political system. These types of issues tend to be handled at the pinnacle of government. These include major foreign policy crises (acute security threats, monetary destabilization, alliance crises), but also less extreme, yet highly consequential and politically divisive foreign issues (such as major international treaty negotiations that may commit the country in significant ways). Groups play a role in this process in two ways: either as the forum where the key decisions are made in a collegial setting, or as crucial advisory bodies to chief executives making individual decisions.[3] In examining the latter, it is important to focus on those cases where groups mediate the executive's access to information and expertise.

A crucial caveat is in order. Establishing that in a particular case of foreign policy decision making the crucial choices were arrived at in a small group setting does *not* imply that the decisions made can be fully explained by small group factors. On the contrary, small groups in politics are always embedded in a web of institutional forces and environments that may provide powerful opportunities and constraints shaping their behavior. The mode of small group analysis advanced in this volume will pay due respect to the embedded nature of small group interaction. We shall return to this point later in this chapter ("Moving beyond Groupthink"). Yet first we will embed this volume in the intellectual context from which it emerged, for example, the pioneering work of Irving L. Janis on groupthink.

The Roots of the Small Group Approach: Groupthink Revisited

The publication of *Victims of Groupthink: A Psychological Study of Foreign Policy Decisions and Fiascoes* by Irving Janis (1972) has proven to be a turning point in our understanding of the role of small groups in foreign policymaking. Janis studied a number of historical fiascoes in American foreign policy, notably the lack of preparedness for the Japanese attack on Pearl Harbor (1941), the escalation of the war in Korea (1950), the failed U.S.-sponsored landing of anti-Castro rebels in the Bay of Pigs (1961), and the escalation of U.S. involvement in the war in Vietnam under President Johnson (1964–68). Each of these episodes went badly: the policymakers did not achieve their major goals, massive violence and many casualties resulted, and the government suffered a serious loss of domestic and international prestige.

Based on his detailed investigation of these episodes, Janis suggested that in each of them, the major decisions that shaped the course of events were reached after insufficient and unsystematic thinking and discussion. To bring this out more clearly, he contrasted them with two cases of policy success where policies had been developed in a more rigorous process (the making of the 1947 Marshall plan and the 1962 Cuban missile crisis). Specifically, Janis argued that in each of the failure cases, the decision-making process had been distorted by what he called *groupthink:* a tendency toward premature and extreme concurrence-seeking within a cohesive policy-making group under stress. In each of the cases, key decisions were made by a cohesive small group composed of a leader (the president, and in the Pearl Harbor case the base commander Admiral Kimmel) and his closest advisers. And in each case, reconstruction of the group's deliberations seemed to show that the group members were keen to preserve the mood of optimism and presumed agreement that prevailed. This desire to minimize controversy compromised the quality of the discussion: crucial information was ignored or misinterpreted, alternatives to the group's preferred course of action were not considered or not taken seriously, and the groups tended to persist in their original policies even when confronted with feedback that the policies were not working out well or that they were fraught with risks.

In his later work, Janis developed his initial hypothesis into a more fully articulated theory of groupthink (Janis 1982), and in turn embedded this in a broader theory of executive decision making (Janis 1989). Parallel to this, a significant number of follow-up studies have appeared. These have ranged from detailed laboratory experiments testing specific parts of the causal chain put forward in groupthink theory, to case studies of other historical episodes of decision making in government and business. Furthermore, various attempts have been made to revise and improve the theory.

In the meantime, groupthink has quickly become a standard item in textbooks in social psychology, organization and management, and public policy-making. This instant popularity must be looked at with caution. It is important to be aware of the limitations of groupthink analysis. For one, we do not know how frequently it occurs. Most of the documented cases of groupthink concern instances of U.S. foreign policy-making, and Janis (1982) speculated—not particularly plausibly—that groupthink would occur twice as much in America as in European countries. Andeweg (1991), observing such national differences, convincingly argues that they can be traced in part to institutional variations in the organization of government. In his view, the lack of continuity in the U.S. presidential staff makes this administrative system more vulnerable to groupthink than Western European systems, in which the government can rely on a more permanent and experienced staff. In addition, vulnerability to groupthink is presumably determined by the amount of political heterogeneity within government. Coalition cabinets, common in many Western European states, with ministers having different political backgrounds and different departmental responsibilities, will be less likely to suffer from groupthink than the generally more homogeneous American presidency, let alone a dictatorial regime. In countries with relatively strong political parties and departments the chances of groupthink may be much more marked at the level of subcabinet factions, including departmental cliques, coalition partners, or factions of hegemonic parties, like the Liberal Democrats in Japan or the Social Democrats in Sweden (Andeweg 1991).

It seems eminently reasonable, therefore, to treat groupthink as a contingent phenomenon, rather than as a general property of foreign policy decision making in high-level groups. Unfortunately, the very popularity of Janis's work has tended to obscure this simple conclusion. A cursory look at the standard textbooks on foreign policy-making will reveal that if they deal with small group decision making at all, the presentation is likely to be dominated by the groupthink phenomenon, inadvertently equating "group decision making" with "groupthink." This is a gross simplification, betraying the enormous variety of groups and group processes that play a part in foreign policy-

making which, ironically, had been recognized by early analysts not infatuated with the powerful groupthink heuristic (Snyder, Bruck, and Sapin 1962;
De Rivera 1968). Moreover, the general preoccupation with "the dangers of
groupthink" found in the foreign policy literature echoes pervasive tendencies
in contemporary social psychology to cling to a negatively biased view of
groups, forgoing an impressive body of evidence detailing the many positive
aspects of group behavior (cf. Moscovici and Doise 1994). Janis is to be
applauded for his explicit concern with drawing practical lessons for policymakers from his analysis, but we must be careful to remember that the lessons
of groupthink analysis are not the only possible prescriptions that may follow
from small group analysis of foreign policymaking (see 't Hart, this volume).

In short, it is time to put Janis's impressive legacy in its proper perspective and go "beyond groupthink" in studying small group decision making in
foreign policy. A crucial first step in this direction is to map out a broader
research agenda. In the remainder of this chapter, we shall attempt to sketch
some key ideas and principles guiding our joint efforts in this volume to
develop this agenda. The core of these ideas is twofold:

1. Policy-making and advisory groups take a variety of shapes and
   forms, and they perform widely different functions in the foreign
   policy process ("Beyond Groupthink [I]").
2. Policy-making and advisory groups are embedded in an institutional
   and political context that constrains and facilitates their performance
   ("Beyond Groupthink [II]").

Beyond Groupthink (I): The Many Faces
of Small Groups in the Policy Process

One of the crucial problems facing small group analysis originates in the sheer
variety of small groups in the foreign policy process. Research in social
psychology has documented extensively, if not ad nauseam, that seemingly
simple factors such as group size, the physical arrangements of the group
discussion, the order of presentations by individual members, the length of
time available for discussion, and the rules of decision making can have a
profound impact on what groups do and how well they do it (Hare 1976; Shaw
1981; McGrath 1984; Forsyth 1990). Beyond that, social psychologists have
detected a wealth of other, less obvious characteristics of group structure and
process that are similarly important (for example Steiner 1972; Gladstein
1984; Turner 1987; Moscovici and Doise 1994). And the list is growing rather
than shrinking.

How does this play out in the specific context of foreign policy-making?
How can we make sense of the dynamics of the widely different types of

groups and group settings that we can find in the foreign policy process? The answer is not obvious: we do not know (yet). We do not at present possess an empirically grounded typology of policy-making groups that can be related to a coherent body of hypotheses or even educated guesses about what sort of interaction is likely to ensue in each type of group involved. There are just too many potentially relevant group properties that could be used as a basis for such a typology. Another way of handling this question is not to start with a typology of groups, but with a differentiation of the various roles that groups play in the policy process. Here, insights from social psychology can be usefully merged with those from research on public policy-making and management studies (Bryson and Crosby 1992; Gaenslen 1992; Meertens and Wilke 1993; Moscovici and Doise 1994, 79; Nutt 1989). As will be shown below, awareness of these various functions provides us with a richer analytical starting point than the conventional exclusive focus on decision making in a more narrow sense. The next step would then be to check whether particular group roles are typically performed by groups with certain properties, and eventually to develop a typology that combines group characteristics with group functions in the policy process. Below we discuss a number of manifestations of groups in foreign policy-making.

Information Processing: The Group as "Think Tank"
When Janis wrote about groupthink as a pathology of the foreign policy-making process, his underlying assumption was that a key task for policy-making bodies is reality testing (Janis 1989; see also Burke and Greenstein 1989; Turner 1991). One reason for working with groups and teams in organizations in the first place is that if they work well as a unit, they are demonstrably superior to individuals when it comes to processing information about novel, complex, and unstructured problems.

These types of problems are typical of high-level policy-making. A common task for foreign policymakers is to interpret events and trends in their domestic and international political, economic, and security environment. This interpretation process occurs at different levels. At the most abstract level of foreign and defense policy strategy, efforts to rethink the basic premises of the hard core of a country's policy are often triggered by major contingencies and crises in the international system, for example the collapse of the Bretton Woods monetary system in 1971, the collapse of communism in Eastern Europe in 1989, and the dissolution of the Soviet Union in 1991.

At the most concrete level of day-to-day policy-making, the organization of the policy process usually provides periodic, predictable occasions for preparation and reconsideration of positions. One example of this would be the process of European Union policy-making with its elaborate rounds of consultation and negotiation, each of which requires issue area specialists in the member states to assess the situation and determine their stance on the problems of the day. But there may also be specific, unscheduled occasions where a close monitoring and interpretation of international events is called for. This occurs when there is bilateral, multilateral, or indeed widespread international tension in such divergent matters as trade (fishing disputes, boycotts), finance (stock market fluctuations, acute balance of payment and debt problems in key countries, major currency de- and reevaluations), environment (transnational pollution accidents), or security (escalation of ongoing disputes, border violations).

The group as think tank metaphor zooms in on the dynamics of group information processing. This encompasses, firstly, the ways in which the group arrives at a common representation of events (Moreland and Levine 1992). Furthermore, it deals with the extent to which during the deliberations, group members come to share information available to them with their colleagues (Stasser 1992). It also looks at the process by which groups make inferences from the information available to them and develop a composite picture of its implications for past, present, and future policies (for example, Poole and Hirokawa 1986; Leary and Forsyth 1987; Hirokawa, Gouran, and Martz 1988).

The upshot of groupthink analysis is that it shows in a dramatic way that the process by which some groups solicit and interpret information as the basis for policy adjustments may be less than optimal. As a result, important events may go unnoticed, serious threats may be played down, potential alternatives to the present policy go unprobed, and latent opportunities pass by unexploited. In the case of the critical episodes investigated by Janis and other groupthink analysts, these flaws in the process of group perception, and, literally, group thinking, turned out to have catastrophic results, thus illustrating the truth of Craig and George's observation that in international diplomacy "disaster is always a single bad decision away" (1990, 201).

Authority and Choice: The Group as "Command Center"
The other powerful assumption underlying groupthink analysis and indeed many other small group analyses of foreign policy-making is that, in the case(s) under examination, the group constitutes the site where "values are allocated authoritatively" (Easton 1965; see Hermann and Hermann 1982, 1989). The picture is one of collective decision making at the pinnacle of government: a well-defined, relatively small-scale unit having the power and responsibility to make authoritative choices about the ends and means of foreign policy and to see to it that these choices are put into practice by the bureaucratic apparatus. In addition, the command center metaphor refers to the idea of a cabinet or high council of government as the key locus of

attempts to control societal images of and responses to major foreign events (Halper 1971; Edelman 1988).

As we have noted above, among the situations that most closely resemble this situation of top-level collegial choice, coordination, and control of policy-making are international crises. When things become politically hot, and especially when there is an acute threat of war, situational pressures, political logic, and constitutional practices combine to produce a contraction of decisional authority at the highest levels of government (Hermann 1963; Brecher 1993; cf. 't Hart, Rosenthal, and Kouzmin 1993). In parliamentary systems, political and military leaders will confer intensively in the context of special cabinet committees or "war cabinets" (Stein and Tanter 1980; Hill 1991; Verbeek 1992; Stern 1992). Although in presidential systems the chief executive tends to be granted sweeping personal powers to deal with these kinds of situations, he will generally arrive at his decisions in the context of intensive formal and informal group meetings with his most senior advisers and national political leaders (George 1980; Rose and Suleiman 1983).

Given this pivotal role for small groups as loci of decision and control in foreign policy crises, it becomes essential to study how these groups arrive at their decisions and coordinate a huge, complex, and error- and resistance-prone implementation process. The information processing that is crucial to the group as think tank notion now becomes merely one among a wider range of factors to be taken into account. A key additional issue raised by the group as command center is leadership and power. A distinction needs to be made between the power *of* the group and power *over* the group.

The *power of the group* refers to the degree in which the group is able to effectively coordinate and control foreign policy actions undertaken on its behalf. Allison (1971) provided colorful descriptions of the problems that Kennedy's inner circle experienced in maintaining control over U.S. military operations during the height of the Cuban missile crisis. Subsequently, a whole range of other analysts have shown that coordination and control in foreign policy implementation are far from given. They are in fact subject to constant enforcement and (re)negotiation in the relationship between political elites and the foreign policy and defense apparatus (Karvonen and Sundelius 1987). During security crises, for example, military leaders and field commanders tend to possess considerable discretion in interpreting political decisions about the use of force, and they tend to do so with reference to powerful norms and routines of their own organizations (Bracken 1983; Steinbruner 1974; Bouchard 1991; Sagan 1991). Likewise, the physical distance between foreign ministries and embassies may be reproduced in considerable social distance between central executives and field operatives, which translates itself in divergent perceptions, assessments, and action propensities regarding outstanding issues with the host country (Metselaar and Verbeek 1995). This "appreciative gap" may produce considerable center-field tensions and a series of attempts by the center group to increase its control (Boin and Otten 1996). It may, however, also compromise the position within the group of the minister or official responsible for that part of the apparatus, in particular when his colleagues begin to form a more generalized impression that he "cannot deliver" or has "gone native."

The issue of *power over the group* evolves around the question of control over group decisions: if the group is (supposed to be) in command of policy, who is in command of the group (Barber 1965; Fenno 1962; Maoz 1990)? One predominant feature of groups in organizational and governmental settings is that their members have unequal status. This goes much further than the truism that there is always a certain leadership in any group, whether appointed or emergent, and individual or collective. Most policy-making groups have a complex, finely tuned informal hierarchy, shaping the interpersonal relations between their members (Thompson 1961; George 1980). Many though by no means all senior political executives can exert great influence upon the composition of their advisory groups, the agenda for discussion, the framing of issues, and the rules of interaction prevailing in the group ('t Hart, 1990/1994, 174). For example, one of the primary sources of influence for British prime ministers is their power of appointment and dismissal of ministers, but perhaps more importantly their control over the composition of cabinet committees, which increasingly have become the spot where the real policy discussions take place (James 1991). Likewise, they can shape the very purpose and nature of group deliberation. De Rivera long ago suggested that there are important differences across U.S. presidents in this regard, a finding subsequently documented by many students of presidential foreign policy-making:

> Often, meetings are conducted in quite a different way . . . President Truman essentially directed a discussion with the aim of helping *himself* make a decision. Neustadt's description of one of President Eisenhower's regular cabinet meetings, shows the President *guiding* a discussion with the aim of having the group make a decision or reach a consensus (De Rivera 1968, 225).

Absent constitutionally powerful or personally dominant formal leaders, however, the scope for informal types of leadership to become prominent increases. Informal leaders may be group members possessing critical resources (such as ministers of finance or military leaders), vital information and specialist expertise, or effective interpersonal skills. They may also effectively use coalitions with other group members. Just as the group as a whole sometimes exerts more of a rhetorical than a real control over the conduct and implementation of policy, however, so do leaders over the behavior of the group. Much depends on whether they observe the limitations placed upon their power by the group's role structure and norms. Although it is commonly held that leaders enjoy considerable "idiosyncrasy credit" (Hollander 1978), empirical research on power in high-level management teams suggests that this is only true up to a point:

> [The] obligation to act within the bounds of a role does not decrease as one assumes higher positions of authority; a role may grant more discretion in how it is enacted, but there are normative constraints to even the highest level positions. The cabinet officers we described had, in some instances, tens of thousands of subordinates and billion-dollar budgets, but they, no less than a clerk, were constrained to perform their roles in such a way as to demonstrate their obeisance to norms. Even chief executives must exercise power within the norms of authority. (Woolsey-Biggart and Hamilton 1984, 548)

In governmental settings, the consequences of norm violation may be severe in terms of reputation damage among peers, bad press, punitive responses by other actors, and even the formation of coalitions of opponents. To study this interplay of positions, powers, and personalities within the group as it interacts with other parts of the foreign policy apparatus is an important challenge for future research.

Social Support for Policymakers: The Group
as "Sanctuary"
The foreign policy-making environment subjects practitioners to powerful chronic stressors. The burdens of office tend to be heavy. Decision makers are often overworked, understaffed, and struggling to cope with one deadline after another. Making strategic foreign policy decisions tends to be full of pitfalls, endangering interests, reputations, and careers virtually overnight. These combined pressures may get to decision makers. At worst, they picture their environment as dominated by personal enemies, political rivals, and ever-present sensationalist mass media, all keen to exploit moments of vulnerability. For this reason, the hostile nature of the policy context has led some observers to liken foreign policy-making to combat, or, to paraphrase Clausewitz, to view politics as warfare conducted by other means.

Furthermore, it is rarely possible to satisfy all or even a large segment of the constituencies affected by major policy decisions. Value trade-offs are inevitable in decisions about war and peace, signing disarmament treaties, joining or leaving alliances or intergovernmental bodies, or major currency reforms. Deep-rooted values and policy principles may clash with organizational expediency and the imperatives of *Realpolitik*. In some cases, they may take the form of tragic choices between equally unattractive alternatives, sure to solicit harmful consequences and widespread criticism. Such trade-offs may evoke decisional conflict and high levels of stress in officeholders (Janis and Mann 1977; George 1980).

Not surprisingly, senior policymakers often develop a need for emotional support. They may find this in several places: in personal assistants and advisers (Woodrow Wilson and Colonel House, Franklin Roosevelt and Harry Hopkins), siblings (John and Robert Kennedy), cronies (Richard Nixon and Bebe Rebozo, Dwight Eisenhower and his golf crowd), spouses (Margaret and Denis Thatcher), personal physicians, priests, truth tellers, and other "fuzzy" outsiders (Nancy Reagan and her astrologist). In many cases, however, small groups of close associates perform this same function. They act as a place of refuge from the pressures and dilemmas of responsibility. Members are drawn together by bonds of joint socialization, party loyalties, personal friendship, joint enemies, and common fate. The group can provide the members (or the dominant leader) with the security and comfort they seek. These typically derive from the individual's knowledge that here is a group of trusted and liked associates who share his worldview, his values and concerns, and who have a first-hand understanding of the predicaments he is facing. Any inner doubts he may have about certain issues or parts of his performance can be held at bay by the confidence and approbation of one's peers.

For groups in the policy process to fulfill this function, they must be close-knit and informal, almost like primary groups. Occasionally, cabinets or councils as a whole may develop strong collegial and personal bonds, especially when they are able to chart a common course in the face of overwhelming external pressures. However, the consensus and cohesion that occur in these rather large and politically stacked groups are often contrived, ambivalent, and easily offset (see for example Woodward 1979, on the U.S. Supreme Court). It is more likely that relatively small circles of innermost advisers or key colleagues will assume the sanctuary role. These groups and their meetings often do not show up on the organization charts and appointment calendars, but they can be tremendously influential. In many cases, their existence is known only to insiders, and it becomes apparent to observers only via painstaking retrospective investigation.

The positive effects of peer-group support on the task performance of high-level policymakers should not be underestimated. Without them it is likely that many more decision makers would fall prey to premature burnout, cumulative exhaustion, and even breakdown. Yet as Janis (1972) so eloquently noted, there is a risk that maintaining such group sanctuaries may have insidious effects on the policy-making process. There may be a thin line between advisers offering emotional support and becoming sycophants to a dominant leader. Leaders and group members may be led to overestimate their own effectiveness, that of their colleagues, and that of the group as a whole. They may come to underestimate the abilities and political potency of rivals. The availability of the group as a place to hide may set in motion processes of social loafing and diffusion of responsibility known to be pernicious to the quality of joint action from social psychology and management studies (Allison and Messick 1987, 111–12; Harvey 1988). One major challenge for small group research is to explore the borderline between the positive and pernicious effects of peer-group support in the policy process. The key issue is to identify the factors that enable a group to perform the sanctuary function, without detracting from the group's reality-testing potential.

Conflict Management: The Group as "Arena"
It may be true, as one Canadian provincial premier once remarked, that "ministries do the fighting in government, not ministers" (White 1994, 255). Apparently, one should not overrate the importance of conflict in collegial political decision making at the pinnacle of government (Burch 1993, 122; Nousiainen 1993, 281). At the same time, however, studies of policy coordination have shown time and again how difficult it can be to achieve a common understanding and consensus on a course of action when powers and responsibilities for handling certain issues are shared between two or more policymakers and agencies (Dunsire 1978; Hanf and Scharpf 1978; Jenkins and Gray 1985).

Political divisions—whether they be intraparty factional battles or squabbles between coalition partners—and bureaucratic politics provide two powerful centrifugal forces that beset collegial decision making (Andeweg 1988). Foreign affairs and national security provide no exception to this rule, despite the strong rhetorical emphasis placed in many countries on the existence of a unitary (e.g., "the") national interest. Ironically, instead of serving as a superordinate goal integrating various agencies and officials in the foreign affairs arena, the insistence upon a uniform and more or less objectively given national interest has tended at times to spark off intensive maneuvering and infighting to get one's own interpretation of "the" national interest accepted as the dominant frame of reference in the collective decision making and policy coordination process (Huntington 1961; Halperin 1974; George and Keohane 1980; Gabriel 1985; Kozak and Eagle 1988; Maoz 1991). A clear example of this process at work can be found in the bitter personal, bureau-political, and interpersonal struggles within the British cabinet over the choice of a manufacturer for new army helicopters (Dunleavy 1990).

Not all of the sensitivities, tensions, maneuvers, stalemates, and interorganizational bargaining that occur in the interagency coordination process escalate to the senior executive level. Yet bureaucratic and political conflicts do form the daily stuff of many subcabinet policy-making groups. Such groups are best thought of as arenas, as stages for the enactment of conflict and negotiation between various institutional stakeholders. Their representatives to the group meeting are acting out their organizational roles, guided by their agency's prearranged briefs and mediated by their personal capabilities, styles, and experiences.

Rather than being sites of predictable and unmitigated "tribal warfare," many coordination committees are more profitably conceptualized as mixed-motive groups. They deal with an ever-changing array of issues, each of which generates a different configuration of incentives for confrontation and cooperation. Consequently, in many cases bargaining and compromise formation, however tenuous, contrived, and implicit, rather than all-out conflict, tend to be characteristic of what goes on in these committees. The key question for research here is how this setting of divergent perspectives and interests, mixed motives, and bureau-political role-playing affects the group's deliberation process and outcomes.

Organizing the Anarchy: The Group as "Sorter"
A seemingly mundane dimension of the practice of policy-making is to organize the flow of work. In all complex, bureaucratic organizations where division of labor is a core feature, a lot of time and effort is routinely devoted by senior executives to making decisions about where certain issues and problems are to be dealt with. The importance of this kind of meta-level or procedural decision making cannot be underestimated (Dror 1968). If one accepts the view of government as an organized anarchy characterized by ambiguous goals, unstable participation, and underspecified technologies for action, it follows that for every problem it addresses, its goals and means have to be discovered and continually adjusted by a variable set of stakeholders (Cohen, March, and Olsen 1972; Kingdon 1984; Bryson and Crosby 1992). From this perspective, determining which issue gets talked about by whom, when, under what circumstances, governed by which procedures, and with what kind of mandate then becomes much more important than as a mere procedural matter. It becomes the key to getting things done, that is, to the management of the policy process (Lynn 1987). Indeed, procedural power is one of the most important sources of power of high office holders and is vital to understanding their success and failure in government (Lewis 1983).

From the sorting perspective, small groups are important in two ways that need further study. On the one hand, they may be the ones doing the sorting, for example when cabinets or senior management teams decide on the prioritization of their policy agendas and then delegate issues and problems to various bodies down the hierarchy. The major challenge to the analyst here is to detect the underlying principles and power relationships governing the sorting process. For example, does the group follow a logic of managerial effectiveness, institutional appropriateness, or political expediency in channeling issues (March and Olsen 1989)? Does the group make these procedural decisions collectively, or is it manipulated by leaders and powerful members playing (bureau-)political games (Maoz 1990)?

On the other hand, groups may be on the receiving end of the sorting process and are charged with handling a particular matter. This happens, for example, when a special cabinet committee or policy planning group is set up, when a parliamentary inquiry is initiated, or when a commission of "wise men" is appointed to advise the government. When this happens, a number of crucial parameters come into play: purposes (what does the delegating leader or body want the group—or its core members—to do: produce facts, give advice, foster support, buy time, subdue controversy?), participation (who is in and who is left out, and why? who leads?), and procedures (what steps can the group take to achieve its mission? when, how, and to whom should it present its products?). All of these are crucial factors determining how the issue will become defined, and what strategies to deal with it will be articulated and considered by the group. Also, these parameters will determine the group's impact, both its nature (substance or symbolism) and its size (from free-floating advice to binding rulings).

Conveying Meaning: The Group as "Ideologue"
One important function of high-level bodies of government (similar to that of corporate management groups) is to articulate and embody the core values and norms advocated by the chief executive, the organization as a whole, or the prevailing policy paradigm. Top-level policy-making groups are highly conspicuous, and their behavior and that of their members conveys important messages to subordinates, interest groups, and other countries. All of these are constantly scanning the groups' behavior for cues about where policy is going. Knowing that their every move will be watched, and that even the smallest indication of internal discord may give the wrong idea to key actors in their environment, policymakers are keen to put up a show of unity.

One very powerful way of doing so is stressing the team-like nature of the group. "Team" is a golden concept; everyone agrees we should have more teamwork in foreign policy-making. Taken from the world of sports, the "teams" and "teamwork" metaphors convey a sense of unity of purpose, high group cohesiveness, mutually complementary skills, effective leadership, equitable participation, resilience in the face of arduous tasks and overwhelming odds, and perhaps even rightness of cause and methods. The imagery seems to project that if foreign policy-making is the product of a united government, one can rest assured that the national interest rests in safe hands. Policymakers know this and will make every effort to cultivate this image. Newly elected presidents talk about it constantly. Once in office and producing major decisions, they often face the press seconded by the members of their "team," who just days or hours before may have fought bitterly over the most desirable course of action.

The need to project and maintain dominant beliefs and values also plays out in the group setting itself. It may act as a normative constraint upon bureaucratic or political game playing between group members with different views and interests. It may, however, also be used as an instrument of power for group leaders and majorities to squash internal dissent. Chief executives know that "being part of the team" is an indispensable asset for their colleagues and may use this fact to their advantage. They can set the boundaries of what they consider to be loyal group behavior ("team play"). Group members who do not conform to these standards can be given numerous subtle and less subtle cues to come back in line, with the threat of demotion in or exclusion from the group as the ultimate sanction looming in the background. Since the loyal member is supposed to subordinate his personal interests to the group's needs and identity, the need to be seen as a loyal team player may place strong pressures on individuals disagreeing with the group's policies (Jackall 1988). The group effectively becomes a kind of "psychic prison" for its members, particularly those having doubts about the group's course of action (cf. Morgan 1986). This was experienced, for example, by George Ball and later Robert McNamara during the Tuesday Lunch sessions of President Johnson and his advisers on the conduct of the Vietnam War (Janis 1972). Ultimately, this may promote a certain insulation of the top-level group, captured so well by C. P. Snow in his famous political novel *The Corridors of Power* (1964, 23). "The danger was that we were listening to ourselves. It was the occupational danger of this kind of politics: you cut yourself off from your enemies, you basked in the echo of your own voice. That was one of the reasons why the real bosses stayed more optimistic than the rest of us."

Legitimizing Policy: The Group as "Smokescreen"
Roger Hilsman once observed the following about John F. Kennedy's style of managing the decision-making process:

> Kennedy said: And now we have the "inner club." He meant that we had together the people who had known all along what we would do about the problem, and who had been pulling and hauling, debating and discussing for no other purpose than to keep the government together, to get all the others to come around. (Hilsman 1967, 6)

In complex organizations, high-level group discussions may not always be what they seem. Many such groups are part of the formal structure of the organization. In government, they may even be rooted in law or the Constitution. Yet that does not mean that for this reason alone, they are actually performing their stated tasks. Like Kennedy, many chief executives and senior policymakers have found it useful at times to conduct an important part of their business in informal groups and settings, while leaving intact the formal system. When this is done on a more regular basis, a dual structure of policy-making develops (Rockman 1978). The formal system of committees and cabinet meetings remains important primarily for symbolic reasons: it reinforces deeply rooted organizational norms and constitutional myths about how collective decisions ought to be made, it provides a platform for marginal actors and dissenters to articulate their positions, it allows key players to make certain statements for the public record (Meyer and Rowan 1977; Feldman and March 1981; Smith 1988; James 1991). In sum, it provides an essential source of legitimacy for the policies and actions of an informal, more closely knit inner circle—where the real decisions are made.

These dual structures of collective decision making are especially relevant in the conduct of foreign policy, where, political leaders are quick to argue, there is often a need for confidentiality, particularly in matters relating to national security (cf. "back channel" tactics of international negotiation). But it is in fact not primarily the fear of leaking that prompts the formation of inner circles. More important are personal and political factors. At the personal level, the management style of the chief executive, prime minister, minister, or senior official is crucially important (Hermann and Preston 1994). For example, leaders may feel uncomfortable in formal group settings; they may have a low tolerance for conflict among their advisers and colleagues, or a strong need for emotional support in handling difficult issues. All of these personal factors will induce them to gather around them a relatively small circle of trusted and like-minded associates and to minimize their reliance upon the more sizable, heterogeneous and potentially conflictual formal bodies. Other leaders are more comfortable in these settings and will even want to avoid inner circles (see Preston, this volume).

Likewise, at the political level, dual structures of inner circles for substantive deliberation and formal groups for rituals of multipartisan consultation may be crucially important in helping embattled presidents or fragile coalition governments succeed in managing controversial and divisive foreign policy crises. In Great Britain, for example, many crucial foreign policy issues are primarily dealt with by the tandem between Prime Minister and Foreign Secretary, sometimes referred to as the foreign policy executive (Hill 1991). At the same time, there will often be a political need to at least discuss the matter at some length in full cabinet. This is done at best to reconsider once more the chosen course of action, but often prime ministers consider it a necessary evil to obtain the support of their colleagues and party factions. At worst, cabinet discussion really serves no other function than to go through the motions of collective decision making (James 1991).

Finally, there are also social-psychological factors that drive this creeping marginalization of formal groups. Especially in more established groups working together over a long time, a good deal of interaction is displaced by anticipation, with group participants preferring to compare notes and work out common positions in informal subgroup meetings before the plenary session (for example, Olsen 1983). As a result, the plenary session of a cabinet, the public meeting of a parliamentary committee, or a body like the U.N. Security Council "can become a mere 'theater session'" about a problem already decided, often with pseudo-arguments given in the discussion, while the real arguments and causes of action remain in the dark, raising major methodological challenges for small group analysts (Stocker-Kreichgauer, cited in Gaenslen 1992, 174).

Functional Patterns

Overviewing these functions, one can discern a certain pattern in them. Some are more directed toward the external performance of the group, whereas others concentrate on the group's performance qua group, for example, primarily internal functions. Accordingly, we can make a distinction between internal and external dimensions of group behavior. In addition, although in most functions groups emerge as instrumental, task-oriented units, there are two which seem to refer much more to the construction of meaning of group activities. This allows us to draw a second dimension of instrumental-substantive versus symbolic-expressive functions.[4] Figure 1.1 summarizes this view.

Although we have to be careful not to confuse metaphors and ideal types with an empirical reality that is likely to be more varied, fuzzy, and hybrid, this review of some key functions of small groups in the policy-making process does suggest heuristically that analysts need to move away from an exclusive preoccupation with group information processing and problem solving. Groups fulfill crucial task-oriented functions, such as conflict resolution, that cannot be captured by the "think tank" metaphor. They also serve crucial emotional and symbolic purposes, and thus relieve pressures on decision makers and maintain organizational identity and integrity.

During the course of their interactions, members of policy groups socially construct which international, domestic, and organizational realities they choose to enact and how they go about it. In doing so, they can slide into different types of performance modes and oscillate between instrumental and symbolic activities. Consequently, these groups can have many different meanings, both to their members and to domestic and international stakeholders in their policy environment. If one accepts this, the idea that one group tends to perform multiple functions at the same time becomes a plausible one.

In sum, it cannot be taken for granted that particular bodies or groups actually have the substantive impact on policy ascribed to them on the basis of

	INSTRUMENTAL-SUBSTANTIVE	SYMBOLIC-EXPRESSIVE
INTERNAL TO GROUP	*Sanctuary:* diffusion of individual responsibility. emotional support	*Ideologue (I):* shaping group beliefs. enforcing group norms
EXTERNAL TO GROUP	*Think tank:* intelligent information processing and problem solving *Command center:* concentration of power, central policy coordination *Arena:* bureaucratic. cabinet. and party politics: conflict resolution *Sorter:* organizing work flow: prestructuring decision making process and outcomes	*Smokescreen:* Concealing informal structures. showcase for outside constituents *Ideologue (II):* projecting and reaffirming society's and organization's core values

Fig. 1.1. Small group functions in the policy-making process

their formal powers and duties. From this perspective the integrating metaphor to characterize policy-making groups operating at or close to the apex of the foreign policy apparatus becomes that of the *garbage can:* the group, its process, and its policies are the product of a constantly evolving set of members, each representing configurations of institutional and personal values, norms, expectations, problem definitions, and behavioral repertoires (Cohen, March, and Olsen 1972; for an application to defense policy, cf. March and Weissinger-Babylon 1986). In the course of the group's interactions, members collide and cooperate, issues and problems become salient and disappear, goals, standards, and procedures are articulated and negotiated, and group policy preferences are shaped. Given the complexity of this process, analysts of group decision making in foreign policy are likely to find a considerable amount of ambiguity, role conflict, actor and issue linkages, and seemingly inconsistent performance. To understand what is going on, then, the analyst needs to put these groups in their proper context, since so much of what groups do is determined directly and indirectly by properties of the organizational and policy arena in which they operate.

Beyond Groupthink (II): Embedded Group Processes

Despite the need to study policy-making groups in their broader institutional context, there is a distinct dearth of studies that follow Janis's example and actually do this. That this is so in contemporary social psychology should perhaps not surprise us much, given its strong emphasis on experimental research methods. The need for control and parsimony in the design and conduct of experiments severely limits the ability to take into account real-world complexities such as time, culture, organization, and politics. One might wish that more experimental social psychologists would be prepared to limit their concern for internal validity of experiments and give greater weight to considerations of external validity when designing their studies. Also, one might chastise social psychologists for their lack of determination to revive the once prominent tradition of field experiments, as embodied in the work of pioneers such as Sherif (1936) and Lewin (1948).[5] At the very least, they could take the laboratory closer to the world of decision makers, and work with more realistic populations of subjects than undergraduate students in Psychology, Business, and Political Science (see Minix 1982).

Yet such critiques are only valid up to a point. Even in the research laboratory, small groups remain an intricate and demanding object of study. Merely describing carefully what goes on during a small group meeting requires an elaborate observation, registration, and categorization effort (Bales 1950). Take the highly reductionist minimal group paradigm, for example. In many of the studies of intergroup behavior that have been conducted with it, the group process that develops in response to the most limited of stimuli is often still quite complex and ambiguous, certainly enough so to warrant sustained and highly focused attention to its fine details (Rabbie et al. 1989).

Those who study high-level foreign policy-making are faced with a multilayered object of study, as captured so well in Hill's observation that "[At the] highest level of responsibility, foreign policymaking is made up of a set of moving relationships, played out within the limits laid down by institutions, precedents, personalities, and the structure of the issue of the moment" (Hill 1991). Other foreign policy analysts have similarly stressed the need to study the embedded nature of foreign policy-making processes. They have adopted insights from contemporary social theory where individual behavior is seen as enabled and constrained by relationships with multiple, overlapping collective identities. Factions, groups, and organizations exhibit structural properties such as norms, rules, and roles, as well as constellations of resources, status, and power. Each is both a structure (looking "inward" to its component agents) and an agent (whose behavior is partly governed by larger sociopolitical forces and structural parameters). The agency-structure problematic noted by international relations scholars is highly relevant to understanding the role and behavior of small groups in the foreign policy process (Wendt 1987; Hollis and Smith 1990; Carlsnaes 1992). First, it highlights the embedded nature of groups in broader organizational, political, and cultural constellations. Second, it points to the role of group-level factors as forces shaping the behavior of group members. Third, it implies that the results of the interaction that takes place within the group may in turn have an impact on the institutional context in which the group operates.

From this perspective, it becomes essential to look at cabinet decision making as embedded in a country's cabinet system (James 1991, 1–10, 53–69). Similarly, one should study the course and outcomes of U.S. National Security Council meetings on a certain policy issue in relation to the institutional makeup of the foreign policy-making system existing at that time (Tower 1987; Moens 1990; Prados 1991). This is no mere play of words. This approach highlights the embedded, institutionalized nature of small groups in the foreign policy process. The logic of the system—as governed by the constitution, law, standard operating procedures, and personal preferences of incumbent office holders—in part determines how groups are formed, which roles they can play, which issues they are confronted with, which information reaches them, and what sort of pressures they have to contend with. Cabinets, for example, can only function properly as central bodies of decision and coordination in foreign policy if they are adequately informed by the various departments involved, if their key members are sufficiently prepared by their advisers, if there is some kind of shared set of major foreign policy principles that they can rely on to evaluate specific proposals for action, if major differences of opinion have been articulated and discussed prior to the plenary meetings, and so on. For all these conditions to be fulfilled, high-level decision groups are highly dependent upon different parts of their institutional environment.

In this context, the institutional environment refers to sets of values, norms, rules, and roles that constrain and facilitate a policy-making group's formation and behavior. *Macro-level* elements of institutionalization reside in the national society and the political-bureaucratic system the group is part of, flowing from their history, culture, and structure (March and Olsen 1989; Ostrom 1990; Vertzberger 1990). Thiebault (1994, 97), for example, observes that

> . . . the relationship between cabinet structural arrangements and cabinet decision-making processes is strong. In Western European cabinets, decision-making process developed on the basis of the different country "cultures" that produced different structural arrangements. These "cultures" appear to be truly alive; in particular they cut across both the distinction between parties of the Right and Left and the distinction between single-party governments and coalitions.

Meso-level opportunities and constraints are embedded in the specific policy arena in which the group operates. More strongly so in some domains of foreign policy-making than in others, certain "decision regimes" (Kegley

1987) or "policy networks" have formed. These consist of patterns of actors, interdependencies, interaction patterns, and policy styles. In agricultural policy-making in the European Union, one can find a clear example of a highly institutionalized, if recently evolving, decision regime. The entire process takes the shape of intergovernmental bargaining, triggered and partly orchestrated by the European Commission, and scripted in terms of a fixed process of discussion rounds, climaxing in the well-known marathon sessions of the Council of Ministers of Agriculture.

Institutionalization is also operative at the *micro level* of the group itself (endogenous institutionalization). It is here that social psychological research has made a major contribution, in particular by generating knowledge about the impact of various components of the group's structure (such as size, composition, decision rules, hierarchy, and deliberation procedures) upon its process and performance (Hackman and Morris 1975; Gladstein 1984; McGrath 1984). The same holds true for more intangible factors that could be considered part of the group's micro culture, such as level of cohesion, norms of participation, informal performance standards, prestige hierarchies, and preferred ways of dealing with conflict among members (Forsyth 1983). More recently, social psychologists have acknowledged that groups may display variable types and degrees of institutionalization and that this may vary over time. Particularly interesting in this regard are theories of group development, which suggest that groups evolve through a more or less distinct set of stages, during each of which they may display particular combinations of structure, culture, and internal and external behavioral propensities (Moreland and Levine 1988; Worchel et al. 1992; see Stern, this volume).

Taken together, these macro-, meso- and micro-level components of the institutional context may serve to mitigate the garbage can–like quality of group activities in the policy process referred to above. Although exceedingly complex, the behavior of high-level policy-making groups is apparently subject to an opportunity structure and a range of constraints and influences that can be studied systematically. All contributors to this book attempt to understand the dynamics of high-level groups and their impact on the process by adopting a multidisciplinary perspective. They seek to compare, contrast, and integrate pertinent concepts and findings from a range of social science disciplines. In doing so, they echo the observation that:

> Social and political psychologists cannot afford to ignore the broader institutional forces that govern the perceptions, calculations, and behavior of real-world policy makers. They do so at the risk of arriving at reductionist explanations and identifying all sorts of biases, irrationalities, and information-processing pathologies, whereas seasoned observers of organizational and political behavior, who are more aware of meso-level considerations and constraints, and of paradigms of gover-

nance that do not accord a central place to its problem-solving and information-processing functions, would find these conclusions to be both overly simplistic and normatively crude. ('t Hart 1994, x)

Moving beyond Groupthink: A Preview of the Book

This volume seeks to refine the agenda of the decision-making approach to foreign policy analysis. Following in Janis's footsteps, it refocuses attention on the importance of small elite groups at crucial junctures in the foreign policy process. Moving beyond Janis's work on groupthink, it presents a range of questions, conceptual frameworks, and empirical explorations that should enable us to understand more fully the different functions that small groups perform in the policy process. It combines a respectful yet critical assessment of 25 years of groupthink-dominated small group research in foreign policy with innovative contributions that should inspire a new wave of research in this domain.

The composition of the volume reflects this twofold strategy. In part 1, entitled *Groupthink and Beyond,* the significance and limitations of group-think analysis are discussed. However, the chapters in this section do more than looking back at Janis's legacy. Each also offers important building blocks for the move "beyond groupthink" that we feel is urgently needed. In part 2, *Political Group Dynamics and Foreign Policy,* four different examples of "post-groupthink" foreign policy analysis are provided. In the final part, *Implications,* we look at the upshot of this volume in terms of its contribution to ongoing efforts to reform and grade the foreign policy-making institutions and processes.

This volume does not report a tightly programmed collaborative research venture guided by a central theoretical framework and division of labor between the authors. However, it aspires to be more than a collection of loosely coupled essays. Table 1.1 illustrates how the various chapters hang together. Several observations on the overall structure are in order. First of all, as figure 1.1 shows, the key emphasis in this volume is on conceptual innovation, that is, to stimulate new ways of thinking about small groups in the foreign policy process. Except for the first and the fifth chapter, the book has relatively little to offer to those seeking new ideas about research strategy and methodology for studying real-world policy-making groups. This is not because we believe such methodological innovation is not important; on the contrary. However, our first priority was on the conceptual side: to break the hold of the "group-think frame" by placing new questions about small groups on the foreign policy research agenda and offering analytical tools to start addressing these questions. Based on the groundwork of this volume, an important next step that should be taken is to revisit and rejuvenate epistemological and methodological debates, to think through the research design implications of the

TABLE 1.1.   Overview of the Volume

Core Features by Chapter	Groupthink Retro	Conceptual Innovation	Methodological Innovation	Empirical Content	Policy Advice
1	•	• • •	•		
2	• • •	•	•		
3	• • •	• •			
4	• •	•		• •	
5	•	• •	• •		
6	•	• •		• •	
7		• •		• • •	
8		• •		• • •	
9	•	• •		•	•
10		• •			• • •

Note: The distribution of the five •'s indicates the extent to which the particular topic is a priority area in the chapter concerned.

"beyond groupthink agenda." Also we should develop better methodological tools for describing and assessing small groups in policy-making settings.

Second, as one moves from front to back, the balance between retrospection and authentic theoretical and empirical contributions shifts in favor of the latter. The chapters of part 2 elaborate segments of the research agenda developed in chapters 1 and 5, the crucial analytical linchpins of the volume. Both chapters have key theoretical and methodological contributions to make. Theoretically, the first chapter has emphasized the need to better grasp the multiple, ambiguous, and overlapping functions that small elite groups may perform in the policy-making process; methodologically, it urges analysts to take into account the embedded (institutionalized) nature of these groups and use multi-level study designs. Chapter 5 takes these ideas one step further. Its main theoretical contribution consists of a careful mapping of the types of interaction patterns (group processes) that may be encountered in foreign policy-making groups; its methodological input lies in the presentation of a six-step research procedure that is sensitive to the embedded nature of group interaction processes in foreign policy-making. Chapters 6 through 9 elaborate different components of this analytical menu and offer empirical illustrations of their descriptive and explanatory potential using case-study data. With these general considerations in mind, let us now briefly introduce each of the chapters individually.

Part 1

In chapter 2, Alexander George takes us back to the roots of the notion of groupthink as developed by Janis. He stresses that groupthink is a coping mechanism for decision makers beset by stress and reconstructs two types of decisional stress differentiated by Janis. George also notes some of the fundamental conceptual and methodological problems associated with the group-think construct. After briefly discussing post-Janis efforts to amend group-think theory, George concludes that the analysis of top-level decision-making and advisory groups should be grounded in an understanding of the broader institutional context (tradeoff dilemmas of executive policymaking; advisory systems; leader–adviser relationships) in which these groups operate.

Sally Fuller and Ramon Aldag review, in chapter 3, the results of group-think research as it has been conducted since 1972. They address some of the conceptual and methodological problems of the field, and argue for a more encompassing and politically astute approach to explaining group decision making in organizations. To this end, they present a generic model of the antecedents, processes, and outcomes of group decision making in organizations that considerably widens the groupthink-dominated research agendas of foreign policy analysts.

In chapter 4 the essential ambiguity of groupthink analysis when applied to a historic case of foreign policy decision making is highlighted in a detailed case study of the Dutch cabinet's policies during its 1950–62 territorial dispute with Indonesia over Western New Guinea. Max Metselaar and Bertjan Verbeek show that although at first sight the decision-making process within the Dutch government showed a number of characteristics commonly associated with groupthink, a closer analysis shows that several key developments in the Dutch position cannot be accounted for by classic groupthink analysis. They mention six "non-groupthink elements" that played a pivotal role, including the political-institutional context in which decision making took place, the role of informal leadership within the cabinet, the cognitive style of key individual decision makers, and the shifting locus of decision making beyond any single dominant group. Arguing inductively from their case, these authors echo both chapters 2 and 3 in concluding that a multi-level approach is needed that highlights the interplay between individual, group, and institutional factors, rather than one that isolates group-level variables.

In chapter 5, Bengt Sundelius and Eric Stern present a bridge between the critical and agenda-setting groupthink retrospectives of chapters 2 to 4 and the theoretical and empirical explorations presented in part 2. Their essential contribution is twofold. In the first part of the chapter, they specify the crucial variable in small group analysis, that is, the group interaction patterns that result from the interplay between different individual, group, and institutional factors. Whereas groupthink focuses exclusively on concurrence-seeking behavior in groups, Stern and Sundelius discern and describe six other interaction patterns. In the second part, they develop a six-step research procedure that can be used to investigate what types of interaction take place in policy-making groups, taking into account the "embedded" nature of these groups.

Part 2

The chapters in part 2 elaborate selected parts of the research agenda sketched in this introduction and in part 1 of the book. Stern's chapter 6 is a detailed application of the two-part contribution by Stern and Sundelius from chapter 5. Using one of Janis's original cases, U.S. decision making leading up to the fiasco of the attempted counterrevolution in Cuba in 1961, Stern applies the six-step research procedure, taking into account a range of institutional factors shaping the Kennedy group's planning process and looking at the different interaction patterns. In his theoretical section, he provides an extensive treatment of one of the seven interaction patterns identified in chapter 5, the so-called newgroup syndrome. He argues that this may have been a more important explanation of the flawed decision making on the Bay of Pigs invasion than the groupthink hypothesis advanced by Janis. Newgroup syndrome refers to the special risks that occur when crucial policy decisions (often under conditions of crisis) are made by newly formed, weakly institutionalized groups.

Following up on Alexander George's call for a contextual process analysis of the nexus between political leaders and their advisers in foreign policy-making, Thomas Preston in chapter 7 shows how various elements of a U.S. president's leadership style play out in the ways in which he structures his advisory system, thus predisposing it toward a particular configuration of group structures and decision-making patterns. Furthermore, he shows how personal style characteristics may predispose leaders toward particular ways of managing deliberations that take place between them and their advisers. Preston develops a framework for systematic inquiry which is subsequently applied to the classic case of President Truman's major decisions at the outset of the Korean War, drawing intensively on declassified presidential documents.

Jean Garrison and Paul Hoyt take up the groups-as-arenas metaphor introduced in this chapter and analyze the political maneuvering that goes on within and around foreign policy decision-making groups (chapter 8). Their chapter highlights the various ways in which leaders as well as individual members can manipulate the group's composition, operating procedures, and interpersonal dynamics to advance their personal objectives and exert decisive influence on the outcome of the group's deliberations. Their empirical analysis focuses on the Carter administration and deals with its handling of the onset of the Iranian revolution, as well as its decision making concerning the presence of a Soviet brigade on Cuba.

Finally, and in contrast to the previous chapters of part 2, Yaacov Vertzberger's contribution is focused more on the dependent variable in small group analysis, that is, the nature of the decisions taken (chapter 9). One of the key properties of group decisions discussed intensively in the literature is risk: how and to what extent do groups perceive and weigh risks associated with their current situation and possible courses of action, and what kinds and levels of risk are they willing to accept in choosing a course of action? Specifically, Vertzberger revisits the familiar social-psychological explanations for risk-taking behavior in groups and examines their relevance in the real world setting of collegial foreign policy-making. He then outlines a number of group attributes not covered by these explanations that may be particularly relevant in political decision groups. Throughout, he illustrates his theoretical arguments with detailed case examples from national security decisions in the Soviet Union, India, and Israel.

Part 3

In the final chapter, Paul 't Hart discusses the practical implications of small group analysis. He argues that before moving from empirical analysis to proposals for institutional reform, small group analysis needs to develop a more explicit normative framework for evaluating group performance in the policy-making process. This kind of framework needs to come to terms with the reality of normative pluralism in assessing group performance, as implied in the multifunctionality of groups in the policy process discussed in this introductory chapter. Secondly, we must pay more attention to the practical feasibility of our proposals, and become more aware of the uses and limitations of academic recommendations to reform policy-making practices. In keeping with the overall philosophy of this volume, this final chapter concludes that in formulating the practical "lessons" of small group research for policy practice, we need both to reconsider and move beyond existing prescriptions to prevent groupthink in the making of foreign policy.

NOTES

For their comments on an earlier draft of this chapter, the authors are grateful to Rick Guzzo, Marieke Kleiboer, and Steve Walker, as well as to the participants of the Small Groups Initiative seminar during the faculty meeting of the Research and Training Group on Political Psychology in Ohio, June 1995.

1. Throughout this volume we use the masculine forms when referring to persons or offices in general. This is done for reasons of consistency and does not reflect any substantive opinion or bias on gender issues.

2. Subsequently, the decision-making approach was extended significantly by, among others, Sprout and Sprout (1965), Paige (1968), De Rivera (1968), Allison (1971), Brecher (1972), Steinbruner (1974), Jervis (1976), Snyder and Diesing (1977), East et al. (1978), George (1980), Lebow (1981), Hermann et al. (1987), Maoz (1990), Vertzberger (1990), and Khong (1992).

3. This implies a different approach from the one pursued by Hermann and Hermann (1989), who present the problem more in either/or terms: multiple autonomous actors, or a single group, or a dominant leader is identified as ultimate decision unit. In the latter case, the analysis concentrates strongly on variables at the individual level and accords only a minor role to the group-level advisory process that frequently provides the setting in which dominant leaders arrive at their decisions.

4. The two dimensions mentioned here could be viewed as a disaggregation of the conventional distinction between task-performance and group-maintenance functions (Shaw, 1981). From our perspective, this old dichotomy does not fully capture the fact that both of these types of functions can be relevant primarily for the group itself or primarily for the social environment in which the group operates. Also, a distinction needs to be made between a "voluntaristic" view of groups, depicting them as instruments at the disposal of leaders and interest groups, to be used strategically for specific purposes (such as postponing tricky problems or legitimizing policies already decided upon), and a "deterministic" view that suggests that the nature and purposes of groups are circumscribed carefully in the institutional structure of the policy process. In practice, we tend to see elements of both.

5. We acknowledge that the strict ethical standards enforced by human subject committees, while serving an important function, are often an obstacle to conducting these types of experiments today.

CHAPTER 2

From Groupthink to Contextual Analysis of Policy-making Groups

Alexander L. George

Introduction

Before going "Beyond Groupthink" and arguing in favor of an alternative approach to studying the role of small groups in foreign policy decision making, as this and the other essays in this volume do, I believe it is appropriate to make an attempt to clarify as best I can what Irving Janis meant by "groupthink" and to identify some of the novel and striking ideas he advanced in his seminal book, *Victims of Groupthink,* over twenty years ago. It is well to recall that this book reflected Janis's long-standing interest in decision making on matters of great importance to individuals, the stresses that often accompany such decisions, ways in which individuals attempt to cope with decisional stresses, and suggestions for how the process of decision making and the quality of decisions might be improved.

In *Victims of Groupthink,* Janis shifted his focus from individual psychology to the ways in which groups make highly consequential decisions. In this work, as in so much of his research before and after its publication, Janis coupled efforts to design as rigorous an empirical method as possible with an openly espoused normative and policy-oriented viewpoint. He explicitly acknowledged and, indeed, cautioned readers of *Victims of Groupthink* to keep in mind that its scope was limited to advancing hypotheses that would have to be subjected to more rigorous assessment than was possible by means of the several historical case studies he presented (Janis 1972, 202, 206).

Janis's stimulating and provocative book made several important contributions to the academic and policy-oriented literature that should be recognized at the outset. Janis challenged the view, then predominant in theoretical and applied social psychology, that group cohesion always results in better performance. Under certain conditions and when a group engages in stressful decisional tasks, Janis argued, strong group cohesion can contribute to defective decision making which, in turn, may lead to a policy disaster.[1] The potentially detrimental effects of group cohesiveness had not received much attention in the earlier work of Kurt Lewin and his students who had been more interested in the positive effects of group cohesiveness.[2] To explain why and how decisional stress experienced by a cohesive group led to defective policy-making Janis, drawing on the work of Wilfred Bion, a group therapist, and his own observations of other groups, identified a different type of group dynamic which he called concurrence-seeking, a concept which I will examine more closely below.

Noteworthy in *Victims of Groupthink* as in his other research was Janis's emphasis on the importance of emotional factors in decision making.[3] This reflected his long-standing conviction that a narrow or exclusive focus on cognitive processes is inadequate and that attention must be given to how psychodynamic processes in individuals and groups affect their decision-making behavior. While unfashionable among mainstream social psychologists during most of his career, Janis's position anticipated and helped to lay a foundation for the exciting wave of research into social cognition which has gained momentum since the early 1980s. Like Janis, much of this more recent work acknowledges the importance of emotionally charged "hot" cognition so common in real-world decision making (see, e.g., Lebow 1981; Abelson 1985; Marcus and Zajonc 1985; Tetlock 1985; Fiske 1993, 175–79; Lebow and Stein 1993).

More broadly, one of Janis's major purposes which the book certainly accomplished was, as he put it, "to increase awareness of social psychological phenomena in decisions of historic importance, so that group dynamics will be taken into account" (vi; original emphasis omitted). It is testimony to his success in this respect that since its publication over twenty years ago *Victims of Groupthink* has stimulated and encouraged a great deal of follow-up research on these questions (see, e.g., 't Hart 1990/1994, 1991; Fuller and Aldag, this volume, for thorough reviews) and that it leads us now to the present task of moving *Beyond Groupthink*.

The rest of this essay will be structured as follows. First, I will provide further clarification of and some critiques addressing Janis's (1972) seminal contribution and discuss some of the critiques raised against it. Then I will take a similar look at the neo-groupthink approach developed by Paul 't Hart in *Groupthink in Government* (1990/1994) and subsequent writings. In the last part of the chapter, I will sketch out some arguments in favor of moving beyond groupthink and toward a more contextual/holistic approach to studying the role of small groups in executive decision-making processes.

Victims of Groupthink: A Critical Retrospective

Janis's theory of groupthink was based on a type of group dynamic—what he referred to as "concurrence-seeking"—that had not received much attention in the literature. It must be said here that the nature of concurrence-seeking and what, in Janis's theory, gives rise to it has not been clearly understood or adhered to in commentaries upon or in subsequent research that has attempted to build upon or to replace his theory. That misunderstandings of what Janis meant by concurrence-seeking have occurred is not surprising. For one thing, as Paul 't Hart (1991) pointed out, the idea of groupthink as an explanation for policy disasters was a beguiling one. Groupthink caught the imagination of other writers and spread quickly into public discourse, leading to vulgarization and stretching of the original concept. A particular flagrant example was the tendency to redefine concurrence-seeking to include any and all efforts to obtain consensus and support within the group for a policy decision.

Janis may have inadvertently contributed to the stretching of his theory insofar as he did not succeed in impressing on his readers that concurrence-seeking emerged under conditions of severe decisional stress. This is, in fact, an integral component of his theory, as he states early in the book: "The central explanatory concept [of the theory] involves viewing concurrence-seeking as a form of striving based on a powerful motivation in all group members [of a cohesive group] to cope with the stresses of decision making that cannot be alleviated by standard operating procedures" (20). (Note, here, the clear reference to concurrence-seeking as a way of coping with decisional stress. I emphasize this because others have used the term "groupthink" more broadly to refer to policy consensus arrived at by a group prematurely without adequate consideration of the pros and cons of the available options.)

Janis elaborated the link between decisional stress and concurrence-seeking by calling attention to the fact that stress often produces a heightened need for affiliation with other members of the group and that this, in turn, contributes to further strengthening of group cohesion. In this context he invoked the sociological concept of "primary group" which had been previously employed in field studies of combat groups, air crews, and disaster control teams. These studies, he noted, supported the findings of social psychological experiments with college students which showed that "external sources of stress produced a heightened need for affiliation. . . . which leads to greater dependency upon one's primary work group." Acknowledging that this phenomenon "can have beneficial effects in morale and stress tolerance," Janis emphasized that under certain conditions it will have adverse effects if it leads to "an increase in concurrence-seeking at the expense of critical thinking" (Janis 1972, 114). Concurrence-seeking, Janis postulated, serves as a

Decisional Stress ————————————————————▷ Coping Mechanism

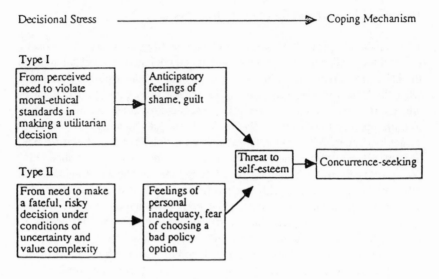

Type I

| From perceived need to violate moral-ethical standards in making a utilitarian decision | Anticipatory feelings of shame, guilt |

Type II

| From need to make a fateful, risky decision under conditions of uncertainty and value complexity | Feelings of personal inadequacy, fear of choosing a bad policy option |

| Threat to self-esteem | Concurrence-seeking |

Fig. 2.1.   **The relationship between decisional stress and concurrence-seeking**

coping device for the members of a cohesive group who experience an en-hanced need for affiliation under severe stress: "participating in a unanimous consensus along with the respected fellow members of a congenial group will bolster . . . [their] self-esteem" (ibid., 203).

Only at the end of chapter 8, in a brief section of hardly more than a single page (ibid., 202–3) titled "Rudiments of an explanatory theory," does Janis finally provide a fuller statement of his theory regarding the relationship between decisional stress and concurrence-seeking that results in groupthink.[4] At this point Janis identifies two types of decisional stress and then attempts to suggest how members of the cohesive group cope with them via concurrence-seeking (see figure 2.1). One type of decisional stress arises from "the threat of losing self-esteem from violating ethical standards of conduct" when policy deliberations "generate within each participant an intense conflict between humanitarian values on the one hand and the utilitarian demands of national or organizational goals, practical politics, and economics on the other . . . " (ibid.). In such situations the individual "realizes that he is sacrificing moral values in order to arrive at a viable policy [and] will be burdened with anticipatory feelings of shame, guilt, and related feelings of self-depreciation, which lower his self-esteem" (ibid.). Such feelings create psychological stress and a need for coping somehow with that stress.[5] This first type of decisional stress was of particular interest to Janis since he was concerned with the use of force as an instrument of foreign policy, as his initial and most important case study, the Bay of Pigs, indicates.

The second type of decisional stress, to which Janis referred only briefly but which deserves considerable amplification, arises "whenever a decision maker is faced with a perplexing choice that he considers beyond his level of competence or that forces him to become keenly aware of his personal inadequacies" (ibid., 203).[6] A fuller characterization of this second type of decisional stress is needed that calls attention, more broadly, to the psychological malaise that many policy-makers are apt to experience when confronted by the need to make fateful decisions involving the welfare of their country, their party, and indeed themselves in situations characterized by the well-known cognitive limits on rationality. These are (1) inadequate information about the situation; (2) inadequate general knowledge of cause-and-effect relationships that is needed for assessing the expected consequence of alternative courses of action; and (3) the lack of a single utility criterion by means of which to deal with multiple competing values and interests embedded in the issue to be decided. These three cognitive limits on rationality give rise to uncertainty and value complexity which make it very difficult for the decision maker to judge which course of action is best. They are the source of considerable potential or actual stress. Concurrence-seeking is one way—but only one way—of trying to cope with decisional stress.[7] Concurrence-seeking, then, "can best be understood as a mutual effort among members of a [cohesive] group to maintain self-esteem, especially when they share responsibility for making vital decisions that pose threats of social disapproval and self-disapproval" (ibid., 203).

Concurrence-seeking is a distinctive type of group dynamics, not to be confused with the more familiar type of group dynamic that takes the form of conformity pressure on dissident or wavering members of the group to bring them into line with the decision that is being taken. It should be noted that evidence of conformity pressure within the group is more easily obtained by researchers than evidence that concurrence-seeking has taken place. Concurrence-seeking is at the core of groupthink, but it is generally not accessible to direct observation. Whether or not it occurs within a group has to be inferred.

The difficulty of direct observation of concurrence-seeking has created special problems for empirical validation of the groupthink theory. Although Janis appears not to have openly acknowledged this difficulty, he was evidently aware of it and was led to try to identify indirect indicators that concurrence-seeking had occurred within a decision-making group. "Defects" in decision making, six of which he identified, could not serve as indicators of concurrence-seeking since these defects could arise not only from groupthink but also from other causes—e.g., "erroneous intelligence, information overload, fatigue, blinding prejudice, and ignorance" (ibid., 10–11). Neither, of course, could the fact that a policy fiasco had occurred be taken as evidence that it was caused by groupthink since policy failures often occur as a result of other flaws. In sum, Janis recognized that groupthink was neither a necessary nor a sufficient condition for the occurrence of policy fiascoes. Rather, the most that could be said was that groupthink was "conducive to errors in decision making, and such errors increase the likelihood of a poor outcome. Often the result is a fiasco, but not always" (ibid., 11–12).

How, then, to find empirically observable indications that concurrence-seeking had occurred in a group's decision making? At various points in the book, Janis referred to one or another "symptom" of concurrence-seeking. Finally, on pages 197–98, he drew these observations together in what he called a "review of the major symptoms" of the "groupthink syndrome" (ibid., 197–98). Here he recognized the need to "operationalize" the concept of groupthink "by describing the symptoms to which it refers." Although not explicitly stated, Janis evidently drew upon the materials in his case studies to identify eight "main symptoms," claiming that "each symptom can be identified by a variety of indicators, derived from historical records, observer's accounts of conversations, and participants' memoirs." Left unanswered for the moment was the question whether a certain circularity had entered into the process of using the historical materials first as evidence that concurrence-seeking and groupthink must have occurred in a particular case and then extrapolating that "evidence" into a listing of general "symptoms" of the groupthink phenomenon.

What remained was the necessary task of specifying how each symptom contributes to ways in which concurrence-seeking copes with the two types of decisional stress postulated by the theory. Janis finally addressed this critical methodological-theoretical question in a brief section entitled "Psychological functions of the eight symptoms" (ibid., 203–6). "Concurrence-seeking *and the various symptoms of groupthink* to which it gives rise can best be understood as a mutual effort among the members of a group to maintain self-esteem, especially when they share responsibility for making vital decisions that pose threats of social disapproval and self-disapproval" (emphasis added). The eight symptoms of groupthink, he argued, "form a coherent pattern if viewed in the context of this explanatory hypothesis. The symptoms may function in somewhat different ways to produce the same result."

Hence, for Janis, it is identifying the psychological function a "symptom" performs in enabling members of the group to cope with the decisional stresses in question that enables him to offer an operationalization of the theory. He provides a brief indication of how each of the eight symptoms fulfills this psychological function. However, one must ask whether these "symptoms" constitute valid and reliable indicators of concurrence-seeking, the group dynamic that lies at the heart of the groupthink theory but which, as I have noted, does not lend itself to direct observation. This critical methodological question received little attention in Janis's writings; evidently he deferred it to subsequent efforts to validate the theory that he recognized as being necessary. I will not attempt to provide a detailed discussion of this important methodological problem, which has received a certain amount of attention in follow-up studies and commentaries. Certainly, Janis's hypothesis regarding the psychological function these symptoms may play to facilitate concurrence-seeking is plausible and, therefore, worth serious consideration.

However, several important questions arise. First, is concurrence-seeking necessarily accompanied by any or all of these symptoms? Here, it may be noted, Janis suggests that not all of the eight symptoms need appear for groupthink to occur: "even when some symptoms are absent, the others may be so pronounced that we can predict all the unfortunate consequences of groupthink" (ibid., 198). In this connection, Janis rests his case on a probabilistic generalization—namely, the hypothesis that the more a group displays such symptoms, the worse will be the quality of its decision.

It may also be noted that Janis's discussion of this point is based on an unstated but important assumption, namely that evidence will be available to the investigator (or the observer of the group) as to whether the symptoms are present. The unavailability of such evidence, however, is not an unlikely occurrence in research of this kind. Accordingly, the absence of available data on symptoms cannot be taken as excluding the possibility that members of the group did experience these symptoms. This could lead the investigator/observer to make a "false negative" judgment that concurrence-seeking did not occur (the possibility of "false negatives" was not mentioned by Janis).

But consideration must also be given to the possibility of a "false positive" finding that concurrence-seeking must have occurred because some or all of these symptoms were present. Relevant to this possibility is a question not really addressed by Janis—namely, are the symptoms exclusive to concurrence-seeking or can they occur also in its absence? If a symptom is not a telltale sign that concurrence-seeking has occurred, then the symptom is not a reliable indicator and cannot provide the basis for a confident inference of groupthink. For example, it is well-known that one of Janis's eight symptoms, conformity pressure exerted by group members against associates who entertain reservations or disagreement, occurs in a variety of situations in which nothing like concurrence-seeking, as he defines it, is present. In fact, conformity pressures are a quite different type of group dynamic that should not be confused with concurrence-seeking. Janis certainly knew this; he may have nonetheless included it among his symptoms to highlight the possibility that those members of a group themselves engaged in concurrence-seeking may resort to conformity pressure against members who do not participate in concurrence-seeking. However, the employment of conformity pressures for this purpose does not make it a symptom or indicator of concurrence-seeking, and it would be better left off his list of symptoms.

Another example of the ambiguous status of one of Janis's symptoms as an indicator of concurrence-seeking may be briefly mentioned. This involves the group's use of negative stereotypes of an adversary. It may be correct to argue, as Janis does, that "stereotypes that de-humanize out-groups alleviate guilt by legitimizing destructive and inhuman acts against them" (ibid., 204). In this assertion Janis identifies the psychological function negative stereotypes can provide to facilitate concurrence-seeking when the members of the group experience the first of the two decisional stresses he posits. One need not challenge this hypothesis to note that since negative stereotyping occurs among policymakers in other contexts as well it cannot be regarded as a solid basis for inferring concurrence-seeking and groupthink.[8]

Another significant methodological problem can be seen in *Victims of Groupthink*. One can approve Janis's effort to use historical case studies for the limited purpose of "hypothesis construction" (ibid., v) but still raise questions about the validity of his explanation that concurrence-seeking was a major contribution to those instances of "policy fiasco." As is the case with so many other theories in the social sciences when they are employed in case studies, the theory of groupthink is more easily used to generate explanatory hypotheses than to assess them rigorously. This familiar, important distinction between hypothesis formation and hypothesis testing is not satisfactorily applied in Janis's historical cases that are said to evince the role of concurrence-seeking and groupthink in contributing to defective decision making and policy fiasco. Readers who are familiar with the requirements for acceptable historical explanation will not be persuaded. Instead, they are likely to conclude as I do, and as Paul 't Hart gently observed, that there is a danger that the theory of groupthink has been "imposed" as an explanation for the cases.[9] This error arises from efforts to find evidence of "defective" decision-making procedures (that do not conform to ideal criteria) and to couple this with whatever evidence exists that there was strong group cohesion and that there were some indications of some of the symptoms of groupthink.

Janis's best case for the role played by concurrence-seeking is clearly the one on the Bay of Pigs, where indeed historical evidence of the various symptoms can be found. The other cases of presumed groupthink at work are, to my mind, distinctly less persuasive. However, neither in the Bay of Pigs case nor in the other cases of policy failure he presents are alternative explanations adequately identified or explored.[10] In fact, Janis's explanation for the Bay of Pigs has been subjected to serious challenge and several plausible alternative explanations have been offered.[11]

From Groupthink to Neo-Groupthink Theory?

If the concerns that have been expressed regarding the difficult, unresolved methodological problems embedded in Janis's theory of groupthink are justified, then its scientific status is diminished and its future must be regarded as highly problematic. One can either continue efforts to deal more effectively with these problems or abandon the theory and move on to other ways of studying decision making in group situations. Still another possibility is to try to absorb as best one can Janis's prototheory into a broader framework for studying various pathologies of the policy-making process. The latter was the choice made by Paul 't Hart (1990/1994) in his impressive effort to develop a revised theory of groupthink.[12]

He opts for a much broader, quite different conceptual definition of groupthink and has indeed produced a useful multipath analysis of how poor decisions can emerge from the deliberations within a small group.[13] This has led 't Hart to substantially redefine "concurrence-seeking" so that it no longer refers to the special type of dynamic that was at the core of Janis's theory. In 't Hart's revised theory, concurrence-seeking seems to refer simply to an effort within the group to arrive at a policy consensus. The problem is not with this definition itself, but rather with 't Hart's effort to characterize aberrant forms of concurrence-seeking. As he and Kroon put it, "rather than rejecting concurrence-seeking altogether, it is more precise to state that only premature, and/or excessive concurrence-seeking is harmful" (1997, 7).

The revised definition of groupthink is closely tied to this characterization of aberrant concurrence-seeking. Thus, he and Kroon speak of "the *premature, excessive* and *rigid* concurrence-seeking that is groupthink" that, they point out, can come about in several ways, not just via the group dynamic upon which Janis focused ('t Hart and Kroon 1997, 27; emphasis added).

But does not this new definition of groupthink raise new methodological and theoretical problems? How does one define and operationalize "premature," "excessive," and "rigid"?[14] These terms clearly imply that when concurrence-seeking assumes this aberrant form within the group, its efforts to arrive at a policy consensus will likely have a harmful effect on the quality of the decision. But how is one to know whether the group's effort to agree on a policy is premature, excessive, and rigid?[15] Sound methodology, of course, requires that the value of the independent variable concurrence-seeking be established or measured independently of the value of the dependent variable, for example, the quality of the decision taken. One cannot allow oneself to infer that concurrence-seeking must have been flawed because the decision taken was of poor quality and may have contributed to a "bad" outcome.

In sum, it appears essential for the further development of the revised theory of groupthink to set forth ways of establishing or measuring directly whether concurrence-seeking is premature, excessive, or rigid. To be sure, concurrence-seeking may be regarded as questionable if it leads to or is accompanied by a failure to meet the requirements of an ideal process for diagnosing problems and identifying, considering, and weighing alternative options. But how exacting should these ideal requirements be? In other words, what departures from ideal requirements can be regarded as meriting the judgment that arriving at a policy consensus was premature, or that a group consensus was excessive or rigid?[16] Is it possible and, in any event, does it make sense, to try to identify the extent of premature or excessive consensus very likely to result in the making of a poor decision which, in turn, will lead to a bad policy outcome?

Toward Contextual Process Analysis

If adequate and generalizable answers to the questions raised in the previous sections are not possible, then it may be necessary to rely upon a more fine-grained contextual analysis of each case. Drawing this conclusion is emphatically not tantamount to a wholesale rejection of theory and endorsement of a purely "idiographic" and descriptive approach. Rather, the function of available general theory becomes that of an aid to both the scholar and the policymaker in making a more discriminating diagnosis of each case in order to judge whether efforts to achieve consensus within the group cut short or distorted vital search and analysis of information and identification and evaluation of policy options before a decision was made.

Without going into to detail on the nature and workings of contextual analysis here, it would include recognition of the following facts:

> Executive decision making must often deal with difficult trade-offs between the quality of a policy, the need for support by others, and the need for timely and economical action.
>
> A thorough canvassing of problems, information, and options is not always necessary to arrive at a sound decision.
>
> Sound decisions by executives do not always require vigilance or consensus within the group.
>
> Executives do not always "consult" advisers in order to receive information and advice; often they do so for very different reasons.

Executive decision making must often deal with difficult trade-offs between the quality of a policy, the need for support by others, and the need for timely and economical action.[17]

One of the most important decisions high-level policymakers are often obliged to make—and sometimes make in a very offhand fashion—concerns which of a number of potentially competing criteria to prioritize in making

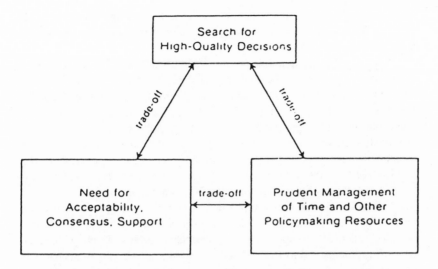

Fig. 2.2.   Trade-off dilemmas in presidential decision making. (Adapted from A. L. George, *Presidential Decisionmaking in Foreign Policy: The Effective Use of Information and Advice* [Boulder, CO: Westview Press, 1980], 2. Copyright © 1980 by WestviewPress. Reprinted by permission of WestviewPress.)

that decision. A perennial problem to be managed is the trade-off that often exists between seeking to maximize the analytical quality of the policy to be chosen and the need to obtain sufficient support for the policy option that is finally chosen. Another familiar, often difficult trade-off problem arises from having to decide how much time and policy-making resources to allocate to the effort to identify the best possible policy option. A third trade-off problem arises from having to decide how much political capital, influence resources, and time to expend in an effort to increase the level of support for the option to be chosen. The three trade-off problems are depicted in figure 2.2.

Academic specialists can easily fall into the error of thinking about high-quality policy decisions in too narrow a framework. Policymakers have to deal with the tension that often exists between policy quality and the need to choose a policy that commands enough support. Very often a measure of quality has to be sacrificed in favor of a decision that will get the kind of political support within and outside the administration that is necessary if the policy is to have a chance of being sustained. At times, executives may perceive an urgent need to procure the support or at least the acquiescence of certain key officials such as cabinet secretaries or ministers, legislative leaders, or even their own advisers, upon whom they have become politically or personally dependent. Compromises in order to increase the likelihood that such support will be forthcoming are then to be expected.[18] Similarly, some executives may place a heavy emphasis on finding a consensus among the members of their advisory group, even at the cost of compromising the quality or integrity of the policy at hand.

Another trade-off in public policy-making is the one between the quality of the decision and the policymaker's sensible use of time and of analytical and political resources. A policymaker who spends a tremendous amount of time trying to arrive at a policy decision of superior quality may incur considerable political and opportunity costs. And if policymakers tie up all the analytical resources at their disposal in order to achieve a higher quality decision, the analysis of other policy issues may be neglected or shortchanged (this trade-off is said to have been a problem with Kissinger's style when he dominated foreign policy-making in the Nixon administration).

Policymakers also face the practical question of deciding how much of the political capital and influence resources at their disposal they should expend in order to gain support for a higher quality decision. Dealing with these trade-off problems requires policymakers to make ad hoc judgments based on their analysis of the political context, since well-defined rules are lacking.

It seems appropriate to note, in passing, that Janis himself recognized the need to take such trade-offs into account in decision-making analysis in some of his later writings. Janis's (1989, 16) last book, *Crucial Decisions,* in fact included a revised and more psychologically elaborated version of the trade-offs model which has been reproduced here as figure 2.3. Janis proposed to incorporate an additional category of egocentric imperatives into the framework. According to Janis, the term *egocentric constraints* refers to factors such as "desire for prestige and other self-serving motives; need to cope with stress, to maintain self-esteem, and to satisfy other emotional needs" (Janis 1989, 16). Janis suggested that trade-offs between egocentric constraints and each of the other three sets of constraints are to be expected.[19]

A thorough canvassing of problems, information, and options immediately prior to choice is not always necessary to arrive at a sound decision.
There are several reasons to be cited in support of this assertion, which may seem provocative to some readers. First, the trade-offs noted above may at times conspire against the launching of such an ambitious and expensive decision process. Executives may accurately and rapidly come to the conclusion that policy or political imperatives rule out many options and potential lines of inquiry, making it easier and justifiable to focus on a particular view of the problem or option. Similarly, analytical resources may be tied up with other equally or even more important issues, making leaders more inclined to "satisfice" than to optimize in their policy choices. Thirdly, executives may decide that a vigorous investigation in the interest of improving decision quality is unnecessary, if they feel that the issue has been adequately studied

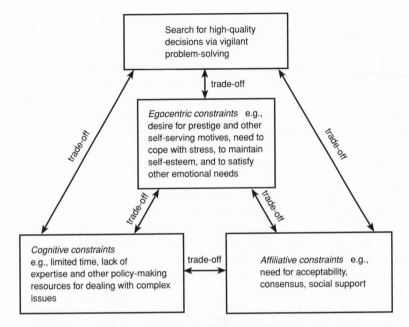

Fig. 2.3. Constraints creating trade-off dilemmas in policy-making. (This figure is based on George [1980], with a category added for ego-centric constraints. Reprinted from I. Janis, *Crucial Decisions,* New York: The Free Press, 1989, 16. Copyright © 1980 by WestviewPress. Reprinted by permission of WestviewPress.)

and well understood in the past and that changed circumstances do not warrant a reopening of the policy question. This last point has important analytical implications. In order to make an assessment as to whether a rapid choice was the result of premature concurrence-seeking or a prior vigilant politico-analytic process, it is necessary to examine the history of the policy issue in question.

For example, a number of scholars (e.g., Lebow 1981, 298–303; Purkitt 1992; Lebow and Stein 1994) have suggested that Kennedy prematurely de-fined away a range of accommodative options during the early stages of the Cuban missile crisis, providing the ExCom with a dangerously restricted mandate. Some have even gone so far as to suggest that groupthink prevailed during this part of the crisis (e.g., McCauley 1989, 255). Yet these analyses tend to neglect evidence suggesting that Kennedy's preliminary decision was in fact based on a careful analysis focusing on the detrimental consequences of an accommodative strategy for the broader constellation of U.S. foreign policy goals (and his own domestic political prospects) in light of previous public commitments not to tolerate Soviet medium-range missiles in Cuba.[20]

It should be recognized that the conscious exercise of leadership in a crisis situation in order to direct the focus of group deliberations away from options already discarded *for good reasons* and toward issues where the executive feels a particular need for group input is a legitimate response to the constraints on decision making outlined above. Thus, the exercise of executive authority is not necessarily inimicable to the maintenance of a sound decision-making process. Setting boundaries or parameters within which a discussion takes place is, after all, a leadership responsibility.

Sound decisions by executives do not always require vigilance or consensus within the group.
As the discussion above has already implied, it is important to keep in mind that the group, while clearly important, is not necessarily the only relevant site for decision activity. An apparently poor-quality decision process within an advisory group is not tantamount to a poor decision process as a whole. Executives may be drawing upon other personal or organizational resources apart from their formally or informally constituted decision groups. It is only when executives do depend upon a particular group or set of groups as the primary source of information and analysis that a flawed group decision process may place the quality of policy-making as a whole in jeopardy. However, it is necessary to look beyond the small group to the broader context and scope of decision-making activity in order to establish whether or not that was the case.

Similarly, it is worth noting that many executives do not particularly expect, desire, or depend upon finding a group consensus. Nor is the soundness of the executive decision process by any means a hostage to the generation of such a consensus. In many systems, not least the U.S. system, the decision-making authority is concentrated to a high degree in the hands of an executive. When the decision rule is executive choice after consultation with advisers, the lack of a consensus may not lead to serious difficulties, particularly if the leader has succeeded in establishing norms which indicate when advocates should break off or tone down their dissent. In fact, as I have suggested elsewhere in my writings on multiple advocacy (e.g., George 1980), a diversity of perspectives can serve to invigorate and improve decision-making processes, particularly when the competition among advocates is balanced and moderated by a "custodian-manager."

Executives do not always "consult" advisers in order to receive information and advice; often they do so for very different reasons.
At least five reasons for executive consultation with advisers can be identified.[21] First, the executive may turn to advisers for information and advice; hence, they may help an executive to satisfy his or her *cognitive needs* prior to

making decisions. Second, as Janis emphasized, a chief executive may interact with advisers in order to obtain the *emotional support* needed to cope with the strains of making difficult, possibly fateful, decisions. Third, consultation with leading foreign policy officials of his administration may be useful to an executive for gaining their *understanding and support* for whatever decision is made, since the advisers then at least have the satisfaction of knowing that their views were solicited and considered. Fourth, an executive who has already made up his or her mind may employ an advisory group as an instrument for *coordination and dissemination of information.* Finally, since it is expected that a leader will consult and take advice from properly constituted officials who share responsibility in foreign policy and national security matters, he or she may want to do so in order to gain greater *political legitimacy* in the eyes of legislative bodies and the public for his or her policies and decisions.

Differences of opinion among scholars regarding a particular decision process often hinge in part upon differing opinions as to an executive's purposes in engaging in consultation. For example, while Berman's (1982) account of the decision-making process which resulted in the Vietnam War portrays LBJ as a manipulative leader, Janis (1982, 129) suggests that the president might have been a victim of groupthink. The former interpretation views LBJ as having made up his mind in advance, and group deliberations as largely driven by considerations of legitimation and support-building. The latter interpretation suggests that LBJ may have leaned heavily upon a dysfunctional advisory group for cognitive and emotional support—with devastating consequences. Burke and Greenstein's (1989) subsequent analysis of key decisions made during the Vietnam conflict shows how difficult it is to account for the complex and overdetermined decision-making process of the Johnson administration using Janis's indicators of groupthink as the sole guidance.

Of course, a leader's incentives for consulting may include more than one of these objectives and the reasons for so doing may vary from one situation to another. It is clear that the extent to which an executive decision process is harmed by one-sided or sterile deliberations within the advisory group depends upon what it is that the executive was trying to accomplish in the small group, as well as upon the extent to which "compensating" information is provided elsewhere.

Taken together, these points indicate that a narrow focus on small group deliberations immediately preceding major decisions may be highly misleading—significant aspects of the policy process occurring previously or outside the small group setting can easily be missed.[22] The same is true of an analysis which focuses exclusively upon the substantive quality of decisions taken in or potentially influenced by small groups and neglects the broader political context in which political judgment is exercised. Such one-sided or skewed analyses may well lead to unfair and unjustified attributions of "pathology" in foreign policy decision making. Only with reference to a well-understood and firmly established general and issue-historical context does it become meaningful to discuss potential shortcomings and pathologies of the decision process, such as those attributed to groupthink syndrome.

It is imperative for foreign policy analysts to attend to the diversity of types of relationships that may develop between executives, advisers, and other autonomous political actors in their attempts to study and evaluate decision-making processes. The results of studies of presidential decision making in the U.S. foreign policy-making setting reveal that these relationships can take a variety of forms—often with characteristic strengths and vulnerabilities. Even greater diversity is to be expected across political systems. Contextual diversity is ignored only at the foreign policy analyst's (and his or her reader's) peril. Contextually sensitive comparative research into the role of small groups in executive decision-making processes promises to provide not only insights into the functioning of other political systems, but also into the functioning of our own.

NOTES

I am heavily indebted to Eric Stern for making substantial improvements to an earlier draft of this chapter, particularly in the concluding section, "Toward Contextual Process Analysis."

1. The reader familiar with Janis's work will recognize that I have not referred to the considerable effort Janis made in the first edition of *Victims of Groupthink* and later in the second edition published in 1982 to identify the conditions that made concurrence-seeking more likely. He obviously felt impelled to do so because he recognized from the beginning that group cohesiveness does not invariably lead to groupthink. "It may be a necessary condition, but it is not a sufficient condition" (Janis 1982, 199). Hence, the need to identify other conditions. Many such possible conditions were discussed. Efforts to evaluate the causal status and importance of these conditions, however, have been handicapped among other reasons because it is necessary first to determine whether in fact concurrence-seeking has occurred in the cases examined, a determination that, as I will argue below, rests uneasily on the validity and reliability of the "symptoms" employed as indicators of concurrence-seeking.

2. See Mullen and Copper 1994 for an integrative review of the literature on the relationship between cohesiveness and performance.

3. For example, the importance of emotion in decision making is a central theme in Janis and Mann's (1977) influential monograph.

4. In his earlier work, such as Janis 1959, he developed a detailed theory of

decision making as a stressful process, largely concentrating on individuals rather than groups as units of decision. In his last main book, Janis (1989) embeds groupthink in a much broader set of decision pathologies.

5. Note that this type of decisional stress assumes that members of the group entertain sufficiently strong commitments to the humanitarian values that they feel obliged to violate. This is, of course, not true of all individuals who become policy-makers. As Willard Gaylin, M.D., has emphasized, the nature of politics and what it takes to be successful in politics—as in business—may attract sociopathic and para-noid personality types: "The capacity to be ruthless, driving and immoral, if also combined with intelligence and imagination, can be a winning combination in politics as well as commerce . . . Sociopathic and paranoid personality traits that are most dangerous in people of power are precisely those characteristics most suitable for the attainment of power in a competitive culture such as ours" ("What's Normal?," *New York Times Magazine,* April 1, 1973).

6. Although not clearly spelled out, Janis was suggesting that when individuals within the group experience these types of decisional stress they tend to rely on each other's opinions and judgments on matters on which there is inadequate information. In this respect Janis echoed an important element in Leon Festinger's theory of informal social communication, which Stanley Schachter later developed in his studies of con-formity pressures. Schachter postulated that "on any issue for which there is no empiri-cal referent, the reality of one's own opinion is established by the fact that other people hold similar opinions." Schachter's "social reality" test, then, plays a role in concur-rence-seeking that tends to replace reality-based estimates of the efficacy and morality of policy options being considered.

7. For a discussion of various analytical and psychological modes of coping with decisional stress induced by value complexity and uncertainty, see George 1980, chapter 2.

8. Ironically, the prior existence of negative stereotypes of a potential adversary may be a *source* of situational stress as well as a means of coping with decisional stress. One need only imagine encountering members of an ethnic group stereotyped as "dangerous" in an isolated place, late at night, in order to appreciate this point. Regard-less of the intentions and actual behavior of the individuals in question, the holder of the stereotype might well experience high levels of stress.

9. Paul 't Hart (1991, 268, emphasis added) makes the critical observation, entirely justified in my view, that Janis "chose cases of (alleged) policy failure first, and then applied groupthink analysis to see whether the decision process was affected by it. If so, groupthink was implied to be one of the causes of failure. This methodology places a high premium on the objectivity of the analyst to withstand (unconscious) biases towards selective interpretation of the case study material."

10. I believe it is appropriate to recall that when, at Janis's request, I read the very rough and quite inadequate drafts of the case studies that later appeared in revised form in *Victims of Groupthink,* I urged that alternative explanations be explored. I also cautioned that he should not overstate the case that groupthink played the dominant role in producing what he referred to as a policy fiasco but be content with the more modest claim that it appeared to have contributed to it.

11. See, for example, Etheredge 1985, chapter 1 and pages 112–16; Vandenbroucke 1984; and Stern (this volume).

12. 't Hart's *Groupthink in Government* is, to my knowledge, the only book-length monograph on groupthink theory aside from Janis's own books. For a useful review, see Stern and Sundelius 1994.

13. My own preference, however, would be to restrict the concept of groupthink and concurrence-seeking to their original formulation by Janis. My hunch is that progress would be facilitated if both concepts were set aside rather than redefined and broadened, but that is not a position to be argued here. Rather, I attempt here, in a constructive way, to point out some aspects of 't Hart's revised theory that appear to be in need of additional attention.

14. In fairness to 't Hart, I should mention that he does provide some guidance relevant to the operationalization of rigidity in his discussion of the literature on "entrapment" and risk taking, which are conceptualized as outputs of groupthink (1990, 96–97, 124–25).

15. It should be noted that 't Hart's discussion indicates an awareness of the subtleties involved in making such determinations. For example, 't Hart (1990, 19) approvingly cites Longley and Pruitt's observation that rapidly shutting off "repetitive" and "low utility" discussions might actually enhance decision quality. Yet such "policing" actions by a leader or other assertive members might well be interpreted by an analyst as indications of "premature" closure.

16. The notion of "prematurity" seems to imply some objective or easily accessible time frame against which the time devoted to the decision-making process can be measured. Yet, as C. F. Hermann (e.g., 1972) and many others have argued, time constraints in crisis may best be conceptualized as subjective and contingent upon the perceptions of the decision makers. In other words, coming to a determination regarding how much time is available is an integral part of the decision process itself.

17. This discussion is adapted from George 1980.

18. Such individuals may or may not be included within the inner circle participating in policy deliberations. Where they are not, they may be highly important "shadow participants" influencing decisions.

19. In Janis's (1989, 16, 149) reconceptualization, groupthink is seen a response to "affiliative constraints" (the need for acceptability, consensus, and social support).

20. For a brief assessment of the broader foreign policy imperatives that led Kennedy to dismiss accommodative options in the initial phase of the crisis, see George 1993, 112–15. Kennedy reportedly was well aware that concessions might be necessary eventually, *after* having clearly demonstrated the firmness of the U.S. resolve to remove the missiles from Cuba. As we now know, Kennedy did ultimately proceed in this fashion. See also George 1991, 233–35, for a further analysis of Kennedy's bargaining strategy and tactics in that crisis.

21. This discussion is adapted from George 1980, chapter 4. See chapter 1 of this volume for an alternative approach to capturing the diversity of roles played and functions fulfilled by advisory and decision groups.

22. This is reminiscent of the debate regarding national security decision making in the Eisenhower presidency. Initial analyses focus upon what was perceived as an

overly formalistic and sterile policy development and implementation system. These analyses tended to miss a second informal policy development track that complemented and buttressed the first, leading many subsequent scholars to revise their assessments of the effectiveness of Eisenhower's leadership and policy-making system. See, for example, Greenstein 1982.

CHAPTER 3

Challenging the Mindguards: Moving Small Group Analysis beyond Groupthink

Sally Riggs Fuller and Ramon J. Aldag

Introduction

We begin with a parable, "The Parable of Gruffthing":

> *Many of the villagers could still remember the first time they had heard of Gruffthing, more than twenty years ago. As portrayed by a storyteller who had passed through the hamlet, Gruffthing was huge, covered with long hair, sporting a yard-long pointed horn in the center of its forehead, living on fermented moose droppings. Gruffthing, the storyteller intoned, was the dark force behind the myriad ills that had been plaguing the village. It made sense to the villagers that such an awful beast would be associated with terrible events; even the name conjured up dark images in their minds.*
>
> *Each time foul deeds took place—the killing of an animal, destruction of part of the nearby forest, a raid on a food cache, unexplained weight gains—the villagers would ask in hushed, respectful whispers, "Was it Gruffthing?"*
>
> *Sometimes, those who had seen the rogue which was responsible for the odious deed would attempt to describe it.*
>
> *"It was big!" they might say, and the other villagers would respond, "Gruffthing is big!"*
>
> *"It was hairy!" they might say, and the other villagers would respond, "Gruffthing is hairy!"*
>
> *"It was covered with feathers!" they might say, and the other villagers would shout, "You must have seen it wrong!"*
>
> *"It killed my sheep!" they might say, and the other villagers would chorus, "Gruffthing could kill sheep!"*
>
> *"It carried a gun," they might say, and the other villagers would respond, "There's no reason Gruffthing couldn't carry a gun!"*

"It flew over my hen house to reach my pigs!" they might say, and the other villagers would respond, "Sometimes Gruffthing sprouts wings to satisfy its blood lust!"

"It wore a false nose and funny glasses!" they might say, and the other villagers would reason, "Sometimes Gruffthing disguises itself!"

None of the villagers could ever remember spotting a yard-long pointed horn during their Gruffthing sightings, and none had ever noticed a conspicuous decline in reports of moose droppings, but these facts were seen as unimportant. Surely any sentient, objective observer could recognize the overwhelming evidence of the ravages of Gruffthing.

The villagers' farms and homes fell into disrepair as they obsessed on Gruffthing, but they had more important things to do than tend familiar fences. They shared a mission to carry word of Gruffthing to neighboring towns—towns that, until now, had remarkably been spared from its awful wrath. A quarter century after entering the minds of the villagers, Gruffthing had become a metaphor for malice, and it was wreaking terror across the countryside.

Anchors serve useful roles, providing comforting security in times of turbulence and uncertainty. They may also permit secure exploration of a limited area. Clinging to an anchor, though, can be constraining. Such constraint becomes counterproductive if the anchor itself is suspect. In this chapter, we argue that the groupthink phenomenon has become an anchor on the small group literature, a metaphor for malice and negligence. Every fiasco is scanned for evidence of groupthink, and disconfirming evidence tends to be discounted. As a result, we argue that strong medicine is necessary to correct imbalance. We urge a cessation of calls for additional groupthink research, refinements, or redirection. Similarly, we reject the dual tendencies to see all flawed decision making as evidence of groupthink tendencies (see George, this volume) and to equate support for any element in the groupthink model as support for groupthink itself. Instead, as the title of this volume suggests, it is time to move beyond groupthink. To do so, it is useful to attempt to draw some lessons from the quarter century history of groupthink dominance in the policy-oriented small groups literature.

In the last two decades there has been a substantial increase in emphasis on groups in organizations in general and on group problem solving in particular. However, surprisingly little attention has been paid to development of comprehensive models of group problem solving. Models are available to suggest when groups, rather than individuals, should be used for problem solving and the appropriate composition and functioning options of problem-solving groups, and several specific group problem-solving techniques have been presented. Further, generic models of group functioning are also available, but do not lend themselves to application specifically to group problem solving (e.g., Homans 1950; Gladstein 1984). However, comprehensive models of group problem solving applicable to the practices of high-level policy decision making are lacking.

The groupthink model (Janis 1971, 1972, 1982) is the most prominent attempt to fill this void. In recent years, acceptance of the groupthink phenomenon has become widespread, and groupthink has entered the popular vocabulary. It has been blamed for such decision-making fiascoes as the Bay of Pigs invasion, the escalation of the Vietnam conflict, the Watergate cover-up, and the Challenger disaster, as well as for flawed group problem solving in business and other organizations. Despite Longley and Pruitt's (1980) warning that both the groupthink theory and related research were problematic, Janis did not significantly alter his original conceptualization, and groupthink continues to be viewed as a defective process to be avoided. With few exceptions ('t Hart 1990/1994), group researchers and theorists have continued to refer to, and rely upon, the unaltered groupthink model. Articles discussing the dangers of groupthink and suggesting remedies have regularly appeared in periodicals aimed at managers, lawyers, medical professionals, and the general public.

Janis chose the term "groupthink" because of its frankly Orwellian connotation, similar to "doublethink" and "crimethink." He wrote that "The invidiousness is intentional" (1982, 9). This view of groupthink as an undesirable phenomenon continues to be evidenced in Janis's most recent work. For instance, Janis (1989) wrote that

> Whenever a policymaking or crisis management group is functioning as a compatible team with a fair or high degree of esprit de corps, take steps to counteract tendencies toward concurrence-seeking or "groupthink". If a leader does this, the decisionmaking process will tend to be of higher quality. (247)

The widespread acceptance of the groupthink model suggests that it has had considerable heuristic value. It has stimulated research on group dysfunctions and encouraged viewing outcomes in problem-solving terms; shown how decision processes may be relevant to a wide range of situations; provided links to other literatures, such as stress and vigilance; and identified potentially important variables in group problem solving. It has provided a base for further development and testing. Nevertheless, the groupthink model has a relatively narrow focus, primarily addressing major decision fiascoes. Also, it has not been adequately revised to incorporate emerging literatures and empirical findings. This chapter develops and discusses a new model of group problem solving, termed the General Group Problem Solving (GGPS) model (Aldag and Fuller 1993) which addresses each of these threats. The GGPS model captures and recasts some elements of the groupthink model; generally, this is a process of liberation of variables from a confining context. Additionally, the GGPS model integrates findings of a groupthink literature review, material from a variety of other literature suggested by a general problem-solving perspective, and a critical examination of groupthink assumptions.

At this point, we should explicitly note that we use the term "problem solving" in this chapter to refer to the problem-solving process (e.g., Huber 1980), a process including problem definition, alternative generation, evaluation and choice, implementation, and control. As we discuss later in the chapter, this process can be applied to any sort of decision group, not merely to narrowly defined problem-solving groups. Such a broad focus permits application of the model to different levels of analysis and varying contexts, including foreign policy-making by high-level groups in government.

In this chapter, we first discuss the basic characteristics of the groupthink model. Next, the research that has examined groupthink is summarized and discussed, a general problem-solving perspective is adopted and other relevant literatures suggested by that perspective are presented, and groupthink assumptions are questioned. We then present the new model, address the allure of groupthink, and provide implications of our literature review and model development for future theory and research on group problem solving.

The Groupthink Model

At the level of the individual, Janis and Mann (1977) argued that thinking about vital, affect-laden issues generally results in "hot" cognitions, in contrast to the cold cognitions of routine problem solving, and that such hot cognitions can result in errors in scanning of alternatives. Such situations induce stress which results in defensive avoidance, characterized by lack of vigilant search, distortion of the meanings of warning messages, selective inattention and forgetting, and rationalizing. Groupthink is seen as the group analog of defensive avoidance, or "a collective pattern of defensive avoidance" (Janis and Mann 1977, 129). According to Janis:

> I use the term "groupthink" as a quick and easy way to refer to a mode of thinking that people engage in when they are deeply involved in a cohesive in-group, when the members' strivings for unanimity override their motivation to realistically appraise alternative courses of action. . . . Groupthink refers to a deterioration of mental efficiency, reality testing, and moral judgment that results from in-group pressures. (1972, 9)

Janis (1982) explicitly defined the context in which groupthink is thought to occur, and divided these antecedent conditions into three categories. First, a moderate to high level of group cohesion is a necessary but not sufficient condition for groupthink. Secondary antecedents that are said to predict situations in which groupthink is likely to occur are structural faults and a provocative situational context. In the structural fault category are insulation of the group, lack of traditional impartial leadership, lack of norms requiring methodological procedures, and homogeneity of members' social backgrounds and ideology. The provocative-situational-context antecedents focus on the role of stress as a situational factor. The first stress factor is characterized as external threats of losses combined with a low hope of finding a better solution than that of the leader. The internal-stress antecedent stems from temporary low self-esteem due to members' recent failures, perceptions that the task is too difficult to accomplish, and the perception that there is no alternative that is morally correct.

There are several supposed symptoms of groupthink (cf. Janis and Mann 1977, 130–31), including: an illusion of invulnerability; rationalization to discount warnings and other negative feedback; belief in the inherent morality of the group; stereotyped views of members of opposing groups; pressure on dissenters; self-censorship; illusion of unanimity; and self-appointed mindguards acting to shield the group from adverse information.

According to Janis, groupthink results in a number of consequences which interfere with effective group decision making. For instance, the group limits its discussion to just a few alternatives. After a course of action is initially selected, members ignore new information concerning its risks and drawbacks. At the same time, they avoid information concerning benefits of rejected alternatives. Members make little attempt to use experts to obtain more precise information. And, because they are so confident that things will turn out well, group members fail to consider what may go wrong and so do not develop contingency plans. These "defects" are seen as leading to impaired performance and other undesirable outcomes. This view of the causal sequence relating to determinants and consequences of groupthink is summarized in figure 3.1.

Janis also suggested a number of strategies to prevent groupthink or minimize the negative consequences. These are presented and discussed in the concluding chapter of this volume.

Underlying Assumptions of Groupthink

At base, the prevailing view of groupthink seems to rest on a set of generally unstated assumptions. As discussed in more detail elsewhere (Aldag and Fuller 1993), at least seven such assumptions can be identified:

1. The purpose of using a group for problem solving is primarily to enhance decision quality.
2. Group problem solving is essentially a rational process, with members

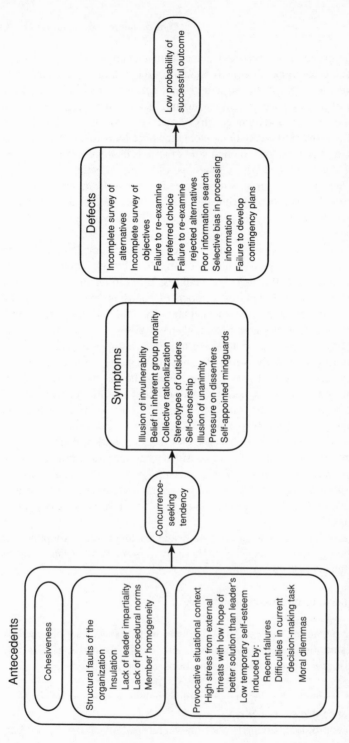

Fig. 3.1. Groupthink model. (Adapted with the permission of The Free Press, a division of Simon and Schuster, reprinted from Irving L. Janis and Leon Mann, *Decision Making: A Psychological Analysis of Conflict, Choice, and Commitment*, New York: The Free Press, 1977, 132. Copyright © 1977 by The Free Press.)

unified in their pursuit of a goal and participating in the group process to facilitate achievement of that goal.

3. Benefits associated with a problem-solving group that functions well are assumed to include: a wide variety of perspectives on a problem; more information concerning proposed alternatives; heightened decision reliability; dampening of biases; and social presence effects.

4. Groupthink characteristics are assumed to prevent the actualization of these potential group benefits by causing group members to passively respond to external pressures in undesirable ways.

5. By taking steps to prevent the occurrence of groupthink characteristics, a more rational and effective group process will result, leading to enhanced decision quality.

6. An illusion of well-being is inherently dysfunctional.

7. Concurrence-seeking attitudes and behaviors ("symptoms" and "defects") result from individuals' psychological agreement-seeking drives and group pressures for consensus.

We shall revisit these assumptions later, but first we shall review the results of the research on groupthink.

The Groupthink Literature in Review

We will review three types of literature relating to the groupthink phenomenon: case analyses, laboratory studies, and conceptual papers.

Case Analyses

Early support for groupthink was based almost entirely on retrospective case studies. For instance, Janis (1971, 1972, 1982) focused primarily on five American foreign policy crises: the Marshall Plan, the invasion of North Korea, the Bay of Pigs invasion, the Cuban missile crisis, and the escalation of the conflict in Vietnam. Through case studies, he categorized these crises by whether evidence of groupthink was revealed. In his 1982 work he also discussed the Watergate cover-up as an example of "how clever manipulators can get caught in an avoidable quagmire."

Tetlock (1979) examined the same five crises considered by Janis. Content analyses were performed on the public statements of key decision makers involved in the crises. Consistent with Janis's theory, groupthink decision makers were found to be more simplistic in their perceptions of policy issues than non-groupthink decision makers and to make more positive references to the United States and its allies. Inconsistent with Janis's theory, groupthink decision makers did not make significantly more negative references to the

Communist states and their allies. Tetlock (1979, 1322) concluded that "the current findings converge impressively with the conclusions of Janis's intensive case studies." He attributed the lack of uniform support to methodological issues, arguing that content analyses of public statements may be insensitive to differences in evaluations of opponents in groupthink and non-groupthink crises.

Subsequently, Tetlock et al. (1992) used a quantitative method (the Group Dynamics Q Sort [GDQS]) for analyzing historical cases of group decision making, employing it to compare Janis's case interpretations with other historical interpretations of the same cases and to test the causal linkages predicted by the groupthink model. The GDQS results showed considerable convergence between Janis's accounts of group decision making and those of independent historical sources. However, Janis reported relatively more conformity and rigidity and less pessimism in the groupthink cases than did other historical observers. A test of the causal sequence of the groupthink model yielded only limited support. For example, group cohesiveness and provocative situational context proved to be only weakly related to concurrence seeking, with structural and procedural faults playing larger roles.

Several other case studies of groupthink have been published. For instance, Manz and Sims (1982) presented three cases to demonstrate groupthink tendencies in autonomous work group settings. Smith (1985a) presented case information describing the attempt by the United States to rescue its hostages in Tehran as an example of groupthink (this example was noted by Janis in his 1982 edition). Hensley and Griffin (1986) applied groupthink to a case analysis of the 1977 gymnasium controversy at Kent State University where trustees decided to build an addition to the school's gymnasium on part of the area of the tragic 1970 confrontation of students and Ohio National Guard members. They concluded "that each major condition of the theory was present in the conflict and that the trustees were indeed victims of groupthink" (Hensley and Griffin 1986, 497). Heller (1983) linked groupthink to the conduct of the Falkland Islands War by the Thatcher government. Rosenthal (1984) found inconsistent evidence of the role of groupthink in several cases of crisis decision making in the Netherlands. Similarly, Etheredge (1985) and Polsby (1984) found inconclusive or negative evidence regarding groupthink's role in their studies of the evolution of the United States Central American policy and several cases of policy innovation, respectively. 't Hart and Kroon (1995) summarize additional case studies linking groupthink to governmental policy fiascoes.

Esser and Lindoerfer (1989) conducted a quantitative case analysis of the Space Shuttle Challenger accident. They coded statements from the *Report of the Presidential Commission on the Space Shuttle Challenger Accident* (1986) as positive or negative instances of the observable antecedents or consequences of groupthink. Positive "instances of groupthink" were reported to be twice as frequent as negative instances. Further, during the 24 hours prior to launch, the ratio of positive to negative "instances" increased and then remained high. Esser and Lindoerfer noted (1989, 175) that "It is possible that the many instances of decision-making defects would be consistent with *any* theory of poor decision-making. We have no comparison group with which to evaluate this alternative." Use of the terminology "positive and negative instances of groupthink" was taken to imply that any statement not directly inconsistent with groupthink was an "instance of groupthink." The authors failed to find statements relating to some groupthink symptoms or consequences. While they speculated that the decision makers constituted a highly cohesive group, no statements provided information concerning group cohesiveness. Finally, the finding of a greater relative number of occurrences of "instances of groupthink" closer to the decision point was interpreted as evidence of poor decision making, rather than as simple convergence on a solution. As noted by 't Hart and Kroon (1995), the results of several other analyses give further reason to question the appropriateness of a groupthink interpretation of the Challenger disaster. For example, it is difficult to pinpoint one crucial decision-making group in the case, and factors other than small group dynamics (such as competition for space dollars among various parties) appeared to play important roles.

In other cases, apparent confirmation of the groupthink model has been found to become suspect upon closer examination. For instance, 't Hart (1990/1994) examined the political and military decision-making process on the Dutch side prior to the German invasion of Holland on May 10, 1940. Although at first glance the case seemed to have all the ingredients of groupthink, closer examination required that such an interpretation had to be discarded. Similarly, Verbeek and Metselaar (this volume) discuss decision making in the Dutch cabinet during the 1959–62 West New Guinea conflict, when the Dutch government attempted to persuade the United States, the United Kingdom, and Australia to form a coalition in order to deter Indonesia from attacking Dutch-controlled Western New Guinea. Verbeek and Metselaar show that symptoms and antecedent conditions of groupthink can be readily identified in the case, but that an adequate analysis of the case requires the consideration of additional variables such as the institutional context, leadership and its consequences, and the simultaneity of issues. In fact, they demonstrate that factors in the institutional context may have created conditions which a more cursory analysis would attribute to groupthink.

Laboratory Studies

Almost fifteen years ago Moorhead (1982, 436) wrote that "Since the publication of Janis's book, there has been no systematic research testing any of its propositions." Even now there have been only a limited number of studies empirically examining groupthink. The Esser and Lindoerfer quantitative case analysis was discussed above. In addition, laboratory studies of groupthink are reviewed below in chronological order.

Flowers (1977) hypothesized that cohesiveness and leadership style should interact in the decision process, so that groupthink is most likely when group cohesiveness is high and leadership style is closed (i.e., the leader presses for his or her own decision and a unanimous decision). Flowers assigned undergraduate students to experimental teams, with leaders trained to take an open or closed style and cohesiveness manipulated by whether students knew each other (high cohesive) or did not (low cohesive). Teams were given a "crisis" decision situation involving a school personnel problem. Open leadership style produced more suggested solutions and use of available facts than closed leadership style, but there was no support for Janis's assumption that cohesiveness is a critical variable. Flowers (1977, 888) argued that "the results of this experiment suggest that poor decisionmaking activities can occur in a wider variety of crisis situations than originally studied by Janis."

Courtright (1978) formed college freshmen into teams and gave them the problem "What is the best method for recruiting new students to the University of Iowa?" Half were told they were chosen to be compatible (high cohesive) and the other half that they probably would not like each other (low cohesive). In addition to cohesiveness, Courtright manipulated "decisionmaking parameters." In the "freed" condition, group members were told that arguing is the best way to solve a problem. In the "limited" condition members were told that cooperation is necessary and that time is limited. In the "no instructions" condition, members were told only of the time limit for discussion. Dependent variables included the number of times each member offered solutions, stated agreement, and stated disagreement. The only significant finding was that groups in the high cohesive and limited parameters condition (the groupthink condition) generated significantly less disagreement than groups in the low cohesive and limited parameter condition. However, Courtright (1978, 229) stated that "the theory as postulated by Janis is essentially correct."

Moorhead and Montanari (1982) developed measures to tap groupthink concepts, including "group characteristics," "symptoms," and "defects," and presented a preliminary study to assess the validity of the indices. Business students competed as teams in a management simulation. After the competition, students completed the Moorhead and Montanari instruments. Largely nonsupportive factor analyses led the authors to conclude that "The measurement and validation of groupthink may not be as simple as Janis's clear and alluring presentation would suggest" (Moorhead and Montanari 1982, 382). They further noted that, while the "group characteristics" measures appeared adequate, "the conceptual uniqueness of the variables described under the

Symptoms and Defects categories can be questioned, based on these data" (ibid., 382) Further, they reported on the basis of intercategory correlations that the "preliminary analysis indicated that some of the relationships proposed by Janis appeared to hold for the groups used in this study" but that others "do not appear to be as strong for this data set" (ibid., 382).

Callaway and Esser (1984), using undergraduate psychology students, manipulated group cohesiveness and adequacy of decision procedures in a factorial design. The authors concluded that their findings provided mixed support for the groupthink hypothesis on measures of decision quality and group processes presumed to underlie the groupthink decisions. In the study, cohesiveness categories were achieved post hoc, and the degree of support for groupthink varied with the group task (the Lost at Sea task was supportive while the Horse Trading task was not). Given the differential support across tasks, the authors reasoned that the Horse Trading task may be inappropriate in a test of groupthink because it has a single correct answer which becomes immediately obvious.

Leana (1985) used teams of college students solving a hypothetical business problem. She tested the effects of group cohesiveness and leader behavior (directive versus participative) on defective decision making. She found that teams with directive leaders proposed and discussed fewer alternatives and discussed fewer alternative solutions than did teams with participative leaders. However, contrary to Janis's groupthink model, members of noncohesive groups engaged in more self-censorship of information than did members of cohesive groups. These findings were interpreted as partially supportive of the groupthink model.

Gladstein and Reilly (1985), using a management simulation called Tycoon, studied group decision making under threat. They hypothesized that threat may result in restriction in information processing and a decrease in breadth of distribution of influence (termed constriction of control). Noting the congruence of these hypotheses with the groupthink model, they stated that "No one has fully tested the groupthink model, although several studies have shown partial support for it" (Gladstein and Reilly 1985, 615–16; Flowers 1977; Leana 1985). While the results indicated a restriction in information processing and increased stress when threat increased, the degree of threat made no significant difference in constriction of control. It was argued that group norms and task demands may have acted to moderate the relationship between threat and constriction of control.

Callaway, Marriott, and Esser (1985) reasoned that, since Janis proposed that groupthink is essentially a stress-reduction process, it might be prevented in cohesive groups if the stress could be diffused by other factors. They investigated the effects of group structure (decision-making procedures) and individual dominance on symptoms of groupthink, anxiety, and quality of group decision making. Students, formed into groups on the basis of dominance scores, participated in the Lost at Sea task (Nemiroff and Pasmore 1975), which permits objective scoring of the "correctness" of the group decision. Decision-making procedures were found to influence time required to reach a decision, but not decision quality nor the process variables assumed to mediate groupthink. Groups composed of highly dominant members made higher quality decisions, exhibited lower state anxiety, took more time to reach a decision, tended to make more statements of disagreement and agreement, and reported more group influence on the members.

Moorhead and Montanari (1986) argued that previous empirical studies of groupthink were flawed both because they failed to successfully produce the antecedent conditions proposed by Janis and because they provided very incomplete tests of the groupthink theoretical framework. They wrote that "The most comprehensive empirical test to date (Courtright 1978) included measures of only two of the seven antecedent conditions, none of the symptoms, three of the seven decisionmaking defects, and outcomes measured on a subjective productivity rating instrument" (Moorhead and Montanari 1986, 402). To provide a more complete test, the authors formed teams of Business Policy students who completed "a highly competitive management simulation exercise" (ibid., 405). Refined versions of the Moorhead and Montanari (1982) measures were administered and path analysis was used to assess the implied causal sequence. The authors concluded that, while several relationships supported the framework proposed by Janis, "the empirically derived model suggests that several linkages were opposite to those predicted by the Janis framework" (Moorhead and Montanari 1986, 408). For instance, cohesion had a negative impact on self-censorship, a positive impact on dissent, and a negative impact on the defect, "few alternatives." Moorhead and Montanari noted that "these data do not show powerful support for Janis's groupthink hypothesis" (ibid., 408) but argued that there were enough significant relationships among variables to warrant further investigation.

Montanari and Moorhead (1989) developed and validated scales to measure groupthink variables.[1] They included three antecedents (cohesion, insulation, and promotional leadership) and all eight symptoms and seven defects. Factor analyses were used to reduce eight symptoms to five, and seven defects to three. The analyses were conducted only on variables within categories (i.e., antecedent conditions, symptoms, and defects), presumably because the sample size ($n = 61$) did not permit a full factor analysis. Even with this restricted approach, there was relatively little support for the structure proposed by Janis. The authors concluded that "Janis's conceptualization of the groupthink variables, when operationalized via subscale items, lacks sufficient stability" (Montanari and Moorhead 1989, 217).

Conceptual Papers

In the first comprehensive critical evaluation of groupthink, Longley and Pruitt (1980) raised several issues including the lack of empirical support and deficiencies in the theory itself. They called for a clearer definition of group-think, more rigorous empirical research, and increased attention to underlying processes and the relationships among variables. Despite these warnings, research on groupthink continued in the same vein, without significant changes to Janis's (1972) original theory.

Whyte (1989) argued that the decision fiascoes attributed to groupthink may be explained by prospect polarization which employs, in addition to the pressures for uniformity of groupthink, the concepts of framing effects and group polarization. While Whyte cited some groupthink research as more consistent with prospect polarization than with groupthink, he did not chal-lenge the general constellation of characteristics said to be associated with groupthink. He suggested that groupthink "although relevant, is an incomplete explanation for the occurrence of decision fiascoes" (Whyte 1989, 54).

Luechauer (1989) provided a brief overview of groupthink and the cri-tiques leveled against it (citing Longley and Pruitt 1980 and Whyte 1989). He then presented a "revised model of the groupthink phenomenon" which sug-gests that the self-monitoring propensity of group members "is a critical personality variable that should be considered in the groupthink formulation and that Fantasy Themes may act as a possible mechanism which propels groups toward groupthink" (Luechauer 1989, 5). Luechauer argued that fanta-sies enable a group to draw a boundary around itself that resists intrusions. He then discussed how such additional variables might act to pull the fantasizing "away from reality and toward groupthink" (ibid., 10). He noted that "Our purpose in presenting this model is not to debunk Janis's work. Rather, it is to expand the model by supplying two elements that Janis does not consider in his treatment of the topic" (ibid., 5).

McCauley (1989) used content analysis to review Janis's descriptions of historical cases. He sought to determine whether groupthink concurrence-seeking was due to compliance (public without private agreement) or internal-ization (private acceptance of group consensus). McCauley interpreted Janis as arguing for internalization, but reasoned that compliance may have also played a substantial role. For each of eight decisions (six groupthink and two non-groupthink), McCauley determined whether compliance and eight hypo-thesized antecedents were present. The results showed evidence of compli-ance in two of the six groupthink decisions and in neither of the two decisions without groupthink. Since all eight cases reflected high degrees of cohesion and external threat, these antecedents were not useful in discriminating between groupthink and non-groupthink situations. The Watergate case was the only example in which all six of the other antecedents were present. Across the six groupthink decisions for the six discriminating antecedents, 21 antecedents were present and 15 absent (that is, without Watergate, these hypothesized antecedents were equally present and absent). In the two non-groupthink decisions, five antecedents were present and seven absent. In only three of the groupthink decisions were more discriminating antecedents present than absent. McCauley concluded that cohesion can lead to both compliance and internalization, and that future groupthink research should attempt to distinguish between them.

Park (1990) provided a critical evaluation of empirical groupthink research. He questioned the model's completeness and the methodologies used to assess it. Criticisms included the researchers' failure to test all of the model's variables and the inappropriate use of modes of measurement. Park's recommendation was to use structural equation modeling such as LISREL to test groupthink. Despite the above criticisms, he appeared to accept the phenomenon as valid without suggesting changes to the original framework.

't Hart (1990/1994) provided the only book-length study of the groupthink phenomenon (cf. 't Hart 1991; 't Hart and Kroon 1996; and chapter 2, this volume). 't Hart's aim was mainly theoretical, that is, putting Janis's *ad hoc* theory of groupthink on a broader theoretical footing, drawing upon literature in social psychology and political science/public administration. He developed a major revision of groupthink theory in three areas. The first deals with the causes of groupthink. Following McCauley (1989) he specified not one but two distinct "pathways" to groupthink: groupthink as a product of high in-group cohesion, sometimes reinforced by deindividuation, and anticipatory compliance of group members to leaders or powerful peers (1990/1994, 115–26, 195–206). Second, 't Hart stipulated that there might be two generically different clusters of situational conditions under which groupthink is most likely[2]: (1) situations of threat and stress as emphasized in Janis's original model, and (2) situations which are perceived by group members as major opportunities (policy windows) requiring rapid and major commitment to a pet project or policy to achieve a major success. According to 't Hart this type of groupthink condition is likely to be encountered during so-called honeymoon periods of new governments, or major infrastructural, architectural, and research and development projects (ibid., 181–93). Third, 't Hart provides a more focused view of groupthink outcomes, hypothesizing that groupthink is likely to foster extreme forms of risk taking (ironically because of the fact that groupthink blinds decision makers to risks involved in their course of action), and in sequential or repetitive decision situations facilitates entrapment in increasingly ineffective and costly policies (ibid., 73–95).

Evaluating the Groupthink Literature

In this section we first present some general comments regarding past group-think literature and then discuss specific lessons which may be drawn from that literature. As suggested by the above review, most support for groupthink (aside from the work of Janis himself) derives from retrospective case studies which have focused on decision fiascoes rather than comparing the decision-making processes associated with good versus bad decisions. Experimental studies of groupthink have considered only a small portion of the model, often without a cohesive group and in situations inconsistent with Janis's antecedents. Further, they have relied exclusively on student samples dealing with hypothetical or simulated decisions, with potential resultant problems for external validity. Military strategists, managers, politicians, or other "real-world" decision makers have never been employed. In the laboratory, many "real-world" group characteristics, including ongoing power relationships and political maneuverings, have been necessarily ignored. While student samples in lab settings may be valuable to address many issues relating to group problem solving, their use to examine groupthink is problematic.

Empirical studies of groupthink have tended to use short-term decision quality as the sole outcome measure and have contained serious threats to internal validity. Based on a rather cursory review of just three laboratory studies of groupthink (those of Tetlock, Courtright, and Flowers), Posner-Weber concluded that:

> In the study of groupthink, each experimenter has tended to start from scratch, either arbitrarily or intuitively deciding what aspects of the groupthink phenomenon will be studied . . . Janis's theory is largely based on intuition; he is well-informed, but his statements are not clearly confirmed. (1987, 124)

Interestingly, Janis apparently discounted these experiments. For instance, Janis (1989) cited none of the experimental studies of groupthink; his discussion of groupthink refers only to case studies and anecdotal pieces. However, Janis (1985) has explicitly recognized the dangers of reliance on anecdote and suggested the "modus operandi" approach (Scriven 1976) as a more rigorous methodology for the analysis of case studies. Studies of groupthink which employ this methodology have not yet appeared.[3]

Studies of groupthink have focused on various combinations of Janis's original antecedents, and have rarely been faithful to the original conceptualization, in which cohesion was a necessary condition. Also, the majority of studies did not operationalize the model as Janis defined it. Another important aspect of prior research concerns the situations chosen for study. The groupthink conceptualization is restrictive, primarily due to the model's antecedents and the international policy context for which groupthink was developed. The narrow focus of the model's antecedents is not surprising given the fact that Janis extracted them directly from the major policy decision fiascoes he examined. Early case evidence provided in support of groupthink was drawn largely from these and similar "hot" decision situations. The ability to generalize from such situations is questionable. For instance, the extremely high group cohesiveness and clearly unified goals in many major military policy decisions or in groups facing a natural disaster are unlikely to be frequently encountered in other settings. Nevertheless, laboratory and survey research on groupthink has typically chosen settings considerably different from Janis's conceptualization. Such issues call into question the appropriateness of most past groupthink research.

Our discussion of prior research suggests that conclusions should be drawn from that research only with caution. Nevertheless, the following lessons appear to emerge from the groupthink research.

General Support for the Model

To assess the level of overall support for groupthink, it would be tempting to conduct a meta-analysis of prior research. However, the relatively small number of empirical studies, variety of methodologies employed, and methodological difficulties associated with many studies make this approach unfeasible (Campbell 1986; Park 1990).

On the basis of our review, it seems clear that there is little support for the full groupthink model. In fact, to our knowledge, no study of groupthink has fully tested the model, and in no study were all results consistent with the model. The McCauley (1989) review raises doubts about Janis's conclusions regarding the prevalence of the antecedent conditions in his initial scenarios. Further, the central variable of cohesiveness has not been found to play a consistent role. Flowers (1977, 895) went so far as to state that "A revision of Janis's theory may be justified, one which would eliminate cohesiveness as a critical variable." This suggestion is diametrically opposed to Janis's view that high cohesiveness induced or intensified by stress (see George, this volume) and an accompanying concurrence-seeking tendency that interferes with critical thinking are "the central features of groupthink" (Janis 1982, 9).

The variable that has received the most consistent support is the directive leadership antecedent (i.e., lack of tradition of impartial leadership). However, almost by definition, leader behaviors which promote the leader's own views and do not allow open exploration of alternatives will be associated with such "defects" as incomplete survey of alternatives and failure to reexamine preferred and rejected alternatives even in the absence of "concurrence-seeking" groupthink. Such domain overlap calls into question groupthink research that finds links between partial leadership and decision-making defects.

Evidence of Grouping of Characteristics

Groupthink's proposed causal chain is based on the premise that sets of variables such as symptoms and defects group together. However, support for the grouping of those characteristics derives from anecdote, casual observation, and intuitive appeal rather than from rigorous research. Because there has been no full factor analysis of groupthink variables, it is impossible at this point to determine whether the groupthink factor structure is as hypothesized. As previously noted, Moorhead and Montanari's (1986) restricted factor analyses appeared to support a simpler model than that presented by Janis (1982). Thus, support for this aspect of the model is lacking.

Presumed Negative Outcomes

Groupthink has been overwhelmingly viewed as an unmitigated evil, leading to uniformly negative outcomes. Indeed, such a view is universally implicit in the language of groupthink (e.g., the common references to "symptoms of groupthink," "victims of groupthink," and "defects of groupthink"). When used in groupthink research, such negative terminology can invite distortions in responses due to scale use tendencies and related psychometric difficulties and can also result in framing effects.

Individuals (whether subjects or researchers) presented with negatively framed terminology may adopt the readily available negative frame and respond accordingly (Bazerman 1990; Tversky and Kahneman 1986). Therefore, even simple attempts by the subjects to give responses that are consistent with the tone of the questions would result in negatively oriented responses. In many cases, failed decisions are examined and characteristics of groupthink are then sought. There is evidence that when individuals are provided knowledge of a negative outcome, they infer a negative process (Guzzo, Wagner, Maguire, Herr, and Hawley 1986). Further, a focus only on the conjunction of groupthink characteristics and negative outcomes invites illusory correlation (Einhorn 1980; Hogarth 1980; Kleinmuntz 1990).

On a more fundamental level, this framing has resulted in a focus on error rather than on decision quality per se. Janis has noted that he began studying fiascoes "for the purposes of studying sources of error in foreign policy decisionmaking" (Janis 1982, 9). However, there is more to the performance of a football team than the absence of fumbles and interceptions, and there is more to group decision quality than the absence of error (cf. 't Hart 1991). A focus on negative outcomes of group processes may divert attention from group synergies. One example is the assembly effect bonus, which, as noted by Collins and Guetzkow (1964, 58), "is productivity which exceeds the potential of the most capable member and also exceeds the sum of the efforts of the group members working separately." There is considerable evidence for this assembly effect bonus, at least in some contexts (Burleson, Levine, and Samter 1984). Thus, we may learn little about superior group performance by a focus solely on fiascoes. Instead, a focus on decisions with a broad range of outcomes, including superior performance, is necessary. In the concluding chapter of this volume, Paul 't Hart (this volume) argues that groupthink characteristics may lead to desirable outcomes such as esprit de corps, quick and easy consensus in the inner circle, and the avoidance of value trade-offs, and that Janis's suggestions for preventing groupthink may thus jeopardize those outcomes.

The consequences of the groupthink literature's preoccupation with fiascoes are doubly ironic. First, the overemphasis on fiascoes inhibits generalization to other decision situations used in virtually all attempts to assess the validity of groupthink. Second, the focus on fiascoes makes it difficult to say anything even about the determinants of fiascoes (cf. King, Keohane, and Verba 1994).

As our discussion suggests, recent scale development efforts such as those of Montanari and Moorhead (1989) are badly needed. That is, Montanari and Moorhead have attempted to develop psychometrically adequate indices while removing the negative labels associated with Janis's variable categories and the associated problems. We see this as an encouraging and critical development. In pursuing such avenues, however, it is critical that researchers do more than simply avoid negative labels; they must also avoid limiting their perspectives to the confines of the groupthink model.

Groupthink Interpretation

Strong and weak interpretations of groupthink have emerged. The strong interpretation, commonly cited, suggests that groupthink is an integrated set of characteristics with rather deterministic linkages. That is, groupthink characteristics cluster due to their common ties to specific antecedent conditions and are linked in a causal chain from those antecedent conditions to symptoms to defects to outcomes. The weak interpretation is sometimes presented in response to the failure of empirical examinations to provide results wholly consistent with groupthink. It suggests that groupthink may be evidenced by the presence of some subset of these characteristics, and that the causal ordering posited by Janis may be suggestive rather than necessary.

When the weak interpretation is presented, it is crucial to ask what characteristics, if any, are unique to groupthink. That is, some "groupthink" characteristics, such as belief in the rightness of a decision and pressures to achieve consensus, are common to many group processes and, in fact, may be beneficial. For instance, Nemeth (1986) has argued that convergence to the majority viewpoint is desirable if the majority viewpoint is correct. Other characteristics, such as mindguards and self-censorship, better discriminate groupthink from other group processes. It is difficult to accept the argument that the presence of characteristics common to most problem-solving groups is supportive of the existence of groupthink.

Janis apparently did not accept this weak form of groupthink. To the contrary, he wrote that

> It does not suffice merely to see if a few of the eight telltale symptoms of groupthink can be detected. Rather, it is necessary to see if practically all the symptoms were manifested and also to see if the antecedent conditions and the expected immediate consequences—the symptoms of defective decisionmaking—are also present. (1989, 60)

Comprehensiveness

Several researchers and theorists have suggested that the groupthink model is incomplete as a model of group problem solving. Some have proposed specific additions, as indicated below, while others have noted that other, unexplored variables may be playing roles (Moorhead and Montanari 1986; Courtright 1978). Among the proposed additions are norms, leader power, task characteristics, and stage of group development.[4] The importance of these factors is evidenced both in the groupthink research and in more general literatures on group problem solving.

Norms
Moorhead (1982) noted after a brief review of the research relating cohesiveness to group performance, and consistent with prior arguments of Seashore (1954) and others, that group norms will moderate the influence of cohesiveness on performance. For this moderating variable was also noted, in passing, by Janis (1982) himself (see also Stern and Sundelius, this volume). When the norms favor high performance, cohesiveness should enhance performance. When norms favor low performance, cohesiveness should lower performance. This suggests that examination only of cohesiveness per se, rather than asking, "Cohesiveness to what?", may be misleading. Further, Gladstein and Reilly (1985) reasoned that the nature of group norms may have prevented the constriction of control they had hypothesized ('t Hart 1990/1994, 37). They

noted that working as a team was a strong norm in the school in which the study was performed, and that the groups in the study appeared to adhere to that norm, making decisions as a group and striving for consensus.

The need to consider norms has also been widely recognized and evidenced in the more general group problem-solving literature. For instance, Bazerman, Magliozzi, and Neale (1985) have noted how norms influence group members' interpretation of problems and their subsequent attention to distributive or integrative solutions. Similarly, Bazerman (1990) has discussed how norms influence choice of third-party intervention procedures in group decision conflict as well as member risk preferences. Further, Howell and Frost (1989) have demonstrated how norms and leadership style may interact to influence performance and other outcomes in group decision making. Thus, norms may play pervasive roles in group problem solving and should be explicitly considered.

Leader Power
Flowers wrote that

> One potentially important factor not dealt with by Janis was the degree of power held by the leader over group members. Janis's groups had powerful leaders who could exercise reward and punishment as well as legitimate, expert, and perhaps referent power . . . over their members, whereas the leaders in this experiment held only certain legitimate power. Adding the variable of power to the operational definition of groupthink might create in highly cohesive groups an increased thrust toward groupthink. (1977, 895)

Similarly, McCauley (1989, 254), in his review of the Bay of Pigs decision, concluded that "compliance with a group norm promulgated by a powerful and attractive group leader" contributed to faulty decision making (cf. 't Hart 1990/1994, 55–63, 161–78; Stern, this volume).

The group problem solving literature has regularly noted the role of leader power. For example, Huber (1980) has argued that a powerful leader is needed to provide the opportunity for control if problem-solving groups begin to engage in dysfunctional behaviors. Clearly, the degree and locus of power in a group setting may have important consequences for group decision processes and outcomes. This point is reinforced by Metselaar and Verbeek (this volume) in their analysis of the West New Guinea conflict.

Task Characteristics
Callaway and Esser (1984) reasoned that the nature of the task might be important. In particular, they argued that a eureka-type task, in which a single

correct answer becomes immediately obvious once insight is achieved by any group member, may be inappropriate in a test of groupthink. This is because the group interaction necessary for groupthink characteristics to occur is circumvented. Thus, whether the task requires a pooling of inputs, or interaction at all, may be important. Further, Gladstein and Reilly (1985) noted that the task they used allowed for a high degree of specialization, and that it was thus difficult for one person to make all the decisions. This suggests that such characteristics as distribution of information and task complexity, as well as specialization per se, may be relevant task characteristics.

Task characteristics have often been examined in group problem solving. For instance, researchers have considered how group influences impact on decision performance in additive, compensatory, conjunctive, and disjunctive tasks (e.g., Steiner 1976; Weldon and Gargano 1985). Similarly, the literatures on such alternatives to traditional interacting groups as the nominal group technique and the Delphi process suggest that group decision processes should be fitted to the task (e.g., Stumpf, Freedman, and Zand 1979).

Leana (1985) argued that the *stage of group* development may be relevant since it may moderate the role of cohesiveness. She noted, building on Longley and Pruitt (1980), that *ad hoc* groups with no previous experience together may be quite susceptible to groupthink symptoms because of insecurity concerning member roles and group norms. However, groups with a tradition of working together may exhibit far fewer symptoms of defective decision making because members are secure enough in their roles and status to challenge one another, but have also developed ways of reaching agreement. This need to consider the stage of group development is made explicit by Stern and Sundelius (1994) in their discussion of newgroup syndrome, a pathological conformity dynamic liable to occur in newly formed policy groups. Newgroup syndrome, further explored by Stern (this volume), may result when uncertainty in newly formed groups, resulting from a lack of procedural norms and of a common group subculture, creates incentives for compliance and internalization. This all suggests that the potential benefits and costs of alternative techniques for group problem solving, including dissonance-induction procedures, may depend upon the stage of group development.

A General Problem-solving Perspective

In the previous section, we highlighted several important factors emerging from research on groupthink that merit incorporation in a general model of group problem solving. In each case, we also noted explicit links to the problem-solving literature. In this section, we suggest how a problem-solving perspective may be further employed to guide development of such a general model. In so doing, we first indicate how the framework of the problem-solving process may be used to recast and expand upon the groupthink model. We then discuss additional sets of variables suggested by the literature related to problem solving and question certain assumptions of the groupthink model. As noted previously, we use the term *problem solving* to refer to the full process beginning with problem definition and concluding with decision implementation and control, rather than as an allusion to narrowly defined problem-solving groups. As such, the perspective is applicable to a wide variety of group types. Indeed, adoption of this perspective was guided in part by the recognition that current models were limited in their breadth of applicability.

Process Orientation

The large literature relating to the problem-solving process suggests that many variables included in the groupthink model are relevant, but that a recasting and expansion is appropriate. Problem solving may be viewed as a multistage process which includes problem identification, alternative generation, alternative evaluation and choice, decision implementation, and decision control (Bass 1983; Elbing 1978). Explicit recognition of these stages is important for several reasons.

First, groupthink "defects" can be viewed simply as difficulties occurring through the stages of the problem-solving process. That is, "incomplete survey of objectives" represents a failure at the problem identification stage, "incomplete survey of alternatives" is a failure at the alternative generation stage, "failure to examine risks of preferred choice" is a failure at the evaluation and choice stage, and so on.

Second, other variables not explicitly noted by Janis are known to be important in the problem-solving process. These include explicit problem definition, quality of alternatives generated, source of the solution, group decision rule, gathering of control-related information, and timing of solution convergence. Concerning the latter variable, the decision stages differ in the degree to which they rely on divergent or convergent thinking. For instance, the alternative generation stage is primarily divergent, while the evaluation and choice stage is largely convergent. As such, premature convergence, rather than convergence per se, is undesirable.

Third, the various stages of the problem-solving process may require different social arrangements, and those appropriate at one stage may be troublesome at another. For instance, while interaction may be facilitative at the alternative evaluation and choice stage, it is often dysfunctional at the alternative generation stage (Taylor, Berry, and Block 1958; Van de Ven and Delbecq 1971; Vroom, Grant, and Cotton 1969).

Fourth, it becomes apparent that groupthink defects focus primarily on the first three stages of the problem-solving process, ending with evaluation and choice. Janis gives less emphasis to implementation and control. Only the "failure to work out contingency plans" symptom relates to the implementation stage, and control is not explicitly considered. This focus is restrictive. For instance, in the event of a faulty decision, if implementation hasn't been considered, it would be impossible to sort out the relative roles of faulty decision making and faulty implementation. As an example, Janis (1985, 81) cited the ill-fated attempt by President Carter to use military force to rescue the American hostages in Iran as an example of the "unsqueaky wheel trap." That is, Janis reasoned that the decision makers neglected to consider the possibility of early abortion of the rescue mission because the "squeaky wheel" on which attention was focused was the obvious danger once the mission reached Teheran. In fact, it is not clear whether this reflects faulty evaluation or lack of attention to implementation.

Finally, an explicit focus on the full problem-solving process emphasizes the importance of multiple decision outcomes. For instance, along with decision quality, the problem-solving literature stresses the need to consider decision acceptability, satisfaction with the decision process, and so on (e.g., Huber 1980). The literature further indicates that the degree of group members' inputs to problem solving, and whether those members feel the ultimate decision reflects their inputs, influences these additional outcomes (e.g., Vroom and Yetton 1973).

Lessons from Related Literatures

The problem-solving literature suggests other elements that should be recognized in developing and interpreting a more general model. Those elements include organizational power and politics, group cohesiveness, social control, and directive leadership—variables that are clearly critical in political decision making.

Organizational Power and Politics

The literature concerning organizational power and politics is an integral part of the study of organizational decisionmaking. Organizations have been described as political coalitions (March 1962), and Pfeffer (1981) states that power, influence, and political activity are all inevitable and important elements of administrative activity. Often, the development and use of power are evidenced not by overt confrontations, but rather by exhibitions of acquiescence. One type of political alignment is the politics of patronage in which little or no conflict is manifest due to the ability of powerful forces to smooth over differences and gain consensus (Lawler and Bacharach 1983). Viewed in this light, certain groupthink characteristics may reflect not passive and maladaptive responses to stressful antecedent conditions but active, conscious efforts to attain personal outcomes. Thus, a broader problem-solving perspective would include consideration of such proactive political action.

Group Cohesiveness

Group cohesiveness is seen as a primary antecedent condition for groupthink and is known to result in dysfunctional forms of conformity behavior. However, there is also considerable evidence that higher levels of cohesiveness may have a variety of desirable consequences. These potential benefits include enhanced communication among members, higher member satisfaction, decreased member tension and anxiety, and higher levels of group task accomplishment (Shaw 1981). Further, it would appear that situational, task, and goal characteristics may moderate the desirability of cohesiveness in group problem solving, and positive effects should not be ignored (see also Stern and Sundelius, this volume).

Social Control

Social control has been defined as "social arrangements employed to keep the behavior of some people in line with the expectations of others" (Hewitt and Hewitt 1986, 155). Informal social controls are unofficial, subtle pressures to conform to norms. Nemeth and Staw (1989) identified five ways in which social control is exercised to achieve uniformity. Several of these mechanisms are particularly relevant to the discussion of groupthink and group problem solving. First, conformity in a group may reflect agreement on the solution that most closely aligns with established norms. Second, powerful individuals often have the ability to achieve conformity to their positions. Finally, uniformity can be the result of a more tacit form of influence, that of agreement with majority viewpoints. These three forms of social control can serve as alternative explanations for the occurrence of groupthink's symptoms and defects.

Nemeth and Staw (1989, 175) also noted that conformity "has both necessary and desirable elements, particularly with regard to attainment of goals and harmony." When the norm of the organization or the wishes of those in power is adopted, there is less strain on individuals as well as greater efficiency because the group can move toward its goals. However, Nemeth and Staw also wrote that, while conformity may serve useful functions, it may also stifle dissent. They noted that "there is evidence that dissent, even when erroneous, contributes to the detection of truth and to the improvement of both performance and decisionmaking" (ibid., 196). Thus, this literature suggests that the determinants and roles of conformity in group problem solving are more complex than is suggested by the groupthink model.

Directive Leadership

Directive leadership is viewed as an antecedent condition of groupthink and thus of negative decision outcomes. The possible effects of directive leadership have been widely examined in the problem-solving literature, perhaps most notably by Vroom and Yetton (1973). The model presented by those authors, as well as related research (e.g., Field 1982; Vroom and Jago 1978), indicates that autocratic styles sometimes result in effective decision making. Further, situational theories of leadership, especially path-goal theory (House and Mitchell 1974), argue that directive leader behaviors may in some instances result in enhanced group performance and member satisfaction. There is considerable empirical support for such views (e.g., Schriesheim and Von Glinow 1977). Thus, it should not be assumed that directive leadership is inherently dysfunctional (see also George, this volume).

The benefits of leader impartiality are also challenged by the literature on transformational leadership (e.g., Bass 1990b). That literature argues that successful leaders communicate their vision to followers and inspire and stimulate them toward the accomplishment of that vision.

Finally, it appears that Janis's "lack of tradition of impartial leadership" antecedent has been used in various, distinct ways in groupthink research, often confounding the leader's promotion of a correct decision process with promotion of a preferred outcome. While the former is often espoused as desirable for the proper functioning of a decision group, the latter may inhibit member inputs (Huber 1980; Peterson 1995).

Examining Past Assumptions

Earlier, we presented several implicit assumptions of groupthink. Our review of the groupthink research and the problem-solving literature provides several theoretical challenges to those assumptions. First, although groupthink assumes that groups are used primarily to enhance the quality of decisions, group decision making is often used specifically to increase the acceptance of a decision (Pfeffer 1981). Also, organizational members may choose to utilize groups for other reasons including socioemotional benefits, and accomplishment of members' own secondary goals (e.g., "hidden agendas").

Second, the assumption that the group process is a rational pursuit of a unified goal is inconsistent with the known complexities of group processes (see 't Hart, this volume). Such processes are characterized by interplays of covert and overt motivations, concern not just about the current problem but also with residues of past problems and the anticipation of future problem-related interactions, and many other subtleties outside the typical focus of the rational model. Processes and outcomes which appear irrational to "objective" observers may in fact be functional from the point of view of individual members and even of the entire group. For instance, such processes and outcomes may serve to maintain the motivation of the group leader, help ensure the continued use of group processes, prevent the defection of certain group members, serve as a means for members to show allegiance to coalitions, and minimize the likelihood of the use of still other political acts. Organizations are inherently political, with shifting coalitions and interest groups, a diversity of goals, and active use of power (cf. Hardy 1985; Lawler and Bacharach 1983; Pfeffer 1981; Hoyt and Garrison, this volume). According to this view, political activity is not only a reality of organizational life, but may be entirely appropriate in some situations.

Third, the assumption that actions taken to prevent or minimize groupthink tendencies will produce a more rational and effective group process is questionable. These remedies may have unintended consequences. That is, attempts to create a micro-rational decision process in an inherently political environment may prove misguided. Other literatures have suggested the dangers of presenting an oasis of change in a nonreinforcing desert. The groupthink remedies are decision-specific, while the causes for supposed group dysfunctions may be systemic. That is, the application of specific techniques to prevent or minimize group difficulties may amount to treating the symptom of a deeper problem.

Fourth, while intuitively appealing, the view of a group's illusion of well-being as dysfunctional should also be questioned. For instance, S. E. Taylor and Brown have argued that such illusions

> . . . appear to promote other criteria of mental health, including the ability to care for others, the ability to be happy or contented, and the ability to engage in productive and creative work . . . These positive illusions may be especially useful when an individual receives negative feedback or is otherwise threatened and may be especially adaptive under these circumstances. (1988, 193)

Thus, this illusion of well-being may be most useful specifically in the "hot" decision situations described by Janis. While the Taylor and Brown review focuses on the individual, the processes which they detail seem equally applicable to groups.

Two of the literatures considered by S. E. Taylor and Brown should be explicitly noted. The first relates to self-fulfilling prophecy (Merton 1948), referred to in some settings as Pygmalion effect (Rosenthal and Jacobson 1968) after the sculptor whose stone image of the perfect woman became real. Recently, attention has focused on the Galatea effect (e.g., Eden 1988; Eden and Ravid 1982), after the sculpted maiden. The Galatea effect refers to the impact of direct manipulation of others' expectations. Pygmalion, Galatea, and similar expectation effects appear to be common in organizational settings (e.g., Sutton and Woodman 1989). Taken together, evidence concerning these related effects suggests that nonveridical perceptions may often yield positive consequences. Second, the literature on optimism–pessimism (e.g., Seligman 1991) leads to similar conclusions. That is, although pessimism is often found to be associated with more realistic worldviews, optimism typically yields superior outcomes. These arguments are not meant to imply that overly positive perceptions are necessarily desirable, only that the opposite should not be automatically assumed.

A final groupthink assumption concerns causes of characteristic groupthink attitudes and behaviors. Rather than, or as well as, stemming from individual psychological factors, conformity behaviors may be politically motivated. They may, for instance, reflect compliance rather than internalization. Thus, many groupthink characteristics could be due to conscious actions by members to subscribe to political norms.

The GGPS Model

We incorporated the elements noted earlier in an expanded decision framework—the GGPS model—that is presented in figure 3.2. The version of the GGPS model in the figure replicates that shown in Aldag and Fuller (1993) with the exception that feedback loops are included to highlight the dynamic nature of the model. We included variables in the GGPS model only if they are suggested by prior research on groupthink, the literature relating to group problem solving, or direct theoretical challenges to groupthink assumptions. The model is primarily descriptive, serving as a visual summary device of our review and as a framework for future theory and research.

Two general characteristics of our model that differentiate it from groupthink should be noted. First, whereas the latter is viewed as pathological and casts all determinants, characteristics, and consequences accordingly, our model presents each element in a more value-neutral manner. For example, we recast "too few alternatives" as "number of alternatives," thus making no assumptions about probable interrelationships. Such a reorientation is important both conceptually and in terms of future empirical analyses.

Second, the GGPS model has a more political orientation than does the groupthink model. For instance, while groupthink antecedents are seen as a relatively small number of external forces impinging on the passively responding group, the GGPS model considers a larger and more varied set of antecedents. Significantly, some of these may involve conscious actions on the parts of group members, and the political realities of group processes are also considered. Similarly, proactive behaviors of group members and political aspects are incorporated throughout the new model.

Antecedent Conditions

Several groupthink antecedents have been incorporated in the GGPS model, sometimes in slightly reworded form, while others have been recast. Those recast include the lack of procedural norms, recast as procedural requirements;

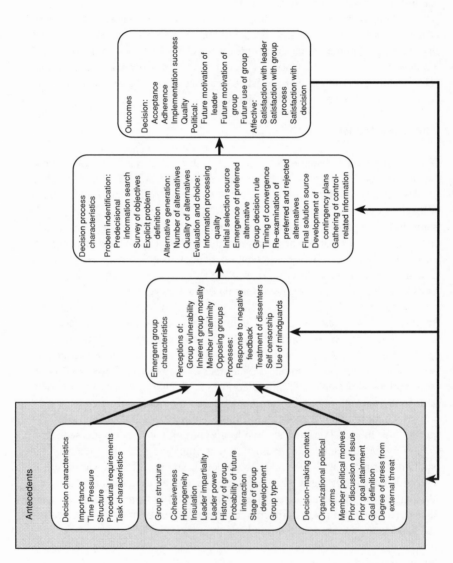

Antecedents

Decision characteristics

Importance
Time Pressure
Structure
Procedural requirements
Task characteristics

Group structure

Cohesiveness
Homogeneity
Insulation
Leader impartiality
Leader power
History of group
Probability of future
interaction
Stage of group
development
Group type

Decision-making context

Organizational political
norms
Member political motives
Prior discussion of issue
Prior goal attainment
Goal definition
Degree of stress from
external threat

Emergent group
characteristics

Perceptions of:
Group vulnerability
Inherent group morality
Member unanimity
Opposing groups
Processes:
Response to negative
feedback
Treatment of dissenters
Self censorship
Use of mindguards

Decision process
characteristics

Problem indentification:
Predecisional
information search
Survey of objectives
Explicit problem
definition
Alternative generation:
Number of alternatives
Quality of alternatives
Evaluation and choice:
Information processing
quality
Initial selection source
Emergence of preferred
alternative
Group decision rule
Timing of convergence
Re-examination of
preferred and rejected
alternatives
Final solution source
Development of
contingency plans
Gathering of control-
related information

Outcomes

Decision:
Acceptance
Adherence
Implementation success
Quality
Political:
Future motivation of
leader
Future motivation of
group
Future use of group
process
Affective:
Satisfaction with leader
Satisfaction with group
process
Satisfaction with
decision

Fig. 3.2.   **General group problem solving model**

lack of leader impartiality, recast as leader impartiality; recent failures, recast as history of group; and difficulties in current decision-making task, recast as prior goal attainment. We incorporated decision importance, time pressure, and structure because Janis (1972, 1982) considered them to be important but did not explicitly include them in his model and because other literature on group problem solving suggests their relevance. The only groupthink antecedent variable not retained was members' moral dilemmas from failing to have alternatives that do not violate their moral norms. We consider this variable to be overly restrictive and difficult to assess directly (McCauley 1989). Nine antecedent variables have been added.

The first of these, suggested by prior groupthink research, is task characteristics. For example, more complex tasks may require a wider range of member inputs and decrease the feasibility and desirability of directive leadership. Task specialization and broad distribution of information may play similar roles. Further, compensatory tasks, where one person's judgments can compensate for another's, may make different demands on group members than conjunctive tasks, where the group is limited by the performance of its weakest member, or disjunctive (including "Eureka") tasks for which a single member's judgment is employed. Groups dealing with these differing tasks would appropriately exhibit dissimilar interaction patterns.

Second, the stage of group development is important for a variety of reasons, as noted previously. It may, for instance, moderate the influence of group cohesiveness. As discussed by Leana (1985) and Longley and Pruitt (1980), the members of a fairly cohesive group in the mature stage are likely to be secure enough in their roles to challenge one another. As noted previously, this point is reinforced by Stern in his chapter in this volume.

Third, we included group type because implications for the decision-making process would differ if the group were, for example, an advisory group as opposed to an ongoing decision group that was responsible for implementation (on a related point, see Preston, this volume). In later chapters in this volume, Vertzberger discusses how group type influences voluntariness of membership and, in turn, group risk preferences, and Hoyt and Garrison consider how group types differing in flexibility of membership may have differential consequences. Although many groupthink characteristics may only be evident in ongoing, fixed-membership, self-contained groups, a general model must be more broadly applicable.

A fourth new antecedent is leader power. As noted in the lessons from prior groupthink research and the discussion of the power and politics literature, a powerful leader can have a crucial impact on the group's functioning. Many groupthink characteristics may result from the exercise of influence by a powerful leader (see Preston, this volume).

Fifth, the organizational power and politics literature suggests that many decisions are influenced by ongoing political activity and reflect shifting power of various coalitions. Therefore, the probability of future interaction of the group is critical. If group members do not interact, and do not anticipate future interaction, some types of political influence may be lessened.

Sixth, we added organizational political norms because the groupthink assumption of rationality may not apply in an organization functioning with a political model of decision making, where political influence is a prevalent part of the decision-making process. In such organizations, for instance, personal power rather than rational pursuit of organizational goals may dictate decision outcomes, control is through shifting coalitions and interest groups, and decisions result from bargaining and interplay among interests (Pfeffer 1981). As Jervis observed, psychologists

> often neglect the possibility that what appear to be errors on the part of politicians are really devious strategies for seeking less than admirable goals. Thus, a statesman who seems inconsistent or confused may be seeking the support of opposed factions. (1989, 442)

Janis (1982, 7) recognized the possibility of political factors in decision making, noting that "members tend to evolve informal norms to preserve friendly intragroup relations and these become part of the hidden agenda at their meetings." However, he viewed this hidden agenda as a source of error, rather than as potentially acceptable or functional.

Seventh, members' political motives are also relevant. Individuals may have a vested interest in certain alternatives, or there may be one or more strong coalitions present; both of these will affect behavior in the group decision-making process. As an example, ingratiation, a type of political behavior, is often manifested as opinion-conforming behavior. Such ingratiation may be used to positively alter the evaluations or attributions of relevant others (Liden and Mitchell 1988). Group members' conformity behavior is often a way for individuals who are seeking upward advancement to gain approval (Nemeth and Staw 1989).

Eighth, whether group members discussed the issue prior to the decision-making meeting can also impact the problem-solving process. Members could have previously discussed the organization's norms as well as what decision would be most consistent with them. Also, previous "deal making" could have occurred, making the decision essentially a political one. Finally, various alternatives could have been explored before the meeting, thereby shortening the observable problem-solving process and giving a false sense of premature closure. Inclusion of these factors make small group analysis more "contextual" as advocated by George in the previous chapter.

Goal definition is the final new antecedent. For appropriate application of the rational model of decision making, there must be agreement on a unitary goal for the group. Goals may be multiple, discrepant, and/or ill-defined, violating this requirement.

Emergent Group Characteristics

The groupthink "symptoms" capture important group characteristics such as perceived unanimity, perceptions of opposing groups, and response to negative feedback, albeit negatively framed. As such, we retained them as our emergent group characteristics. However, in the GGPS model, they have been reworded to avoid negative connotations and have been categorized into group perceptions and processes.

Decision Process Characteristics

In the GGPS model, we group decision process characteristics in terms of the first three stages of the problem-solving process: problem identification, alternative generation, and evaluation and choice. We do not explicitly include the implementation and control stages here because they follow the actual decision, although we do include variables which prepare for those stages (i.e., development of contingency plans and gathering of control-related information). The groupthink defects, recast in value-neutral terms, as well as eight additional decision process characteristics, are included in the GGPS model.

The first new factor is explicit problem definition. Group members may fail to explicitly define the problem because a focus on the problem is uncomfortable, because they are anxious to move on to choice, or for other reasons. However, failure to adequately define the problem may result in an "error of the third kind," solving the wrong problem. If a problem has been inadequately defined, the "solution" cannot be adequate (Elbing 1978, 110).

Along with the quantity of alternatives generated, alternative quality must also be considered. Processes which enhance alternative quantity will not necessarily enhance alternative quality. While some group processes, such as brainstorming (Osborn 1963), are based on the premise that a large quantity of alternatives improves the prospects for identification of a superior alternative, it is conceivable that defective processes may result in the generation of large numbers of hastily considered, low-quality alternatives. This could both complicate choice making and lead to poor decision outcomes.

Furthermore, the source of the initial selection of a preferred alternative may be important. Group member reaction to the initially preferred alternative may vary considerably depending on factors such as whether it was selected by the leader, mandated by a person external to the group, or used in the past. Also important is whether the group identifies a preferred alternative early in the decision-making process or converges on a solution much later. If there is no preferred alternative during much of the process, several of the groupthink "defects" simply would not apply.

The group decision rule is also important. A decision rule identified early in the process could influence other decision process characteristics. For instance, with a consensus decision rule, each member recognizes that dissent may preclude, or at least jeopardize, problem resolution. With a majority decision rule, such dissent may be more acceptable. However, even such a statement is an oversimplification. For instance, political norms may dictate the group decision rule. In addition, if the decision is to be chosen by the majority, silent agreement-seeking behavior may be indicative of members who acknowledge that they are in the minority and thus cannot have an impact.

The timing of convergence is also critical. Consensus-seeking behavior should not always be considered negative. Indeed, the choice stage of problem solving is inherently convergent; reaching a consensus is the goal. 't Hart and Kroon (1996) make this point, noting that "concurrence-seeking as such is not always bad, it is even a necessary element within each collective decision process (especially when unanimity is called for). At a certain point in the deliberative process, discussions need to be concluded and actions taken. Moreover, early concurrence seeking, or the use of simple cognitive decision rules like 'satisficing' . . . may be an efficient strategy for simple, routine decision problems." Therefore, the important variable to examine is not if convergence is displayed, but whether or not it is displayed prematurely. Unfortunately, determination of whether convergence is premature can generally only be determined *ex post,* potentially resulting in circular reasoning (that is, a poor outcome is taken as evidence of premature convergence, which in turn is taken as evidence that premature convergence is undesirable).

We noted above that the source of the initial selection may be relevant. Similarly, the source of the final solution, which may or may not be the same as the initial selection, should be important. The problem-solving literature suggests that the source of the final solution should influence outcomes such as decision acceptance and implementation success. For instance, solutions proposed by group members during group discussion will likely result in greater understanding and acceptance of the decision and greater likelihood of implementation success.

The gathering of control-related information should also be considered. For instance, proper control requires gathering of data prior to implementation of the decision to permit assessment of change, as well as determination of the specific variables for which subsequent monitoring is important (e.g., Huber 1980). Further, lack of consideration of decision control may result in failure to recognize the consequences of feedback, thus underestimating the dynamic aspects of group problem solving.

Outcomes

Although groupthink views outcomes primarily in terms of a narrow assessment of decision quality, the GGPS model goes further, including an array of decision, political, and affective outcomes. Decision outcomes include acceptance of the decision by those affected by it and/or who must implement it, adherence to the decision (that is, whether the decision is subsequently overturned), implementation success, and decision quality. The political outcomes include future motivation of the leader and group and future use of the group. Finally, the affective outcomes include satisfaction with the leader, group process, and decision. The model does not assume these outcomes to be independent.

Incorporation of this array of outcomes recognizes that a "good" decision is not only one that appears so from an objective, rational evaluation immediately following the decision. Rather, it is also necessary to consider whether the decision is functional to the organization in the long term. The outcomes explicitly recognize that group members may bring a variety of goals to the problem situation (and thus that a single decision outcome may be misleading, or even artificial) as well as that basically political outcomes (such as the likelihood that the group leader will refuse to use the group process in the future, or that the group's decision will subsequently be unilaterally reversed by the leader) may be critical. They recognize also that affective reactions may influence group cohesion and future group functioning.

Moving beyond Groupthink

The GGPS model is meant to be applicable to a broad range of group problem situations. Using the groupthink model as a starting point, we have drawn on lessons from past groupthink research, literatures related to problem solving, and a direct assessment of groupthink assumptions to create this new model. Here, we consider the allure of groupthink and present implications of our analysis for group problem solving.

The Allure of Groupthink

We have argued that, whatever its actual validity, the groupthink phenomenon has been accepted more because of its intuitive appeal than because of solid evidence. The allure of groupthink in the absence of convincing supporting evidence is intriguing and deserves discussion. We suspect that the reliance on anecdote in many studies of groupthink probably contributes to the availability heuristic, playing on our preference for case, as opposed to base, data (Tversky and Kahneman 1973); a concrete instance of the appearance of groupthink "symptoms" in a fiasco may be seen as compelling evidence, especially in the absence of base data.[5] Further, we have argued that the focus of groupthink anecdotal evidence on fiascoes has fostered illusory correlation.

It may also be the case that the groupthink perspective is consistent with our implicit theories of groups. Indeed, our references to the intuitive appeal of groupthink suggest that the phenomenon is somehow consistent with our preconceptions of effective, or ineffective, group functioning. The roles of implicit theories in influencing responses have been widely documented (cf. Sternberg 1985). Staw (1975) warned that implicit theories may distort informants' reports of organizational phenomena. One important characteristic of implicit theories is their "gap-filling" function (Bower, Black, and Turner 1979; Graesser, Gordon, and Sawyer 1979). In the context of groupthink, individuals observing a situation in which some groupthink characteristics are present may assume the existence of others.

As further evidence of the role of implicit theories, several researchers have found that feedback given to group members or observers about group performance affects the characteristics ascribed to those groups (Binning and Lord 1980; Downey, Chacko, and McElroy 1979; McElroy and Downey 1982; Staw 1975). Guzzo, Wagner, Maguire, Herr, and Hawley (1986) found feedback about group process to affect evaluations of outcomes and feedback about outcomes to affect evaluations of process. Individuals who were told that a group had performed poorly were more likely to report instances of "poor" interaction processes, such as lack of willingness to hear other members' views. Thus, the focus on poor decision outcomes in groupthink research may lead to reports of instances of poor group functioning.

Factors that may have contributed to the allure of groupthink, including availability, illusory correlation, and implicit theories of group processes, should be explicitly considered in future theory and research on group decision processes.

Implications

Our discussion to this point has a number of implications for group decision processes and related research. These relate to the potential for disconfirmation, importance of both the rational and political perspectives, decision outcomes, a typology of problem types, and choice of prescriptions for effective group functioning.

Potential for Disconfirmation

Perhaps most important, we consider it critical to address examination of group decision processes with an open mind. Starting with a statement such as the Janis (1982, 9) definition of groupthink (i.e., "Groupthink refers to a deterioration of mental efficiency, reality testing, and moral judgment that results from in-group pressures") invites the search for confirming evidence. Disconfirmation is the stuff of science. Greenwald, Pratkanis, Leippe, and Baumgardner (1986) stress the dangers of research that is theory confirming, rather than theory testing, and warn against the conduct of studies in which the researcher holds a strong prior belief about the outcome.

Rational and Political Perspectives

Group processes are seldom purely rational. Our discussion suggests that it may be inappropriate to ignore the political aspects of group functioning, and artificial to treat the rational and political perspectives as mutually exclusive. Our integrative perspective of group problem solving sees the two aspects as coexisting and views political behaviors as entirely rational in some situations (and vice versa). Most organizations may "operate under the guise of rationality with some elements of power and politics thrown in" (Pfeffer 1981, 344). Therefore, there may be more going on than meets the "objective" eye. This need to explicitly recognize the key roles of political perspectives is broadly echoed in the other chapters in this volume.

Decision Outcomes

Our discussion has stressed the need to consider many outcomes of group problem solving. As Pfeffer (1981, 156) pointed out, "In ongoing organizations, implementation of and commitment to the decision may be as important, if not more so, than the decision itself." Additionally, we have argued that future motivation of the group and leader, future use of the group, affective responses, and other dependent variables may also be important outcomes for groups and/or group members.

Typology of Problem Types

A typology of problem types would help to foster a more systematic appraisal of group problem solving. Some dimensions of that typology—not necessarily independent—have been suggested by our discussion to this point: crisis versus noncrisis, recurring versus nonrecurring, important versus unimportant, and successful versus unsuccessful. The need for such a typology is evident from the groupthink literature. Case support for groupthink has been drawn largely from crisis, nonrecurring, important, unsuccessful decisions. Conversely, many group problems, such as decisions by individuals at high levels in organizations, may be noncrisis, important, recurring or nonrecurring, successful or unsuccessful.

Others have called for and developed typologies of problem types. For instance, to illustrate the failure of psychological experiments to fully and adequately address the domain of intellectual tasks, Edwards (1983) presented a taxonomy of intellectual tasks and their performers. It included dimensions such as easy versus difficult, realistic versus unrealistic, time pressures versus lack of time pressures, tools available versus tools unavailable, and laboratory versus job versus life. Several other task typologies have been proposed (e.g., de Vries-Griever and Meijman 1987; Fleishman 1982; Shaw 1973; Steiner 1972) focusing on dimensions such as information-processing requirements, coordination requirements, required task behaviors, and ability requirements. However, such typologies have not been constructed specifically for application to group problem solving, and we feel they fail to incorporate important dimensions.

Choice of Prescriptions for Effective Group Functioning
Our discussion suggests that prescriptions for appropriate group functioning must consider cost, feasibility, and scope (see also 't Hart, this volume). First, some of the proposed remedies for groupthink may be costly or infeasible. For instance, as noted by Luechauer (1989), once groups have begun to engage in dysfunctional modes, it may be too late for the recommendations to be used because the groups will simply not perceive a need for them. In addition, regardless of the objective value of application of these remedies, they will not be used if the group decision process is consciously being manipulated for political ends.

Perhaps most important, as noted previously, a focus on specific remedies for specific decision situations may be misguided. It may be more appropriate to assess and potentially alter organizational culture or contingencies of reinforcement rather than to implement specific techniques in the hopes of overcoming the consequences of the group's decision environment. This suggests the need for explicit consideration of system changes.

Directions for Future Research

We have already identified several directions for future research, but a few others deserve explicit consideration. It may be infeasible to attempt simultaneous use or testing of the entire GGPS model. Just as a variety of prescriptions may be appropriate for the effective psychological and physiological functioning of the human body, multiple prescriptions for effective group functioning may emerge from future research. Similarly, just as it may be infeasible to test a model of the entire human body, it may be necessary to examine portions of the model most congruent with the focus of the researcher.

Although the complexity of the GGPS model makes a test of the full model difficult, it permits testing of important issues on which the groupthink model is silent. For instance, the political perspective would suggest that the presence of self-censorship may reflect a conscious strategy by members to adhere to a politically advantageous alternative. As such, research should further consider alternative determinants of particular conformity behaviors. In addition, the GGPS model allows examination of the relation between presumed negative factors such as cohesion and member homogeneity and potential positive consequences such as member satisfaction. Furthermore, emergent group characteristics may influence fundamental aspects of the decision process beyond the suggestions of groupthink. For instance, perceived member unanimity may lead to increased use of a consensus decision rule, which may influence factors such as the role of dissent.

Movement beyond groupthink will require the use of an expanded set of methodologies to capture the richness and complexity of group decision making. Studies should include actual problem solvers in a variety of ongoing, real-world decision situations as well as use of behavioral simulations and qualitative methodologies. In addition, the use of recalled-problems methodology may permit group members to provide "thick" descriptions of actual decision situations in which they have been involved. In addition to choice of appropriate methodologies, it will be necessary, as noted earlier, to pay additional attention to issues of measurement and operationalization as well as to movement toward prescription.

Furthermore, it is common practice to call for longitudinal studies of a phenomenon of interest; we do so here. Such studies would permit more adequate examination of the group problem-solving process, including timing of convergence to a group decision. They could, for instance, permit differentiation between convergence, which is inherent in the choice-making stage of the problem-solving process, and premature convergence, which may be pathological.

Finally, we suggested earlier that implicit theories may help explain the appeal of the groupthink phenomenon. It would be instructive to directly address implicit theories of group problem solving, perhaps through use of cognitive mapping procedures (Aldag and Stearns 1988). This would permit examination of how antecedent conditions, emergent group characteristics, decision process characteristics, and outcomes are associated in such implicit theories.

Conclusion

Group problem solving is a complex and challenging phenomenon. Comprehensive models are needed to guide researchers and practitioners in dealing with this phenomenon. The groupthink model has served a valuable role in generating interest in group problem-solving processes and in acting as a catalyst for associated theory and research. However, the model has not incorporated two decades of theory and research, has received limited empirical support, and is restrictive in scope. Recent theory and research, as well as critical evaluation of the model, have suggested the need for an expanded, integrative model of group problem solving.

Building in part on the groupthink model, we offer the GGPS model as such a framework. On the basis of a problem-solving perspective and incorporating prior theory and research, it is intended for a broad range of problem situations. The GGPS model relaxes restrictive assumptions of groupthink, recasts certain groupthink variables, employs less value-laden terminology, and includes several additional process and outcome variables. Further, it explicitly recognizes the roles of political factors in group problem solving.

We present the GGPS model as a foundation for further testing and refinement. Researchers should recognize the complex, dynamic nature of group problem solving and use a broad range of methodologies and problem situations while avoiding explicit search for confirmation. Indeed, we will consider the GGPS model to have played a useful role if rigorous research, however disconfirming, leads to new knowledge concerning group problem-solving processes. The need to be open to dissonant information is, of course, a central lesson of Janis's work.

The evidence we have reviewed clearly documents the fact that groupthink *per se* is a phenomenon lacking empirical support and resting on generally unsupported assumptions. Indeed, perhaps the most remarkable aspect of the groupthink model is its continuing appeal in the face of nonconfirming evidence. Failures to support groupthink predictions have regularly been viewed as evidence of partial support, or as signals that the research methodology was flawed. In our view, group researchers and theorists have unwittingly acted, in Janis's terms, as virtual mindguards for the groupthink phenomenon.

As such, it is time to move on, to get beyond groupthink. In our opinion, this can best be accomplished by resisting the temptation to call for further tests of groupthink, additions to the groupthink model, or other adjustments from the groupthink anchor. Groupthink has served a purpose but must now be cut loose, however seductive its continuing intuitive appeal. There is no question, of course, that groups may exhibit severe dysfunctions, that premature concurrence-seeking may be harmful, that conformity pressures play important roles, and so on. What we must recognize, though, is that exploration of all these areas predated groupthink and will survive it. Research and theory on conformity pressures, insularity, stereotyping, rationalization and other mechanisms for dissonance reduction, leader dominance, or other elements appropriated into the groupthink model, should continue, but outside the artificial confines of that model. Groupthink, in our view, has provided an alluring path down which researchers and theorists have ventured, a path that has led to some discoveries but has also diverted attention from more fundamental small group issues. As the following chapters make abundantly clear, there is a rich territory to be explored in the region beyond groupthink. To explore them, we must discard groupthink as a metaphor for malice and negligence. We must get off the groupthink path, remove the groupthink blinders, cut free from the groupthink anchor, and mix as many other metaphors as are needed to drive home this important, but remarkably elusive, point.

NOTES

This chapter is an updated and revised version of R. J. Aldag and S. R. Fuller, "Beyond Fiasco: A Reappraisal of the Groupthink Phenomenon and a New Model of Group Decision Processes," *Psychological Bulletin,* 1993, 113:533–52. Copyright © 1993 by the American Psychological Association. Adapted with permission. Quotes from Janis 1989 reprinted with the permission of The Free Press, a division of Simon & Schuster. Copyright © 1989 by The Free Press. The authors made equal contributions to this chapter. They are indebted to the Graduate School of the University of Wisconsin-Madison and to Tom and Judy Pyle for providing funding to support the chapter.

1. Although Moorhead and Montanari's 1982 paper is nowhere noted in Montanari and Moorhead's 1989 article, the papers are essentially identical (i.e., the latter is apparently a journal version of the former).

2. Throughout his book, 't Hart (1990/1994) emphasizes the contingent and relatively rare nature of groupthink in high-level political and bureaucratic decision-making groups.

3. This approach attempts to determine the probable cause of undesirable events with high certainty even though the available data do not come from controlled experiments or quasi-experiments. It involves formulating all the known causal sequences that might account for an observed outcome and then attempting to determine which of them appears to be implicated. However, although this approach is intriguing, it continues to focus only on sources of error. Also, because many causal sequences may lead to similar consequences, expected causal sequences may be "confirmed" when other, unexamined sequences are actually playing roles.

4. Although others (e.g., Luechauer 1989; Whyte 1989) have suggested additional variables, those variables were presented as alternative explanations for groupthink rather than as supplements to the model. For instance, Luechauer argued that self-monitoring propensity may be important, whereas Whyte emphasized the potential role of prospect polarization.

5. Although Janis (1989) did discuss the availability heuristic, he discussed it as a factor influencing whether policymakers take warnings seriously rather than in this context.

CHAPTER 4

Beyond Decision Making in Formal and Informal Groups: The Dutch Cabinet and the West New Guinea Conflict

Max V. Metselaar and Bertjan Verbeek

Introduction

Things are not always as they appear. This banal yet fundamental observation applies to historical analysis as to other life situations. Even a case which at first sight seems a clear example of groupthink leaves unanswered several questions which point to deficiencies in Irving Janis's original groupthink conceptualization.[1] The case in question is Dutch Cabinet decision making during the last stages of the so-called West New Guinea conflict in 1961 and 1962. During this period the Dutch Government tried to persuade the United States, the United Kingdom, and Australia to form a coalition in order to deter Indonesia from attacking Dutch-owned West New Guinea (currently the Indonesian region of Irian Jaya). Specifically, we will argue that small group analysis would benefit from taking into account four key factors which are commonly overlooked. These are: (a) institutional characteristics of the political system in which the group is operating, (b) the occurrence and nature of formal and informal leadership within the group, (c) specific traits of informal leaders, such as their information style and their cognitive belief system, and (d) the dynamic interplay of several, partly overlapping formal and informal groups.

The West New Guinea Puzzle

The analysis takes as its point of departure prima facie the hypothesis that groupthink may have significantly affected the decision-making process. In our view, this requires the analyst to make a plausible claim that the group in question misinterpreted relevant information that should have led the group to choose a different policy alternative, or that the group could have easily obtained such critical information (Verbeek 1994). Such a claim in turn generates a research puzzle: why did this occur? For Dutch Cabinet decision making during the later stages of the West New Guinea conflict (November 1961– April 1962), such a puzzle can be found in the assessment of the likelihood that American support, deemed essential for the success of Dutch policies, would be forthcoming.

The striking element in that decision-making process is the nearly unanimous belief of cabinet members that the United States would fully support the Dutch government in the event of an Indonesian attack on West New Guinea, despite the availability of massive evidence to the contrary. It was not until late February 1962, when Robert Kennedy visited The Hague during a fact-finding mission which had taken him to Jakarta a few weeks earlier, that the Dutch were forced to face the fact that the United States would not back the Dutch in such a contingency. The Attorney General's blunt statements were met with disbelief and disarray.[2] Yet, full awareness of the weakness of the Dutch position was not achieved until President Kennedy's letter of April 2 to Dutch Prime Minister Dr. Jan de Quay confirmed the fears provoked by Robert Kennedy's visit.[3] At that point, the Dutch had little choice but to accept the plan put forward by the American former diplomat Elsworth Bunker, which envisaged a transfer of West New Guinea to the Indonesian Republic after a nine-month transition period during which the area would be administered as a UN trusteeship.

Thus ended a conflict that originated in the 1949 Round Table Conference that had provided for Indonesian independence from the Netherlands, but had left West New Guinea outside the agreement. Between 1949 and 1962 the conflict between the Netherlands and Indonesia over the sovereignty of West New Guinea slowly escalated, roughly divided in the following phases:[4]

Phase 1 (1949–52): Bilateral diplomacy aimed at settling the issue failed when the Dutch Cabinet resigned in 1951 due to internal divisions regarding the desirability of returning the area to Indonesia.

Phase 2 (1952–55): This was a period of relative calm during which Indonesia was unable to get the issue on the United Nations agenda. A conference in Geneva failed to bring the two countries close to an agreement.

Phase 3 (1956–60): The conflict slowly escalates. Indonesia in 1956 unilaterally withdraws from the Dutch-Indonesian Union, which regulated the mutual preferential treatment of both countries. Indonesia initially put Dutch enterprises under surveillance and then nationalized them. Massive emigration of Dutch citizens from Indonesia followed. Indonesian leaders regularly called for the liberation of West New Guinea and attempted to mobilize popular support (1958–60). The diplomatic battle of the late 1950s evolved into gunboat diplomacy with a Dutch flotilla of warships, including the navy's only air carrier *Karel Doorman.*

Phase 4 (1960–1962): The conflict escalates further as Indonesia broke diplomatic relations with the Netherlands in 1960 and, six months later, ended the representation of Dutch interests by the United Kingdom. There was an increase in Indonesian infiltrations of West New Guinea. Small scale coastal naval battles took place, and the Dutch reinforced their troops in the area (cf. De Geus 1984; De Beus 1977, 244–403; Henderson 1973). On the political front, the Dutch government installed the so-called New Guinea Council, a preliminary advisory body clearly aimed at preparing the Papua's for self-governance.

The events of the case are summarized for the reader's convenience in table 4.1.

Recognizing that full defense of an area so distant from the Netherlands would never be possible, the post-1956 strategy of successive Dutch cabinets, and especially Secretary of Foreign Affairs Luns, was to build a coalition of the United States, the United Kingdom, and Australia to deter Indonesia from a full-scale attack. The support of the United States was seen as crucial, providing key logistical, diplomatic, and economic resources. Fully aware of the lack of such support at the height of the conflict, the Dutch cabinet in 1962 had to abandon its policy. The decision to withdraw was painful. Partly because the Catholic Party had become more involved in the West New Guinea affair, the rationale behind Dutch policy gradually changed from colonialism to moralism (Lijphart 1966). Most of the cabinet members felt increasingly morally committed to deterring Indonesia as long as required to permit native Papuan inhabitants to exercise their right of self-determination.

The puzzling element in this case is the availability of evidence that American support would not be forthcoming. Thus, Dutch policies aimed at deterring an Indonesian attack long enough to build national self-consciousness among the Papuans were doomed to fail. The Dutch ambassador to the United States, Dr. J. van Roijen, had for some time been sending lengthy telegrams to The Hague warning his superiors about the prevailing mood in Washington. These messages could have reached the Cabinet in two ways. First, the Dutch foreign secretary, Mr. Joseph Luns, could have informed the cabinet during the foreign affairs briefings he held at cabinet meetings. Second, since copies of the most important telegrams from the Dutch ambassador in Washington were directly transmitted to the office of the prime minister (De Quay) and the deputy prime minister (Korthals), both could have decided to share their contents with the rest of the cabinet.

Evidence from various sources suggests that important pieces of infor-

TABLE 4.1. Chronology of Events

Events in the Netherlands	Events in Indonesia	International Events
		1950 Failure of Dutch-Indonesian talks on the status of West New Guinea.
1951 Dutch Cabinet resigns because of West New Guinea policy.		
	1956 Indonesia unilaterally dissolves the Dutch-Indonesian Union; the Indonesian government puts Dutch enterprises in Indonesia under surveillance.	**1956** Failure of the Dutch-Indonesian talks in Geneva. **1956** Failure of the Indonesian attempt to put the issue on the agenda of the United Nations.
1957 The Netherlands sends reinforcements to West New Guinea.	**1957** Forced emigration of Dutch citizens from Indonesia.	
	1958–60 Increased mass mobilization to fight against "Dutch Imperialism."	**1958** Foster Dulles vaguely promises American support in the case of an Indonesian attack on West New Guinea.
1959 De Quay's Government formally announces West New Guinea to be part of the Kingdom of the Netherlands.		
April 1960 The Netherlands sends aircraft carrier to West New Guinea	**August 1960** Indonesia severs diplomatic ties with the Netherlands.	
	1961 Indonesia terminates representation of Dutch interests in Indonesia by the United Kingdom.	**1961** American pressure on the Netherlands to agree to a diplomatic solution of the conflict. **1961** Failure of Dutch UN resolution calling for an international authority for West New Guinea.
	December 1961 Indonesian President Sukarno calls for the liberation of West New Guinea.	**December 1961** American pressure on the Netherlands to accept bilateral negotiations.
	January 1962 Military battle off the West New Guinean coast.	
February 1962 Dutch Cabinet shaken by bluntness of Robert Kennedy.		

(continued)

TABLE 4.1. (*Continued*)

Events in the Netherlands	Events in Indonesia	International Events
March 1962 Further secret reinforcements of Dutch forces on West New Guinea.	**March 1962** Small naval battle off the West New Guinea coast.	**March 1962** Start of Dutch-Indonesian negotiations in Middleburg (USA) chaired by Elsworth Bunker. **August 15, 1962** Signing of an agreement envisaging the handing over of West New Guinea to Indonesia after an interim U.N. administration of 8 months.

mation provided by Van Roijen were not transmitted to the full cabinet. Several years after the conflict, finance minister Zijlstra acknowledged that the cabinet was not aware of the full contents of Van Roijen's messages because the Dutch ambassador reported to Luns rather than to the cabinet directly (Gase 1986). During the crisis Van Roijen's close assistants at the Embassy (Schiff and Huydecoper) noticed, through their contacts at the Foreign Office, that important warnings had never been passed on (Huydecoper 1990).[5] Moreover, not every telegram that actually reached Prime Minister De Quay and Deputy Prime Minister Korthals was distributed to their colleagues.[6]

It will be shown that decision making by the De Quay cabinet was defective in at least three regards. First, members of the cabinet were reluctant to bypass Foreign Secretary Luns and look for alternative sources of information that could shed new light on the exact nature of American support. Second, despite the fact that various messages from Van Roijen that did reach the cabinet cast much doubt on American support, its members continued to play down the negative aspects of these messages. Third, to the extent that some ministers did conclude that American support was highly unlikely, none made an attempt to press the matter in the cabinet.[7]

The Dutch Cabinet: A Likely Victim of Groupthink?

A first analysis of Dutch cabinet decision making during the last phase of the West New Guinea conflict (1960–62) could well be cast in terms of Irving Janis's groupthink phenomenon. According to the groupthink explanation, the cabinet led by Prime Minister De Quay, the central Dutch decision-making unit during this conflict, drifted into a fiasco because of premature and extreme consensus-seeking. To back up this claim, it is necessary to check the case evidence for both symptoms of groupthink and the occurrence of ante-cedent conditions.[8]

Symptoms of Groupthink

The available primary and secondary sources indicate the presence of symp-toms of groupthink at various stages of cabinet decision making. Examples of at least six different symptoms can be found:

1. An unquestioned belief in the group's inherent morality. The De Quay cabinet firmly believed that it was safeguarding the Papuan population's right of self-determination. This consideration provided an important defense against outside critics who pointed to the lack of economic gain that could be expected from holding on to the area and the economic losses that Dutch enterprises suffered from Indonesian measures against their investments in the country. Many members of the Cabinet professed to believe in the primarily moral nature of the Dutch policy.[9] They felt strongly committed by their promises to the Papuans. For instance, when in early 1962 one of his party advisers informally urged him to hand over West New Guinea, Prime Minister De Quay called this line "cowardly" and "dishonest" (De Quay Diary, XVII: 1, 47, 5074).

Another moral issue that affected the group decision-making process was that many cabinet members felt it their moral duty to defend the international order of justice and its legal principles against regimes ignoring or even "raping" this system. There was no doubt among them that Sukarno was an immoral dictator and aggressor like Hitler had been in 1938 (cf. Cabinet Minutes, January 6, 1962). More than once, ministers like Korthals, De Pous, Visser, Klompé, and Toxopeus stressed that "Might should not be superior to right. To make sacrifices for this principle will surely be significant" (Korthals in Cabinet Meeting, January 6, 1962).

Both moral issues affected the decision-making premises, the discus-sions, the doubts (and lack thereof), and the calculations in the cabinet. Most of the cabinet members (including at times even such a consummate *real-politiker* as Luns, the main champion of the Dutch policy) increasingly de-fined the conflict as a struggle between a conscientious, morally superior, but vulnerable government and the opportunistic and cynical power politics of its "allies" (the United States, the United Kingdom, and Australia). Neither moral issue was ever seriously questioned. However, in the periods in which the cabinet was confronted with the likelihood of a major Indonesian military attack on New Guinea (in April and August 1962) several cabinet members agonized over a series of difficult questions. Which political and military risks and how much bloodshed would be justified in defending these moral and judicial principles in the hope that a firm stand would finally convince potential allies (the United States, United Kingdom, and Australia) that it was both a moral imperative and politically expedient for them to support the Dutch? How long would it be realistic, and politically and militarily acceptable, to stick to one's principles, instead of sacrificing them in the face of an untrustworthy, opportunistic aggressor? How long was it reasonable to hope that, given the righteousness of one's moral principles, international support would eventually be forthcoming?

2. Illusion of unanimity. Partly because of their moral convictions, members of the De Quay cabinet felt that there was no major conflict on the issue within the cabinet; all ministers shared the view that Dutch policies should be aimed at securing the right of self-determination for the Papuan population of West New Guinea and that a continued Dutch presence on the island rather than Indonesian sovereignty would be the best guarantee of Papuan involvement. The Dutch government had thus formally abandoned other motives for clinging to West New Guinea, such as keeping the island to secure a Dutch presence in the Pacific, or developing it as a settlement area for pro-Dutch immigrants from Indonesia (De Geus 1984, 193–214; Lijphart 1966, 39–66). In fact, strategic goals were never mentioned in the weekly and sometimes daily cabinet discussions on West New Guinea during the crucial year of 1962. Discussions in the cabinet basically centered on tactical questions: which military reinforcements were necessary and acceptable; how much international diplomatic support could be mounted for the Dutch case; when would an Indonesian attack be likely?

This illusion of unanimity disguised differences between the individual motivations to hold on to the area as long as possible, such as Foreign Secretary Luns's interest in maintaining Dutch international prestige by securing a Dutch presence in the Pacific, or the general feeling shared by a majority of Dutch politicians in the 1950s that West New Guinea was a crucial source of late-colonial national self-esteem, necessary after the loss of Indonesia (Lijphart 1966, 288–89). Becoming the protector of Papuan rights thus served also as a collective rationalization of a variety of less lofty motives for holding on to the area.

3. Self-censorship. From late December 1961 until August 1962 West New Guinea became the dominant issue at the weekly Friday cabinet meetings. In addition, an increasing number of special sessions were devoted to it, sometimes twice a week. At first sight these discussions appear very open and free. Every member could speak his or her mind without being criticized by his or her colleagues. Many relevant aspects of the American attitude were put forward, including the possibility that support would not be forthcoming. Yet, at the same time, it is remarkable that all members of the cabinet seem to have been reluctant to address the painful implications of that critical contingency, almost as if one was forbidden to talk about the possible and necessary consequences.[10] Serious personal feelings of some of the cabinet members that the Dutch West New Guinea policy was a lost and hopeless cause (e.g., Zijlstra, Beerman, Cals, and Schmelzer) were seldom discussed explicitly during the cabinet meetings. It seems illustrative that a clear remark that "We won't make it" by one of the cabinet members who seriously questioned the chances of American political and military support, CHU minister Beerman, during a cabinet meeting on August 8, 1961, did not provoke any reactions from his colleagues (Gase 1984, 82; Gase 1986). At the same time, there was a strong tendency to bolster even the smallest signals that hope for American support was still realistic, despite the fact that all odds seemed to be against this option.

4. Self-appointed mindguards.   At various instances, most notably in 1962, Foreign Secretary Luns attempted to prevent Ambassador Van Roijen from having direct access to cabinet decision making, minimizing the risk of the cabinet being exposed to the assessment that American support would be out of the question. On January 30, 1962, for instance, Luns warned Prime Minister De Quay against personally receiving Van Roijen, airing his mistrust of the ambassador in Washington and arguing that Van Roijen should not be appointed as the Dutch negotiator during the secret meetings with Indonesia that were soon to start (De Quay Diary, XVII: 1, 47, 5081). In several instances, Luns, possibly in collusion with Prime Minister De Quay and Deputy Prime Minister Korthals, did not mention nor pass to the cabinet important telegrams sent by Van Roijen referring to significant changes in the American position. During a consultation with nearly all cabinet members at Luns private home, on the evening of June 7, 1962, Van Roijen was surprised that most cabinet members had never before been confronted with an important memorandum that he had drafted (the so-called credo-Van Roijen). He also discovered that they knew nothing about a very relevant, strategic analysis by UN ambassador Schürmann regarding Dutch opportunities in the UN and the assurances which Secretary of State Dean Rusk offered to Luns in a letter dated April 26 (Huydecoper 1990, 126).

5. Collective rationalizations.   Starting with Robert Kennedy's visit to The Hague in late February 1962, it was slowly dawning on the Dutch that American support would not be forthcoming. Most cabinet members then sought comfort in the notion that the attorney general was the evil genius behind the apparent change in the American attitude toward the conflict. President John Kennedy was thought to be leaning toward the opinion suggested to him by his brother. Other American officials believed to be more sympathetic toward the Dutch position, such as Secretary of State Dean Rusk, were ignored (Hansen 1967). At first, it was hoped that a direct presentation of the Dutch case to President Kennedy (particularly Luns's visit to the White House in early March 1962) could restore the balance. President Kennedy's letter of early April 1962, however, made the Dutch cabinet realize that the United States wanted a swift resolution of the conflict, which meant the transfer of sovereignty within a very short period of time. The anger, despair, and feelings of treachery among the members of the De Quay cabinet testify to the forlorn hope that arguing one's case directly would convince the American president of the moral strength of the Dutch point of view.

Another example of a collective rationalization shared by members of the Dutch cabinet was their long-lasting assumption that, given the limited strength of Indonesian forces at the time, a full-scale Indonesian attack on West New Guinea would not become possible until 1964, allowing the Dutch ample time to build up a deterrent coalition. This assessment soon proved to be illusory, as later observed by Finance Minister Jelle Zijlstra (Puchinger 1978, 99).[11]

6. Stereotyped views of enemy leaders. Generally, the Dutch tended to separate the "bad" Indonesian leaders from the "good" Indonesian people (Lijphart 1966, 129–30, 181–82). In this context, the temptation was to consider the "radical" Sukarno as the single leader and decision maker in Indonesia, thus ignoring internal divisions in the Indonesian ranks. The influential army general Nasution, for example, was increasingly considered by the Americans as a significant moderate, pro-Western factor in Indonesian politics. The Dutch, however, preferred to ignore these complexities and persisted in an uniform, unmitigated enemy image of Indonesian leaders.[12] Such stereotyping was needed in order to maintain the rationalization that Dutch presence in West New Guinea was the main safeguard against Indonesia turning communist, the main Dutch claim vis-à-vis the United States. This may explain why so little attention was being paid to the shift in the American attitude toward Indonesia from 1958 onward, when supporting Nasution came to be considered the best way of stemming the communist tide in the area.[13]

Antecedent Conditions of Groupthink

The presence of several of the antecedent conditions that Janis originally distinguished gives further credibility to the suggestion that the Dutch cabinet may have been a victim of groupthink during the latter stages of the West New Guinea conflict.

Decision Makers Constitute a Cohesive Group
First and foremost, the members of the De Quay cabinet can be said to have
formed a very tight group, though consisting of members from four different
parties.[14] This was due largely to Prime Minister De Quay's success in creating a personal bond with and between all members of his cabinet.[15] Strong ties
had developed among the members of the cabinet, even obstinate ones such as
Social Affairs Minister Veldkamp (cf. Veldkamp 1993, 47–48).[16] The survival of a deep crisis in December 1960, caused by internal divisions over the
construction of state-subsidized houses, had given the cabinet a strong sense
of competence and cohesion (Zijlstra 1992, 129–34). Finance Minister
Zijlstra records how the bonds of affection united all cabinet members in their
defense of Prime Minister De Quay whenever he was attacked. Moreover, he
notes how individual members preferred to solve their disputes outside the
formal cabinet meetings in order not to embarrass De Quay with discord
(Zijlstra 1992, 111, 134). De Quay's top aide played an active role as a
troubleshooter "behind the scenes" using his long-standing personal ties with
Luns to preempt and "dampen" conflicts in the cabinet.[17]

Insulation of the Policy-making Group
Three factors support the idea that the cabinet operated under a certain degree
of insulation. First of all, the De Quay cabinet considered itself an "extraparliamentary cabinet" not bound by any formal agreement to its constituent
parties (Van Raalte 1977, 56–57). More than half of the cabinet members
were recruited from outside Parliament. Not only the key players in the West
New Guinea decision-making process (Luns, De Quay, Zijlstra) but also most
of the other cabinet members who played a more or less significant role
(Visser, Klompé, De Jong, Bot, Van Houten, Calmeyer) belong to this category (see table 4.2).

Second, three of the constituting parties (ARP, CHU, VVD) strongly
observed the tradition of dualism in relations between cabinet and parliament.
The two branches of Government were supposed to have separate responsibilities. A cabinet was to be judged on its proposals and should not assume
automatic parliamentary support. As a consequence of this tradition, informal
contacts between members of the government and the governing parties'
members of parliament were relatively scarce. The fourth party (KVP) formally observed the same rule.[18] Within that party existed an important informal network around parliamentary leader Carl Romme which permitted the
Catholic leader to influence cabinet policies through his informal meetings
with Catholic ministers in the cabinet, especially Klompé, Luns, Cals, and
even Prime Minister De Quay. Romme had even managed to launch one of his
protégés, Norbert Schmelzer, as secretary of state at the prime minister's
office. This official served as both a guardian angel and a watchdog to the

TABLE 4.2.   The De Quay Cabinet (1959–63)

Ministers	Department	Parliamentary Experience	Government Experience	Previous Employment
De Quay (KVP)	Prime Minister	none	1945	Provincial Governor
Korthals (VVD)	Deputy Prime Minister; Transport	1945–59		
Luns (KVP)	Foreign Affairs	none	1952–59	Diplomat
Cals (KVP)	Education	none	1950–59	
Marijnen (KVP)	Agriculture/ Fishery	none	none	Secretary Union of Catholic Employers
Veldkamp (KVP)	Social Affairs	none	1952–59	Civil Servant, Local Labour Council, Breda
Klompé (KVP)	Social Work and Public Health	1948–56	1956–59	Secondary School teacher of chemistry
Toxopeus (VVD)	Home Office	1956–59		
Visser (VVD)	Defense	none	none	Secretary Union of Dutch Employers
Beerman (CHU)	Justice	none	none	Lawyer at Rotterdam
De Pous (CHU)	Economic Affairs	none	none	Secretary to the Union of Christian Employers; member of Council of State
Zijlstra (ARP)	Treasury	none	1952–59	Professor of Economics
Van Aartsen (ARP)	Public Housing	none	1958–59	Alderman, The Hague

politically inexperienced Prime Minister De Quay (Ammerlaan 1992, 71–92).[19]

Third, the cabinet did not receive all relevant information regarding the American attitude toward the West New Guinea conflict. A crucial position in the cabinet was taken by Foreign Secretary Luns who was the main source of information for the cabinet regarding international affairs. Much of what was known about the position of other states was transmitted by Luns during his lengthy briefings. As a matter of fact, Luns had given orders to the Communications Department at the Foreign Office to distribute telegrams regarding West New Guinea to three people only: himself, Permanent Under Secretary ("Secretaris Generaal") Baron van Tuyll tot Serooskerken, and Luns's special adviser regarding Indonesia, Nico Blom.[20] Although members of the De Quay cabinet asked Luns several times to show them important telegrams so they could form their own opinions regarding the American position, Luns persistently refused to do this. Thus, the cabinet remained isolated from many relevant telegrams and memos. Toward the height of the crisis, when Van Roijen was leading the Dutch delegation to the secret negotiations with Indonesia, he was occasionally invited to cabinet meetings and was thus able to state his dissenting views about American attitudes. Even so, Luns's opposite opinion would long carry the cabinet. Circumventing his direct chief, Ambassador Van Roijen would subsequently establish direct contacts both with key cabinet members and, in 1962, with party leaders of one of the Protestant coalition partners. Slowly the wall of protection around the cabinet, partly erected by Luns, partly enabled by the complacency of the cabinet members themselves, was being torn down by Van Roijen's minority advocacy.

Lack of Norms Requiring Systematic Procedures

De Quay's inexperience as a national politician and his personal leadership style had two important consequences for the nature of decision making in his cabinet. First, De Quay tended to prolong deliberation as long as possible until consensus among the members of his cabinet could be reached. "Keeping the club together" seems to have been his major concern. The result was often procrastination. Notwithstanding the increasing Indonesian military threat and mounting time pressures, crucial decisions about strengthening Dutch military capabilities were postponed time and again. In fact, until June/July 1962 De Quay acted purely as a technical chairman. He would refrain from expressing his personal views on the matter. Rather, he would prolong debate until all members were united in one position. De Quay explicitly wanted his ministers to convince each other of their views.[21] From July 1962 onward De Quay's leadership style became more assertive as he became more confident and more explicit in his views.

Second, De Quay's leadership style promoted highly unequal individual influence by the ministers. At first glance, De Quay's handling of cabinet meetings appears effective in avoiding the trap of *directive leadership* (Janis 1982, 235–38). However, De Quay's insecurity, and his "open forum" approach to cabinet deliberation, produced an unmistakable informal hierarchy of speakers: Luns and to a lesser extent Zijlstra dominated discussions on foreign affairs, while Zijlstra alone dominated discussions of economic and financial policies.[22] As a matter of fact, until December 1961, it rarely occurred that all cabinet members gave their personal views, even in matters regarding West New Guinea.[23]

High Stress

The cabinet had to cope with multiple forms of increasing stress. First and foremost, they were confronted with the fact that time seemed to be working against them. Cabinet members gradually realized that both international and domestic support for the Dutch position was decreasing step by step.[24] For instance, in July 1960 they became aware that by 1961 they would no longer be able to prevent Indonesian resolutions from being adopted by the General Assembly of the United Nations. Because of decolonization, the Afro-Asian states had then become able to reach a two-thirds majority.[25] These situational changes produced ever more explicit decisional dilemmas. The cabinet members were increasingly pressed to revise their policies toward West New Guinea, but were acutely aware that both a continuation and a change of the current course of action would be costly and painful.

Another notable source of stress was the unsettling balance between the increasing time the cabinet invested in the West New Guinea problem, and the lack of positive results from this increased commitment. From December 1961 onward, many cabinet members felt increasingly obsessed and haunted by the West New Guinea conflict (Ammerlaan 1992, 96; Hansen 1967, 26; Gase 1984, 61, 87, 94, 100, 104). A typical diary entry of Prime Minister De Quay from this period reads as follows: "Evening at home. A lot of telephone calls. Everything is dominated by New Guinea. Difficult. Hold on and do not yield . . . " (Diary of Prime Minister De Quay, January 30, 1962).

A third, and in this case, more incidental form of distress was caused by the military encounters with Indonesian forces that were taking place in West New Guinea. In late 1961, the first Dutch casualties were recorded and the prospect of a bloody war seemed real (Puchinger 1979, 98–99; Ammerlaan 1992, 105). Similar peaks occurred in March/April 1962 and July/August 1962. During these periods of acute military threat, some of the cabinet members harbored serious doubts about the policy. For instance, when the analytical finance minister Jelle Zijlstra heard about the first Dutch casualties, he contemplated resignation for the first time since joining the Government in 1952. Zijlstra stayed on, convinced that the cabinet should remain united in finding a solution for the West New Guinea conflict (Zijlstra 1992, 155; Gase 1986). Minister of Foreign Affairs Luns, Defense Minister Visser (Liberal Party), State Secretary of the Navy De Jong (Catholic Party) and Prime Minister De Quay himself all contemplated resigning during such periods of stress.

Deficiencies of a Groupthink Analysis

The analysis presented in the preceding section suggests that a groupthink-relevant research puzzle can be constructed and that evidence of groupthink can indeed be observed in the Dutch cabinet deliberations. Nevertheless, these empirical findings need to be qualified and elaborated. This leads us to submit a number of theoretical considerations, which so far have been neglected in much of the groupthink literature. These modifications can be divided into four categories: the institutional context within which the group is operating (see 't Hart; Stern and Sundelius, this volume); the ascendance and impact of formal and informal leaders within the group; the specific traits of informal leaders, such as their information style and their cognitive beliefs system; and the dynamic interplay among several, partly overlapping formal and informal groups.

The Institutional Context

Several institutional features of the Dutch political system affected cabinet decision making during the New Guinea conflict. After a discussion of these elements, we will indicate what they contribute to solving the empirical puzzle we have constructed.

Political Culture

Three elements of Dutch political culture, each operating at a different level of political life, are relevant to crisis decision making. The fundamentally dualist relationship between parliament and cabinet is primary. One of the antecedent conditions of groupthink, relative isolation of the small group, was a strong cultural feature of Dutch politics until the early 1970s. The accepted norm was that cabinets and coalition partners in parliament have separate responsibilities, despite the fact that a cabinet may be founded on an initial coalition agreement between parliamentary parties covering important policy areas (Andeweg en Nijzink 1992, 163–67). This process encouraged individual ministers to identify with the cabinet rather than with their political party. This tradition of dualism was especially strong in the ARP, CHU, and VVD coalition partners.

Second, Dutch cabinets have a distinct culture of reciprocal nonintervention. Specialized ministers tend to focus on their departmental portfolios and refrain from criticizing the policies of their colleagues, in turn expecting them to do the same when their own policies are being proposed (Andeweg 1991). Of course, the West New Guinea conflict may have been considered too important for this rule to be applicable because it was generally perceived as a threat to Dutch national interests. Moreover, the measures to be taken clearly concerned several departments, notably Defense, Foreign Office, Finance, and Economic Affairs. Nevertheless, there are indications that at least until December 1961 the nonintervention norm affected West New Guinea policymaking by successive Dutch governments since 1951 (Meijer 1994, 495). After December 1961, when tensions over West New Guinea increased and cabinet sessions devoted to the matter increased both in number and in length, all ministers participated in the debate, and, occasionally, raised doubts about American support. However, Luns's authority in foreign affairs was never challenged and decisions were never taken in his absence.

Third, the internal party culture of the dominant coalition partner had an impact on the cabinet process. One of the major parties of Dutch politics, the Catholic Popular Party (KVP), long cultivated an ambiguous posture consisting of a dualist relationship between the party's parliamentary faction and the cabinet, and, on the other hand, the development of a strong informal network between the top of the party (especially the parliamentary leader) and Catholic members of the cabinet. In particular, during the New Guinea conflict, a strong bond existed between parliamentary leader Carl Romme and several of his protégés in the De Quay cabinet, such as Luns, Klompé, Cals, Schmelzer, and to a certain extent, De Quay himself. These individuals often met informally before, after, and in between cabinet meetings and always kept Romme informed by phone calls or letters. This network of dependencies and information exchange proved to be crucial in maintaining the cabinet consensus.

The Nature of Coalition Government
Governments of the Netherlands have always been coalitions between various parties. On the one hand, this could be instrumental in preventing the occurrence of groupthink, since it strongly promotes differences of opinion at cabinet meetings (Andeweg 1991; Blondel 1988; 't Hart 1990/1994, 139). On the other hand, when the survival of the government is threatened and coalition partners estimate that the government's downfall may produce serious negative electoral consequences or may otherwise harm party interests, they may engage in feverish consensus-seeking.

The West New Guinea conflict certainly posed a threat to the De Quay cabinet, and, in addition, to the Catholic Popular Party itself. In 1951 a previous cabinet had fallen over the West New Guinea issue after Dutch-Indonesian negotiations had failed and the Dutch cabinet had considered transferring sovereignty to the United Nations. Thus, New Guinea clearly was a dangerous topic for any Dutch cabinet, a fact of which De Quay was fully aware. His cabinet was founded on a painstakingly negotiated consensus between the coalition partners, where they agreed that Dutch sovereignty over the area was indisputable. The long-term objective of guiding the Papuan population to self-determination became the cornerstone of Dutch policy (Gase 1984, 62–63). From the outset, therefore, the De Quay cabinet had defined its own stakes in terms of the Papuans' right to self-determination.

Second, the Catholic party had a strong stake in the survival of the De Quay cabinet. In December 1960, Carl Romme, the party leader and the center of its informal network, had fallen ill and had to withdraw from active politics. The Catholic leaders who were part of the government, notably Cals, Marijnen, and Schmelzer, considered the new Parliamentary leader, De Kort, unfit to become party leader as well. Many of them had leadership aspirations themselves.[26] They judged an eventual fall of the cabinet before the expiration of its electoral mandate in 1963 as too early. None of them would before then have mounted enough internal party support to beat De Kort in a leadership contest (Ammerlaan 1992, 84–87).

Third, Foreign Secretary Luns's position appears to have been an important element as well. The foreign secretary was the author of the compromise formula regarding West New Guinea that formed the basis of the coalition. Luns had made clear to Romme, who could make or break the new cabinet, that he would not join any cabinet that adopted a formula that might risk the handing over of West New Guinea to Indonesia "through the front, the side, or the backdoor.[27] The parliamentary leader of the Protestant ARP, Bruins Slot, secretly approached Romme and told him that they could live with the formula only if Luns were at the helm of the Foreign Office.[28] More than once during cabinet meetings, Luns threatened to resign over the government's West New Guinea policy. Both the governing coalition and the chances of Catholic runners-up to the party top were thus affected by the position of the minister who had defined his main mission as implementing the delicate formula he had helped to formulate.

Several actors had important stakes in preventing the fall of the government. This gave several hard-liners within the government an important weapon. At various instances during the spring of 1962 they threatened to resign if the issue of military reinforcements to West New Guinea were not put on the agenda.

It has been shown above how a groupthink analysis should be complemented with exploration of the institutional setting in which decision making takes place. Aspects of political culture and context such as imperatives of political survival strongly affected the De Quay cabinet throughout the period under scrutiny. Three important aspects of the puzzle of West New Guinea cannot be understood unless these factors are taken into account.

First, it took a long time before the cabinet fully took notice of the assessment by important Protestant (ARP) members of parliament that international support of the Dutch position was very unlikely in case of an international crisis. Chairman Berghuis visited Australia in the autumn of 1961, while Biesheuvel traveled to the United States during the same period (Houwaart 1988, 86–88; Jansen van Galen 1984, 125–28). No reassessment took place within the cabinet. Part of the explanation can be found in the culture of dualism and the extraparliamentary character of the De Quay cabinet which isolated it from its supporting parties in parliament (Gase 1986).

At the same time, political survival was an important consideration, not only for the Catholic members of the cabinet, but also for the full coalition, given their stake in preserving Dutch sovereignty over West New Guinea and eventually ensuring the Papuas' right of self-determination. It is important to note that "political survival" is based on considerations of both the well-being of the group as a whole and on individual calculations of future political careers.

A third factor was proving that the cabinet could govern and manage extremely difficult tasks like the New Guinea conflict without the Socialist Party (PvdA) as a coalition member. This was a major challenge to many KVP politicians. As Schmelzer, one of the key KVP members and protégés of KVP leader Romme, wrote in his diary, "We must stick to our coalition with the liberal party [VVD] because of political-tactical motives" (Ammerlaan 1992, 81). The idea was that the Catholic Party would conquer an ideal center position in Dutch politics if it succeeded in keeping the cabinet together until the next election in 1963. All of these pressures pushed in the direction of trying to maintain group consensus and cohesion even at high cost.

Formal and Informal Leadership and Its Consequences

Any analysis of Dutch decision making in the West New Guinea conflict should take into account the central role of Foreign Secretary Luns. This points to the importance of leader–follower relations in small group analysis (Tetlock, Peterson, McGuire, Chang, and Feld 1992). Two important elements play their part: the strength of the institutional position of the Dutch prime minister and the informal leadership of Luns.

Formally, the Dutch prime minister is first among equals. Although one can speak of an informal hierarchy between departments, and consequently between ministers, the opinion of relatively unimportant ministers, however, cannot be ignored. The cabinet operates as a collective body in which decisions are usually taken by consensus and in which votes are unusual. Over the last twenty years the role of the prime minister has become more important, especially in foreign affairs. This is not least because of the prime minister's role in matters regarding the European Union. Yet, in the late 1950s and early 1960s, the prime minister had no overriding influence because of his constitutional position.

We have already observed that De Quay was a highly insecure Prime Minister without experience in either national or international politics, who felt that he had no knowledge of the important policy areas of economic and foreign affairs. This allowed powerful ministers such as Zijlstra and Luns to dominate discussions in their respective policy sectors.

One important additional tool of influence, however, is the supply of information to the cabinet: the prime minister decides which pieces of information will go to all members of the cabinet (Rehwinkel 1991, 233). Potentially, this gatekeeping position gives a prime minister the opportunities to frame the perceptions and preferences of the other cabinet members (Maoz 1990). However, De Quay preferred to rely on Luns to manage the supply of information in this policy issue: the telegrams from the Washington Embassy that reached De Quay through Luns were not distributed automatically to his colleagues. This practice reinforced Luns' informal leadership. In the cabinet, Luns used his privilege to spend hours lecturing on foreign policy and his diplomatic adventures.

This suggests that De Quay's hesitant formal leadership did not result in the avoidance of directive leadership (and thus of a condition of promoting groupthink) but rather reinforced Luns's informal leadership. Luns's informal leadership was not simply based on the inexperience of the prime minister or the tendency of specialized ministers not to interfere with other departmental policies. Rather, Luns's prestige had grown since he first became foreign secretary in 1952. After a difficult initial period (1952–56) in which he had to share responsibility for foreign policy with a second foreign secretary, Jan Beyen, Luns had developed into the foreign policy expert of successive cabinets and was to remain in place until 1971.

Specific Cognitive Traits of Informal Leaders

Under certain circumstances the information style of key decision makers can have far-reaching consequences for small group decision making (Driver et al. 1990; Streufert and Swezey 1986). Especially when they are placed in central strategic positions in the information network, the way informal leaders scan and interpret information can have an important impact on the dynamics and the outcomes of small group decision-making processes.[29] Given Luns's prestige and De Quay's and Korthals's tendency not to pass on information to the cabinet, as well as the long-standing tendency of most cabinet members to be reluctant in seeking and creating alternative information channels themselves, Luns became an important gatekeeper in providing information to, or withholding it from, the cabinet. This was the case regarding the question of forthcoming American support in the event of an Indonesian attack on West New Guinea. Luns's central position suggests that explaining the empirical puzzle of West New Guinea requires answers to the following questions: (1) How did Luns collect and interpret information; (2) How did Luns pass on information to the cabinet; (3) How did the cabinet judge the information provided by Luns?

How Did Luns Interpret Information?
In order to understand how Luns processed incoming information it is important to know his fundamental views about the nature of international relations. To this end, we have constructed Luns's *operational code* (George 1969;

Walker 1990). Between 1949 and 1952 Luns was stationed as a diplomat at the Dutch representation to the United Nations in New York. He had known Catholic Party leader Carl Romme since the 1930s, when both were members of the same student fraternity in Amsterdam. Luns and Romme had remained in touch since then, and between 1949 and 1952 Luns sent Romme at least 20 hand-written, personal letters. In these he gave Romme advice on international politics, and in particular, on the issue of West New Guinea.[30] On the basis of those letters the following elements seem important to Joseph Luns's cognitive belief system (Metselaar and Verbeek 1995, 239–46):

> The Netherlands had been following a neutralist foreign policy since the Napoleonic wars. The Second World War proved that neutralism was a mistake. Yet, the Dutch diplomatic and political elite is not geared to (a) assessing the Dutch position in the world and (b) playing the power game of international politics.
>
> Dutch diplomats and politicians assume a conciliatory attitude guided by a strong belief in international law and/or morality. This produces an attitude in which diplomatic negotiations are considered as meetings that, one way or another, *have* to succeed. By consequence, Dutch diplomats and governments are often the first to make concessions rather than defining and defending the national interest.
>
> Dutch diplomacy has acquired the international reputation of eventually giving in if pressed long enough. This is fatal for the defense of Dutch national interests. Rather, the Netherlands should be prepared to follow the example of countries like Britain, France, South Africa, and Israel, and simply say no to the United Nations or to pressures from third parties (as a result, Luns had become very distrustful of Van Roijen who had been practicing the traditional style of Dutch diplomacy during the 1949 Round Table Conference on Indonesian independence, and of those politicians and diplomats that were about to commit the same mistakes during the 1950–51 negotiations on West New Guinea).
>
> The national interest should take precedence over international conciliation. The Dutch national interest requires us to keep West New Guinea as long as possible, because it is one of those "imponderable elements" of international power and prestige that make the Netherlands more than a small power. Possession gives automatic access to all important international forums in the Pacific. It constitutes an important tool for influencing Indonesia and making sure that it respects Dutch possessions in the area.
>
> The maintenance of West New Guinea, however, requires the construction of an effective extended deterrent by building a coalition with the

United States, the United Kingdom, and Australia. Defense of the area is impossible without outside support. In building this coalition, it is essential to show resolve, to make sure that the Netherlands is not going to give in and that it will go very far in defending the area. This requires that the country be united: internal dissensus would be fatal to keeping the deterrent intact.

Good economic relations with Indonesia are not more important than holding on to the economically unattractive area of West New Guinea. Indonesia cannot be trusted, and the transfer of West New Guinea will actually induce Indonesia to be even tougher with the Dutch.

How Did Luns Pass on Information to the Cabinet?

The cabinet was dependent on Luns's account of international diplomacy, and especially of his interpretations of American guarantees to support the Netherlands over the West New Guinea issue. After the last Dutch-Indonesian diplomatic attempt to settle the matter, Luns started in 1956 a permanent campaign of building and maintaining a coalition between the United States, the United Kingdom, and Australia. He claimed to have obtained guarantees from successive secretaries of state, such as Dulles and Herter, and the promise of newly elected President Kennedy that all pledges by the Eisenhower administration would be honored also by him.

How Did the Cabinet Judge the Information
Provided by Luns?

The question of the nature of American guarantees was frequently raised in the cabinet, but Luns again and again could remain very vague in his answers. Members of the cabinet preferred not to press the matter and did not question the exact nature of guarantees and the precise conditions under which the Americans could be expected to keep whatever promises they had made.

The Dynamic Interplay of Overlapping Groups

Thus far the analysis shows the existence of various formal and informal decision-making units. At the cabinet level, we find the full body meeting formally. In addition, the cabinet often met informally over lunch and dinner. Moreover, an informal KVP network existed of Catholic ministers and their parliamentary leader, Romme. At the departmental level, a small inner circle operated around Foreign Minister Joseph Luns. At the formal interdepartmental level we find a group consisting of Prime Minister De Quay, Minister of Foreign Affairs Luns, Minister of Domestic Affairs Toxopeus, Minister of Defense Visser, State Secretaries Calmeyer, De Jong, and Bot, and the joint chiefs of staff (De Geus 1984, 185). At the informal interdepartmental level there was a long-standing friendship and informal relationship between Luns and the most senior aide to the Prime Minister, Permanent Undersecretary Fock. Fock and Luns frequently contacted each other before meetings of the cabinet, especially when potential conflicting issues were placed on the weekly agenda. Luns personally acted as the major *trait d'union* between his department and the cabinet. Finally, primary sources suggest that many informal meetings between De Quay and Luns preceded, and followed, formal cabinet decision making.

This constellation of informal groups does not permit us to conclude, however, that the *locus of decision making* cannot be found in the cabinet. None of the informal groups was powerful enough to be able to make decisions without the cabinet. The cabinet remains the central decision unit (cf. Hermann and Hermann 1989). Many of the decisions were settled by consensus and some of them by voting. An important informal decision rule in the cabinet was that no crucial decision was taken as long as Minister of Foreign Affairs Luns was not present at the cabinet meeting. This meant that the most important functions of the other overlapping groups were: to collect, process, and disseminate information; to prepare or implement the decisions; and to manage potential conflicts and to build consensus to prevent crises in the cabinet itself.

On the other hand, the network of overlapping informal groups did provide important opportunities for actors to influence the general thrust and substance of the cabinet decision making. In this respect, it is important to note that Luns was a dominant, well-informed and proactive member of all of the overlapping groups mentioned above. Another important factor that may have influenced the interplay between the groups, as well as the decision making process in the cabinet, was that some crucial decisions were made (for example the decision on April 6, 1962 to strengthen the military presence in West New Guinea) while some of the more skeptical cabinet members (Zijlstra and especially De Pous) were absent from the meeting (see Garrison and Hoyt, this volume).

Concluding Observations: Moving Beyond Groupthink

Any analysis of Dutch decision making during the later stages of the West New Guinea conflict should take into account the interplay between explanations at the individual and group levels rather than accentuate the one at the expense of the other. At first glance, the case seemed to be a clear-cut example of groupthink. The Dutch De Quay cabinet indeed suffered from defective decision making. It did not make use of relevant information at hand and it processed available relevant information in a biased way. This contributed to its misjudgment of the likelihood that American support, indispensable for deterring Indonesia from attacking West New Guinea, would be forthcoming. Several symptoms of groupthink could be detected as well as a number of its antecedent conditions, including insulation of the group, high cohesion among its members, and perceptions of increasing stress. At the same time, it became evident that the decision-making process was also shaped by factors not contained in groupthink theory. Some of those elements pertain to the role of key individuals, others to group dynamics. Furthermore, all of these individual and group elements should be analyzed within the institutional context of cabinet decision making in the Netherlands. In sum, we note at least six "non-groupthink" elements:

1. Stages of the group process. Before Indonesia put real pressure on the Netherlands in December 1961, when the first armed battle occurred, West New Guinea surfaced as a routine issue on weekly cabinet meetings. During these sessions discussions were dominated by a small group of ministers who had been members of previous governments (Luns, Zijlstra, Klompé, and Cals). Luns's prestige made him the informal leader of cabinet discussions on foreign affairs. The prime minister, De Quay, made few attempts to use his weight as chair and put his mark on the debates. After December 1961, the other cabinet members became more assertive. Yet Luns retained enough prestige for his opinions to continue to carry much weight. Nevertheless, more and more dissenters, like Van Roijen, started doubting his analyses and made themselves heard. This development increased the danger of the cabinet falling apart and thus, paradoxically, increased the influence of the weak prime minister, De Quay. He was hesitant to draw conclusions from discussions and continued postponing important decisions, such as the controversial reinforcement of Dutch defenses at West New Guinea, in order to prevent a breakup of the cabinet. This analysis suggests that a decomposition of stages of group decisions may be a useful tool (Burnstein and Berbaum 1983). It also appears that group dynamics may be affected by the distribution of old and new members within the group (Stern, this volume).

2. Political calculations. The predominant concern with political survival among many of the De Quay cabinet members suggests that political group dynamics are not only influenced by the strength of affective relations between group members, but also by political calculations dictated by the institutional conditions under which small groups in politics operate. In this case, the imperatives of coalition government were the most salient. Two aspects seem particularly relevant. First of all, the pivotal party in Dutch politics in the 1950s, the Catholic KVP, had two important reasons to prevent the collapse of the government. The power vacuum within the party caused by the illness of its leader, Carl Romme, made the prospect of early elections less attractive to the KVP ministers jockeying for party leadership (Cals, Marijnen, Schmelzer). Moreover, the KVP wanted to prove that it could govern smoothly without their traditional coalition partner, Labor (PvdA). Secondly, the structural condition of wanting to prevent the fall of the government gave several hard-liners within it (notably Defense Minister Visser and Secretary of State for the Navy De Jong) an important weapon. At various instances during the spring of 1962, they threatened to resign if reinforcements were not put on the agenda. This analysis suggests that 't Hart's expansion of Janis's group-think construct by including political calculations is a valuable modification ('t Hart 1990/1994, 129–91).

3. Informal groups.   The importance of the survival of the government to the KVP points to a key element of cabinet decision making: the role of informal groups. Decision making within the De Quay cabinet cannot be fully under-stood unless the elaborate informal network at the top of the Catholic party is taken into account. KVP members of government met frequently with the party elite (including Romme, Beaufort, and Beel) and kept in close touch by private letters. Cabinet decision making was often preceded or followed by informal meetings between Prime Minister De Quay, Deputy Prime Minister Korthals, and several cabinet members. Yet at no time could it be said that a more or less durable inner circle orchestrated cabinet decision making.[31] Rather, these informal meetings served to strengthen the bond between the members of the cabinet, helped to work out new compromises, and thus contributed to maintaining cabinet unanimity.

4. The role of individuals.   One is struck by the central role played by For-eign Secretary Joseph Luns. Due to his prestige as an experienced foreign secretary and his crucial position in the communications network between the Dutch Embassy to the United States, the Prime Ministerial Office, and the full cabinet, Luns was extremely influential. Furthermore, Luns was a participant in the informal KVP network as well. One could surely call him a gatekeeper. Because of this privileged position, certain individual traits of Luns are impor-tant in understanding his biased selection and forwarding of information to the (deputy) prime minister and the full cabinet. His cognitive belief system and specific mode of information gathering are important elements in explaining which type of information actually reached the cabinet. Eventually, Luns's powerful position was weakened. First domestic political support eroded when members of the Protestant ARP party initiated contacts with the Dutch Embassy in Washington. Second, the Dutch ambassador to the United States, Dr. van Roijen, attempted to circumvent Luns and the Foreign Office and contacted the Dutch prime minister directly.

5. Coincidence.   A final element should not overlooked: the accidental presence or absence of key players at crucial cabinet sessions without any deliberate attempt by others to manipulate the decision-making process. At several instances, the De Quay cabinet was exposed to "correct information" about the United States' position while major critics happened to be absent. This happened when Ambassador Van Roijen flew to The Hague in February 1962 to inform the cabinet directly of the American attitude. Important doubters, such as Zijlstra and Cals, were abroad or ill. As a matter of fact, De Quay noted in his diary that things had gone smoothly because, luckily, Zijlstra and Cals had been absent (De Quay diary, February 2, 1962, XVII: 5084). When Cals returned, he scribbled a personal note to himself, noting "I was told [they] were happy that [I] was away" (Cals Papers, box 186).

6. Institutional context of decision making.   Individual and group elements cannot contribute to a full account of decision making unless embedded within their institutional context (see George, this volume). For a political system such as the Netherlands, this implies that analysts should pay attention to the rules governing coalition politics. Some of these rules pertain to the relationship between government and parliament: in Dutch politics governments can only be coalition cabinets. One would expect tendencies toward groupthink not to be weaker in coalitions. Presumably, the very idea of coalition governments implies that different policy views meet in a cabinet, thus reducing the danger of tunnel vision. On the other hand, this pressure for relatively open discussions is mitigated by the fact that, at least until the mid-1960s, Dutch governments operated in relative isolation from the parliamentary parties supporting them. This was because of the informal practice of dualism. Group isolation and opportunities for building high cohesion within the cabinet were thus fostered by the institutional practices of Dutch politics.

In our view, this empirical analysis of a Dutch case of cabinet decision making has important theoretical implications. Reification and isolation of the small group from its wider organizational-institutional context may be profoundly misleading. Important insights may be generated via exploration of the individual—group nexus (see Preston, this volume) and the ways in which institutional factors affect intragroup dynamics. This topic will be explored further in the following chapter by Stern and Sundelius.[32]

NOTES

The authors wish to thank the editors and many other members of the *Small Group Initiative* for their helpful comments on various drafts of this chapter. Further, they would like to thank a number of former civil servants who have provided us with useful background information, as well as the curators of the archives of the Ministry of Foreign Affairs in The Hague, the *Algemeen Rijksarchief* at The Hague and Den Bosch, the *Katholiek Documentatiecentrum* in Nijmegen, and the *Public Record Office* at Kew, United Kingdom.

1. We assume that the reader has a fair knowledge of Janis's groupthink hypothesis. We adopt Janis's original definition in which groupthink refers to "a mode of thinking that people engage in when they are deeply involved in a cohesive in-group, when the members' strivings for unanimity override their motivation to realistically appraise alternative courses of action" (Janis 1972, 9). See the chapters by George and Fuller and Aldag (this volume) for more detailed introductions.

2. All available memoirs and diaries of Dutch ministers attest to their anger, disbelief, and revulsion to Robert Kennedy's attitude: "a tough man," according to Prime Minister De Quay (De Quay Diary, XVII, 1, 47: 5104), "impolite, rough," Finance Minister Zijlstra judged (Zijlstra 1992, 158); "an incouth lout" (Luns). Robert Kennedy himself later recalled having been "quite frank" with the Dutch (Guthman and Shulman 1988, 320).

3. This letter caused feelings among the Dutch cabinet of having been cheated by the Americans, as evidenced, for instance, in De Quay's diaries (XVII, 1, 47: 5135). In a conversation with Foreign Secretary Luns and Ambassador to the United States Van Roijen, De Quay concluded "that the United States has deserted us, the United Nations will give us nothing, and that, therefore, we have been sold out. In my opinion this is caused by Dutch half heartedness. In this world blackmail pays; poor country, poor world" (XVII, 1, 47: 5141).

4. Analyses of the conflict in English include Henderson 1973 and Lijphart 1966. In some textbooks on international organizations the settlement of the conflict is heralded as a major example of peaceful settlement via the United Nations (e.g., Bennett 1980, 175–76).

5. In the course of 1962 the American government became aware of this and occasionally bypassed the Foreign Office by contacting De Quay directly (Koster 1990, 85).

6. Evidence that De Quay did not forward these telegrams to his cabinet colleagues comes from the testimony of a senior civil servant at the prime minister's office (interview, March 10, 1994).

7. The first two points refer to symptoms of defective decision making, commonly known as "poor information search" and "selective bias in processing information at hand" (Janis 1982, 175). The third aspect is rarely observed in the groupthink literature, but could count as a form of self-censorship.

8. In this chapter, we prefer not to engage the discussion about Janis's eight symptoms, in which questions have been raised about the minimal number of symptoms to occur for groupthink to be attributed, the sequence of their occurrence, and the completeness of the symptoms included. Rather, we follow Janis's original formulation (1982, 174–97; see Aldag and Fuller, this volume).

9. Former Finance Minister Zijlstra suggests that those cabinet members who most deeply believed in the Dutch obligation to protect the rights of the Papua population (Klompé [Social Work], Toxopeus [Interior], and Korthals [Deputy Prime Minister,

Transport]) were the ones who also felt that American support was forthcoming (Zijlstra 1992, 157).

10. It is, for example, illustrative that the shocking Kennedy visit in February and the U.S. president's letter in April 1962 were hardly even mentioned in the cabinet meetings directly afterward. However, their diaries, their remarks in informal meetings, and many remarks in interviews afterward show that both events had an impressive impact on the cabinet members. Later, these two moments were often defined as crucial turning points. It has been suggested that it was only then that most ministers realized that American political and military support was an illusion and that Luns had been wrong (Hansen 1967; Gase 1984; Ammerlaan 1992, 109–10). Yet, a thorough analysis of the cabinet minutes suggests that these remarks may well have been post hoc rationalizations. On the one hand, it is certainly true that both messages were serious blows to their confidence in American support. On the other hand, however, especially during the cabinet meetings, selective avoidance, bolstering, and wishful thinking continued as if nothing had happened.

11. Partly due to this misperception, most members of the De Quay cabinet were surprised completely by messages of the minister of defense, Visser, and the secretary of marine affairs, De Jong, that a massive Indonesian military attack could be expected around April 1, 1962 (*Minutes of the Cabinet,* March 1, 1962; March 2, 1962); and later on by messages that a major Indonesian military attack was prepared in August 1962 (*Minutes of the Cabinet,* July 21, 1962; July 27, 1962; see also Huydecoper 1990, 112, 145–48, 154).

12. This is clear, for instance, in De Quay's recording on October 27, 1960, of his discussion with a Catholic missionary (Father Kersten) who tried to convince De Quay that Nasution was heading the anticommunist faction in the Indonesian government. In his diary De Quay strongly doubted that Luns and the others would ever accept such an analysis (De Quay Diary, XIV, 4707).

13. During the summer of 1958, Luns in a personal letter to the leader of the Catholic Popular Party, Carl Romme, gave an analysis of the Dutch position in the international arena. Luns dismissed American attention to Nasution, who had suppressed a communist revolt in early 1958, as "being deprived of much hope" (Luns to Romme, August 29, 1958, Romme Papers, Box 92).

14. The De Quay cabinet was a coalition between Catholics (KVP), Protestants (ARP and CHU), and liberals (VVD).

15. It may well be that De Quay's efforts can partly be explained as an attempt to compensate for his lack of experience in national politics and his poor personal power basis within his party (Catholic Popular Party, KVP).

16. In fact, primary sources show that this strong inner bond between the cabinet members was kept alive for years afterward. There was a regular correspondence between most of them, and they frequently socialized with each other.

17. As noted in several interviews with a former senior official at the department of general affairs and former members of the department of foreign affairs between March and May 1994.

18. Indeed, in the mid-1950s several top KVP politicians around party chairman Harry van Doorn judged that the KVP had been excessively formalistic in its dualistic

attitude. It was proposed to have more regular contacts between ministers, party officials, and members of the KVP parliamentary faction; letter of minister of housing to Ministers Klompé, Luns, Cals, and Struyken, October 30, 1957, *Cals Papers,* Box 90.

19. De Quay, partly because of his insecurity, wanted to bring Schmelzer to cabinet sessions regularly. This caused a lot of tension within the cabinet. Ministers fiercely opposed this (Veldkamp 1993, 48), as Dutch secretaries of state do not usually participate in deliberations. As for the assessment of the American attitude, they may have deprived themselves of a useful observer, as Schmelzer was a doubter—albeit self-proclaimed—of American guarantees. Schmelzer was never invited for the New Guinea debates in the cabinet. Moreover, the highest civil servant in the department of the prime minister, Mr. Fock, having a strong formal and informal power base in the department, seemed to be more and more successful in removing Schmelzer from the inner circle of advisers around De Quay.

20. Thus, no top civil servant at the Dutch foreign office was aware of Ambassador Van Roijen's warnings against the lack of American support. Van Roijen learned of this situation himself only in 1984 (letter, Baron Van Boetzelaer to Van Roijen, January 24, 1984, *Van Roijen Papers,* Box 35).

21. This was De Quay's own interpretation of his ability to bridge differences between conflicting individuals in his cabinet (hence his nickname "Mending-Jan"). Conversations with J. de Quay, *De Quay Papers,* no. 092.01: 84–85.

22. This can be deduced from De Quay's notes in his diary from the start of his cabinet. He would be relieved whenever Zijlstra or Luns were absent from cabinet meetings, because their absence allowed for proper discussion (*De Quay Diary,* passim). Social Work Minister Marga Klompé complained to Catholic Party leader Carl Romme about the consequences of De Quay's leadership style, Klompé to Romme, January 10, 1961, *Romme Papers,* Box 83.

23. After an important meeting on January 6, 1962, De Quay notes how useful it had been that at long last everyone had given their opinion (*De Quay Diary,* XVII, 1: 5062).

24. See, for example, cabinet minutes of August 7, 1960; April 14, 1961; March 12, 1962.

25. This was a major reason why the cabinet contemplated transferring West New Guinea as a trusteeship to the United Nations. The primary sources, especially De Quay's diary, do testify to various instances at which cabinet meetings took place. *De Quay Diary,* XIV: 4628.

26. Indeed, two of them were to become prime minister (Marijnen [1963–65], Cals [1965–66]), while the third was to be parliamentary leader between 1963 and 1971.

27. One of the backdoor solutions that Luns opposed was to hand over Western New Guinea to the United Nations (Luns to De Quay, April 13, 1959, a copy of which Luns sent to Romme, *Romme Papers,* Box 82).

28. This is clear from the diary Romme kept on the formation of the De Quay Cabinet in 1959. De Quay first wanted to leave Luns out of the cabinet, preferring to give the foreign office to the Liberal VVD, because he held a different opinion on New Guinea from Luns's. Only the influence of Father Beaufort, an influential KVP senator and a good friend of Luns's, made De Quay accept Luns as his foreign secretary (Diary

of the 1958–59 cabinet formation, esp. 17–24 covering the April 4–13, 1959 period, *Romme Papers,* Box 82).

29. Individuals develop their information styles within the context of standard organizational procedures for collecting and passing information. After Luns became minister in 1952 the institutionalized procedure at the foreign office was for all incoming information that had any relevance to West New Guinea be automatically sent directly to the minister's office. Most of the time a small, stable, and cohesive group of civil servants within the ministry was involved in the preselection of the enormous quantity of telegrams, memos, telephones, reports, and news from media all over the world concerning the West New Guinea conflict. These were sent to the minister's office every day solicited and unsolicited.

30. The letters are scattered throughout the voluminous Romme Papers at the National Dutch Archives in The Hague. The first letter is dated September 9, 1949, the last June 24, 1952 (*Romme Papers,* Boxes nos. 37, 40, 71, 80, 92).

31. This happened, for instance, in Great Britain during the 1956 Suez crisis (Verbeek 1994).

32. See also the chapter on collective risk taking by Vertzberger (this volume).

CHAPTER 5

Understanding Small Group Decisions in Foreign Policy: Process Diagnosis and Research Procedure

Eric K. Stern and Bengt Sundelius

The Importance of Group Process in Foreign Policy-making

Before outlining our own research strategy for taking small group analysis a step beyond groupthink, let us pause for a moment to take stock of the main thrust of the preceding chapters of this volume. Despite the differing disciplinary backgrounds and empirical domains represented, there is considerable agreement on a fundamental, empirical point. Small group processes matter a great deal in politics. As the eminent political psychologist Philip Tetlock and his associates (Peterson, McGuire, Chang, and Feld) have argued, "Most political decisions in the world today are the product of a collective decision-making process. One can make a strong prima facie case that how this group decision-making process unfolds plays a crucial role in determining the fate of governments" (1992, 403). The survival or prosperity of very-large-scale collectives such as nations often depends upon decisions made by a handful of individuals engaged in intensive communicative interaction. Deliberative and political processes taking place within and across small groups in governmental settings may profoundly affect the decision makers' view of their situation and its possibilities, constraints, and imperatives.

When groups make consequential decisions or when executives depend heavily upon groups for information and advice, small variations in group interaction—assumptions left unchallenged, questions unasked or ignored, dissenters excluded—can have dramatic effects on the choices made (or not made) and, indirectly, even upon "the fate of nations." As Moscovici and Doise (1994, 122) have observed: "In the field of decision-making modest causes have great consequences." Thus, for foreign policy scholars, delving into the "black box" of group decision processes remains a pressing task.

A practical problem for the researcher intent upon making use of a small group perspective for the analysis of one or more historical cases is the bewildering flora of theoretical constructions and research findings from several disciplines bearing on group interaction in governmental settings. This potpourri is the result of the efforts of a diverse community of scholars working in different traditions toward a variety of programmatic ends. There is a need to weave together and integrate the existing body of research in order to facilitate comparison and cumulative understanding of real-world decision making in group settings. In other words, intellectual bridges from the realm of laboratory and simulation studies to the realm of historical and field studies are required.

One such bridge, Fuller and Aldag's synthetic General Group Problem Solving model, was presented earlier in this volume. They consider the manner in which decision characteristics, group structure, and decision-making context generate emergent group characteristics (cf. Gladstein 1984). These shape the group decision process that, in turn, produces group choices. While Fuller and Aldag point to a broad range of task, contextual, and group variables impacting on group decision processes, they do not focus on the important problem of how to diagnose the group decision-making processes identified in the analysis of particular historical cases.

Alexander George concluded his contribution to this book with a call for contextual process analysis reembedding the small group in the broader policy-making system of which it is a part. In that spirit, this chapter will focus on the task of formulating a contextually sensitive empirical research strategy for group process diagnosis. First, we will develop a diagnostic set of group interaction patterns from the rich, multidisciplinary literature. Then we will present a step-by-step, analytical procedure for examining the institutional and intragroup context of small group decision making, the importance of which was clearly demonstrated empirically by Metselaar and Verbeek in the preceding chapter. The objective of this systematic approach is to facilitate the diagnosis of the group interaction pattern (or patterns) manifested in a particular historical case of foreign policy making, patterns which may profoundly affect decision outputs and outcomes. For easy access and reference, the diagnostic set and the research procedure are summarized in tables 5.1 and 5.2 respectively.

Group Interaction Patterns: Developing a Diagnostic Set

One of the most enduring and compelling insights from cognitive psychology is the importance of *availability* in interpretation and attribution. When a belief, proposition, or explanation is readily available—because it has been recently used or stands out as particularly vivid or important—individuals are likely to make use of that notion when attempting to interpret new and ambiguous situations (e.g., Nisbett and Ross 1980). Foreign policy analysts are clearly not immune from the downsides of such basic psychological heuristics. As George (this volume) has pointed out, there is good reason to believe that Janis "imposed" the groupthink hypothesis on a number of his cases of foreign policy misadventure. If Janis did indeed fall prey to the perennial academic temptation to consciously or subconsciously "massage" the data a wee bit, a contributing factor may have been the fact that his analytical repertoire in his groupthink studies consisted essentially of only two alternative group interaction patterns—groupthink and vigilant decision making (Fuller and Aldag, this volume). It seems reasonable to argue that an analyst will, all other things being equal, be less inclined to favor a particular interpretation or explanation in his or her analysis of empirical cases if a broader and more nuanced repertoire of alternative interpretations is available at the outset. Then the question becomes not whether groupthink fits or can be made to fit the "facts" of the case in question, but rather which of a number of competing or complementary group interaction patterns best captures what went on in the decision group or groups under study.

The set of patterns developed in this section should be seen as a kind of menu which may alert the case analyst to a selection of the best established or most promising interaction patterns to be found in this vast literature. Because these interaction patterns are drawn from differing discourses and idiosyncratic conceptualizations by individual authors, together they do not yet meet the standard typological criteria of mutual exclusiveness and collective exhaustiveness. Thus what we offer is *not* yet a formal typology. While an integrative reconceptualization in order to produce mutual exclusiveness may be promising, it is a daunting task.[1] With regard to exhaustiveness, additional interaction patterns, identified in the vast interdisciplinary literature bearing upon group process, may need to be added.[2]

The following discussion of group interaction patterns is organized around the issues of conformity and conflict in the small groups setting. We wish to emphasize that the relationship between these basic dimensions of social interaction in groups is complex and multidimensional. As a result, we will devote particular attention to exploring a number of important hybrid patterns exhibiting various mixes of convergent and divergent tendencies (Moscovici and Doise 1994).

Simple Conformity

In developing our diagnostic set, let us begin with one of the most central topics in the small groups literature: the issue of *conformity*. Classic experiments by Sherif, Asch, Schachter, Bales, and others produced the disturbing conclusion that group members are often willing to suspend their own critical judgment and even the evidence of their own senses in order to avoid deviating from what they perceive to be an established or emergent group norm (Turner 1991; Moscovici 1985; cf. Deutsch and Gerard 1955). This is particularly likely to occur when members of the group actively "police" the norm and apply pressure to those airing deviant views. In extreme cases, deviants may even be physically expelled from the group. Importantly, the example set by the treatment of dissenters may serve to discourage others from airing differing views.

Tendencies toward conformity may decrease the diversity of perspectives brought to bear in group deliberations and lead to less differentiated understandings of the problem before the group and the merits and liabilities of alternative solutions. Members may engage in self-censorship and withhold information that seems incompatible with the way they see the proverbial winds blowing in the group. In other words, conformity may lead to a restriction and homogenization of the information base available to the group and to premature closure of the decision process. Beneficial short-term and longer-term impacts resulting from the airing and serious consideration of minority views may be lost if the pressures toward conformity become too strong within the group (Moscovici 1985; Nemeth and Staw 1989; Moscovici, Mucchi-Faina, and Maass 1994).

Groupthink

Irving Janis's (1972, 1982) groupthink syndrome may be seen as bearing a family resemblance to the basic conformity pattern described above. Since Janis's work has been described at length in the chapter by Aldag and Fuller, let it suffice to say that Janis's work emphasized the role of stress-induced or reinforced cohesion (such as that associated with crisis situations) in producing conformity, stereotyping, and risk taking, to the detriment of the procedural "quality" of the decision process. In particular, such groups were alleged to be subject to an insidious, largely unconscious erosion of the critical capacities of group members.[3]

Post-Janis reformulations of the groupthink notion tend to amalgamate groupthink and simple conformity and deploy an alternative distinction between internalization and compliance. Internalization refers to the case where group members come to adopt group consensual views without private reservations (McCauley 1989; 't Hart 1990/1994). Compliance refers to the situation where individuals do not express private reservations about what they perceive to be the group consensus on a particular issue. In his multipath reformulation of groupthink, 't Hart (1990/1994) argues that the route to groupthink most relevant to groups operating in political/administrative settings is *anticipatory compliance,* which refers to the tendency to those lower down in the hierarchy to take positions which conform to the (real or perceived) predispositions of superiors.

Newgroup Syndrome

Another type of group dynamics associated with conformity is a pattern which Stern and Sundelius (1994) have labeled *newgroup syndrome.* Since newgroup syndrome will be treated at length in one of the chapters below (Stern), a brief description here should suffice. This is a pattern linked to the stages of group development and that may operate at varying levels of cohesion and conflict within the advisory group. In ad hoc or newly institutionalized groups (i.e., in the *forming* stage, to use Tuckman's [1965] terminology), a common group subculture and well-developed procedural norms tend to be lacking. This vacuum creates uncertainty among the members, which works to the advantage of group leaders and other assertive individuals and contributes to the emergence of tendencies toward conformity in the group as a whole. Longley and Pruitt (1980, 87) have argued that in newer groups:

> Group members are uncertain about their roles and status and thus are concerned about the possibility of being made a scapegoat or even excluded from the group. Hence they are likely to avoid expressing opinions that are different from those proposed by the leader or other powerful persons in the group, to avoid conflict by failing to criticize one another's ideas, and even to agree overtly with other people's suggestions while disagreeing covertly. Such actions sound very much like groupthink.

This interaction pattern clearly belongs to the "family" of conformity dynamics. Newgroup syndrome may appear even in only moderately cohesive groups and may in fact be exacerbated by the defensive mentality associated with policy environments rife with personal, factional, or bureaucratic politics–style conflict. The general susceptibility to conformity we have noted suggests that new groups may be particularly ripe for manipulation attempts as well (see below).

It is important to recognize that virtually all new groups are thought to have these latent propensities. Yet, not all new groups develop newgroup *syndrome.* As Burnstein and Berbaum (1983, 551) have suggested, a key factor is whether or not leaders intervene actively in order to set norms and ground rules that suspend extragroup status considerations and encourage broad, forthright, and critical participation from the very start. Alternatively, explicit group discussion and negotiation of participation norms by members may serve the same function.

At the other end of the scale are conflictually driven dynamics within small advisory and decision groups. These evolve around the balance of power (and "skill") among the "players." Intragroup bargaining and other forms of political gamesmanship tend to generate choices that reflect a political logic, sometimes to the detriment of policy feasibility, moral defensibility, or other standards of evaluation. A substantial body of literature in political science and organizational theory suggests that the withholding of information as a result of latent or open conflict is quite common (George 1980; Vertzberger 1990; Maoz 1990; Pfeffer 1991). The result of such gamesmanship may well be the diminished differentiation in the understanding of a policy problem and alternative responses to that problem.

Cabinet and Bureaucratic Politics

Conflictual group dynamics patterns may take several forms including bureaucratic and cabinet politics, naysaying, and manipulation. Several researchers have noted during the last decade that the literature on organizational and bureaucratic politics was relevant to group decision making (Hermann 1988; Vertzberger 1990; 't Hart 1990/1994). In particular, the fact that bureaucratic or cabinet political struggles are commonly fought out in the small group arena—at all levels of government—led to the realization that factional conflict could be a driving dynamic in group decision making (Vertzberger 1990). Tactical withholding or deployment of information could have highly significant effects on the choices made by faction, "nonaligned," and leading group members. When small group decision making is driven by personal and organizational conflicts of interest, final decisions may reflect the balance of power and influence within the group—they may be "resultants" produced by "pulling and hauling" (and, counterintuitively, also by tactical compromise and coalition building)—rather than via a task-driven analytical process.

The contending positions in such conflictual interaction may be represented by individuals (often representing outside constituencies) or by *factions*. Factions are subgroups within the group, bound together by various combinations of personal relationships, perceptions of common interests, ideological homogeneity, or career interdependencies (such as mentor–protégé relationships). Factions tend be more cohesive than the wider groups of which they are a part and they may exert particularly strong pressures toward conformity on members. They are also thought to be particularly susceptible to groupthink. Conformity within the faction and the tendencies of factions to withhold or selectively provide information in order to promote factional interests may have a negative impact on the wider group's information processing (cf. Vertzberger 1990, 246–49).

Following up this line of thought, let us digress briefly to consider whether bureaucratic politics and conformity are fundamentally incompatible. A number of scholars seem to suggest that this may be the case. For example, George (1980, 91) notes that

> pressures against conformity in policymaking groups often arise from motives inspired by bureaucratic politics and the institutional loyalties of individual members rather than on the basis of the objective merits of a particular proposal.

While plausible, this is only half the story. We agree that the defensiveness associated with bureaucratic and partisan politics is likely to inhibit uncritical internalization of group viewpoints. However, there is no reason to believe that bureaucratic or partisan political orientations generally inhibit compliance at the individual level or conformity at the factional or group level (McCauley 1989). In fact, the desire to avoid making enemies, to save political capital for organizationally (or factionally) more important issues, and to be associated with the "winning" side in deliberations may induce compliance behavior among particular group members, thus supporting the emergence of conformity dynamics or even full-blown classic groupthink in the rest of the group. Furthermore, as Vertzberger (1990) and 't Hart (1990) have noted, conflict with rival groups or factions may increase cohesion and the likelihood of conformity within an embattled faction or group.

As a result, one may question Hermann's (1989, 375–76) assertion that "It is noteworthy that groupthink postulates very different dynamics for group decisionmaking than does bureaucratic politics. Clearly, both conditions cannot occur simultaneously in the same group." Once the possibility of subgroup factions is taken seriously it becomes clear that a manipulative faction might strategically exploit stress-induced cohesion experienced by some or most of the other members—generating dynamics at the group level which resemble groupthink.[4] We will return to this point below.

Nay-saying

Perhaps the most extreme conflict-driven dynamic noted in the literature is the *nay-saying* pattern. Nay-saying is characterized by a situation where group deliberations exhibit a pervasive negativism, a crippling contrariness, which inhibits effective group decision (Vertzberger 1990; Rosenthal, 't Hart, and Kouzmin 1991). In such an atmosphere, decision makers are frustrated and exhausted by battles over even the most minor substantive or procedural points. This pattern is thought to result from a passive or discredited group leadership and/or an embedded and stalemated factionalism based on irreconcilable ideological, personal, or other differences.

Manipulation

The literature suggests that at least two major group interaction patterns straddle the distinction between conformity and conflictual dynamics set out above: manipulation and "balanced critical deliberation." *Manipulation* or "rigging" of meetings by one or more group members entails the implementation of a hidden agenda through the deliberate structuring of the process or the substantive information base for decision making available to the group (Janis 1989, 55–56; see also Hoyt and Garrison, this volume). While any member can in principle engage in manipulation, group leaders commonly enjoy advantages in this regard (cf. Berman 1982). In this perspective, competition or conflict within the group setting is implied. If resistance to the sought-after objective was not anticipated, Machiavellian machinations would not be required. Yet, in successful manipulation attempts the underlying conflicts may remain latent and, not uncommonly, invisible.

The clubby atmosphere commonly associated with socially cohesive groups may create a decision environment especially conducive to exploitation by the manipulator who may turn tendencies toward conformity to his or her own ends. Intentional suppression of information can contribute to the emergence of premature closure by restricting and homogenizing the information base available to members during group deliberations (Vertzberger 1990, 235).

Manipulation may also appear as a "managed" form of conflictual interaction, which at first sight resembles ordinary bureaucratic or cabinet politics. In this configuration, a manipulator might attempt to incite or stage a conflict between extreme views in order to frame a preferred alternative as reasonable and moderate. A manipulator may deliberately introduce one or more "red herring" alternatives in order to break up a potentially winning coalition developing around a course of action he or she finds objectionable. Whether successful or not, such manipulation affects information flows and political alignments within the advisory group.

Manipulation may be facilitated by aspects of the group setting and organizational context. Maoz (1990, 93) argues that manipulative leverage is enhanced when asymmetries of information exist among the membership:

> An individual [or a faction] who is the only source of information about the events requiring decision and the data necessary for the evaluation of

the various options is in a unique position to frame the issues in a manner which suits his or her goals without actually distorting the information or presenting it in a selective manner. Others may find it difficult to challenge the definition of the situation, especially if the data given to the group sounds credible.

The allocation of "expert" status to particular members may provide leverage and enhanced credibility which may be turned to manipulative ends. The high levels of stress (and not uncommonly confusion), and the norm of "rallying around the flag" make crisis situations particularly ripe for manipulation.

The tendencies toward policy entrapment noted above may be deliberately exploited by the manipulator, who may attempt to induce a leader or a policy group to accept a commitment which would have been rejected out of hand had the full implications and full extent of the project been revealed from the start. This manipulative strategy is nicknamed "the salami tactic" in the literature:

> With the salami tactic one innovates by breaking down the novel course of action into a series of gradual policy options. Although each change deviates only marginally from the previous policy, each one also sets the stage for the subsequent decision in the series. Instead of taking one sharp departure from the previous policy, the group takes a series of steps which results in the same effect as the "innovative" alternative the manipulator desired all along. (Maoz 1990, 90)

Balanced Critical Deliberations

The discussion thus far has emphasized various ways that a decision process may be negatively affected by conformity or conflict. In fact, moderate levels of conformity and conflict may be seen as having a positive effect on decision making. In the absence of a will to constructive dialogue and in due course to achieve closure, deliberations become an empty, exhausting, and ritualistic exercise as in the nay-saying pattern noted above. At the same time, in the absence of some degree of divergent thinking and conflict, deliberations become stagnant, deprived of the "motor" of diversity and dialectic exchange (Moscovici and Doise 1994).

This line of thought suggests that another, happier, hybrid pattern should be added to our growing list. In so doing, we follow the example of Janis (1982) who, as a contrast to the groupthink pattern, also set out a model of "vigilant" group decision making.[5] We have chosen to label this interaction pattern "balanced critical deliberation" in order to emphasize the challenge of

TABLE 5.1. A Diagnostic Set of Group Interaction Patterns

	Conformity Patterns
Simple conformity	Derives from overt or covert pressure from leaders, other members, or the rest of the group on individual group members. Deviance from group norms leads to sanction and, in extreme cases, to exclusion from the group. May lead to reduced differentiation in the decision process via censorship and self-censorship.
Newgroup syndrome	Ad hoc or newly institutionalized groups lack stable norm, role, and status structures, which tends to generate member uncertainty, dependence on leaders and other assertive members, and coordination difficulties detrimental to the decision process.
Groupthink syndrome	The basic mechanism is an unconscious concurrence-seeking tendency—deriving from defensive avoidance and stress-induced or reinforced cohesion—which undermines the critical thinking capacity of group members and, in turn, the "quality" of the decision process.
	Conflictual Patterns
Cabinet/bureaucratic politics	Group interaction is characterized by adversarial relationships among individuals and subgroup factions. Outcomes represent the resultant of the balance of political power among the contestants. Coalition-formation in order to achieve political preponderance may lead to tactical cooperation as well as conflict, both of which may have implications for information processing and bargaining.
Nay-saying/paralysis	The group is deeply divided by acute personal, organizational, or ideological conflicts. Patience and energy are sapped by disputes over even small procedural and substantive issues. Opposing factions can veto decisions to which they object. Communication may become ritualized and geared toward constituent consumption rather than persuasion and pursuit of cooperative solutions.

(continued)

navigating between the Scylla of extreme conflict and the Charybdis of extreme conformity. When this can be achieved, group discussions may facilitate the emergence of a more differentiated view of the values implicated in a given situation and the relative prospects of alternative courses of action. Deliberations may contribute to integrating these perspectives by identifying value trade-offs inherent in the various problem representations and alterna-

TABLE 5.1. (*Continued*)

	Hybrids
Manipulation	Asymmetries of information and control over the decision-making process are exploited by devious members in order to circumvent opposition to a preferred course of action. May take various forms and can be difficult to distinguish empirically from other patterns. For example, group tendencies toward conformity can be exploited by a manipulator. Alternatively, a manipulator may orchestrate factional conflict in order to frame a favored option as a moderate compromise position.
Balanced critical deliberations	Members maintain a task orientation characterized by constructive conflict focused primarily upon differences of opinion regarding the character of the problem and merit of possible solutions. Group members engage cognitive and organizational resources to develop a richer understanding of the problem and share their insights with the group.

tives generated (Lawrence and Lorsch 1967; Nemeth and Staw 1989; Moreland and Levine 1992; Moscovici and Doise 1994).

It has been suggested that balanced critical deliberations tend to be associated with more open, democratic, and facilitative leadership styles. They are more likely to be found in group cultures emphasizing task achievement. Finally, they require a rough balance of power, influence, and policy-making resources among members of the group. Alexander George's (1980) multiple advocacy arrangement is an example of an attempt to foster balanced critical deliberation and guard against excesses of power imbalance, conformity, and conflict in highly competitive policy-making environments. Table 5.1 summarizes the menu of group interaction patterns presented above.

Developing a Procedure for Small Group Decision Analysis

Both the interaction patterns outlined in the preceding review and more general attempts at modeling small group decision making (Gladstein 1984; Aldag and Fuller 1993; Fuller and Aldag, this volume) call our attention to some critical contextual and group structural variables which serve to channel group interaction toward one or more of the patterns noted above. We propose a systematic six-step research procedure as an aid to diagnosing group decision-making processes in specific historical cases. The procedure *presupposes* that a preliminary analysis of the decision process in a particular case indicates that one or more small groups may have played a significant role shaping the decision making in that case.[6]

Before proceeding to a more detailed justification and explication of each step, let us reiterate that a fairly accurate diagnosis of the processes leading to the adoption of a particular foreign policy posture is of vital importance for the analyst. Even the most subtle and seemingly modest shifts in the way policy problems and potential solutions are framed and the character of information brought to bear in the decision-making process may have drastic consequences for choices taken, and indirectly, for foreign policy outcomes. This is the case in part because crucial policy decisions commonly depend upon contested or potentially contestable judgments regarding matters such as overall problem representation and salience, the capabilities and intentions of adversaries, and other types of difficult risk assessments. It is not possible to understand how such differences of opinion are suppressed or resolved without delving into the decision process. Thus such crucial choices cannot be properly understood without reference to the process and context which produced them.

Step One: Investigate the Extragroup Setting

The literature suggests a number of factors which are likely to be relevant to understanding the role of the wider institutional context in shaping the group setting and process. These include the placement of the decision-making group in relation to wider organizational constellations, the influence of organizational cultures or subcultures on the group, and patterns of intergroup conflict.

Placement refers to several closely related factors which may influence group decision making. The first, boundary management (Gladstein 1984), refers to the extent to which channels of communication between the group and the wider organizational environment are maintained or shut down in the name of operational secrecy. Members may refrain from consulting outside experts (or qualified generalists, for that matter) or sources of information such as those available via other organizations, groups, or networks to which the members may have access. In foreign policy, the classic case here is the self-imposed isolation of cabinet members from departmental expertise on particularly sensitive issues. In particular, the alleged need for secrecy and an excessive interpretation of the need-to-know principle may deprive senior policy groups from potentially useful information. Alternatively, the monopolization of information at the top level can deprive officials at lower levels from the possibility of being able to fulfill their responsibilities (Stern 1990).

Several scholars have argued that insulation of the group is a key antecedent condition to groupthink (e.g., Janis 1982; 't Hart 1990/1994; Aldag and Fuller 1993). Similarly, differential degrees of member control over communication flows to and from the environment is a precondition for manipulation of the information base (Maoz 1990). Leaders or other privileged members may be able to act as gatekeepers selectively providing information to the group in order to promote their own agenda.

Decision-making groups, and their individual members, are typically the products of multiple socializations. The cultures or subcultures that result play "a cognitive mediation role by providing members with a benchmark and a sense of direction for coping with and understanding their complex environment" (Vertzberger 1990, 195).[7] Over time, groups are likely to develop a group-specific decision culture if they endure (see below). At the same time, to the extent that the group is lodged in a broader organization or multi-organizational network, the decision makers may be also be influenced by broader organizational cultures. For example, a senior decision-making group within a ministry is likely to be influenced by the culture of that ministry. Alternatively, in an interorganizational group such as a cabinet or interagency coordinating committee, members may be highly influenced by their respective departmental cultures with regard to both substantive and procedural questions. The well-known adage "where you stand depends upon where you sit" captures this dynamic nicely, as does the oft-maligned tendency of individual cabinet secretaries or ministers to "go native" and adopt the prevailing views of their departments ('t Hart 1990/1994; Andeweg 1993). Thus organizational socialization may be an important precondition for bureaucratic (or cabinet) politics.

Finally, patterns of intergroup conflict may have important implications for the level of cohesion exhibited within decision groups, a key variable emphasized in the classic (Janis) groupthink pattern (Tajfel 1982; 't Hart 1990/1994). Perceptions of competition or threat originating from outside groups (such as rival intragovernmental groups, domestic political adversaries, or foreign adversaries) are likely to produce heightened cohesion within the decision-making group. Similarly, subgroup factions may be involved in conflictual relations with extra- (as well as intra-) group formations.

Step Two: Investigate the Intragroup Setting

A number of key group composition and structural variables are thought to influence group processes. First of all, the degree of heterogeneity among the group membership has implications for the quality of group interaction and the breadth of perspectives brought to bear in group problem solving (Janis 1982, 1989; Gladstein 1984; Aldag and Fuller 1993). For example, Janis (1989, 99) suggests that "a moderate degree of heterogeneity in basic attitudes and beliefs among the members of a policymaking group" in combination with member commitment to vigilant problem solving yield the highest degree of likelihood that conceptual errors and faulty assumptions will be corrected in group deliberation. Alternatively, excessive homogeneity may contribute to the likelihood of groupthink; this may be due to direct effects on the information base or indirectly via tendencies toward heightened cohesion in homogeneous groups.

A related factor is the specific politics of group formation, recruitment, and exclusion. The answers to the following questions are likely to provide clues to power relations and factional constellations within the group (more on these topics below). What rules for admittance governed the group entry of each individual member or, alternatively, on what basis were individuals excluded? Were the participants included at the sufferance of a formal or de facto leader? Were they admitted as representatives of extragroup interests, responsible to an external constituency? To the extent that discretion over admission to or exclusion from a group is in the hands of the leader or particular members, homogeneity and conformity are more likely, barring the presence of countervailing norms for recruitment and deliberation. Manipulation may be facilitated by such asymmetries of control.

Third, group power and status structures are important factors which shape group interaction. In particular, a robust body of research suggests that groups rapidly develop informal pecking orders which strongly affect communication within the group (Bales 1950; Moscovici 1985; Nemeth and Staw 1989; Levine and Moreland 1992). High-status members tend to set the norms to which others conform and may feel free to deviate from emergent or established norms to a greater extent than lower-status members (Hollander 1965). Status patterns within the group may reflect differences in external status and access to outside resources, differences in levels of experience, or differences in the strength of personal relationships to powerful individuals within or outside the group. They may also be based upon a range of seemingly irrelevant personal characteristics such as appearance, demeanor, age, gender, race, social background, and so forth. Such informal status rankings may or may not correspond to formal roles in hierarchical groups. Attending to patterns of power and status within the group helps the analyst understand the outcomes of intragroup power struggles. Severe asymmetries of status and power such as those associated with strong formal or informal group leaders are conducive to conformity dynamics (including groupthink). Power over the form of the decision-making process is also, as we have seen, a precondition for some types of manipulation.

Fourth, the allocation of "expert" status to some group members matters. Wrong (1988, 52) discusses a source of power labeled "competent authority" that is the source of leverage available to those deemed "expert" (cf. French and Raven 1959). George (1980, 21) addresses the case where decision makers are generalists and technical reports are submitted by "experts" out-side the decision unit. He suggests that "expert advocacy" within the unit may be necessary in order to appreciate the subtleties and uncertainties associated with complex issues and to maintain critical distance in assessing analyses. Expert monopolies may create strong pressures toward conformity as nonex-perts may be reluctant to question an expert analysis that is not balanced by a competing analysis of comparable credibility.

It is also possible that expert advice may originate from within the small decision group. Rosenthal and 't Hart (1991) note that experts tend to glide into decision-making roles in crisis situations. This situation may recreate the uni-source problem George has identified. In fact, it may create a potential for group manipulation by those members with a monopoly on expert competence (Maoz 1990, 93). Deference accorded experts in group deliberations is likely to be especially important when the problems addressed are complex and have important technical dimensions. Thus it is important to consider whether any of the group members enjoyed "expert" status, which made them relatively immune to challenges by others in the group. If so, did their status inhibit group debate, deliberately or inadvertently?

Group norms and decision rules are likely to be extremely important factors generating distinctive group interaction patterns. Norms "are shared expectations about how group members should behave" (Levine and More-land 1992, 600). Norms of deliberation and choice may be mandated by constitutional arrangements, set by leader fiat, by an initial voting procedure, or generated by the common experience of group interaction over time. In particular, norms may regulate the degree to which the agenda is open or constrained (such as by leader mandate), the length of time taken in delibera-tions, the amount of information considered, and the number of alternatives considered or reconsidered (George 1980; Janis 1982; Burnstein and Berbaum 1983; Betthausen and Murnighan 1985). Norms may also regulate the extent to which dissenting views are expressed and the kinds of intra- and extragroup strategies that may be legitimately employed in persuasion and other forms of influence attempts. Norms of accountability may have a highly significant effect on the amount of cognitive effort expended by members (Tetlock 1985a). Procedural models for "quality" or vigilant decision making may be seen as general normative systems designed to promote a critical and analyti-cal decision-making process (George 1980; Janis 1982, 1989). Group norms may encourage members to maintain a task orientation or, alternatively, en-courage them to engage in the kind of gamesmanship associated with the conflictual dynamics outlined above.

One particular kind of norm, the decision rule, deserves closer attention. Decision rules are fairly specific procedural prescriptions regarding how to aggregate and weight member preferences in order to reach closure on an issue and enable collective action. Decision rules are thought to have a dramatic impact on group deliberation processes. For example, a unanimity rule may result in the application of strong pressure in order to bring a minority into line with an apparent majority. At the same time, such a rule would tend to protect the rights of the minority to be heard, by providing them with a veto. A consensus rule would tend to have similar, though slightly weaker effects, as a dissenting fringe might not necessarily block a choice favored by the bulk of the members. In contrast, majority or plurality rules may result in the marginalization of minority views. Coalition builders may focus their attention predominantly on those with closely aligned views in order to reach the magic 51 percent or to become the largest of the contending blocs (Kaplan and Miller 1987, 311; Hermann 1993). Another common decision rule (particularly in the U.S. foreign policy-making setting) is executive choice (George 1980), which may result in communication patterns focused on the group leader.

Thus decision rules are highly significant in pushing deliberative processes toward various forms of conformity and conflict. A given decision rule or, more subtly, discretion over which rule will be applied in situations where the appropriate decision rule is not obvious, may be exploited by prospective group manipulators. For example, additional options may be introduced in order to break apart an objectionable coalition that appears likely to "win." A manipulator on the verge of being caught in a minority might be able to shift the rule to "consensus" and improve his or her bargaining position (Burnstein and Berbaum 1983, 550–52; Thompson et al. 1988; Scharpf 1989, 153).

Finally, let us note once again that group development factors play a significant role in influencing group interaction patterns (Tuchman 1965; Longley and Pruitt 1980; Aldag and Fuller 1993; Stern and Sundelius 1994). Tuckman and Jensen's (1973) revised theory of group development, subsequently supported by research findings, suggests that groups develop and decline in five stages—forming, storming, norming, performing, and adjourning—exhibiting characteristic behavior patterns. For example, in the formative stage, members may be uncertain, anxious, tentative, and inclined to seek direction from a leader figure (Moreland and Levine 1988, 155–56) making them prone to newgroup syndrome. Groups in the storming stage are likely to exhibit conflictual group dynamics. Groups in the performing stage may be best positioned to sustain balanced critical deliberations.

Step Three: Investigate Group Leadership Practices

The literature suggests that the character of group leadership practices may have profound impacts on interaction patterns in the group at large.[8] While the literature on group leadership is vast, we will focus on one important dimension: the extent to which leadership is directive as opposed to facilitative in group discussions. Directive leadership refers to situations where the (formal or informal) group leader promotes personal views strongly in deliberations. Those expressing deviant views may be denigrated or ultimately excluded from the group. Characterizations of the situation or suggested courses of action at odds with those of the leader may be rejected out of hand, without giving the rest of the group an opportunity to consider the independent merits of the idea in question. Leaders may deliberately or inadvertently grant privileged positions to advocates of a particular view, placing the burden of proof on dissenters and making it difficult for them to be heard. A classic example of this phenomenon is Kennedy's "sponsoring" of the CIA representatives in the Bay of Pigs Case (e.g., Wyden 1979; Janis 1982; Vandenbroucke 1992; Stern, this volume). Highly assertive leadership practices may be associated with conformity in general, and with conformity in newly formed groups in particular (Burnstein and Berbaum 1983; Stern and Sundelius 1994). Directive leadership practices are an important antecedent of both classic (Janis 1982) and reformulated ('t Hart 1990/1994) notions of groupthink.

Facilitative leadership stands in bold contrast to directive leadership. Facilitative leaders may attempt to refrain from personally affecting the course of group deliberations through their interventions. They seek to avoid placing advocates in privileged positions. They may attempt to conceal their initial preferences in order to draw out other members' views. Facilitative leaders may even choose to withdraw from deliberations in order to avoid influencing debate by their mere presence. They may take pains to encourage timid or lower-status members to participate. In fact, they may emphasize the responsibility of each member to bring their knowledge, judgment, and analytical resources to bear in probing the issue under discussion. Such leaders may be wary of a rapid consensus and suggest that more rigorous inquiry might be needed prior to choice. Facilitative leadership is associated with what we have called balanced critical deliberations in the set of diagnostic patterns set out above.

The substantive character and the level of engagement on the part of group leaders may have a highly significant impact on the extent to which group members internalize a group identification (see below) and maintain a task orientation. Cabinet and bureau-political group dynamics are thought to be particularly likely to emerge when leaders are disengaged or are incapable of creating a common group identity and task-orientation that transcends more parochial interests (Rosati 1981; Hermann 1989). Group identity provides a natural transition to the next step which focuses on group cohesion.

Step Four: Examine the Type and Level of Cohesion in the Group

One of the variables that has figured most prominently in the literature on group decision making is cohesion (or cohesiveness).[9] This variable broadly refers to the forces, or balance of forces, holding groups together. A classic definition was submitted by Festinger:

> Cohesiveness of a group is here defined as the *resultant* of all the forces acting on members to remain in the group. These forces may depend on the attractiveness or unattractiveness of either the prestige of the group, members in the group, or the activities in which the group engages. (1950, 274; emphasis added)

Cohesion as defined by Festinger may consist of member–member, member–group, or member–leader ties. By defining cohesion as a resultant, tendencies holding the group together (centripetal tendencies) and tendencies pulling the group apart (centrifugal tendencies) are amalgamated producing a "net" cohesion assessment (cf. Andeweg 1988). In other words, cohesion and conflict are posed as opposite ends of a single dimension.

For our present purposes, Festinger's expansive definition of cohesion is far too broad to be useful. We argue that it is necessary to at least partially disentangle the morass of motivations lumped together by Festinger if insight into the genesis of group interaction patterns is to be gained. In real-world situations of high-level decision making, in contrast to some controlled laboratory settings, elements of group affiliative and conflictual motives commonly coexist. The challenge facing the observer is to be sensitive to the subtleties occurring in the interface between these two basic elements of group interaction. The analyst should keep in mind that groups are multidimensional in character, as are their individual members. As a result, we begin by treating centripetal and centrifugal dimensions separately.

Returning to the question of cohesion, it is also advisable (to the extent possible based upon the available empirical evidence) to separate out the impact of different types of attraction that may bind groups together. This is particularly important as several recent analyses focus on the distinction between social and instrumental cohesion on the one hand, and task cohesion on the other. Social cohesion refers to the intrinsic appeal and attractiveness of the group, the other members, and/or the leader (cf. Holsti 1989, 21). Instrumental cohesion refers to the desire to maintain group membership in order to attain other types of goals, such as monetary reward or career advancement. Task cohesion refers to attraction to the group arising from the goals or purposes to which the group is perceived as being dedicated. The latter is thought to have very different effects on group performance than the former two (e.g., Bernthal and Insko 1992; Mullen and Copper 1994).[10]

These recent findings support an argument made more than a decade ago by Janis where he notes that not all types of cohesion are associated with conformity. Janis submits that high social or instrumental cohesion tends to contribute to the development of groupthink syndrome, while cohesion springing from a high degree of common commitment to group tasks is not likely to do so:

> Concurrence seeking tendencies probably are stronger when high cohesiveness is based primarily on the rewards of being in a pleasant "clubby" atmosphere or of gaining prestige from being a member of an elite group than when it is based primarily on the opportunity to function competently on work tasks with effective co-workers. In a cohesive group of the latter type, careful appraisal of policy alternatives is likely to become a group norm to which the members conscientiously adhere. (1982, 247–48)

McCauley further develops this line of reasoning, pointing out that the relationship between cohesion and conformity is in fact even more complex and likely to be mediated by members' perceptions of the security of their position within the group:

> Cohesion, defined as attraction to the group, must be distinguished from uncertainty about approval from the group. Increased cohesion leads generally to more compliance and more acceptance [of group views], as indicated by Cartwright (1968), but an individual can be strongly attracted to a group and yet be so confident of group support and approval to have no need to comply with group expectations . . . even high cohesion, understood as attraction to the group will not lead to compliance unless an individual experiences some uncertainty about group approval. (1989, 252)

Other scholars note the "idiosyncrasy credit" that may be at the disposal of some group members, allowing them to deviate from apparent majority views or group norms without sanction (Hollander 1965).

To summarize, when assessing group cohesion it is important not only to make overall assessments of the level of cohesion in the group, but also to make an effort to ascertain which types of cohesion seem to be most relevant in binding members to each other, to the leader, to factions within the group,[11] and to the group as a whole. Furthermore, one should keep in mind that each member may be attracted to the group or to a subset of the membership for different reasons and have varying degrees of personal confidence in the approval of the group. These factors are likely to be of importance in making judgments regarding member internalization and compliance (at the individual level) and the extent of conformity in group interaction.

Step Five: Examine the Type and Level
of Conflict or Rivalry in the Group

In this step the analyst seeks to survey the group for indications of negative affect or competitive relationships within the group. These relationships may take any of several characteristic forms in policy decision groups: bureaucratic rivalry, political and ideological rivalry, personal rivalry, and antagonism. Any of these may form the basis for the formation of factions within decision-making groups.

In the literature on foreign (and domestic) policy-making in both the United States and Europe, the potential for organizational rivalries to emerge in intragovernmental interaction have been heavily emphasized (Halperin 1974; Welch 1992; Andeweg 1988, 1993; Rosenthal, 't Hart, and Kouzmin 1991). Portrayals such as Allison's (1971) Model III governmental politics paradigm focus on tendencies among department and agency officials to compete for power and influence. Generally speaking, organizational actors are depicted as imperialistic, seeking bigger budgets, broader mandates, and increased autonomy in policymaking. Anderson (1987, 304) suggests that governmental "subcomponents" tend to interpret problems in light of organizational subgoals, identify actions within their own repertoire of competence on the basis of that interpretation, and seek ratification of these actions at broader multiconstituency decision meetings. In their attempts to do so, they may easily come into conflict with other organizations pursuing different agendas. Alternatively, it should be noted, when a problem is seen as insoluble or politically dangerous, organizations may seek to evade responsibility and compete to avoid being stuck with a political "hot potato."

As we have already noted, such battles over bureaucratic turf are commonly fought out in the small, interagency group setting. In fact, to the extent that department or agency heads go native and are socialized into the subcultures associated with their organizations, bureaucratic politics may easily spill over into cabinet or "court" politics (Destler, Gelb, and Lake 1984; Blondel and Müller-Rommel 1993). At the latter levels, conflicts may also originate in ideological differences, such as those between "hawks" and "doves" or in negative personal relationships among particular individuals. It is easy to underestimate the impact of such antagonisms in the political setting. Yet practitioner memoirs are filled with references toward the impact of the personal factor on political decision making. In systems characterized by strong executives, as in the United States or Britain, cabinet members and other aides may compete with each other for the leader's ear and favor, producing at times bitter conflicts over policy issues.

The phenomenon of coalition government so typical of parliamentary systems such as Sweden, Germany, the Netherlands, and Israel also creates the potential for conflictual relationships among the coalition partners (Andeweg 1988; Blondel and Müller-Rommel 1993). The bedfellows in such marriages of convenience may have an interest in advancing their own interests at the expense of their present allies or attempt to curry the favor of opposition groups with an eye to future governmental constellations. At times these conflicts may be sufficiently powerful, singly or in combination, as to create a policy-making deadlock as in the "nay-saying" dynamic noted above.

Thus, a key question to ask is to what extent are group members acting as committed advocates for competing organizational, political, or personal constituencies? Are informational resources being deployed strategically, and with what effect on the information base available to the group as a whole? If so, what are the entrenched positions of the key actors and how do those differences and their respective efforts at exerting influence over outcomes translate into political resultants?

It is important to realize that such competitive or conflictual relationships may often be difficult to detect. A seemingly cordial surface atmosphere may conceal layers upon layers of conflict below. Like tectonic plates beneath the earth's surface that can exert tremendous pressure on each other, which may or may not ultimately result in an earthquake, so too can conflictual relationships hidden beneath a seemingly cordial surface have significant impacts on group decision making, without such conflict necessarily reaching the light of day in any dramatic way. This is often the case in successful cases of manipulation, which, as we have seen, can take forms resembling either conformity or conflict dynamics.

Step Six: Engage in Group Process Diagnosis by Comparing the Portrait Generated by the First Five Steps above to the Repertoire of Interaction Patterns Outlined in Table 5.1

The final step in our procedure is to weigh the answers to the previous questions in order to establish the nature of the dominant group interaction pattern in a particular decision. In some cases, the results of the framework may clearly indicate that the group decision making process revealed through empirical research matches neatly with one of the seven patterns in table 5.1. However, the analyst should be sensitive to the possibility that the factors examined in the six-step procedure may indicate that the group process in fact exhibits traces or substantial commonalties associated with more than one pattern. This is not surprising. The depiction of a given episode which emerges from intensive historical research is often complex and multifaceted. Interaction patterns falling in between those mapped out above are to be expected.

It is illustrative that the application of our analytical framework to Swedish decision making during a crisis triggered by the stranding of a Soviet submarine on the Swedish coast led to the identification of several of the patterns set out in table 5.1 (Stern and Sundelius, forthcoming). Middle-range dynamics such as simple conformity, newgroup, manipulation, bureaucratic/partisan politics, and balanced critical deliberation appeared. The more extreme and dramatic patterns, classic groupthink and nay-saying, did not. Why did the results cluster in this fashion?

A number of possible explanations come to mind. The characteristics of Swedish political culture explain partially the moderation of conflict dynamics. Norms of leader behavior grounded in the Swedish constitution and administrative practice discourage openly promotional leadership and encourage broad consultation and respect for professional expertise, factors largely incompatible with groupthink. The prevalence of mixed member motives and loyalties in the group settings studied inhibited extremes of insulation and cohesion conducive to classic groupthink effects. The group interaction patterns were thus generated by particular combinations of cohesion, conflict, and group structural properties such as the stage of group development and the character of group norms.

Given the complexities of real-world decision-making processes, a challenge put to the researcher will be to generate a sufficiently fine-grained account of the case under study to be able to distinguish reliably between patterns with substantial similarity of effects. This is reminiscent of the problem George has termed *equifinality*—different causal sequences can result in seemingly similar outcomes. In this case, apparently similar group level dynamics may arise out of different contextual, group structural, or individual-level factors. In table 5.1, we chose to cluster simple conformity, groupthink, and newgroup syndrome together as conformity patterns. Should a decision-making process in an empirical case seem to exhibit a low degree of critical interaction and a rapid consensus regarding the nature of the problem, the values implicated, and/or the appropriate means of dealing with that problem, the analyst should see whether the contextual and structural variables noted above seem to rule out or highlight a candidate interaction pattern.

For example, if the decision-making group was one of long-standing and substantial stability in terms of membership and subculture, newgroup syndrome could be ruled out. Similarly, if the group seems to exhibit low levels of social and instrumental cohesion, does not appear to have been under particularly high levels of stress, and was not insulated from its organizational environment, then classic groupthink could probably be ruled out. By such a process of elimination, one might end up with simple conformity due to group pressure on the individual. This sequence might be the most common one, as the requirements for diagnosing classic groupthink are stringent, entailing the

TABLE 5.2.   A Procedure for Empirical Small Group Decision Analysis

Step 1: *Investigate the extragroup setting* to locate the group within the wider political and institutional contexts.

Step 2: *Investigate the intragroup setting* to establish the composition, internal structure, and culture of the group.

Step 3: *Investigate group leadership practices,* which commonly exert important influences in shaping the intragroup setting and in facilitating or hindering deliberations among the members.

Step 4: *Examine the type and level of cohesion,* which bind group members and their groups together, as this element helps determine group interaction and performance.

Step 5: *Examine the type and level of conflict or rivalries,* which pull members and their groups apart, as also this element helps determine group interaction and performance.

Step 6: *Engage in group process diagnosis* by comparing the portrait generated by the first five steps above to the repertoire of interaction patterns outlined in Table 5.1.

---

simultaneous manifestation of multiple situational and group structural conditions, which probably appear together relatively infrequently ('t Hart 1990/ 1994).

Let us also note that it may be difficult to distinguish one form of manipulation (classed as a "hybrid") in table 5.1 from conformity dynamics. Should tendencies toward conformity or concurrence-seeking in the group as a whole be exploited by a devious group member (or faction), then the group level process would give every appearance of being a conformity-based interaction pattern. However, the conformity would be "steered," and one would have to look to the individual consciousness and behavior of the manipulator in order to appreciate the conflictual game being played beneath the surface.

Ironically enough, it may also be difficult to distinguish between the other form of manipulation (orchestrated conflict) and conflict dynamics such as bureaucratic politics and nay-saying. A manipulator seeking to block action might deliberately create the kind of a deadlock associated with nay-saying. Similarly, "hardball" forms of bureaucratic politics characterized by intensive advocacy might entail gatekeeping and selective presentation of information bordering upon manipulation. This empirical research procedure is summarized in table 5.2.

Reflections and Implications

Looking Backward

In this chapter, we have argued for the need to develop more discriminating diagnostic aids to be used in characterizing group decision and deliberative processes. Further, we have crafted some preliminary analytical tools that we hope will facilitate the kind of empirical analysis we believe to be necessary if one is to understand decisions taken or heavily influenced by policy-making groups. Our review of the literature and the results of two empirical applications reinforce our conviction that the groupthink-vigilant decision-making dichotomy advanced by Janis and the tripartite division of small group interaction patterns (groupthink, bureaucratic politics, and leader-driven critical deliberation) favored by some scholars (Hermann 1988) are too general to be of much use in dissecting real-world decisions. More delicate instruments, like the ones developed in this chapter, are required.

We have also emphasized the importance of taking into account the political-institutional context in which small groups operate. We have attempted to develop a fairly comprehensive, step-by-step approach intended to capture the most salient features of decision groups and their environments and a number of the most important dimensions of group interaction. We are aware that our approach is not parsimonious according to conventional understandings of that term. Yet we believe that understanding a complex, social phenomenon such as the operation and impact of policy-making groups requires taking a wide range of intra- and extragroup personal, political, and institutional factors into account. To refrain from so doing risks the generation of superficial and misleading accounts of crucially important processes. Prescriptions based upon such flawed accounts are almost sure to do as much or more harm than good (see 't Hart, this volume).

Looking Ahead I: Relaxing the Single Group/Unitary Problem Assumptions

Much of the above discussion, like the bulk of the small group literature, is directed at the case where a single, stable, easily identifiable, and (in the case of the foreign policy literature) top-level decision group, is the relevant decision unit. In practice, small groups in foreign policy often have shifting memberships caused by stratification into inner and outer circles, chronic cabinet and staff turnover, and the ad hoc incorporation of experts into the decision unit or units. Furthermore, multiple groups lodged at various levels of administrative hierarchies may affect the decision making with regard to a given foreign policy issue.[12] Let us now consider the analytical implications of relaxing these conventional assumptions.

In the U.S. system, a given issue may be treated initially by interagency groups at the assistant or deputy-secretary level prior to treatment at the so-called principals level. To take a recent example, policy-making toward Iraq prior to the invasion of Kuwait was largely in the hands of the NSC Deputies committee. Then deputy national security assistant (soon to be CIA Director) Robert Gates was assigned responsibility for liaison between the two groups, attending meetings of both. After the invasion, the issue quickly rose on the agenda and the Gulf Crisis was managed primarily by an inner circle around George Bush at the principals level. However, if one wishes to study the role of group deliberation processes in the run-up to the crisis, it is the former body that would probably be of primary interest (Woodward 1991). It is quite common for issues to move up and down in the hierarchy during the course of their persistence on the policy agenda. Thus as one extends the time perspective, it becomes quite likely that multiple groups will emerge or that the membership of a relevant group will shift due to turnover effects.

As a result, the composition of group decision units may shift through any given decision issue.[13] This is highly significant as groups composed of different individuals and representing different constituencies are likely to exhibit different group dynamics. A succession of radically different interaction patterns might well emerge if one tracked group decision making over time through the course of a particular crisis or policy problem.

Identification of any specific group unit as the primary decision locus is to some extent arbitrary. The choice depends on an observer's preference, often a priori or theory-driven, to emphasize parameter-setting by professional staff, the bureaucratic-political interaction, or political decision making. An excessive preoccupation with the process of formal ratification of prior commitments may direct analytical attention away from key decision points. Formalistic views focusing on the concluding stages risk missing significant explanatory aspects. Parametric constraints and a broad range of behind-the-scenes maneuverings by political and bureaucratic actors would be omitted from this type of decision analysis.

Let us also note that what we commonly refer to as a crisis, such as the Cuban Missile Crisis or the Whiskey on the Rocks Crisis, can also be seen as a series of related issues actualized by the broad crisis theme. These subproblems making up the crisis may have different properties. For example, they may have varying degrees of technical complexity or involve different geographic areas. As a result, different individuals may be able to lay claim to expert status and speak with particular authority depending upon the substantive character of the issue. Since, as we have seen, power and status are important determinants of group interaction patterns, we must be alert to the possibility that the same group might develop alternative interaction patterns as the topic of discussion shifts from one topic to another. This shift might be particularly dramatic if an expert monopoly led to deference and conformity with regard to one issue while opposing experts might facilitate balanced critical deliberations on another issue.[14] This finding, deriving from the small group setting, parallels studies in political science focusing on the importance of issues in determining the character of political processes in larger-scale arenas.

Looking Ahead II: Theoretical Enrichment via Empirical Case Analyses

Foreign policy practitioners are fond of noting that, when it comes to political deliberations and policy questions, the devil is in the details. Foreign policy analysts can draw some valuable lessons from this mindset. Experimental control and theoretical parsimony can generate valuable interpretive heuristics; they are not, however, substitutes for contextually grounded and empirically rich accounts of crucial real-world decision-making phenomena. The tasks of process-tracing and diagnosis are time-consuming, costly, even hazardous as the analyst risks being led down the garden path by imperfections in or manipulation of the available historical record. Despite these obstacles and pitfalls, it is imperative that scholars embrace this difficult but rewarding task.

In the next section of the volume, three such attempts at theoretically motivated, historical case analysis are presented. In chapter 6, Eric Stern explicitly applies the analytical procedure developed in this chapter and uses it to structure his analysis of the Kennedy administration's decision-making processes in the Bay of Pigs case. In addition, he delves deeper into and reconceptualizes one of the group interaction patterns identified here—new-group syndrome. In chapter 7, Tom Preston examines the leader–advisory group nexus (a factor strongly influencing emergent patterns of group interaction) in a case study of the Truman administration's management and mismanagement of the Korean crisis. In chapter 8, Paul Hoyt and Jean Garrison focus upon another of the interaction patterns highlighted in this chapter—manipulation—in their study of group decision making in the Carter administration. This section of the volume concludes with Yaacov Vertzberger's broad-ranging analysis of collective risk taking. Here, theoretical constructs from psychology and organizational theory are coupled to numerous empirical illustrations drawn from the foreign policy experience of Israel, India, the Soviet Union, and the United States.

Thus, in the rest of the volume, as in the preceding chapter by Metselaar and Verbeek, the authors practice what is commonly preached, more seldom achieved, and most conducive to leaps of insight—a marriage of theoretical constructs and rigorous empirical analysis.

NOTES

The authors are grateful for valuable comments from numerous colleagues including Paul 't Hart, Alexander L. George, Yaacov Vertzberger, Stephen Walker, Raymond Cohen, Sally Riggs Fuller, Berndt Brehmer, Kjell Goldmann, Magnus Jerneck, Tom Preston, Jean Garrison, Bertjan Verbeek, Max Metselaar, and Paul Hoyt.

1. In fact, there may be a disadvantage in presenting a neatly compartmentalized typology. It may encourage the already strong tendency among researchers to seek unitary parsimonious "either/or" explanations, when reality may in fact have more of a "both/and" character. For a parallel argument, see Ripley 1995.

2. For example, a heuristically promising set of 12 interaction patterns is described in Tetlock et al. 1992, 406–7. Unfortunately, the patterns are very eclectic (embodying broad political cultural and group process patterns) and are described in very sketchy fashion in the article.

3. A number of commentators including George (1980) and Gaenslen (1992) argue that this is the most central and distinctive aspect of Janis's contribution.

4. See Metselaar and Verbeak (this volume) for poignant and empirical examples of this possibility.

5. An oversight in Janis's model was to neglect to emphasize the importance of problem representation in decision making. Janis apparently assumed that the character of the problem was relatively unambiguous in the situations he studied. In their recent reformulation, Aldag and Fuller (1993) include a discussion of problem definition in their rendering of the decision-making process as do scholars such as George (1980) and Burnstein and Berbaum (1983).

6. See Hermann, Hermann, and Hagan 1987, Hermann and Hermann 1989, and Stern 1993 for alternative approaches to performing such a "triage" operation in order to determine the relevant decision unit configuration or configurations in a given case. See also Janis 1982, 194, and 't Hart 1990, 210–11, for some diagnostic questions tailored toward establishing the relevance of groupthink analysis, but of considerable heuristic value nonetheless.

7. National cultures may be highly relevant sources of socialization affecting group interaction as well, of course. See, e.g., Markus and Kitayama 1991, Sampson 1987, and Vertzberger 1990, chapter 5.

8. There is a close interrelationship between leadership and group norm formation. In some settings, such as the U.S. foreign policy-making setting (George 1980; M. Hermann and Preston 1994) powerful leaders may have a high degree of leverage in shaping group norms. Other policy-making settings may be characterized by lesser degrees of hierarchical leadership and enduring institutional norms resistant to executive impacts ('t Hart 1990/1994). For a useful overview of the literature on group management, see Nutt 1989.

9. While a number of researchers have attempted to investigate cohesion as a dependent variable (see, e.g., Hogg and Abrams 1988 for a review) much of the research relevant to decision making addresses the question of the relationship between cohesion and performance and views cohesion as an independent variable. See also 't Hart 1990/1994 and Mullen and Copper 1993.

10. These authors emphasize that high levels of task-oriented cohesion are associated with high performance. Bernthal and Insko (1992) confirm Janis's hypothesis that high social cohesion can decrease performance in decision-making tasks.

11. Vertzberger (1990, 246–49) has identified several properties of factions within the small group setting that generate tendencies toward conformity in group informa-

tion processing. For example, lower-ranking faction members may refrain from challenging the faction leader in wider deliberations.

12. It is often overlooked that Janis's (1982) case study of the U.S. decision making prior to the Pearl Harbor attack identified several relevant decision groups located both in Washington, DC and on-site in Hawaii.

13. This finding is in keeping with Levine and Moreland's (1990, 589) recognition of the importance and complexity of the functioning of multiple, interlocking, and interdependent groups. See also Burnstein and Berbaum's (1983, 547) empirical findings in their case study of the Skybolt affair.

14. Empirical findings from our study of the Whiskey on the Rocks crisis suggest that this proposition is highly plausible. See Stern and Sundelius (forthcoming).

Part 2
Political Group Dynamics and Foreign Policy

CHAPTER 6

Probing the Plausibility of Newgroup Syndrome: Kennedy and the Bay of Pigs

Eric K. Stern

Groupthink or Newgroup Syndrome in the Bay of Pigs Fiasco?

Still flushed with the thrill of victory in the November 1960 presidential election, John F. Kennedy and his advisors committed the United States to an abortive attempt to overthrow covertly the Castro regime in Cuba making use of an invasion force of Cuban exiles trained by the CIA. The name of the landing site chosen for the operation that took place in April of 1961, the Bay of Pigs, has become an enduring symbol of foreign policy fiasco.

This incident is puzzling. Kennedy, whose life and presidency was cut short by a sniper's bullet, stands out as one of the most respected, revered, and emulated presidents of the postwar period. Kennedy's advisers, a carefully selected and relatively diverse group, are often considered to have been among the "best and the brightest" minds of two generations. Elder statesmen, cunning bureaucrats, captains of industry, and academic luminaries placed their talents, knowledge, and considerable experience at Kennedy's disposal. Yet, despite (or perhaps because of) extensive group deliberations, Kennedy went ahead with a flawed plan based on a series of highly questionable assumptions. The result was an outcome that proved highly detrimental to United States interests in Latin America, to the U.S.–Soviet relationship, and to Kennedy's own reputation and political position.

The case raises a number of highly significant questions. Why were the underlying assumptions subjected only to cursory scrutiny, and why were the hard questions rarely asked and the answers shrugged off? As Kennedy himself would later ask, "how could I have been so stupid as to let them go ahead?" (Vandenbroucke 1984, 491). Furthermore, why did his advisory group prove unable to prevent Kennedy from embarking upon this course of action? Thus, in a nutshell, the puzzle of the Bay of Pigs is how so many individually smart and experienced policymakers could make such a poor group decision.

The present author is, of course, not the first analyst to take up these questions, nor the first to look to the operation of the advisory group and its relationship to the broader institutional context as a source of possible answers. In fact, Irving Janis (1972, 1982) formulated and launched the notion of groupthink in part as an attempt to answer these questions and to understand the tragedy of the Bay of Pigs (see also George, this volume). Yet, as we will see, the fit between this case and Janis's groupthink hypothesis is far from perfect. As a result, reopening the case and applying a more broadly based small group research strategy along the lines advocated by Stern and Sundelius (this volume) seems worthwhile.

In particular, an alternative hypothesis will be explored. This hypothesis draws heavily upon the social psychological literature on group development and emphasizes the "newness" of the Kennedy advisory group.[1] Perhaps the Kennedy group fell victim to "newgroup syndrome" instead of, or in addition to, the groupthink dynamics postulated by Janis. Many social psychologists have long believed that groups tend to behave differently and have characteristic behavioral patterns and problems at different stages of development. This literature suggests that newly formed groups or groups subjected to drastic changes in membership or in mode of operation may be particularly susceptible to pathologies of group deliberation. This line of thought has serious implications for political decision making.

New groups are a common feature in political settings for at least three reasons. First of all, a substantial amount of research suggests that acute nonroutine decision problems such as domestic or international crises are commonly handled by ad hoc groups, the members of which may have little experience in working together. Second, it is important to remember that changes of administration are likely to lead to the formation of new groups, which may be forced to deal with pressing issues on short notice and with little opportunity to reflect upon their mode of interaction. Thirdly, and paradoxically, existing groups can become "new" as the membership changes and the preexisting group culture and practices are destabilized. In the political setting, this may occur when cabinets are reshuffled as one or more key players leave the scene or are forced to adopt a new role or ministerial portfolio. The potentially negative consequences of such transience and turnover on policy-making have been noted in the literature:

> Much more important than the experience or inexperience of political appointees is their transience as a group. Cabinet Secretaries may bring with them a cadre of personal acquaintances to fill some of their subordinate positions, but in general public executives will be strangers with

only a fleeting chance to learn how to work together. . . . Rapid turnover intensifies all of the other problems of political teamwork. (Hugh Heclo 1977, 104)

Thus, the second and more theoretically oriented purpose of this chapter is to provide a richer and more elaborated conceptualization of one of the group interaction patterns identified by Stern and Sundelius in the preceding chapter: newgroup syndrome. First, however it is necessary to lay an analytical foundation by taking a closer look at the broader notion of group development.

Groups over Time

As suggested in chapter one, the small group can and should be seen as a small-scale social institution with a developmental history and temporal perspective of its own. Small groups "have a critical context which includes their history, their expectations for the future, their structure, their purpose, and their relationship to other groups" (Worchel, Coutant-Sassic, and Grossman 1992, 183). In this sense, the small group is isomorphic with larger social formations such as organizations, states, or international regimes.

Groups are not static; nor do they emerge, like the mythical Athena, fully formed in an act of divine creation. Rather, groups are convened at a particular point in time, from which they embark on a social trajectory of varying scope and duration. Some groups are characterized by extreme longevity; others are temporary constellations assembled for a single meeting or the duration of a single crisis. Some groups are spontaneously convened and short-lived, enduring only for minutes, hours, days, or weeks. Others may endure for years, decades, or even centuries.

Just as a number of influential theories—such as those by Piaget and Kohlberg—suggest that individuals progress through a series of recognizable developmental stages in the journey from childhood to well-adjusted adulthood, many scholars believe that groups pass through characteristic developmental phases (Tuckman 1965, 396–97; Tucker 1973; Worchel, Coutant-Sassic, and Grossman 1992). Group developmental theory is based on observation of a wide range of group types, tasks, and settings—therapy, so-called T-groups (sensitivity training), laboratory groups, and work groups in the natural setting. On the basis of this diverse empirical experience base, theorists have attempted to model characteristic phases through which groups tend to pass during their "life cycles" (Tuckman 1965; Moreland and Levine 1988).

The term *development* has a strong normative connotation in many of the contributions to this literature (Moreland and Levine 1988, 155). Groups are seen as maturing (generally viewed as a positive quality) and increasingly sophisticated as they "progress" through the developmental sequence (cf.

Tuckman and Jensen 1977; Moreland and Levine 1988 on termination and "regression"). At each of these stages, groups are thought to exhibit characteristic patterns of conflict and cooperation. At some point, following some sequence of preliminary stages, these theories suggest that groups may reach a stage characterized by a salutary mix of individual differentiation and collective integration conducive to improved performance in the realm of the group's endeavor. Developmental perspectives treat many of the same variables emphasized in the wider literature on group decision making and performance. Group development addresses the question of how group structural characteristics change over time as a group acquires a history of prior interaction. Characteristics such as the level of cohesion, the clarity of group norms, role and status systems, and the strength of group identity are thought to change across the life cycle and historical experience of a given group (Moreland and Levine 1988, 154). Let us briefly introduce each of these central variables in the small groups literature and their relationship to group decision making and development.

Cohesion

Cohesion is a variable that has been the object of much attention and conceptual dispute among social and organizational psychologists and management theorists for some fifty years. Festinger (1950, 274) provided a seminal definition:

> Cohesiveness of a group is here defined as the resultant of all the forces acting on members to remain in the group. These forces may depend on the attractiveness or unattractiveness of either the prestige of the group, members in the group, or the activities in which the group engages.

Thus cohesion may consist of member–member, member–group, or member–leader ties. While a number of researchers have attempted to investigate cohesion as a dependent variable (cf. Hogg and Abrams 1988), much of the research relevant to decision making addresses the question of the relationship between cohesion and performance. As a result, cohesion is treated as an independent variable.

A first wave of studies based on work by Lewin, Festinger, Schachter, and others suggested that cohesiveness contributes to member feelings of security, minimization of disruptive conflicts, and task coordination and thus is generally positively related to performance. This view was ultimately challenged by critical findings from several realms (Tannenbaum 1966/1992; Janis 1972, 1982) suggesting that the impact of cohesion is modified by the content of group norms, having the potential for both positive and negative impacts on performance (George 1980). A recent metareview integrating a large number of empirical studies, reviews, and conceptual work suggests that commitment to group tasks (as opposed to purely emotional or status attractions) is the key element in a modest cohesion–performance effect:

> the studies integrated here suggest that what distinguishes groups that perform well is not that their members interact with smooth coordination, like one another, or are proud of their group but that they are committed to successful task performance and regulate their behavior to that end. (Mullen and Copper 1994, 225; cf. Bernthal and Insko 1992)

Mullen and Copper also found evidence of a performance-based developmental effect. Successful performance was found, predictably, to induce increased cohesion over time (Mullen and Copper 1994, 225): "although cohesiveness may indeed lead the group to perform better, the tendency for the group to experience greater cohesiveness after successful performance may be even greater." Another line of research argues that groups subjected to external stress, such as that associated with intergroup conflict, may develop an increased need for affiliation and become increasingly cohesive (Janis 1982, 109–10; Tajfel 1982; 't Hart 1990/1994, chapters 2, 7). Ironically, it has been suggested that situational provocations including "recent failures, such as an unanticipated poor outcome resulting from a prior decision for which members of the group feel responsible, which makes the members aware of their personal inadequacies" (Janis 1982, 255) may lead to low self-esteem, increased attraction to the group, and a susceptibility to collective avoidance ('t Hart 1990/1994, 201).

Status

Relatively robust research findings from laboratory and other group settings suggest that groups quickly develop tentative status hierarchies (or power-prestige orderings) that may be revised to some extent over time (Bales 1950). The content of early contributions to group discussions and external status indicators such as disparities in rank, social class, education, and power provide cues for such rankings. Demeanor (confident or tentative) and physical characteristics are also thought to be significant. Subtle dominance contests (such as staring games) may be used to settle those rankings that may be unclear on the basis of the previously mentioned criteria. Generally speaking, high-status members tend to participate more frequently and authoritatively and are more influential than lower-status members in group deliberations (George 1980; Moscovici 1985; Levine and Moreland 1990, 598–99). The implication of the literature on group development is that groups at higher levels of development tend to have, by definition, relatively stable and well-understood pecking orders, having previously resolved questions of status.

Roles

Roles have been recently defined as "shared expectations about how a particular person in a group should behave" (Levine and Moreland 1990, 601–603). Informal group roles may include "newcomer" and "oldtimer," "ambassador," "scapegoat," "devil's advocate," "constituency representative," "expert," and "leader." Role systems are highly relevant to the achievement of coordination, division of labor, and accountability. More highly developed groups tend to have more differentiated and less ambiguous role systems.

Norms

Group norms are central to the notion of group development. Norms are prescriptions indicating the appropriateness of particular attitudes or forms of behavior within a social setting. Norms may be substantive or procedural. Substantive norms may suggest that the holding of particular views define the view-holder as beyond the pale and indicate exclusion from the community in question (Lebow 1981; Steiner 1989). Substantive norms regarding risk taking are central in some contexts such as foreign or military policy-making. "Boldness" or "caution" may be the order of the day in a particular group or situation, depending upon group experience and context. Norms operate in conjunction with role and status systems in the regulation of participation by group members in discussions. Norms regarding the degree of conflict that will be tolerated and the diversity of opinions that will be solicited are extremely important and may vary across groups. It has been hypothesized that group experience determines norms such as willingness to process large quantities of information and consider a wide range of alternative solutions (Burnstein and Berbaum 1983, 551).

Decision Rules

Decision rules are procedures for the achievement of closure and the aggregation of individual preferences into an expression of collective will or action. Decision rules discussed in the literature include unanimity, consensus, majority, plurality, and executive choice. These rules tend to generate characteristic patterns of interaction with regard to conflict management, coalition formation, and the decision-making process. As a result, they affect not only the choice stage of a decision process, but also the previous deliberation (George

1980; Gaenslen 1980; Scharpf 1989; Hermann 1993). Ambiguities regarding decision rules in newly formed groups may create opportunities for powerful and devious members to manipulate outcomes by shifting to a particularly advantageous rule in mid-stream. (cf. Maoz 1990; Hoyt and Garrison, this volume)

Stages of Group Development

A considerable body of theoretical and empirical evidence supports the contention that groups do indeed pass through recognizable stages of development with characteristic properties (Cissna 1984). One influential theory, formulated in two steps by Tuckman (1965; Tuckman and Jensen 1977) on the basis of an exhaustive literature review of previous theoretical formulations and empirical findings, suggests that groups develop and decline in five stages—forming, storming, norming, performing, and adjourning:

> Groups initially concern themselves with orientation accomplished primarily through testing. Such testing serves to establish the boundaries of both interpersonal and task behaviors. Coincident with the testing is the establishment of dependency relationships with leaders, other group members, or preexisting standards. It may be said that orientation, testing, and dependence constitute the group process of forming. The second point in the sequence is characterized by conflict and polarization around interpersonal issues, with concomitant emotion responding in the task sphere. These behaviors serve as resistance to group influence and task requirements and may be labeled as storming.
>
> Resistance is overcome in the third stage in which ingroup feeling and cohesiveness develop, new standards evolve, and new roles are adopted. In the task realm, intimate, personal opinions are expressed. Thus we have the stage of norming.
>
> [T]he group [then] attains the fourth stage in which the interpersonal structure becomes the tool of task activities. Roles become flexible and functional, and group energy is channeled into the task. Structural issues have been resolved, and structure can now become supportive of task performance. This stage can be labeled as performing. (Tuckman 1965, 396)

Tuckman and Jensen's (1977, 426) characterization of the final adjourning stage in the life cycle of the group is rather sketchy. Moreland and Levine (1988, 156) provide a more cogent summary: "During this stage, everyone gradually disengages from both socio-emotional and task activities within the group. This disengagement reflects group members' efforts to cope with the end of the group" (cf. Worchel et al. 1992).

Tuckman's theory has a number of key strengths but also some omissions and ambiguities that should be recognized. Among the strengths are simplicity, a considerable degree of intuitive plausibility (Tuckman 1965, 396), parallels with individual developmental theory, and the fact that a wide range of independent empirical studies seem to support the basic notion (if not every aspect) of developmental stage theory. Weaknesses include the over-representation of therapy, T-, and laboratory groups, and the underrepresentation of natural groups in the heuristic basis for and subsequent "testing" of the theory. Furthermore, key ambiguities persist. For example, Moreland and Levine (1988, 156) point out that: "The theory might be made more precise by specifying how long each stage lasts or why different kinds of groups develop in different ways but that might be asking too much of a theory meant to apply so broadly."

Another contested issue in this literature is whether or not the sequence of progression through the stages should be seen as invariant or contingent. For example, Tucker (1973, 264, 267) takes a dialectic view and argues that the basic sequence is invariant, as it is only through the enactment and resolution of characteristic conflicts (thesis, antithesis, synthesis) that development may take place (cf. Ziller 1977). Worchel et al. (1992) take a similar though somewhat softer position, emphasizing the order of stages. Tuckman (1965, 397) himself suggested that sequencing may depend on differences within and among particular group settings with regard to the content of the stages, the rate of progression through the sequence, and the order of the stages. It should be noted, however, that the dispute over the sequencing of the later stages of group development hides a broad consensus regarding the basic character of the forming stage that remains logically prior to the others.

The rate of development is another issue worthy of consideration. A seeming strength of Tuckman's model is that it seems to subsume broad patterns of developmental progression noted in work as diverse as that of Bion (1961) and Bales (1950). While Bion studied therapy groups that endured for many months or even years, Bales studied laboratory groups convened for hours up to several days. On the one hand, the parallels among the developmental trajectories noted seem striking. On the other hand, the notion that the rate of development can be hundreds or thousand of times faster in short-term groups is startling. Tuckman submits some explanations for this rate differential. He argues that short-term laboratory groups are forced by situational constraints to engage in problem solving almost immediately. This rapid engagement is facilitated by "the impersonal and concrete nature of the laboratory task" (1965, 397). In addition, guidance and explicit instructions provided by the experimenter may reduce ambiguity and accelerate orientation. In contrast, Tuckman (1965, 379) notes that "emotionality and resistance are major features of therapy group development and represent personal and interpersonal impediments to group development and solution attainment as a function of the highly emotionally-charged nature of the therapy group task." Where does that leave real-world policy-making groups? Generally speaking, they would seem to fall somewhere in between. Like therapy groups, real-world policy groups must face up to potentially high levels of affect (positive and negative) that accumulate during the course of political or bureaucratic interaction. Constellations of prior personal relationships and enmities are likely to affect group interaction and faction formation, thus affecting the rate of development. For example, it has often been suggested that Jimmy Carter's Georgians and Ronald Reagan's Californians formed cohesive subgroups that impacted heavily upon decision making, particularly in the early days of the two presidents' administrations. Similarly, in top-level decision making the stakes are commonly high in terms of career prospects, ideological commitments, and valued personal relationships—values that may be placed in jeopardy in group interaction and may exacerbate conflicts. Both the Carter and Reagan administrations developed bitter rivalries of epic proportions among advisers such as the Vance–Brzezinski and Weinberger–Shultz feuds. While policy problems commonly are ill-structured (as in therapy groups), members may be guided to a considerable extent by precedent or explicit instruction (as in some laboratory settings).

Another issue commonly glossed over in the group development literature is the question of membership turnover (cf. Ziller 1977; Moscovici and Doise 1994). The point of departure seems to be the notion of a group with a stable membership that travels intact through the stages. However, where group boundaries are fluid and members move in and out during the period of time in question, major questions arise. As membership shifts, at what point does the old group cease to exist and a new one appear? Moreland and Levine (1988) provide some guidance in this regard through their work on member assimilation and group accommodation. They suggest that a two-way influence process takes place when membership change occurs within a group. Groups exert pressure on new members to conform (assimilate) to group norms and practices. New members may demand that the group adapt (accommodate) to their presence by changing norms and practices. Where accommodation outstrips assimilation, one might say that a new group has been formed out of the remnants of the old one. It seems reasonable that in such a situation, a group undergoing radical membership change might well regress in its development as uncertainties and interpersonal unfamiliarity reemerge. Paradoxically, in such situations a group can become "new" in an important sense.

New Groups

Given the thrust of the group development literature that emphasizes that groups must pass through the preliminary stages prior to achieving optimal readiness for performance, how do newly formed groups manage their interaction and coordinate the contributions of individual members? This is a highly policy-relevant question since ad hoc, newly established, or newly restaffed groups, committees, and task forces are a common feature of the political-administrative landscape.

Such bodies litter the policy-making field during periods of political transition. Even though such groups may not yet have progressed very far in their development, they may be called upon to make critical decisions on short notice. For example, the Clinton administration took over the reins of power with several foreign policy crises (Bosnia, Haiti, Somalia, Iraq) in progress, as well as an agenda overloaded with other pressing domestic and foreign policy issues.

Moreland and Levine (1988, 64) note, in keeping with the conventional thinking in the group development literature, that "before it reaches the performing stage, the group has not yet evolved a clear set of norms." While plausible, this characterization is somewhat misleading for several reasons. First, while a clear set of group-specific norms may not yet have evolved, typical adult group members bring with them a wealth of experience of group interaction. Such experience may derive from wider organizational or societal cultures and practices as well as from previous membership in other groups. This is, of course, particularly true of governmental decision makers.

Therefore, early group interaction is affected in important ways by the extragroup cultural baggage imported by members, particularly during the early stages of group formation and development. As Bettenhausen and Murninghan observe, "uncertainty over appropriate behavior leads members to use their past experiences in similar settings as scripts for choosing behavior in the current situation" (1985, 350). Where individual member experience and normative-procedural scripts appear to converge, early interaction may proceed (or appear to proceed) relatively smoothly. However, significant differences among member scripts and role conceptions may go unnoticed for some time and have a negative effect on task coordination, performance, and longer-term group stability.[2] Important matters may fall through cracks in the system, if mutual expectations are not made explicit through some kind of communicative process.

Many scholars have emphasized that coordination of policy-making processes in complex, multilayered institutional systems such as the U.S. presidency is a difficult matter under the best of circumstances. For a variety of reasons, the newgroup context may be far from the best of circumstances.

To the extent that the group persists, it will be increasingly affected by an emergent group-specific culture. This culture is the product of repeated interaction, experience, and patterns of power distribution and hierarchy within the group:

> Depending upon the similarity of the members' scripts, a common basis for action is either taken for granted or negotiated within the group. As the members interact they tacitly revise their beliefs about appropriate action, implicitly agreeing with the direction, or overtly attempt to pull the group toward their own interpretations through challenges to the implied norm. (Bettenhausen and Murninghan 1985, 350)

These authors suggest, on the basis of experimental evidence, that groups respond to a high degree "to their own precedents, set early in their initial interactions" (1985, 352).

Extragroup norm imports are not the only source of normative guidance that may be available to newly convened decision-making groups. To the extent that such groups are characterized by internal or externally sustained hierarchies, a formal or emergent leader figure may have the power to set initial ground rules more or less by fiat (cf. George 1980; Bettenhausen and Murninghan 1985, 351). This is particularly likely to be the case where the leader is also the group convenor, enjoying wide powers over the recruitment and exclusion functions as in the U.S. presidential setting. Thus leaders may serve as precedent- and norm-setters, reducing uncertainty during the early period of group existence. From the perspective of enhancing group information-processing and problem-solving capacity, such leader norm-setting may have positive or negative impacts, depending upon the content and strength of the norms he or she establishes. To draw another illustration from the U.S. presidential setting, George Bush was relatively successful in establishing norms generally conducive to balanced and critical advisory group interaction from the very start of his presidency. In contrast, the norms set by Carter did not inhibit what several observers have suggested was excessive conformity among advisers during the early part of his administration (Moens 1990; George and Stern, forthcoming).

What happens if the leader (or some surrogate process manager) does not exercise this prerogative? In that case, there is a serious risk that group interaction will spontaneously evolve in a fashion leading to excessive degrees of conformity or conflict (an abrupt shift into the "storming" stage), either of which may have negative effects on group decision making. The issue of conflict in newly established groups will be put aside for the time being in favor of a focus on new groups and conformity.

New Groups and Conformity in the Political Setting

The tendency of individuals to conform to various forms of overt or covert group pressure is well documented in the small groups literature. These findings are extremely robust—classic experiments by Sherif, Asch, Schacter, and others have been replicated, modified, and elaborated by large numbers of researchers in a variety of cultural contexts (Moscovici 1985; Nemeth and Staw 1989). There is reason to believe that pressures toward conformity are particularly strong in newly formed small groups. In fact, as has been recently noted in the literature, many of these experiments have been conducted upon artificial ad hoc groups existing for very short durations of time (often minutes or hours, cf. Ziller 1977, 307; McGrath et al. 1993, 415). As a result, it is possible that conformity effects associated with new groups may have influenced their results. On the other hand, group phenomena such as conformity are generally regarded as weaker in the laboratory setting than in natural groups where affect and salience, such as moral or instrumental considerations (e.g., career prospects), tend to be of a far greater magnitude (Mullen and Copper 1994).

As has been noted by scholars in several disciplines, the so-called shadow of the future, a vivid metaphor for the expectation of future interdependence, is extremely relevant to questions of cooperation/conflict and conformity/deviance. Where the shadow of the future is short, indulging impulses toward conflict and idiosyncrasy may be highly attractive. The short-term benefits promised by the behavior may predominate. However, as the shadow of the future lengthens and prolonged interaction is contemplated, the costs of such behavior and the benefits of cooperation or conformity may take the upper hand in decision-making calculations. Robert Axelrod (1984) makes a version of this argument in *The Evolution of Cooperation,* suggesting that making the Prisoner's Dilemma an iterated, rather than single-play game leads to cooperation between the players as the dominant outcome. Social psychologists have made similar arguments. For example, Ziller (1977, 305) draws on exchange theory and reports experimental results supporting the hypothesis that "conformity in small groups increases when an individual believes there will be an opportunity for future interaction with the same group." This is based on the notion of conformity as paying in advance for future benefits; a prerequisite for which is the expectation that the social relationship will be sufficiently stable and durable so that collection can take place at some unspecified point in the future.

All other things being equal, the shadow of the future would seem to be longest at the beginning of a particular endeavor, tending to increase conformity incentives in newly formed groups. Such pressures are likely to be particularly strong in newly formed groups where members share the expectation of a longer-term and highly salient interaction. Of course, in groups formed with the expectation of holding together for only a very brief period this effect might not be very strong.

U.S. presidential advisory groups tend to operate with frames of reference measured in years, and membership is generally highly salient to members who may view the experience as the pinnacle of their careers. In such groups, conformity pressures tend to be particularly strong at the outset.[3] Why is this the case? Individual advisers are likely to try to avoid squandering political capital and their access to a newly elected president by taking unpopular stands, defying the executive who just appointed them, or deliberately or inadvertently offending some powerful figure. While such hierarchies are being worked out and procedural and substantive uncertainties prevail, caution and compliance would seem to be the order of the day.[4]

It has been suggested that the key to compliance is the level of an individual's confidence in group approval (McCauley 1989). Hollander (1958) coined the term *idiosyncrasy credit* to capture the latitude granted a leader or particularly esteemed group members to deviate from group norms. The context of newly formed groups is one in which relatively limited opportunities for earning idiosyncrasy credit are likely to have presented themselves. For most members, the account is likely to be empty. Members of a newly formed group tend to be uncertain about the support of the other members and therefore are relatively likely to conform to nascent group norms or the preferences implied or expressed by the leader or other assertive figures within the group.

Stern and Sundelius (1993, 1994) have coined the term *newgroup syndrome* to capture a hypothesized pathological conformity dynamic liable to occur in newly formed policy groups. As has been suggested above, in ad hoc or newly institutionalized groups, that is, those in the forming stage (to use Tuckman's terminology), a common group subculture and well-developed procedural norms tend to be lacking. This vacuum creates uncertainty among the members who are likely to be anxious, tentative, dependent, and, therefore, particularly inclined to take direction from a leader or other assertive group members within the group (Moreland and Levine 1988, 155–56; Wheeler and McKeage 1993, 65–66). These conditions create incentives for both compliance and internalization on the part of the individual member, which in turn results in a tendency toward conformity in the group as a whole. Longley and Pruitt have argued that in newer groups

> Group members are uncertain about their roles and status and thus are concerned about the possibility of being made a scapegoat or even excluded from the group. Hence they are likely to avoid expressing opinions that are different from those proposed by the leader or other power-

ful persons in the group, to avoid conflict by failing to criticize one another's ideas, and even to agree overtly with other people's suggestions while disagreeing covertly. Such actions sound very much like groupthink. (1980, 87)

Longley and Pruitt suggest that these behaviors may be, in part, the result of what they term "false cohesion" based on the insecurities of the situation and member motivations to maintain their membership and maximize their acceptance by the group. Note that according to the definition of cohesion adopted above, such motivations are legitimate components of cohesion, despite the lack of close personal relationships.

Actually, newgroup syndrome may appear even in only moderately cohesive groups and may in fact be exacerbated by the defensive mentality associated with policy environments rife with personal, factional, or bureaucratic politics-style conflict. There are indications that larger newly convened deliberative groups may be especially liable to excessive conformity. This susceptibility to conformity suggests that new groups may be particularly ripe for manipulation attempts as well (Stern and Sundelius 1993; 1994; Hoyt and Garrison, this volume).

Virtually all new groups are thought to have these latent propensities. Yet, not all new groups develop newgroup syndrome. As Burnstein and Berbaum (1983, 551) have suggested, one critical factor is whether or not leaders intervene actively in order to set roles, norms, and ground rules that suspend extragroup status considerations and encourage broad and forthright participation from the very start. Alternatively, in less or non-hierarchical new groups, constructive ground rules empowering the membership can be established through a collective negotiation process (Bettenhausen and Murninghan 1985).

Some Potential Critiques of the Newgroup Concept

In the spirit of balanced critical deliberation, it seems prudent to present some observations from the relevant literature that seem to question the underlying assumptions of newgroup syndrome.

Normative Ambiguity Motivates Critical Thinking

Philip Tetlock, in his influential study of accountability, suggests that individuals tend to take the cognitive path of least resistance. Therefore, when the views of others are known, they tend to conform, applying the "acceptability heuristic," rather than take the social risk and expend the cognitive effort required to adopt a dissenting or critical posture (Tetlock 1985a, 311). Alternatively, in situations characterized by normative ambiguity, individuals are motivated to expend more cognitive effort in making decisions: "Accountability to others of unknown views has been found in a number of studies to 'motivate' people to become more vigilant, complex, and self-critical information processors . . . " (Tetlock 1985a, 314). By extension, in newly formed groups (relative to well-established ones) it could be argued that members are more likely to be ignorant of the views of others and therefore more vigilant.

On the other hand, it has already been suggested that internal structures of individual responsibility and collective coordination are often poorly developed in newly formed groups. Therefore, members seeking the course of action that offers both safety and cognitive least resistance may well adopt passivity rather than vigilance under these circumstances. As a result, new groups may be particularly liable to social loafing (Levine, Resnick and Higgins 1993, 589–90). Thus the logic of accountability can be turned in defense of the newgroup notion as well. Furthermore, there is reason to believe that social loafing may affect group decision making as profoundly as the tendencies toward conformity already noted.

Group Freshness Can Sometimes Be a Virtue

In a study of "collective mind," Weick and Roberts (1993, 375–76) extol the virtues of newly formed groups in terms of their capacity for alert and heedful thinking, arguing that institutionalization tends to decrease vigilance in high-reliability cultures and some other special contexts. These scholars point to newly formed, short-term groups exhibiting a high level of coordination (such as in crisis participants, ad hoc projects, aircraft cockpits, and jazz improvisation), suggesting that such groups are highly vigilant despite low levels of bonding and prior interaction. They quote a study by Eisenberg, who asserts that such groups are based upon a "non-disclosive intimacy" that: "stresses coordination of action over alignment of cognitions, mutual respect over agreement, trust over empathy, diversity over homogeneity, and strategic communication over unrestricted candor" (Weick and Roberts 1993, 375).

Explicitly engaging the group development literature, Weick and Roberts suggest these as examples of highly sophisticated and structured interaction subversive of conventional notions of group development:

> If people are observed to contribute, represent, and subordinate with heed, these actions can be interpreted as operations that construct a well developed collective mind; however, those actions can also be seen as the orienting, clarifying, and testing associated with the early stages of a group just beginning to form. By one set of criteria, that associated with group formation, people engaging in forming are immature. By another set of criteria, that associated with collective mind, these acts of forming

represent well developed mental processes. These opposed criteria suggest that groups may be smartest in their early stages. (1993:376)

Their argument, then, is that for tasks requiring vigilance, new groups may be
likely to outperform more developed or institutionalized groups.[5]

How subversive of the notion of newgroup syndrome is this argument
and these examples? First of all, many of the examples (airline cockpits and
jazz improvisation especially) are taken from situations where temporary
group constellations are drawn from members of wider subcultures, where
individuals are likely to have a high degree of convergence in their operative
"scripts." Such convergence is the result of common aspects of formal and
informal training, and common experience of prior similar situations, a possibility that was recognized above. Several of these situations also commonly
exhibit strong leader figures, such as airplane captains, who may provide
members with covert or overt cues, helping to reduce rapidly normative ambiguity. It is also interesting to note that the bulk of these situations (as described in general terms) seem to exhibit short time frames and shadows of the
future, tending to decrease pressures for conformity. Finally, the character of
the task and the clarity of performance indicators may facilitate coordination
in some of these situations. Uncoordinated musical performances produce
cacophony, suggesting that coordination failures are likely to be detected and
corrected immediately through tacit or explicit communication. Similarly,
uncoordinated and faulty performances in flying an aircraft are likely to produce immediate and recognizable feedback. Such relatively structured tasks
and clear feedback are less common in the realm of policy-making, where
tasks tend to be ill-structured and feedback (like other informational resources) ambiguous at best (Senge 1992).

In sum, these potential critiques—while cogent and reasonable when
taken upon their own terms—do not appear to warrant dismissing the newgroup concept in the political context (summarized in table 6.1). Let us now

TABLE 6.1.   Newgroup Syndrome: A Schematic Summary

Ambiguous Intragroup Context	$\longrightarrow$	Tendencies toward Member	$\longrightarrow$	Susceptibility to Group Pathologies
Norms		Uncertainty		Excessive conformity
Rules		Passivity		Manipulation
Roles		Diminished accountability		Social loafing
Responsibilities		Tactical "caution"		Malcoordination
Power Structure		Compliance and internalization		
Social relationships				

turn to a real-world empirical case in order to probe the plausibility of new-group syndrome.

A Newgroup Plausibility Probe: The Bay of Pigs Case Revisited

Having fleshed out and critically examined the newgroup interaction pattern briefly noted in the previous chapter, it is time to reconsider the puzzle of the Bay of Pigs case described in the opening section of this chapter. The inquiry into the case will be structured by the systematic process-diagnosis procedure presented by Stern and Sundelius (this volume). While an important motivation for this exercise was to probe the plausibility of newgroup syndrome, the case analysis presented here is relatively generic and geared toward identifying the range of group interaction patterns observable in this case. It will not focus exclusively on the manifestation/nonmanifestation of newgroup syndrome.

Only months into his presidency, Kennedy stumbled into a major foreign policy fiasco: the Bay of Pigs. This episode has been described by knowledgeable observers in terms such as "a perfect failure" and "among the worst fiascoes ever perpetrated by a responsible government" (Janis 1982, 14). The compelling aspect of the Bay of Pigs story is, as we will see, that the failure seems entirely avoidable. While it is always tempting to make such judgments with the benefit of hindsight, a strong argument can be made that raising a few serious questions regarding the more obviously dubious assumptions behind the Bay of Pigs invasion plan should have been sufficient to alert the president to the excessive risks entailed by the operation. Yet these questions were asked rarely if at all, and even then the implications of the answers were dismissed more or less out of hand.

In the spring of 1961, the newly elected President Kennedy reportedly perceived himself to be under pressure from constituencies inside and outside the government to do something about the rapidly radicalizing Castro regime in Cuba. Kennedy had inherited from his predecessor a CIA covert operation in advanced stages of preparation. This was based on the idea of landing a modest force of exile Cubans on Cuban soil in order to overthrow Castro. The force was based in training camps in Guatemala. CIA intelligence reports given to the president and to the advisory group suggested that such a landing would trigger a "spontaneous" revolt and a wave of sabotage against Castro's forces. Castro's ability to retaliate could be crippled by air attacks (by obsolete U.S. planes with Cuban markings) against Cuban airfields in the early stages of the operation. A disinformation effort including a show defection of a "Cuban" pilot to Miami would help to obscure the U.S. involvement.[6]

A number of highly questionable assumptions and assessments escaped critical scrutiny during the group deliberations. First, Kennedy and his advisers seemed to believe that the administration could maintain the secrecy or plausible denial of U.S. involvement in the operation despite the fact that the plans had become an open secret known even to a number of journalists prior to the operation (Reeves 1993, 83–84). They assumed that the operation would enjoy the element of surprise when in fact Castro himself had gotten wind of the plan. Second, they failed to question the likelihood of the spontaneous-rising assessment. As it turned out, Castro had penetrated the resistance network and rounded up potential rebels prior to the landing of the exile force. Third, the Kennedy circle labored under the misconception that the exiles would have an escape route to the Escambray mountains should the landing prove unsuccessful. However, a change of venue in the latter stages of the planning foreclosed this possibility. Fourth, Kennedy reportedly assumed that an overt U.S. intervention would likely trigger Soviet retaliation in Berlin, an assumption that was never subjected to rigorous questioning by experts. Finally, on a more general level, Kennedy apparently incorrectly assumed that the information he received from the intelligence and military experts was balanced, impartial, and informed by special professional competence beyond question by nonprofessionals.

What were the results of the decision to go forward on the basis of these assumptions? The April 1961 Bay of Pigs operation should be seen as nothing less than a political and military disaster. Within two days, the U.S.-sponsored exile expeditionary force was decimated and forced to surrender in the face of overwhelming Cuban loyalist numerical and air superiority. One hundred and fourteen exiles lost their lives and the other 1189 were captured by Castro's forces. Furthermore, the short- and longer-term political consequences were severe. Feeble U.S. attempts to deny involvement were generally met with disbelief by the international community, damaging the nation's international credibility. The U.S. action was denounced at the United Nations by allied and political rival countries alike. The Latin American countries were, understandably, in light of the U.S. history of intervention in the region, particularly incensed.

The poor U.S. performance led to a questioning of Kennedy's courage, will, moral fiber, and competence at a critical juncture of his presidency and the ongoing Cold War with the USSR. The abortive intervention attempt also served, ironically enough, to further cement the developing ties between the Castro regime and Soviet Union leading to a detrimental change in the local security environment. The administration's clumsy execution of the operation and apparent lack of resolve may well have encouraged Khrushchev to believe that he could get away with the strategic gambit that would ultimately trigger the Cuban missile crisis of 1962 (Janis 1982, 15).

This historical episode presents us with a puzzle of sorts. As Kennedy reportedly lamented after the disaster, "How could I have been so stupid to let them go ahead?" (Vandenbroucke 1984, 491). Furthermore, why did such a dedicated, talented, experienced, and professional group of advisers allow Kennedy to place himself in such a position? Ironically, these may well have been, for the most part, the right persons in the right positions at the right time. Many of the them would go on to perform admirably in subsequent crises. Somehow, in this situation, the individual intellectual horsepower and combined experience of these advisers failed to translate into an effective advisory group performance. What went wrong? The puzzle of group information processing in the Bay of Pigs case then, to put it crudely, is how could so many individually smart and experienced policymakers make such a poor group decision?

In an attempt to explore the role of small groups contributing to this failure, a systematic analysis of the functioning of Kennedy's advisory group and its relationship to the wider institutional structures in which it was embedded will now be presented. The analysis will be based on the six-step analytical scheme developed in chapter 5.

Step One: The Extragroup Setting

The key decisions in the Bay of Pigs case were taken by Kennedy in consultation with a small group of top-level advisers. However, in order to understand the group's mode of operation and "working conditions," it is important to examine the wider temporal, political, and organizational context.

First of all, the Bay of Pigs decisions were, as noted above, taken in the first three months of the Kennedy administration. In fact, it is quite fair to describe the general atmosphere of that time as a "honeymoon in Camelot." Kennedy's public approval ratings were high and had improved dramatically since the election.[7] This was not, by any means, an administration under siege.

This is not to say that Kennedy and his advisers did not see potential rivals and enemies within and outside the government. Following an election in which he narrowly defeated a more conservative opponent, Kennedy was mindful of his right flank. In fact, Kennedy's campaign had emphasized Cold War themes and criticized the Eisenhower administration for passivity and complacency in the face of the Soviet threat. The spurious (but politically volatile) "missile gap" and the Castro regime in Cuba became symbols for the previous administration's alleged shortcomings in this regard.[8] In an important sense, Castro had become a politically loaded enemy figure for the new administration.

It is also important to keep in mind that like many U.S. presidential advisory groups, the Bay of Pigs group was interorganizational and informal in character. Participants were drawn from various agencies including the

CIA, the State Department, the Defense Department, the Armed Services and the White House staff. Thus no common organizational subculture appears to have been shared by the members. In addition, since the members came from different "parallel" organizations, most of the principals may be seen as formal equals though, of course, subordinate to the president.

However, where more than one participant from a particular agency was involved, intraorganizational status is potentially relevant. For example, Allen Dulles (the CIA Director) was formally superior to Richard Bissell (the CIA Deputy Director for Plans). Such relationships may be significant with regard to questions of inclusion and exclusion from the group. For example, Dulles and Bissell chose to exclude representatives from the CIA's directorate of intelligence from the decision group in particular and from the planning of the operation in general. Even the Deputy Director for Intelligence, Robert Amory, was excluded despite his extensive experience in amphibious landings of the type under consideration in what developed into the Bay of Pigs operation (Schlesinger 1965; Andrew 1995, 261).

As a result of this penchant for secrecy, much of the CIA's area expertise was never brought to bear in an in-depth and systematic analysis of the political situation in Cuba. The operation was viewed as so sensitive that participants in the decision-making group were discouraged from consulting experts at lower levels in their respective organizations. This applied not only to the CIA experts, but also to those affiliated with the State Department. As one analyst noted, "excluded [from the decision making process] were most of the government's Latin America experts, both within the CIA's Directorate for Intelligence and the State Department. In addition, the non CIA officials reviewing the project were mostly generalists who knew little about Cuba or Latin America" (Vandenbroucke 1993, 28). Similarly, Secretary of State Dean Rusk exercised gatekeeping privileges, deciding whether or not his subordinates (such as Chester Bowles or Roger Hilsman) would be allowed to study the project or have access to deliberations or to the president himself (Wyden 1979). As it turned out, the insulation of the decision-making group from relevant expertise served to prevent or weaken challenges to some of the operation's more dubious assumptions.

The proximity to the presidential transition had important implications for the functioning of the advisory group. Disdainful of Eisenhower's formalistic national security policy-making apparatus, which had been heavily criticized by the Jackson Committee, Kennedy ordered it dismantled. He wanted the Eisenhower system replaced with a more ad hoc and collegial organization (George 1980, chapter 8). As a result of this reform process, top level policy-making was significantly deinstitutionalized during this period, depriving the president of the systematic evaluation and implementation routines established by his predecessor. As noted by the Taylor Commission subsequently appointed by Kennedy, "Top level direction was given through ad hoc meetings of senior officials without consideration of operational plans in writing and with no arrangement for recording conclusions and decisions reached" (Wyden 1979, 317). Under these conditions, it was relatively easy for important matters to escape careful scrutiny; a clear allocation of responsibility and accountability for the various aspects of the problem and various stages of the decision-making process was lacking among the members of Kennedy's advisory group (Reeves 1993, 84; Prados 1991, 99–103).

This reorganization was allegedly absorbing most of National Security Assistant McGeorge Bundy's time during the run up to the Bay of Pigs. Other officials were also preoccupied with getting a handle on their new jobs and launching institutional reform programs. Secretary of Defense Robert McNamara was heavily involved in attempting to master the Pentagon bureaucracy. Given the other pressing tasks at hand, it was difficult for these senior officials to focus on the relatively arcane CIA plan (Wyden 1979).

Finally, it should be noted that the Bay of Pigs was far from the only foreign policy problem on the agenda during the early months of 1961. United States–Soviet relations in general, tensions in Berlin in particular, and most notably the situation in Laos were perennial distractions from the Cuba project. In fact, the Bay of Pigs project was often a secondary issue under discussion in the meetings of Kennedy's foreign policy advisory group. It has been alleged that at no time during the decision process prior to the invasion attempt did Kennedy and his advisers concentrate on the Bay of Pigs for more than 45 minutes at a time (Neustadt and May 1986, 1; Andrew 1995, 260).

Step Two: The Intragroup Setting

A natural transition from the external to the intragroup setting is the question of admittance to the group. In this case, it is clear that the president acted as convenor. While the group did include virtually all of the NSC principals, most of deliberations did not take place in formally constituted meetings of that body. As a result, NSC principals could conceivably have been excluded from the inner circle, as has been the case with some subsequent presidents such as Nixon. Other participants, such as Special Assistant Arthur Schlesinger, were included as aides to the president. Thus, unlike in some other political systems and settings, the group leader's control extended to the recruitment/exclusion function. In addition, as noted in the previous section, gatekeeping responsibilities vis-à-vis the major organizations represented were delegated to the ranking participants from those bodies.

The group composition exhibited elements of both homo- and heterogeneity. As was the custom at that time (and during most of U.S. history for that matter), all of the major participants were white males. Most had similar educational backgrounds, with Ivy League degrees. The East Coast foreign policy establishment was heavily represented. It is interesting to speculate whether a greater degree of diversity might have altered the decisions reached. For example, the presence of females in the group might have contributed to diluting the "macho" atmosphere of the deliberations. Perhaps one or more Latin Americans or other minorities in the group might have encouraged questioning of some of the stereotypes that contributed to underestimating the efficiency and competence of the Castro regime.

Apart from the high degree of social, gender, and ethnic homogeneity, relatively diverse experiential backgrounds were represented among the participants. Expertise of various kinds including military science, intelligence, and (to a far lesser extent) regional (Latin America) were at hand. Some of the participants had made their careers in public service, others in academia, still others in the private sector. Politically speaking, the group ranged from moderate republicans such as McNamara to liberal democrats like Schlesinger.

Let us now turn our attention to the group culture in an attempt to identify aspects of the norm, rule, and role structures in the group that may have significantly affected the outcome of deliberations. First of all, a number of analysts have suggested that a norm of "boldness" associated with the "New Frontier" mentality (in contrast to the perceived timidity of the Eisenhower administration) permeated the proceedings (Schlesinger 1965; Janis 1982). Another important norm appears to have been "rally to the President" when his "project" came under the criticism of outsiders. The most dramatic example of behavior apparently stemming from this norm was the reaction of the group to Senator William Fulbright's scathing criticism in the key meeting on April 4. The group reportedly closed ranks in support of the project and rejected the arguments made by the legislative interloper. Another apparent norm that proved dysfunctional was "deference to experts." Finally, an emergent norm of deference to the leader is noticeable, a norm of which the president himself appears to have been unaware.

The literature suggests that decision rules may have important consequences not only for choices, but also for the character of the deliberations and "political" action that precede them (e.g., Gaenslen 1980, 1992; Hermann 1993). The decision process in the Bay of Pigs case was characterized by an overall decision rule of executive choice following extensive consultation. In fact, as has been pointed out by Wyden (1979), the final decision to go ahead with the project was not made in a group setting. However, the plan had been shaped and reshaped in group deliberations and the president's thinking had been profoundly affected by these processes.

It is interesting to note that in the final plenary meeting of April 4 a pseudo-voting procedure was used. This meeting produced what Kennedy perceived to be a near-consensus in favor of proceeding with the Bay of Pigs operation. More than a dozen of Kennedy's top foreign policy and military advisers were assembled. Following a presentation by CIA deputy director Bissell and a critique of the plan by Senator Fulbright, each participant in turn was asked for a yes or no answer. "Ifs," "ands," and "buts" were discouraged; at one point Kennedy interrupted a junior member who tried to give a more nuanced response. After a long string of "yes" votes from the senior participants, Kennedy broke off the procedure, saying "Gentlemen, we'd better sleep over it" (quoted in Wyden 1979, 150). Several of the junior participants including Schlesinger were not given a chance to vote. A number of the participants later suggested that the circumstances and the format were inconducive to serious critical discussion about the plan (Wyden 1979, 146–51).

As the Bay of Pigs decision took place in the first few months of the Kennedy administration, the participants generally had little experience in working together in general and working as a group in particular. This created a potential for misunderstandings regarding the roles of the individual members in the deliberations. For example, Dean Rusk's somewhat idiosyncratic conception of the role of the secretary of state in policy deliberations was apparently poorly understood by the president and other participants. This may have contributed to the growing momentum in favor of the proposed Cuba initiative. Rusk

> sought to be Kennedy's chief advisor on questions men "should approach on their knees." No one must overhear or interfere with the advice the Secretary of State gave the President. In large meetings, he would deliberately "act the dodo" while others spoke. When they were done he would summarize what had been said, let the meeting end, and then follow Kennedy into the oval office to offer his own views in private. (Wyden 1979, 48; cf. Beschloss 1991, 71, 108)

Rusk's passivity in the group setting was apparently interpreted as tacit assent by the other parties. He failed to serve as an effective counterweight to the passionate advocacy of the CIA representatives in group deliberations and failed to hearten other potential critics (Janis 1982, 38). It is has also been suggested that National Security Assistant McGeorge Bundy may have initially interpreted his role as primarily directed at managing the policy process, inhibiting him from engaging in substantive critical advocacy on the basis of private skepticism regarding the Cuban project (Vandenbroucke 1984, 482). To the extent that others may have misunderstood Bundy's role conception, this would have had roughly the same effect as in Rusk's case.

This survey of the intragroup setting will conclude with an examination of the intragroup power and status structure. In the U.S. system, the formal position of the president with regard to foreign policy-making is one of unrivaled power. To the extent that a president wishes to be assertive, as did Kennedy, an abundance of means are at his disposal. In addition, the president has a great deal of institutional latitude with regard to the structuring of the policy-making process after his personal preferences. These factors place the president in a firm leadership position vis-à-vis his cabinet secretaries and other advisers, all of whom serve at his pleasure. However, this important hierarchical dimension is just the beginning of the story.

In practice, this highly asymmetrical power relationship may be modified by issue-related and contextual factors of various kinds. "Players" may have outside constituencies or other power resources that may limit the president's freedom of action, as exemplified by the conflict between Truman and Mac-Arthur. Experience and age differentials are potentially significant as well. Kennedy, as a relatively young president and new in office, may well have been respectful toward, if not quite intimidated by, veterans in public service, such as Allen Dulles who was kept on from the Eisenhower administration.

Dulles had an almost mythic reputation as an intelligence practitioner based on his previous successes including the overthrow of the Arbenz regime in Guatemala in 1954. This wider reputation translated into a position near the top of the intragroup pecking order. As Wyden (1979, 316) neatly put it, "one doesn't trifle with a legend." Bissell, despite relatively junior formal rank in this context also had a privileged position in the group. This position derived from a number of personal factors including Bissell's towering intellect and charisma, his previous history of bold and spectacular successes, and his command of the details of the operation. These assets were buttressed by personal relationships to several of the key players (see below) and by the fact that Kennedy had already made a preliminary decision to offer Bissell the CIA directorship upon Dulles's retirement. Thus both Bissell and Dulles were seen as veteran "experts" in a group dominated by generalists, and generalists new to their jobs at that. Kennedy's personal respect for Bissell and Dulles was matched by his positive image of the CIA as an innovative, flexible, and highly useful institution.

Similarly, Kennedy and several of the other participants including McNamara were inclined to view the Joint Chiefs as having expert status on these issues. McNamara himself had spent fifteen years in the private sector and had initially been reluctant to take on the defense portfolio, feeling that his knowledge of the military realm was out of date. Thus McNamara tended to endorse the chiefs' views on military matters, rather than contributing independent views of his own. Kennedy's view of the military will be discussed below in the section on leadership.

The State Department representatives may have also benefited from the power resources that accompany expert status. In particular, Kennedy proved highly receptive to arguments regarding the need to preserve the deniability of the U.S. role in the operation in light of concern for preserving good relations with regional (and extraregional) powers. However, it should also be said that Kennedy had a rather negative opinion of the State Department as an institution. This fact may have tended to weaken the position of participants affiliated with that organization (particularly the more junior ones) in the group deliberations.

All in all, one sees a situation where the CIA representatives appear to have been in a privileged position, without, however, enjoying a monopoly of relevant expertise. In particular, it seems probable that the Joint Chiefs would have had the prestige and knowledge to mount a serious challenge to the operation had they so desired. In fact, those resources were brought to bear only in relatively marginal and ambiguous ways, which tended to strengthen the hand of the CIA. An illustrative detail in this regard is the fact that Bissell, rather than a military officer, was given responsibility for briefing the decision makers on the findings of the JCS study assigned to assess the CIA plan (Wyden 1979, 95).

Step Three: Group Leadership Practices

In relatively informal, yet hierarchically organized groups of this kind, there is an intimate relationship between leadership style and the formation of group culture (George 1980; Janis 1982; Hermann and Preston 1994a, b). Let us now examine the potential impact of Kennedy's leadership style on deliberations. Kennedy's group leadership had two distinct traits. First, he exhibited a laissez-faire style with respect to process. Second, and ironically, he also showed tendencies in this case toward promotional and directive leadership on substance.

Kennedy, having little previous management experience, reportedly had a relatively simplistic view of small group and organizational management. He placed a premium on talent, believing that this quality was the key to achieving policy and political success. In other words, he believed that it was enough to assemble a number of talented people, throw them in a room together, and wait for good things to happen. JFK's management philosophy upon taking office has recently been described (Reeves 1993, 23) as follows: "Kennedy believed that problem solving meant getting the right man into the right place at the right time. If things went wrong, you put in someone else." In keeping with this general orientation, Kennedy did exhibit a laissez-faire group leadership style with regard to the Bay of Pigs decision-making process. As a result, he did not engage in active norm-setting designed to enhance the critical rigor of deliberations.

A number of the participants including Secretary of State Rusk were reportedly discomfited by the lack of systematic procedures characteristic of

Kennedy meetings during this period. Rusk was disturbed by the egalitarian and informal style encouraged by Kennedy. It galled him that junior participants were often allowed by the president to participate on a relatively equal footing with NSC principals (Wyden 1979, 147–48). Ironically, junior participants such as Paul Nitze and Chester Bowles (who substituted for Rusk when he was abroad) appear to have been unaware of Kennedy's preference in this regard, or alternatively, were inhibited out of deference to higher-ups from their own organizations (Wyden 1979, 120, 148).

Yet it has also been suggested that Kennedy engaged in subtly promotional leadership that granted the CIA advocates a privileged position and allowed them to dominate the discussions (e.g., Schlesinger 1965; Janis 1982, 42–44). For example, the CIA advocates were often allotted substantial time for formal presentations and briefings. Others were allowed to respond and comment, but not in a sustained fashion. As his commitment to the venture increased, Kennedy reportedly became increasingly perceived as a proponent of the Cuban initiative and as easily irritated by doubters, disheartening and disarming potential critics of the venture (Beschloss 1991, 114).

Lacking governmental management experience, JFK reportedly exhibited a naive confidence in the expertise and professionalism of the intelligence and military communities. He accepted the analyses of hand-picked experts as beyond question by civilians uninitiated in the arcane mysteries of these domains (Beschloss 1991, 24; Janis 1982, 31). He apparently had a particularly positive view of the CIA as a motivated and responsive organization, in contrast to his view of the State Department as ponderous and hidebound (Vandenbroucke 1993, 20). Thus Kennedy himself contributed to setting the norm of deference to experts in the group deliberations, as noted above.

Step Four: Type and Level of Cohesion

Kennedy's key advisers in the Bay of Pigs did, for the most part, not know the president or each other well. This may be surprising to some readers; it was a surprise to the author. Part of the myth of Camelot, a myth reinforced by the myriad accounts of the decision making during the 1962 Cuban missile crisis, is the notion of an easy familiarity born of long acquaintance between the president and his talented and trusted men. The fact that Kennedy's management style and organizational model has often been described as "collegial" (e.g., George 1980) reinforces this impression. However, this widely accepted image does not fully capture the personal context of the transition and the first few months of the new administration. Many of the key decision makers were new to their positions and unsure of the strength of their relationships to the newly elected president and the nature of their roles in the decision-making process.

Kennedy lacked a close personal relationship with the major foreign policy players in his administration. Secretary of State Rusk met Kennedy for the first time in December 1960 (Reeves 1993, 80; Beschloss 1991, 71). Defense Secretary McNamara also reportedly met Kennedy at about the same time (Schlesinger 1965, 108). National Security Assistant McGeorge Bundy knew Kennedy only slightly from some brief contact at Harvard functions. Bundy subsequently suggested that had he at the time enjoyed the kind of rapport with Kennedy that later developed, he would have questioned what he perceived to be the president's sudden shift in favor of the Bay of Pigs project in early April.[9] Ironically, those advisers with whom Kennedy did have a close personal relationship were, for the most part, kept out of this decision-making process. Robert Kennedy and Theodore Sorensen did not play important roles in the run-up to the Bay of Pigs operation.

Arthur Schlesinger heavily emphasizes this unfamiliarity factor in his account of the Bay of Pigs decision making. He writes that Kennedy "could not know which of his advisers were competent and which were not. For their part, they did not know him or each other well enough to raise hard questions with force and candor" (1965, 216). Thus it appears that in this case, as in many new groups, the members lacked "idiosyncrasy credit" (Hollander 1965), increasing their susceptibility to conformity.

This overall picture should not be interpreted as ruling out the impact of social ties on the deliberations. For example, both Bundy brothers and Walt Rostow (Deputy National Security Assistant) knew Bissell from his teaching days at Yale University. The Bundys both took economics courses with him; Rostow worked as his teaching assistant. McGeorge Bundy worked briefly for Bissell as a consultant on the Marshall Plan in 1948 (Prados 1991, 100). These prior relationships probably helped compensate for Bissell's relatively junior formal status, as did the sponsorship of Dulles and Kennedy himself.

Of course, personal relations are only one basis for group cohesion. Others include loyalty to the president who appointed them, a desire to contribute to and share in the success of common projects, a sense of shared destiny, and pride in being a part of an elite group. It should, however, be noted that these various types of cohesion may have different effects on policy deliberations. Loyalty to the president might well lead to conformity and support for him when his project is questioned by "outsiders." It could also lead to a desire to protect him from an embarrassing failure by candidly pointing out the flaws in the proposed operation. Thus loyalty and task cohesion may be interpreted as coincident or divergent by members.

Members may handle perceived conflicts of this kind in various ways. At the plenary meeting on April 4, many participants have later professed to have harbored doubts. Some, like McGeorge Bundy, reportedly voted "yes" out of solidarity with the team. Schlesinger was silent at the meeting, but followed it up with a conversation with Kennedy after the meeting and a memo summarizing his grounds for opposition to the venture.

Empirically speaking, it is a very difficult matter to attempt to sort out the motivations of the individual members in order to understand the forces binding the group together. Let it suffice to say that the evidence suggests that the group members did anticipate working together in the future. There is every reason to believe that they valued the cooperation and good will of the other members and the president, not least as a means of pursuing their own public and private agendas.

Step Five: Type and Level of Conflict/Rivalry

Scanning the record of the deliberations prior to the decision to go ahead with the Bay of Pigs operation reveals little in the way of overt and virulent conflict. In general, the tone of the deliberations were cordial and characterized by an apparent willingness of virtually all parties to make compromises. No obvious personal or political animosities among the select group of decision makers involved in the case are apparent from the available source materials. However, this is not to say that other forms of conflict and rivalry did not affect the decision making in this case.

It is important to note that significant differences regarding policy preferences are noticeable among the "players." The CIA contingent (most notable Dulles and Bissell) were committed advocates of the intervention. They favored a relatively bold operation, and tended to be less concerned with concealing the U.S. role. Given trade-offs between military and political risks, they tended initially to favor reducing military risk. However, when pressed by others (particularly Kennedy himself and the State Department representatives) they were prepared to accept greater levels of military risk in order to get the go ahead. In fact, they were so eager to get the project ratified that they at times took direct action to prevent negative assessments from reaching the president and his other advisers (see the discussion of manipulation below).

The defense department, led by a distracted Robert McNamara (who was then concentrating on taking control of the Pentagon bureaucracy), tended to support the CIA view. The other participants from the defense sector, the Joint Chiefs of Staff, tended also to emphasize minimizing military risk. Yet it should be noted that the military apparently treated this issue as one of relatively low organizational salience. They were very aware that what ultimately became the Bay of Pigs Operation was a CIA project from start to finish. As such the CIA would take credit for an eventual success and take the primary heat for a failure. Having procured assurances from the president that conventional U.S. forces would not be used under any circumstances and having successfully vetoed the notion of using the Guantanamo base as a platform of operations (raised by the State Department), the Joint Chiefs provided only ambiguous and muted criticism of the operation (Wyden 1979; Vandenbroucke 1993).

The State Department, represented at the top level by Secretary Rusk, ultimately favored a relatively small-scale and "quiet" operation that would conceal the U.S. role and maintain a posture conducive to plausible deniability. This should not be surprising in light of the departmental responsibility for maintaining relations with Latin America and other foreign governments that might be highly critical of another instance of heavy-handed U.S. intervention in the region.

Similar considerations combined with a high degree of skepticism regarding (a) the viability of the plans and (b) the possibility of keeping the U.S. role secret led two other participants to oppose the proposed operation. Both Senator William Fulbright (Chairman of the Senate Foreign Relations Committee) and Special Assistant Arthur Schlesinger wrote eleventh-hour memos to the president outlining these critical arguments and urging President Kennedy to refrain from this course of action. Fulbright, who was permitted to attend what has been described as the "climactic" meeting of Kennedy's advisory group on April 4, 1961, made an impassioned speech opposing the plan on moral grounds. Schlesinger did not air his views in the wider group at that meeting.

Thus it is clear that a fairly diverse set of competing views were conveyed to the president during the decision process, although a number of key dissents or criticisms took place outside of the group setting, such as those of Schlesinger and Rusk. The discreet communication of criticism may have led the president and his other advisers to overestimate the degree to which a consensus in favor of this course of action had been attained in the advisory group as a whole.

Step Six: Observed Interaction Pattern(s)

Let us begin by checking for indications of newgroup syndrome. Kennedy received his first in-depth CIA briefing on the proposed operation only eight days into his presidency; the operation was conducted less than three months later (Vandenbroucke 1993, 19, 40). As a result, it was a relatively newly convened advisory group that Kennedy consulted on this issue. In such new groups, as we have seen, there is a serious risk that ambiguity regarding the intragroup context may lead to characteristic "malfunctions" that may undermine group deliberations.

Was the intragroup context ambiguous? The balance of evidence suggests that this was the case. Given Kennedy's relatively laissez-faire management style, he did not attempt to guide consciously and clarify the group decision culture in order to reduce uncertainty and promote critical interaction. He appears to have been unaware of the effect of his person and the weight of his office upon his colleagues (Wyden 1979, 316). Similarly, the evidence suggests that he was insufficiently conscious of emergent group norms (unwittingly reinforced by his own conduct) of deference to the president and to "experts."

Many participants were rendered cautious and relatively passive due to their uncertainty regarding their mastery of their organizational portfolios, their role in the decision group, and their relationships to the president and other potentially powerful players. As Schlesinger observed in the quotation above, they simply did not yet know each other well. Wanting to give new colleagues the benefit of the doubt and to avoid unnecessary confrontations, the New Frontiersmen guarded their political capital, and wholeheartedly or reluctantly gave their consent to the CIA's plan. The qualms that were aired were often communicated outside the group setting and tended to originate from outsiders or relatively low-status members.

These observations suggest that Kennedy and his men did fall prey to some of the classic pitfalls associated with new groups such as excessive conformity, social loafing, and serious coordination difficulties. These behavioral patterns go a long way in accounting for the Kennedy administration's poor performance in the Bay of Pigs case (cf. Longley and Pruitt 1980, 87).

New groups are thought to be particularly susceptible to manipulation (Stern and Sundelius 1993). The available evidence suggests that the CIA-based advocates of the operation (Dulles and Bissell) did in fact engage in manipulative tactics in order to secure authorization for their pet project. Their manipulative leverage was enhanced by their ability to use the alleged need for secrecy as a means of limiting the information available to potential critics, particularly concerning the details of the invasion plan. Papers related to the operation were routinely collected by the CIA representatives at the close of meetings. Allegedly, the CIA also actively sought to suppress the expression of views critical of the project (Wyden 1979; Vandenbroucke 1993, 27).

The most flagrant example of the resort to manipulative tactics on the part of the CIA was probably the assurances given the president that the operation could be successfully accomplished without the overt involvement of additional U.S. forces. Privately, they believed that such involvement could very well prove essential and that Kennedy would then be forced to authorize open intervention to avoid failure of the initiative. Therefore, in order to secure presidential authorization for the operation, they avoided openly questioning the restrictions Kennedy was placing on the operation. As Dulles later wrote, he and Bissell did not want to raise these issues—in an academic discussion—which might only harden the decision against the type of actions we required. We felt that when the chips were down—when the crisis arose in reality, any action required for success would be authorized rather than permit the enterprise to fail.[10]

This suggests that the CIA advocates of the operation attempted (ultimately unsuccessfully) to entrap the president, through a variant of the salami tactic described by Maoz (1990).

More conventional bureaucratic and cabinet politics within the advisory system appear to have contributed to the policy failure as well. For example, it has been suggested that the Joint Chiefs may have avoided pressing doubts regarding the military viability of the Bay of Pigs operation in order not to antagonize CIA colleagues or the president who seemed kindly disposed to the plan. Their decision not to "rock the boat" may have been facilitated by the fact that this was a CIA operation and by the president's assurances that regular U.S. forces (and the Guantanamo base) would not be used under any circumstances. Despite serious problems identified during two separate rounds of evaluation resulting in two relatively critical written reports, the JCS did not actively oppose the plan. Vandenbroucke (1993, 25) concludes that

> Having put their reservations on paper, the JCS did not raise them again. There is no evidence the JCS mentioned to the president the findings of the evaluation team. Indeed, the military rarely spoke up about the project. As a result, the civilian decision makers were left with the impression that the Joint Chiefs approved the scheme.

Lacking operational responsibility and having covered themselves with the written reports, the Chiefs' posture contributed to the "consensus" supporting the operation.

It is also possible to interpret the final version of the Bay of Pigs plan as a political resultant established in group deliberations primarily reflecting a mix of the CIA representatives' preference for a larger-scale operation and the preferences of the "State Department representatives [who] fought to reduce the scale and visibility of the operation, while not criticizing the basic idea itself" (Vandenbroucke 1984, 483). The compromise operational configuration that was ultimately adopted was also influenced by the wider constellation of preferences among the consulted "players" (including the vehement opposition of Senator Fulbright) and, most importantly, by Kennedy's own views. Unfortunately, the willingness of many of the stakeholders to compromise, a seemingly commendable trait, resulted in this case in an unbalanced and unstable "worst of all worlds" policy (George 1980).

Could groupthink syndrome have played a role as well? Janis (1982, 35–36) argues that this was the case, citing Arthur Schlesinger's characterization of the Kennedy White House atmosphere during the first few months as "buoyant optimism" consistent with the groupthink illusion of invulnerability: "Euphoria reigned; we thought for a moment that the world was plastic and the future unlimited." Janis asserts that this mood may have undermined the group's critical thinking capacities, serving to prevent the subjection of the key (and faulty) assumptions behind the Bay of Pigs plan to careful scrutiny.

Janis (1982, 38–39) also finds evidence of the groupthink illusion of unanimity, again drawing on Schlesinger's account: "Our meetings took place in a curious atmosphere of assumed consensus." He suggests that the illusion could only be sustained through members' suppression of their private doubts. Janis also cites Sorensen's assessment that senior officials in the White House and State Department held their tongues "partly out of a fear of being labeled 'soft' or undaring in the eyes of their colleagues."

Another key precondition of groupthink, insulation of the decision-making group from outside sources of information and critical analysis, is prominent in this case as well. According to one credible account:

> Excluded [from the decision-making process] were most of the government's Latin America experts, both within the CIA's Directorate for Intelligence and the State Department. In addition, the non CIA officials reviewing the project were mostly generalists who knew little about Cuba or Latin America. (Vandenbroucke 1993, 28)

Thus the decision-making group in this case appears to have been effectively insulated from expert criticism regarding the military viability of the plan and from essential expertise regarding crucial assessments of the local political situation, such as the likelihood of spontaneous risings against Castro in response to an operation of this type.

Still, there are some aspects of the case that do not fit well with Janis's theory. The cornerstone of the theory, and the point that separates groupthink from more basic notions of conformity deriving from group pressure on the individual, is the notion of stress-induced cohesion as a source of extremely strong and largely unconscious conformity pressures (George 1980). This defensive avoidance tendency at the heart of groupthink is labeled concurrence-seeking by Janis. An interesting question is whether Kennedy's advisory group was subjected to unusual levels of stress prior to or during the deliberations on the Bay of Pigs.

It is certainly true that the early days of a presidency may be stressful for the chief executive and his top advisers. The pace of policy-making, the awesome responsibilities of leadership, and the demands of the media weigh heavily on newly appointed top officials. On the other hand, the atmosphere of optimism during the Kennedy "honeymoon" period suggests that the burdens of office still sat relatively lightly on group members during this period. Reading through accounts of this period does not give an analyst the impression of an "embattled" primary group. Quite simply, the Kennedy group does not appear to have been under siege in general or on the Cuba issue until after the operation was in progress. Therefore, the question arises whether Janis's strict version of the groupthink hypothesis—as opposed to noting some symptoms and indications of a low-quality decision process—really fits well with this situation.

Paul 't Hart's reformulation of groupthink neatly sidesteps these problems ('t Hart 1990/1994). First, 't Hart (following McCauley 1989) stretches the groupthink notion to include both unconscious (internalization) and deliberate (compliance) variants of conformity. Therefore, the issue of whether group members were actually carried away on the wave of enthusiasm for the project or merely playing a tactical-political game becomes less central (cf. Janis 1982, 39–40). Second, 't Hart distinguishes between two types of groupthink—collective avoidance (close to Janis's original formulation) and collective overoptimism. The latter type is driven by high levels of group and individual confidence and expectations of dramatic successes. This is an offensive, rather than defensive, avoidance resulting in concurrence-seeking tendencies and group conformity. To the extent that groupthink played a role in this case, it seems that collective overoptimism is the more plausible variant.

This exploration of the decision processes leading up to the Bay of Pigs intervention suggests that (a) newgroup syndrome contributed significantly to the fiasco, (b) the relationship between newgroup syndrome and other patterns of group dynamics noted in the literature is complex, and that (c) several such dynamics may operate simultaneously or in turn across a decision process lasting several months.

Reflections

The Bay of Pigs Case is widely regarded as the strongest of Janis's original groupthink case studies (George 1980; McCauley 1989). Following a suggestion from Longley and Pruitt (1980), this classic case was reopened and confronted with the newgroup perspective and other theoretical constructions from the small group decision-making literature. Clearly, the notion of a newgroup syndrome does help to shed light on the Bay of Pigs puzzle, as do several of the group dynamics patterns previously noted in the literature and incorporated into the synthetic analytical scheme developed by Stern and Sundelius in chapter 5, including manipulation, bureaucratic politics, and basic conformity, as well as groupthink. These theoretical notions proved highly relevant to the task of developing a richer understanding of the unhappy constellation of institutional structure and group process that contributed to the all-too-spectacular policy failure in that case.

A major finding of this case application is to support the theoretical argument made by Stern and Sundelius in the preceding chapter that multiple group dynamics patterns can coexist, interacting in complex ways, to the detriment of the quality of the policy process. Previous notions of the incompatibility (George 1980; Hermann 1989) of bureaucratic politics and conformity dynamics are in need of some revision and clarification. While bureaucratic or cabinet-level political considerations may indeed introduce constructive conflict into the decision-making process, they may also lead to avoidance of responsibility, compliance, and amiable compromise to the detriment of policy feasibility (Vertzberger 1990). Embattled factions within groups may be even more subject to conformity and concurrence-seeking than the wider groups of which they are a part ('t Hart 1990/1994).

Similarly, the relationship between manipulation and conformity patterns such as groupthink and newgroup syndromes is worthy of examination. Stern and Sundelius (1993; 1994, 104) advanced the proposition that tendencies toward conformity such as those associated with groupthink and newgroup syndromes may be exploited by manipulative group members. The case findings here strongly support that proposition as do findings from a previous Swedish crisis decision-making study. The manipulative tactics employed by the CIA advocates of the Cuban intervention went unnoticed and largely unchallenged in good measure due to conformity pressures deriving from a mutually reinforcing combination of newgroup syndrome and elements of groupthink syndrome. It is also worthy of note that even ultimately unsuccessful attempts at manipulation may affect decision processes in highly significant ways. Dulles and Bissell's attempt to entrap Kennedy was ultimately stymied by Kennedy's unexpected (for them) willingness to accept failure of the venture rather than escalate the U.S. involvement. Still their rosy assessments and efforts to stifle critics affected the substantive information base available to Kennedy and his advisers and served to undermine considerably the quality of the decision process.

Decision-making and advisory groups may be particularly susceptible to newgroup syndrome during transitional "honeymoon" periods. Flushed with a string of victories from the campaign trail and the election, they may understandably acquire the "illusion of invulnerability" noted by Janis in his work on groupthink. That, in conjunction with the long shadow of the future together facing group members and the primitive and chaotic group institutionalization typical of such periods, may create pressures for conformity and collective overoptimism. If unchecked by the leader or the group as a whole, this may have extremely negative consequences for the quality of decision processes and make performance failures more likely ('t Hart 1990/1994).

Leadership practices are an essential determinant of the character of group deliberations in virtually all settings. In new groups, where members tend to be especially malleable, leadership practices may well be even more crucial than in more institutionalized group contexts. Formal or de facto leader figures can use their leverage to engage in explicit and implicit norm-setting and coordination. Such group norms may empower members and encourage them to place their knowledge and critical/analytical capacity at the group's disposal, or they may promote passivity and conformity. Unfortunately, a laissez-faire leadership mode in such groups may result in "spontaneously generated" norms leading to excessive conformity and premature closure.[11]

Another function often, but not always, associated with group leadership is coordination and oversight of the division of labor in the group. It is unrealistic to assume that a comprehensive and rigorous analysis will arise spontaneously within the group on the basis of an emergent role system and division of labor. The suggestion on the part of Weick and Roberts (1993) that newly formed groups are more likely to engage in heedful interrelating than more developed/institutionalized groups was not borne out in this case investigation. On the contrary, serious difficulties associated with excessive conformity, inadequate structures of accountability, and role ambiguity emerged from the analysis of the Bay of Pigs case. These findings are in harmony with the basic propositions in the group development literature reviewed above.

This chapter will conclude by considering the subsequent functioning of Kennedy's advisory group over a more extended time perspective. Some eighteen months after the Bay of Pigs fiasco, seemingly very different group dynamics were revealed during the Cuban missile crisis of 1962. Several authoritative assessments (e.g., Janis 1972, 1982; George 1980) of the performance of the Kennedy group in that later crisis suggest that individual and collective learning processes, group development, and a more effective set of leadership practices, division of labor, and group interaction norms resulted in a superior process and outcome.[12] This depiction is quite a contrast to the description of the uncoordinated and conformity-ridden process described above. Perhaps the contrast between the two cases is the difference between a group in the forming stage, which fell prey to newgroup syndrome, and a group in the performing stage, which rose in vigilant fashion to a crucial decision occasion (Longley and Pruitt 1980, 87)? This is a question worthy of further consideration.

The potential for drawing upon the group development literature in order to understand better the functioning and malfunctioning of decision-making groups in the political setting has just begun to be tapped. Comparative synchronic and diachronic studies of such groups offer a highly promising line of inquiry and one with a high degree of potential policy relevance.

NOTES

The author wishes to acknowledge helpful comments and suggestions from many colleagues, including Paul 't Hart, Alexander George, Fritz Gaenslen, Tom Preston, Yaacov Vertzberger, Richard Moreland, Philip Tetlock, Charles Hermann, Walter Carlsnaes, Bengt Sundelius, Michael Karlsson, Bertil Nygren, Sally Riggs Fuller, Jean Garrison, Paul Hoyt, Max Metselaar, Bertjan Verbeek, Helen Purkitt, Bob Billings, Roger Bobacka, and Kjell Engelbrekt.

1. Following the official post mortem, Janis (1982, 31) recognized the newness of the administration as a possible contributing factor. However, in a subsequent section (1982, 33) he dismisses this factor as inadequate even combined with "political calculations," exclusion of experts, and conformity based on a desire to preserve political capital within the group. Janis's assessment may, however, have been led astray in part by his neglect of the emerging literature on group development, which is discussed below.

2. Bettenhausen and Murninghan (1985, 369), call this state "pluralistic ignorance" and suggest that (coordination difficulties aside) the condition is associated with latent group instability and relatively poor performance. Individual views are likely to harden, impairing the group's ability to cope with future threats, challenges and controversies.

3. Conformity pressures would also be expected to wane as the end of a second term approaches, the president becomes a "lame duck," and the group moves into an "adjourning" phase.

4. It is, of course, possible to find examples of political figures who proceed aggressively from day one in group policy-making. General Alexander Haig's brief tenure as secretary of state in the first term of the Reagan administration comes to mind. However, the brevity of that tenure also illustrates the potential risks of not taking the time to feel out the political landscape and emergent norms developing in a policy group. Haig's early attempts to dominate the foreign policy process served to alienate key constituencies and pave the way for his downfall (Smith 1988; Cannon 1991).

5. Weick and Roberts (1985, 376) suggest that groups steadily lose "mind" as they become institutionalized, and must "reform" periodically in order to maintain the capacity for "heedful inter-relating." Bernthal and Insko (1993, 85) have recently made a similar argument suggesting that assembling diverse combinations of individuals drawn from an available pool of talent into short-term task groups might be a better approach than maintaining "long-standing teams."

6. For detailed accounts and analyses of the Bay of Pigs fiasco, see Schlesinger 1965; Wyden 1979; Janis 1982, chapter 2; Vandenbroucke 1983, 1993; Beschloss 1991; Higgins 1987; and Reeves 1993.

7. A poll conducted by Lou Harris on March 23 found that "Public popularity has

risen to perhaps record heights," apparently surpassing both F. D. Roosevelt's and Eisenhower's ratings at that point in their presidencies (quoted in Reeves 1993, 73).

8. In fact, in what would become a historically controversial incident during the campaign, Kennedy called for strong support for Cuban exiles geared toward toppling Castro. Nixon was reportedly furious, feeling that Kennedy had exploited his national security briefing by Dulles for political purposes. In order to avoid compromising the secrecy of the covert operation in preparation, Nixon was forced to bite his tongue and refrain from rebutting Kennedy. It remains to this day unclear whether or not Kennedy had been specifically informed of the mission at the time. Kennedy claimed, in any case, that the statement in question was actually drafted by one of his aides and released prior to his having seen the specific wording (e.g., Wyden 1979, 66–67).

9. Kennedy reportedly committed to the intervention upon his return from a trip to Florida where he met with his father and several other anti-Castro intimates (Beschloss 1991, 107–8). These individuals may have been significant members of Kennedy's reference group for this decision, though not a part of the official advisory system at all.

10. Vandenbroucke 1993, 33, 192, fn. 60. Vandenbroucke cites Dulles's handwritten notes, box 244, x, y of the A. W. Dulles papers collection at the Princeton University library.

11. Another possibility is that a newgroup managed on a laissez-faire basis in a competitive or antagonistic situation will rapidly shift into a mode of interaction characterized by excessive conflict, a state reminiscent of the storming stage of Tuckman's group development model.

12. There are those who challenge the characterization of the Kennedy administration's management of the Cuban missile crisis as vigilant decision making. See, e.g., Lebow 1981; McCauley 1989; Welch 1989; Purkitt 1992; and Lebow and Stein 1994. Many of these arguments are rebutted in George 1993.

CHAPTER 7

"Following the Leader": The Impact of U.S. Presidential Style upon Advisory Group Dynamics, Structure, and Decision

Thomas Preston

Introduction

In September of 1950, President Harry S. Truman and his advisers made the decision to cross the Thirty-eighth Parallel and occupy North Korea. Although the situation was "framed" by Truman and his staff as an opportunity to reunify Korea, end the threat of further aggression from the North, and answer domestic critics of the Administration's foreign policy, within three months the decision had deteriorated into an abject policy failure. The massive intervention by Chinese forces on November 25 resulted in the worst military defeat in American history and a full-scale rout of United Nations forces back to the Thirty-eighth Parallel (Janis 1972, 14). On the other hand, when Truman and his Blair House Group made the initial decision to intervene in Korea to halt the North's unexpected invasion of the South in June of 1950, it was widely seen as an example of decisive presidential leadership and successful decision making. United Nations forces succeeded in halting the North Korean advance, prevented the fall of South Korea, and provided the United States with a golden opportunity to demonstrate its commitment to Containment policy. How were these two pivotal decisions made? Was Truman's leadership style a decisive factor? The policy outcomes were strikingly different in the two cases. Was the advisory process similar in both decisions, or did Truman's advisers fall victim to serious group malfunctions in the ill-fated September 1950 decision? It should be noted that I do *not* mean to imply a perfect correlation between process and outcome "quality"! Yet, enriching the decision process by increasing access to information, debate on options, and so on does promise to improve the chances of achieving desired outcomes. (See Fuller and Aldag, this volume; 't Hart, this volume, for discussions of multiple standards of evaluation.)

Clearly, national leaders tend to receive the lion's share of the credit, or the blame, for foreign policy decisions and their outcomes. Policy failures, like the decision to cross the Thirty-eighth Parallel, are usually blamed on the "leadership," or lack thereof, of the president. On the other hand, leaders are also given credit for favorable policy outcomes, like the original intervention decision. Often such policies originate from the advisory groups surrounding the president. In fact, many of Truman's other notable foreign policy successes, such as the enactment of the Marshall Plan, establishing the Truman Doctrine, and the decision to aid Greece and Turkey, have been attributed to his effective policy leadership. Although such claims represent gross simplifications of the foreign policy process and fail to take into account factors separate from the leader, such as advisory group composition, structure, and the external policy environment, they touch upon a critically important question relevant to group dynamics. Specifically, *what effect do the characteristics of individual leaders have upon the structure and interactional dynamics of their advisory groups, and in turn upon the policy decisions (or outputs) of these groups?*

Why is it that in some cases presidents and advisers work together efficiently as a decision group, seek information, tolerate adviser dissent, and actively consider and debate a number of different policy options, and in other cases they do not? What is it that leads some advisory groups to consider only a narrow range of information or policy options, exclude dissenters, and limit debate to a very small inner circle around the president? In the case of Truman's decision to cross the Thirty-eighth Parallel, why did Truman receive a policy paper from his staff recommending him to cross the parallel which failed to adequately outline opposing views and potential dangers in the action? Why did Truman's NSC group, or the president himself, fail to fully discuss or debate the assumptions within the proposal? And finally, to what extent were the structure and interactional norms of Truman's advisory group, and their subsequent decisional outputs, affected by Truman's own individual characteristics and style preferences?

The central role played by individual leaders in shaping the structural characteristics and dynamics of advisory groups is of critical importance to our efforts to better understand the processes involved in collective political decision making. This "leader–group nexus" represents a multifaceted intersection involving the impact of leader personality and style upon the characteristics of advisory groups at both the structural ("foundational") level and at the process ("interactional") level (cf. Stern and Sundelius, this volume). At the "foundational level" of groups, leader characteristics impact upon the nature of the organizational matrix (i.e., through the creation of initial group structures, selection of members, establishment of formal and informal influence channels for advice). At the "interactional level" of groups, leader characteristics impact upon the internal dynamics of groups (i.e., through the establishment of group decision rules, the types of advice encouraged, tolerance of group conflict, establishment of general norms regarding leader–adviser relationships). Thus, what leaders are like in terms of their personalities, decision making and interpersonal styles, preferred modes of information processing, and their previous policy experience may fundamentally affect both the structure and dynamics of advisory groups, as well as their effectiveness.

U.S. presidential foreign policy decision making is an excellent venue for observing the importance of this "leader–group nexus" on advisory groups. The reason for this is that American presidents face fewer institutional constraints in the realm of foreign policy than they do in domestic policy, where congressional involvement is normally required to make or implement policy decisions. In foreign policy, with the exception of Congress's role in ratifying treaties and declaring war, U.S. presidents usually serve as the chief architects and executors of the nation's policies. Further, the president determines which institutional actors will be invited into the White House "inner circle" (where foreign policy is formulated and decisions taken), whether the NSC or ad hoc groups of White House advisers will be utilized, and who among his staff will participate in the decision groups. Thus, American presidents possess a great deal of discretion over the shape of their advisory systems and control over the internal dynamics within their advisory groups, perhaps more so than in other comparable western societies.

However, it is important to note that this presidential influence over advisory systems takes place within the much broader arena of interactions between the leader–advisory group and the surrounding policy environment. This policy environment involves both: (1) the *policy context* (i.e., the leader's relationship with advisers, outside domestic policy actors, the public, and foreign actors); and (2) the *problem context* (i.e., the substantive characteristics of the policy problem itself, such as the condition of the economy or the military situation on the ground). The universe of potential paths of interaction and feedback from this broader policy environment, illustrated below in figure 7.1, is not a static representation. Instead, it changes across individual presidents with different characteristics and leadership styles, and it changes across time as the "problem context" and "policy context" both alter in response to policy decisions taken by the president and his advisory group. Sometimes the characteristics of the policy environment constrain the actions of presidential advisory groups and force them to take certain decisions. Sometimes presidents and their advisers are not attentive to the policy environment, choose to ignore its implications, or simply misperceive its nature.

Again, the leader–group nexus emerges as the critical variable. The effectiveness of a leader's information gathering system in a particular case is

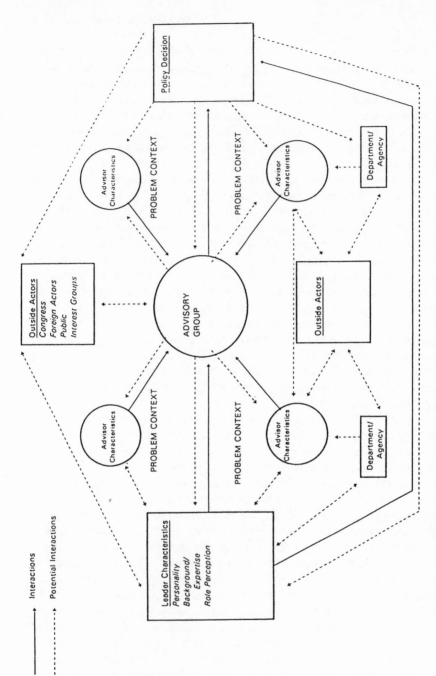

Fig. 7.1. Potential interaction patterns between leaders, groups, and the policy environment

often determined by parameter-setting decisions made by the president regarding the basic organizational structuring of the advisory system itself (i.e., its openness to input from actors outside the executive branch or the thoroughness of procedures within the advisory group for identifying and considering alternative policy perspectives or interpretations). Even if the leader's advisory system is reasonably effective with regard to gathering input from the policy environment, leaders and advisory groups may still misperceive the information or selectively interpret it to fit into preconceived notions. In addition, the degree to which presidents or advisory groups find information salient or attend to it may be affected by whether they are interested in the policy area, have previous experience, or are preoccupied by other matters. Thus, depending upon how sensitive or attentive presidents are to feedback from the environment, the context will have either more or less of an impact upon their policy behavior (cf. Hermann 1986; Hermann and Preston 1994a).

The Foreign Policy Play: Presidential Directors and Advisory Actors

As the director of the foreign policy play, the president works from a script provided by the outside environment (i.e., the policy and problem contexts). Indeed, the surrounding context forms the stage upon which the play will be performed and provides many of the sets, props, and limitations on the size of the productions that can be staged there by the director. Sometimes the president is able to select the foreign policy play to be performed, and sometimes the script is forced upon him by outside producers beyond his control. For example, Lyndon Johnson had the freedom to select his own script in deciding to intervene in Vietnam in 1965, whereas Harry Truman had the script on involvement in Korea essentially forced upon him in June 1950 by the actions of the North, as well as by domestic political forces that severely limited his ability to "turn down" staging the production.

Once selected, each foreign policy script has a set of available roles for actors (advisers to the president) which must be filled by the director. The presidential director "casts" the specific individual actors he feels are "right for the part," often advisers he has confidence in due to their loyalty or past personal relationships with him, the leader's comfort in working with them on an interpersonal level, or their policy expertise. Sometimes the policy environment, or outside producers, may conspire to force the president to "cast," or include, an adviser to his "company" of actors against his wishes, or he may "inherit" the cast of a deceased predecessor's production. However, even in these cases, the president still essentially controls the "rules of the play" regarding which advisers will be more influential, what types of advisory feedback will be accepted, and how much control over the production will be demanded by the presidential director. In this way, "Roosevelt men" were eventually replaced by "Truman men," and "Kennedy men" were replaced by "Johnson men," until the new president had an advisory group he was comfortable with in terms of membership and that provided him with the sort of advice and information required by his own leadership or decision style. Thus, although the context often shapes the nature of the stage, scripts, and actors available to the presidential director, it is the director who makes the final, crucial decisions regarding what use to make of these resources in structuring the foreign policy play.

As a result, the degree to which presidents can "learn" and adapt their advisory systems to a changing policy environment is likely to be related to their sensitivity to the surrounding context. Presidents with a high level of cognitive complexity, such as Eisenhower, Kennedy, and Clinton, are more likely to respond to and change their policy behavior based upon environmental stimuli than are less cognitively complex leaders like Truman, Johnson, or Reagan. Further, since presidents play a major role in structuring and utilizing their advisory systems, leaders who are less sensitive to the environment, and who place less value on diverse information while making decisions, are more likely to set up advisory systems which are less sensitive to the surrounding environmental context.

For example, Truman and Johnson were both very consistent across time with regard to the structure of their advisory systems and their patterns of information gathering in foreign policy decision making, even in the wake of serious policy reverses in Korea and Vietnam. Despite the failure of their advisory systems to adequately provide them with an accurate picture of the policy environment or to warn them of the impending policy setbacks, neither president responded by, or even perceived the need for, adapting their somewhat insular advisory structures to broaden information search and the consideration of alternative perspectives. On the other hand, Kennedy and Clinton, who both favored less structured, ad hoc advisory structures early in their administrations, responded to policy reversals, such as the Bay of Pigs and Somalia, by gradually moving toward more structured, less ad hoc advisory arrangements. In other words, both of these leaders adapted to perceived shortcomings in their advisory systems by altering them to better reflect the policy environment by considering policy information and competing alternatives in a more structured setting (cf. Stern, this volume).

In summary, the degree to which policymakers actually take into account the nature of the policy environment (i.e., policy or problem contexts) is often dependent upon: (1) the cognitive sensitivity, or attentiveness, of leaders to the external environment; (2) the effectiveness of their advisory systems in gathering information from the operational policy environment to inform policy deliberations. As many scholars of American foreign policy have observed, limitations or malfunctions in the information processing or advisory systems of presidents have often resulted in ill-considered or inappropriate policy decisions being taken. These have been based, not upon the "actual realities" of the policy environment, but upon the "faulty perceptions" of that environment held by the decision makers themselves (cf. Sprout and Sprout 1956; Thomson 1968; Janis 1972; George 1980; Berman 1982; Janis 1982; Burke and Greenstein 1989).[1] Given this empirical record, it is important to understand how the characteristics of leaders such as presidents affect the structural and interactional nature of advisory groups during foreign policy decision making.

How Do Leaders Affect Groups?

A leader's personality and preferred leadership style often critically affect how the advisory group is structured, the roles of group members, the nature of debate and information processing within the group, and the quality of the decisions emerging from the group (cf. George 1980, this volume; Greenstein 1982). As Hermann and Preston (1994a) have noted, the style preferences of leaders often set up the "rules of the game" regarding leader–adviser interactions, their characteristics, and the roles advisers will be allowed to perform within the decision process. Further, they provide critical insight regarding how leaders will choose to organize their primary information-processing, advisory, and decision-making structures once in office and the impact such structures will have upon the policy process (cf. Johnson 1974; Hess 1988; Burke and Greenstein 1989).

As Hess (1988) noted in his study of presidential organization in the White House, the management styles selected by presidents change from one administration to the next. They reflect the leader's work habits, the way he likes to receive information, the type of people he prefers to have around him, and the way he makes up his mind or takes decisions (Hess 1988, 188). Similarly, George (1980) observed that presidents are likely to develop distinctive leadership styles shaped to a large degree by preferences developed through previous administrative experience and self-confidence derived from their knowledge and competence of policy matters (George 1980, 147). That presidents tend to play toward their strengths rather than their weaknesses in setting up their policy agendas, or their leadership styles in office, has been noted by many other scholars (cf. George 1980; Cronin 1980; Hess 1988). Indeed, previous policy experience or knowledge is often seen as an important factor in the formation of leader policy preferences (cf. George 1980; Hermann 1986/1988).

A variety of leadership style variables have been identified by the presidential literature as being important to how leaders structure and utilize their advisory systems (see Hermann and Preston 1994a), I shall here focus upon five specific dimensions of leadership style: the *authority-structure, information-management, information-processing, interpersonal,* and *conflictual orientations* of leaders. Although sharing some overlap, and in the aggregate often interacting together in reinforcing or complementary ways, these five dimensions refer to conceptually distinct orientations relevant to improving our understanding of the leader–group relationship.

The first of these dimensions, the leader's *authority structure orientation,* refers to the degree of control over the policy-making process preferred by the leader. For example, if the president wants to ensure that his own policy preferences dominate policy debate and that he controls all final policy decisions, he is likely to prefer a hierarchical system with himself at the apex of the formal chain of command. In this way, the leader can control where policy debate and decision occurs, who participates in the process, and the general "rules of the game" regarding the overall policy process. On the other hand, leaders who need less control over the process tend to prefer a decision-making process based upon consensus or concurrence within advisory groups and a less rigid hierarchical structure for the advisory system. Lyndon Johnson and Richard Nixon are examples of the former type of authority pattern, Dwight Eisenhower and John F. Kennedy of the latter.

The leader's *information management orientation* (cf. Metselaar and Verbeek, this volume) refers to the structural rules preferred by the leader for managing information. If the leader wants information to be tightly controlled and organized, with the details of options debated before they reach his or her desk, a more hierarchical advisory network with gatekeepers might be preferred. On the other hand, if the leader likes to be in on the generation and evaluation of options, the advisory system is more likely to be organized less hierarchically, with the leader operating as the "hub of the information wheel." For example, Nixon preferred to manage information through a formal, hierarchical advisory structure, with Kissinger synthesizing the various options and information generated by different departments or advisers before they reached the Oval Office (cf. George 1980; Hess 1988). This effectively limited information and adviser access to Nixon, reduced the ability of departments to participate in policy debate, and allowed Nixon to avoid political conflict. On the other hand, both Eisenhower and Kennedy preferred to be actively involved in the process of option generation and policy debate, and, as a result, managed information by operating as the "hub of the wheel" in their advisory systems.

These differences in how leaders prefer to manage information basically distinguishes between what the presidential literature has often described as formalistic versus collegial styles (Johnson 1974; George 1980). Thus, in an organizational sense, the leader's information-management orientation relates to the leader's need to be in control of, or "manage," the flow of information and structure of debate within the advisory system. However, it should be noted that this orientation is conceptually distinct from, albeit related to, the next orientation to be discussed, dealing with the leader's need for information and how they use it in a "cognitive sense" in reaching decisions.

The *information-processing orientation* (cf. Metselaar and Verbeek, this volume) of leaders involves their *need for cognition* and preferences regarding the amount and type of information they require for decision-making tasks, and also *the relative emphasis or value placed by these leaders* upon broad information search and openness to competing or divergent information and viewpoints. Unlike the leader's information-management orientation, which focuses purely on preferences for managing or structuring information flows within the advisory system in an "organizational sense," the information-processing orientation relates to the cognitive needs and preferences of leaders themselves for information during the decision-making process within group contexts. Does the leader seek only information which confirms his or her own views or those of the advisory group, or is there an active search for contradictory information or alternative policy options? Further, does the leader recognize complexity in the environment and the need to gather detailed information from a variety of sources, or is the world viewed in absolute, black-and-white terms which limit the need for information search? For example, both Reagan and Truman viewed the world in absolute terms and utilized simplistic stereotypes or analogies to understand ongoing events (Glad 1983; Donovan 1977). As a result, each was more willing to make decisions based on limited information search or policy debate. On the other hand, presidents with a more complex view of the environment, like Eisenhower, Kennedy, or Clinton, tend to place greater emphasis on broad information search, the generation of competing options, and open policy debate within their advisory systems.

The *interpersonal orientation* of leaders refers to the emphasis of and preferences regarding social interactions with advisers and groups. A leader's interpersonal orientation includes their need for affiliation and their relative emphasis upon adviser, group, or constituent needs as opposed to task accomplishment considerations. Further, it also involves the leader's preferences regarding interpersonal interactions with others. As Stogdill and Bass (1981) have observed, "individuals differ in preference and ability to initiate and sustain interactions with other persons . . . some individuals are more comfortable in a face-to-face situation, small informal group, or large gathering/audience" (Stogdill and Bass 1981, 101). Further, when individuals are uncomfortable with particular types of interpersonal interactions, these stressful or unpleasant types of interactions are avoided whenever possible (ibid.,

101). As a result, by understanding a president's interpersonal preferences, we gain a greater understanding of how they are likely to organize their advisory structures and interact with advisers during the decision-making process.

For example, Lyndon Johnson was most comfortable interacting one-on-one with advisers or in very small groups, where the "Johnson Treatment" could be administered to greatest effect. As a result, Johnson tended to take advice and make decisions in small groups of close advisers, such as the "Tuesday Lunch" group, or directly with individual advisers. On the other hand, Dwight Eisenhower, perhaps as a result of his experiences with the Army staff system, enjoyed interacting with larger groups and was comfortable in such settings. Predictably, Eisenhower's advisory system emphasized larger group meetings within the National Security Council, as well as considerable interaction with other staff groups, during the formulation and implementation of policy decisions. Instead of the Johnson emphasis on dominating social interactions, Eisenhower emphasized staff teamwork and greater equality of social interactions. Thus, the leadership style of presidents sets down the "rules of the game" for leader–adviser task group interactions and allows the leader to structure the advisory environment so as to avoid interpersonal interactions which are stressful or unpleasant to that particular individual.

Closely related to a leader's interpersonal orientation, the *conflictual orientation* addresses what George (1980) described as the leader's tolerance or acceptance of political conflict within advisory groups (i.e., the degree to which the president is able to tolerate face-to-face disagreements and confrontations among advisers or close associates). Richard Nixon was uncomfortable in an environment characterized by political infighting, open conflict, and aggressive advocacy between advisers, and he was unlikely to favor the sort of competitive organizational style employed by Franklin Roosevelt, who encouraged these kinds of group interactions. Instead, Nixon put into place an advisory system characterized by rigid hierarchy, centralization of policy debate and decision making within the White House, and the use of "gatekeepers," such as Henry Kissinger, to eliminate such conflict before it reached him (cf. George 1980).

Obviously, the president's orientation to conflict within an advisory system could lead to serious information-processing or policy outcome ramifications, since divergent viewpoints and broad information search may be avoided if a leader's tolerance of conflict is low. For example, advisers who know that the president takes criticism of his policy proposals personally or tends to react negatively toward advisers who strongly oppose positions taken within the group are unlikely to risk alienating the leader or being expelled from the group by engaging in conflictual interactions. On the other hand, leaders with a higher tolerance of conflict in groups, like Eisenhower and Kennedy, accepted adviser dissent and were sensitive to the need for divergent

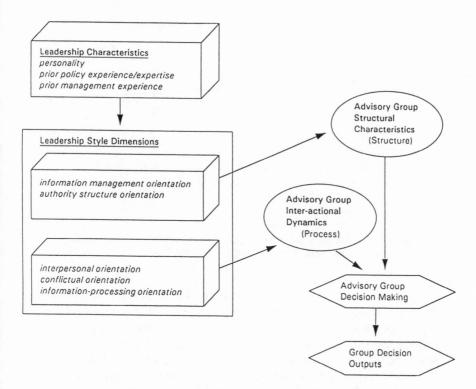

Fig. 7.2. Leader impact upon advisory group structure and interactions

viewpoints. As a result, their advisers were much more confident of voicing concerns or reservations regarding policy and provided more critical evaluation of and debate over policy options during the decision-making process. In addition, the leader's orientation to conflict helps to define the degree of loyalty that will be expected from advisers, as well as the type of role advisers will perform (i.e., active policy advocate, sounding board, policy implementor, or consensus-builder) within the administration.

As illustrated in figure 7.2, these five leadership style dimensions impact upon groups at either the structural or process levels. Specifically, the authority-structure and information-management orientations of leaders are seen to most directly impact upon the "foundational" (or structural) level of groups; whereas the information-processing, interpersonal, and conflictual orientations of leaders more directly affect the "interactional" (or process) level of groups.

This essentially reflects a relationship between leadership style variables

Authority Pattern

		Formal	Informal
	Focus on Political Process	The Chief Executive Officer (Truman and Nixon)	The Team-Builder and -Player (Johnson, Ford, and Carter)
Focus of Policy Coordination			
	Focus on Substance of Problem	The Director/ Ideologue (Reagan and Wilson)	The Analyst/ Innovator (Franklin Roosevelt and Clinton)

Fig. 7.3. Typology of presidential patterns of authority and policy co-ordination. (Data from Hermann and Preston 1994b.)

and groups proposed earlier in Hermann and Preston 1994a, which noted differences between individual presidents regarding the degree of control they desire over the policy-making process and how they prefer to coordinate their advisers. The two types of authority patterns and the two ways of coordinating policy proposed create a four-fold typology of advisory systems based on the president's leadership style (see figure 7.3). These types of leadership styles are described in more detail in Hermann and Preston 1994b.

Each combination of authority pattern and focus of policy coordination suggests different presidential roles within the policy process (i.e., Chief Executive Officer, the Team-Builder and -Player, the Director/Ideologue, and the Analyst/Innovator). Further, these differing leader styles are suggestive of the kinds of advisers which presidents are likely to select and the nature of the relations they are likely to develop with these advisers (see figure 7.4).[2]

As noted in figure 7.3, presidents differ with regard to "authority-pattern," or the degree of control they desire over the policy-making process and in how they prefer to manage information within the advisory group. Leaders who want to make the final decisions and ensure that their preferences prevail within the policy process are likely to organize authority into a hierarchical system characterized by a formal chain of command. On the other hand, leaders more comfortable with decisions made by consensus or concurrence tend to employ a loose hierarchical system that facilitates the president's building of a consensus. In many cases, leaders in loose hierarchical systems become information managers by putting themselves at the hub of the communications network, thereby having some control over who gets what infor-

Authority Pattern

		Formal	Informal
	Focus on Political Process	Advisers used as sounding board. Procedures well-defined & highly structured; Interested in focusing on important decisions; Interested in evaluating rather than generating options; Leader-dominated groupthink possible; Loyalty to leader important	Advisers seen as part of team; Procedures often ad-hoc & less rigidly structured; Sharing of accountability; Group cohesion is valued; Advisers provide psychological support; Options sought that minimize conflict & disagreement Loyalty to group positions important
Focus of Policy Coordination	Focus on Substance of Problem	Selects advisers who share cause/concern/ ideology; Advisers seen as loyal advocates & implementors of cause; Advisers tailor information to fit biases; One or two advisers play gatekeeper roles for information & access; Decisions shaped by shared vision; Disagreements center on means rather than ends	Wants experts as advisers; Advisers seen as providing information & guidance; Open to using bureaucracy to get information; Time spent on generating options & considering consequences; Seeks "doable" solution to problem; Disagreement is valued & may center on both means and ends

Fig. 7.4.   The influence of presidential leadership style on advisory selection and organization. (Data from Hermann and Preston 1994b.)

mation, as well as direct knowledge regarding what others know. Who participates in decision making and how structured the process is varies with the situation and problem. Although the president is still on top, he has chosen to involve others directly in decision making and to use informal channels of authority.

Burke and Greenstein (1989), in their examination of Eisenhower and Johnson's decisions on Vietnam, noted that differences between these two leaders along these lines influenced the ways in which their advisory groups were structured and how decisions were taken. Eisenhower utilized essentially

a formal system of authority in which there were rules, routines, and procedures by which policy choices were defined, discussed, and selected. Those
involved in the process understood and worked by these rules. Differences
between advisers were not "papered-over," but were actively discussed within
the NSC and officially recorded on policy papers. The system was organized
to present Eisenhower with well-thought-out problems and options for his
decision. On the other hand, Johnson utilized a more informal system of
authority which lacked the formal structuring of information and advice found
in the Eisenhower system. For Johnson, there were no explicit operating rules
and procedures. Although Johnson was a voracious consumer of information
and was constantly communicating with advisers, former colleagues in the
Senate, or friends, the information was not managed in a structured fashion.[3]
As a result, information supportive of his views was more plentiful than that
which contradicted them within his advisory system, and opposing perspectives were not generally heard. Essentially, advisers had access because of
who they were and their position on the war.

Along the other axis of figure 7.3, the "focus of coordination" in the
White House seems to take one of two forms—either a focus on concurrence
among relevant advisers or a focus on accomplishing a task (Hermann and
Preston 1994a, 84). According to the group dynamics literature, leaders play
two major functions in groups—either facilitating group interaction, participation, and satisfaction, or helping the group work through a task (e.g., Bass
1985; McGrath 1984; Stogdill 1974).[4] Burke and Greenstein (1989) differentiate between two aspects of political reality testing—"the political component of selling policies and mustering the support necessary to win approval
and the substantive component of devising and analyzing policies and the
means of implementing them" (Burke and Greenstein 1989, 290). For example, Eisenhower was predisposed toward tackling the problem, which
meant a focus on substantive and policy analysis; whereas Johnson was predisposed toward the process, which meant a focus on the political and building
support. Burke and Greenstein observed that each president was more comfortable dealing with one focus over the other and subsequently tended to
shape their advisory systems to reflect this difference.

Three specific leadership style dimensions seem directly relevant to this
notion of "focus of coordination": the leader's interpersonal, conflictual, and
information-processing orientations. A president's "interpersonal orientation"
(his emphasis upon group/adviser needs versus task considerations, and preferences regarding interpersonal interactions with others) is suggestive of the
way a leader is likely to want to coordinate policy. For example, a president
uncomfortable interacting in large groups (like the NSC) is more likely to
prefer smaller advisory groups or individual advisers when gathering advice

or making decisions, and vice versa. Similarly, those interested in task accomplishment over interpersonal considerations (such as group cohesion) will likely emphasize group interactions that focus upon the substantive details of policy; whereas a more interpersonally oriented president might emphasize group teamwork and political considerations (such as adviser or constituent needs) over substantive policy issues.

Similarly, a leader's "conflictual orientation" (tolerance of direct conflict or disagreement in interactions with others) impacts upon whether advisory group processes will allow competitive advocacy and full policy debate, or whether group interactions will emphasize loyalty to leader preferences or group consensus/cohesion. Further, the leader's "information-processing orientation" impacts upon group process by helping to determine the relative value placed by the leader upon broad information search, generation of competing policy options/perspectives, and the critical consideration of diverse information and alternatives within the advisory group. Clearly, these three dimensions have a substantial impact upon how leaders coordinate their advisory groups within the policy process.

Leaders and Foreign Policy Advisory Groups

Leaders and Group Structure

The structural characteristics of advisory groups are fundamentally affected by the authority-structure and information-management orientations of individual presidents. In fact, much of the existing literature on presidential leadership style focuses upon how presidents structure their relationships with close advisers, staffers, and associates, and upon the effects of differing types of management styles and modes of information management on the functioning of presidential advisory groups (Johnson 1974; George 1980; Porter 1980; Pika 1988; Burke and Greenstein 1989). For example, Johnson's (1974) and Porter's (1980) well-known management style typologies focus primarily upon the basic organizational and information-management structures of presidential advisory systems. Other scholars have emphasized the degree to which presidents do business personally or through institutionalized routines, the proactive versus reactive nature of their policy-making, or the degree to which they believe the executive branch bureaucracy will faithfully implement their decisions and programs (C. Campbell 1986; Crabb and Mulcahy 1988; Smith 1988). A more detailed discussion of these leadership style variables found in the presidential literature, and their hypothesized impact upon advisory group structures and processes, is found in Hermann and Preston 1994a.

A few illustrations should underscore how these variables impact upon the authority-structure and information-management characteristics of advisory groups. For example, how "hands-on" a president is often determines the degree to which he will tend to conduct policy business personally, like Lyndon Johnson serving as his own desk officer during the Dominican Crisis or determining the location of air strikes in Vietnam (Kearns 1976; Burke and Greenstein 1989). On the other hand, the more presidents prefer to delegate the details of policy implementation to others, or to have the substantive elements of policy options resolved by staff in advance, like Ronald Reagan, the more they are likely to work through institutionalized routines (Glad 1983; Smith 1988; Talbott 1984).

Presidents like Kennedy, who trust the surrounding executive branch bureaucracy to faithfully implement their policy decisions, often prefer less hierarchical control over the policy process, consider more recommendations originating from inside those agencies, and are more likely to utilize interagency commissions and task forces. On the other hand, presidents like Nixon, who lack such confidence in the bureaucracy, often centralize authority within the White House under trusted aides in order to end-run their opponents (George 1980; Hess 1988; Smith 1988). A consequence of this information-management style is that the more advice and decision making are centralized within the White House, the greater becomes the loss of information, expertise, and competing policy perspectives to the advisory groups. Such information processing malfunctions have been argued to have serious implications for both organizations and groups in terms of decision quality. They are particularly dangerous for presidential advisory groups, where serious policy consequences can result from the poor management of information (see Wilensky 1967; Downs 1967; Kaufman 1971; Janis and Mann 1977; George 1980).

The psychological literature suggests that individual characteristics of leaders, such as the need for power, prior managerial background, self-confidence, and locus of control, should have an effect upon the "authority-structure" or "information-management" orientations of presidents. The need for power or dominance is a personality characteristic that has been extensively studied in the psychological literature and linked to specific types of behavior and interactional styles with others (Donley and Winter 1970; Winter 1973; Winter and Stewart 1977; Etheredge 1978; Hermann 1980, 1987; McClelland 1987; House 1990). Specifically, one would expect leaders with progressively higher needs for power to be increasingly dominant and assertive in their leadership styles in office and to assert greater control or dominance over subordinates and policy decisions (Adorno et al. 1950; White and Lippitt 1960; Winter 1973, 1987; Burns 1978; Etheredge 1978; Hermann 1980, 1987).[5]

The prior experience or expertise of leaders has also been argued to have a significant impact upon the nature of their group interactions and how forcefully they will assert their own positions on policy issues (George 1980; Hermann 1986; House 1990).[6] For example, Hermann (1986) argues that past experience provides leaders with a sense of what actions will be effective or ineffective in specific policy situations, as well as which cues from the environment should be attended to and which are irrelevant (Hermann 1986, 178). Further, it influences how much learning must be accomplished on the job, the inventory of behaviors (standard operating procedures) possessed, and how confident the leader will be in interactions with experts (ibid.).

Self-confidence also affects how leaders structure their interactions with their advisory groups (Hermann 1987, 15). Vertzberger (1990), for instance, has argued that self-esteem leads to greater openness on the part of individuals to the absorption of new information because they feel more confident of their ability to deal with it. However, high self-esteem can also have the negative effect on leaders of breeding overconfidence that their beliefs and theories are correct, even in the presence of dissonant information (Vertzberger 1990, 173). Further, individuals with a lower self-confidence tend to be more open to persuasion and to changing their positions in the face of new information (ibid.). Thus, lower self-confidence works to prevent overconfidence on the part of the decision maker, leaving them more receptive to the advice of experts.[7]

Finally, the locus-of-control beliefs of leaders have significant implications for information management style and the structuring of advisory groups. For example, the works of Rotter (1966), as well as Davis and Phares (1967), suggest that individuals with an external locus of control (i.e., the belief that events are fundamentally beyond the ability of the individual to influence or control) tend to place lower value upon information in general because of its perceived lack of utility in allowing for some control over policy situations, foreign events, or the behavior of other policy actors (Rotter 1966; Davis and Phares 1967). Thus, externals would tend to be less attentive to the environment, require less information for decision making, and prefer a simplified advisory structure that would generate specific options telling them how to deal with the situation. On the other hand, individuals with an internal locus of control (i.e., the belief that events are within the ability of the individual to influence or control) tend to place greater value upon information in general because it is seen to have utility in assisting the individual to have influence over or control policy situations, foreign events, or the behavior of other policy actors. Thus, internal locus of control leaders would tend to be more attentive to information from the policy environment and to favor advisory systems that provide a broad range of information and options for consideration during policy-making.

Leaders and Group Processes

The interactional characteristics of advisory groups are fundamentally affected by the information-processing, interpersonal, and conflictual orientations of individual presidents. Some presidents tolerate conflict or dissent better than others, some focus more upon accomplishing specific policy tasks than upon the needs of constituents or followers, and some require greater amounts and more varied types of information than others to reach decisions. These individual differences create important nuances in presidential leadership style and impact upon group interactional dynamics. Supporting this view, the psychological literature suggests that the individual characteristics of leaders, such as the need for affiliation, task versus interpersonal focus, and cognitive complexity, can affect leader preferences for different kinds of interactions with groups for policy-making purposes.

Information Processing
In terms of the information-processing orientation of leaders, the cognitive complexity of decision makers has long been thought to have a significant impact upon the nature of decision making, style of leadership, assessment of risk, and character of general information processing within decision groups (cf. Stewart, Hermann, and Hermann 1977; Tetlock 1985b; Hermann 1987). Vertzberger (1990), among others, has noted that as the cognitive complexity of individual decision makers rises, they become more capable of dealing with a complex decision environment and information that demands new or more subtle distinctions (Vertzberger 1990, 134; Scott 1963; Bieri 1966; Suedfeld and Rank 1976; Suedfeld and Tetlock 1977). Cognitively complex individuals tend to be higher in need for cognition, are more attentive to relevant incoming information, prefer systematic over heuristic processing, and deal with information overload better than their less cognitively complex counterparts (Vertzberger 1990, 134; cf. Schroder, Driver, and Streufert 1967; Nydegger 1975). Further, in terms of interactions with advisers and acceptance of feedback, several studies have also shown that more complex individuals tend to be more interested in and incorporate into their decision making both positive and negative feedback from others more easily than less complex individuals (Hermann 1984, 64; cf. Nydegger 1975; Ziller et al. 1977).

As Hermann (1984) has observed, the more complex or sensitive the individual is to information from the decision environment, the more receptive the leader is to information regarding the views of colleagues or constituents, the views of outside actors, and the value of alternative viewpoints and discrepant information. On the other hand, leaders with a low sensitivity to contextual information will be less receptive to information from the outside environment, will operate from a previously established and strongly held set of views on the environment, will selectively perceive and process incoming information in order to support or bolster this prior framework, and will be unreceptive or closed-minded toward alternative viewpoints and discrepant information (Hermann 1984, 54–64). Similarly, Vertzberger (1990) and Glad (1983) have noted that individuals characterized by low complexity tend to evidence symptoms of dogmatism, view and judge issues in black-and-white terms, ignore information threatening to their existing closed belief systems, seek belief system–confirming information, and have a limited ability to adjust their beliefs to new information (Vertzberger 1990, 173; Glad 1983, 38; cf. Rokeach 1954; Kleck and Wheaton 1967; Hermann 1984). In terms of its impact upon a leader's advisory structures, cognitively simple leaders appoint advisers into their inner circle of foreign policy advisers who are "like-minded" and agree with "all the highest foreign policy positions within the administration" (Glad 1983, 71).

Interpersonal Relations
However, the cognitive complexity of individuals not only affects a leader's information processing orientation, but also the character of his or her inter-personal orientation. In the same way that some individuals tend to be more sensitive than others to the information environment, some individuals tend to have a greater sensitivity to the interpersonal environment than others. Self-monitoring theory suggests that there are two characteristic interpersonal ori-entations (high and low self-monitoring) and that "high self-monitors" are more sensitive and attuned to the nuances of the interpersonal environment than are less sensitive, "low self-monitors" (Snyder 1987, 33; cf. Jones and Baumeister 1976). In terms of leadership styles, one would expect high self-monitors to be more sensitive to the political situation (the views of constitu-ents, political allies, and opponents, the political climate, etc.), to actively seek this information on the political situation from advisers, and be "chameleon-like" in modifying their own behavior and policy decisions to conform to the existing environment. On the other hand, low self-monitors would be ex-pected to place much less emphasis upon the political situation with regard to their own behavior or their policy positions, passively receive information on the political situation from advisers, and be driven more by their own views and beliefs regarding policy rather than by a desire to conform to the existing political environment. To illustrate using American presidents, if measures of complexity can also be linked to the notion of self-monitoring, Bill Clinton would be expected to evidence a leadership style characterized by high self-monitoring, and Truman one typified by low self-monitoring.[8]

In terms of interpersonal orientation, several individual characteristics have been suggested to affect leadership style. For example, Winter and Stewart (1977) have noted that presidents high in the need for affiliation tend to surround themselves with advisers who are selected on the basis of perceived similarity rather than on the basis of expert knowledge or political sensitivity. Highly affiliative presidents tend to be readily influenced by these advisers and show a high degree of loyalty to them. As a result, it is argued that leaders with a high affiliation motive will receive relatively low-quality advice and possess an ineffective information processing system, leading to poor policy performance (Winter and Stewart 1977, 44–61). In addition, it has been observed that inspiring and interpersonally effective presidents, such as Franklin Roosevelt and Lyndon Johnson, are characterized by a low affiliation motive and high achievement and power motives (ibid., 52–61). A possible explanation for this is found in Browning and Jacob (1964), who note that individuals high in the need for affiliation tend to seek approval more often than others and are overcautious, dependent on others for decisions, and rated as relatively unpopular by their peers (Browning and Jacob 1964). In other words, affiliation is not the same thing as sociability or liking to be with people. High affiliation needs can create anxieties that manifest themselves in behaviors that are not usually admired or liked (approval seeking, excessive caution, vacillation, etc.) and politicians particularly effective on an interpersonal level would not be expected to be high in affiliation motive (Browning and Jacob 1964; McClelland 1975; McClelland and Burnham 1976; McClelland and Boyatzis 1982; Winter 1987).

Another individual characteristic directly relevant to the *interpersonal orientation* of leaders is their relative focus upon either task accomplishment or interpersonal considerations during group decision making (cf. Stogdill and Bass 1981; Nutt 1986; Winter et al. 1991). Task orientation is defined by Hermann (1987) as the "relative emphasis in interactions with others on getting the task done as opposed to focusing on the feelings and needs of others." For example, substantively oriented (high task) leaders focus first upon problem definition, examination of problem/policy specifics, the generation of policy options and alternatives, and questions of task accomplishment or implementation. These substantive concerns override considerations of more process-oriented factors, such as maintaining harmony and group cohesion, pleasing constituents, or playing politics (Winter et al. 1991, 222). On the other hand, process-oriented leaders focus more upon interpersonal relations or political considerations than upon substantive policy matters or task accomplishment.[9] The maintenance of harmony and consensus among followers, as well as the establishment of good personal relations with other policy actors, is valued much more highly by such leaders than is accomplishing policy tasks or setting out an elaborate agenda.

Conflict

The conflictual orientation of leaders impacts upon the internal dynamics of groups by influencing the degree to which advisers are able to dissent from or challenge policy positions favored by the leader or the group without risking punishment by or exclusion from the group. Further, it also influences the degree to which leaders will seek to avoid political conflict in the wider policy environment, either between themselves and their advisers, or with outside constituents, allies, and political opponents (George 1980; Hermann and Preston 1994a). Although discussed primarily in terms of its impact upon the internal dynamics (interactions) of groups, the conflictual orientation of leaders also bears some relationship to the information-management orientation discussed earlier involving group structure. The reason for this is that leaders who are characterized by a low tolerance of political conflict within their interpersonal environments are likely not only to consider information and interact with advisers in ways that minimize conflict within their advisory groups, but they also structure their advisory systems in ways to minimize conflict as well. Thus, depending upon the leader's tolerance of conflict, his or her advisory system will be structured to allow varying degrees of access, by advisers and information, to their inner policy circles in order to control (or manage) conflict. In this sense, the conflictual orientations of leaders reinforce their information-management orientations.[10]

However, from the standpoint of internal group dynamics, the leader's conflictual orientation is critically important because all individuals vary in the degree to which they can tolerate open conflict in their interpersonal environments, whether directed at themselves or among their close advisers and associates. As a result, leaders who dislike open debate or face-to-face disagreements among advisers are likely to favor leadership styles which shield or limit their direct exposure to such conflicts through emphasis upon teamwork or formal analytical procedures in lieu of partisan advocacy and debate (George 1980, 148; Stogdill and Bass 1981). Several individual characteristics could be argued to play a role in shaping a leader's conflictual orientation. Leaders with lower needs for power (defined in terms of the need to dominate and control their decision and personal interactional environments) would be expected to tolerate more ambiguity or conflict among advisers in their inner decision circles than leaders with a high need for power and control. Similarly, leaders with higher complexity would be expected to appreciate the value and need of vigorous debate and opposing points of view during the formulation of policy, and to tolerate conflict within their advisory groups much more than lower-complexity leaders. In terms of advisory group structure, low-tolerance leaders would be expected to prefer strict hierarchical advisory organizations, emphasize personal control, and discourage adviser participation in direct advocacy or open dissent with leader/group policy preferences. On the other hand, high-tolerance leaders would prefer less hierarchical, more informal structures; value partisan advocacy and debate within advisory groups; and allow more open information processing (Hermann and Preston 1994a, 75–95; Johnson 1974; George 1980).

Further, the leader's preferred strategies (or decision rules) for resolving conflict within decision groups (i.e., leader preferences, unanimity/consensus, or majority rule) also influence the nature of the internal dynamics of groups (cf. Kotter and Lawrence 1974; Hermann 1987). Such strategies for resolving conflict are part of a leader's conflictual orientation and influence how advisers are chosen and the way in which the decision-making process within the group operates. Leaders preferring to focus on ensuring their own preferences would be expected to create strictly hierarchical advisory/decision-making structures, discourage active advocacy by advisers or challenges to leader views, and emphasize selection of "like-minded" or loyal advisers to play primarily an implementing role in policy-making. In this way, the leader is able to maintain maximum control over policy and limit the degree to which advisers affect policy decision or debate. On the other hand, a consensus-building strategy requires leaders to provide a less hierarchical environment, allowing advocacy and negotiation/bargaining by advisers within the advisory system in order to build "agreed upon" group decisions, while not alienating colleagues or constituents. Further, since a consensus-building strategy is directed toward developing the "best" policy solution based upon a broad review of relevant information and opinions, it requires leader tolerance of divergent views and conflict between advisers.

Leadership and Advisory Group Dynamics under Truman

Before discussing the leadership style of Harry S. Truman and his structuring and use of advisory groups during the Korean War, it is necessary to briefly note the results of some initial measurements of Truman's individual characteristics and the kinds of impact we might expect from them based upon the above literature.[11] In terms of factors affecting a leader's authority-structure and information-management orientations (i.e., group structure), we find that Truman has a higher than average need for power (or control) and lower than average level of self-confidence (efficacy). Further, Truman scores low in terms of foreign policy experience or expertise, especially compared to Eisenhower or Bush. Thus, one would anticipate Truman to prefer more formal or hierarchical advisory arrangements that ensure his direct involvement and control over the policy process. In addition, one might also expect the advisory system to emphasize managing information through the use of

TABLE 7.1. Hypothesized Impact of Truman's Personal Characteristics and Leadership Style Orientations upon Advisory Group Structure and Process

Leader Characteristic	Hypothesized Preferences for Advisory Structure and Process
High need for power	Authority-Structure • Preference for formal, hierarchical structuring of advisory system • Preference for direct personal control over policy decisions Information-Management • Preference for direct personal control over discussion and debate of policy within advisory group Interpersonal • Preference for assertive interpersonal style Conflictual • Low tolerance of conflictual interactions and dissent within advisory system
Low need for affiliation	Interpersonal • Preference for assertive interpersonal style within advisory group • Emphasis by leader during policy process upon substantive or political considerations over the needs and concerns of advisers • Leader more effective/popular on interpersonal level with advisers
Low self-confidence	Authority-Structure • Delegation of policy formulation and decision to advisers Information-Processing • Leader more open to information and advisory input
External locus of control (i.e., low belief in ability to control events)	Information-Processing • Preference for reactive rather than proactive policy making
High ethnocentrism	Information-Processing • Closed information processing pattern with regard to data on outside actors/groups • Lack of sensitivity toward information about nature/needs of other nations/groups
Low expertise (policy experience)	Authority-Structure • Preference for less direct personal control over policy decisions • Preference for less personal involvement in policy formulation tasks and substantial use of delegation Information-Processing • Relatively open to advisory input (higher emphasis upon use of expert advisers and upon policy debate)
Low cognitive complexity	Information-Management • Closed information-processing system characterized by limited search and few access channels Information-Processing • Low sensitivity to the policy and problem context

(continued)

TABLE 7.1. *(Continued)*

Leader Characteristic	Hypothesized Preferences for Advisory Structure and Process
	• Low sensitivity to multiple policy dimensions/perspectives
	• Decisive, less deliberative decision style
	Conflictual
	• Low tolerance of conflictual interactions and dissent within advisory system

expert advisers who can offset his lack of expertise and self-confidence, perhaps manifesting itself in a willingness to delegate policy formulation to experts or staff.

In terms of factors affecting a leader's information-processing, interpersonal, and conflictual orientations (i.e., group process), Truman's scores on cognitive complexity and need for affiliation are far lower than average and considerably lower than the scores of Eisenhower, Kennedy, or Johnson. As a result, one might expect Truman to be a low self-monitor, generally process information in simple, black-and-white terms, utilize stereotypes and enemy images frequently, and not actively seek out alternative perspectives or disconfirming information. Further, one could expect decisive decision making, since seeing the world and processing information in absolute terms make decisions much clearer and easier to formulate for the individual. In addition, a low tolerance of conflict within the advisory group and interpersonally would likely be indicated, as would an emphasis upon group task accomplishment given Truman's average score on task orientation and his low need for affiliation.[12]

Table 7.1 summarizes Truman's scores on a series of individual characteristics suggested by the literature to be relevant to the five leadership style orientations discussed earlier. Also presented are the hypothesized effects that these individual characteristics should have upon both the structure of Truman's advisory groups and the nature of their group interactions during decision making across two Korean War policy cases: the June 1950 decision to intervene in Korea and the September 1950 decision to cross the Thirty-eighth Parallel. These case studies are based upon in-depth archival research of documents collected at the Truman Library, as well as from the diaries, memoirs, oral histories, and interviews conducted with close associates of President Truman who served as policy advisers during his administration.[13] Across both policy cases below, the archival record will be examined to determine whether observable evidence of the predicted patterns of advisory group structure and interaction in the Truman administration (see table 7.1) existed that support the hypotheses linking leader characteristics and groups.

Group Structure

The archival record appears to support the prediction of a fairly formal, hierarchically organized advisory system characterized by advice and information being centralized around an inner circle of White House advisers. In addition, as was predicted given Truman's lack of foreign policy expertise and low self-confidence, a consistent pattern of delegation regarding the formulation of policy specifics emerges within that circle. The structure of information management and pattern of authority within the advisory system involved the presidential control over all final policy decisions, while allowing his expert advisers, departmental heads, or their immediate staffs to formulate both policy specifics and most recommendations regarding policy options. As a result of this willingness to delegate some authority over policy formulation to advisers, Truman's essentially formal, hierarchical advisory system had some characteristics of an informal, more loosely organized system with greater adviser participation. However, the overall pattern remains one of a fairly formal, hierarchical pattern of authority with centralized information-management structures.

Upon becoming President with the death of Roosevelt in April 1945, Truman, who had strongly disliked his predecessor's manner of organizing his advisory system, decided that his own advisory group would move away from a competitive model emphasizing conflict and address policy in a more formal, structured way.[14] Recognizing his own inexperience and lack of expertise in foreign affairs, Truman decided to select expert advisers who could provide him with policy recommendations and advice. Essentially, Truman believed that as long as his advisers followed his general policy guidelines and referred key policy decisions to him, each should be given discretion to operate independently with minimal interference.

As a result, Truman's structuring and use of his advisory system has often been described by his former advisers as being quite informal in nature, at least in terms of the interactions between the president and his advisers during policy meetings. Although Truman instituted orderly procedures for dealing with policy deliberations and used formal venues for policy discussions, and although some staff members were more influential than others, there was no set staff hierarchy in the administration and senior advisers reported directly to Truman (Donovan 1982, 269–70). George Elsey, who was administrative assistant to the president, recalls that the Truman administration never was a "static institution" with a table of organization and precise duties, but instead varied from year to year.[15] Truman actively used formal cabinet meetings and weekly cabinet luncheons as a forum for receiving advice, hearing alternative viewpoints, and shaping policy decisions (Donovan 1982, 21). In addition, Truman instituted an orderly procedure into his decision-making process by having all the departments or agencies affected by any policy decisions to be taken by his advisory group on a specific issue present at the policy meeting so that they could be heard and their concerns taken into account by the decision group (Acheson 1969, 733). Thus, Truman's simple procedure of ensuring representation of departments and agencies affected by a particular policy served to provide him with more information with which to make decisions. Further, Truman also acted as his own chief of staff, chaired morning staff meetings, issued directions and assignments to advisers, and reserved major policy decisions for himself (Donovan 1982, 22–23).

At the same time, Truman remained fully accessible to his staff and allowed cabinet officers full responsibility over their own departments without presidential interference. According to White House Appointments Secretary Matthew Connelly, when Truman appointed any cabinet member, he would tell them, "This is your job, you're not going to have any interference; you run it, period. You can pick your own people."[16] As Secretary of State Dean Acheson later remarked, "President Truman's strength lay not only in knowing that he was the President and that the buck stopped with him, but that neither he nor the White House staff was the Secretary of State, or Defense, or Treasury, or any other . . . he made the ultimate decisions upon full and detailed knowledge, leaving to lieutenants the execution" (Acheson 1969, 733). Thus, each cabinet member was responsible for his own department, and whatever information, advice, or policy recommendations that reached the president from that department came exclusively through that cabinet member.[17]

The president's daily morning staff meetings were highly informal, with advisers seated in a large semicircle around the president's desk and "free to chime in if they had anything that they thought would be helpful or useful to the President in connection with that meeting."[18] Truman would usually ask each adviser in turn whether there was anything on his mind or anything which should be taken up by the group as a whole, and often staff members would ask to meet with the president after the meeting instead of bothering the whole group.[19] Elsey describes the atmosphere in these meetings as very friendly and relaxed, with even junior members having the right to take matters directly to the president in the presence of everybody else.[20] In fact, Truman had many private sessions with individual advisers during the course of a day, sometimes initiated by him and sometimes by the staffers, to discuss assignments or policy developments.[21] Advisers had complete access to Truman whenever they wanted to see him and were never denied an appointment, though Connelly would sometimes have to schedule the appointment for the next day due to the president's other commitments.[22]

Cabinet meetings, on the other hand, were formal, stereotyped affairs that provided Truman the chance to keep everybody in tune with the issues of the various departments, allowed cabinet officers to bring issues to his attention that needed his direction, and provided a venue to discuss the status of particular battles on Capitol Hill.[23] If an issue required debating at great length or a serious analysis of various policy options, Truman would meet with that cabinet officer outside of cabinet in a smaller group comprised of Truman, his Special Counsel, and the cabinet officer and his staff.[24] As Clark Clifford observed, Truman "did not use his Cabinet as a board of directors" with regards to policy decisions, which he reserved for himself, but as a source of opinions on policy which were under consideration.[25] As former Special Counsel Charles Murphy noted, Truman did not regard cabinet meetings as a place where decisions were made or policies were discussed at any depth.[26]

Regarding the circle of advisers who were most influential with Truman on foreign policy matters, Truman maintained his pattern from domestic policy matters and emphasized only those close advisers who had departmental responsibility for facets of the foreign policy problem at hand. According to Elsey, there were no experts on foreign affairs on the White House staff and Truman looked to the secretary of state, secretary of defense, and the Joint Chiefs of Staff for recommendations, advice, and information when he needed to formulate foreign policy decisions.[27] As Elsey noted, "no one on the Truman White House staff was the person who was *the* principal adviser on *any* one of the policy areas," because Truman looked to his cabinet officers and agency heads for advice on substantive areas that fell within their departmental portfolio.[28] However, that being said, Truman had such respect for the expertise of Acheson and Marshall that they clearly were more influential than other advisers on foreign policy matters.[29]

Thus, in terms of foreign policy, because Truman lacked substantive foreign policy expertise, he developed a pattern throughout his administration of depending upon his secretary of state to formulate U.S. foreign policy and to provide direction regarding which policy approaches should be authorized by the president. For example, although the relationship between the two men was strained, Truman allowed James Byrnes, his first secretary of state, to essentially run U.S. policy toward Germany in 1946 (Donovan 1982, 250). Similarly, Truman's relationships with his next two secretaries, George Marshall and Dean Acheson, also exhibited this pattern of Truman delegating the general formulation of U.S. foreign policy and proposals for policy actions to his secretaries while reserving the final, authorizing decisions for himself.

In terms of his pattern of information management, Truman did not reach down into departments and agencies the way Kennedy later would, to obtain his own independent information regarding the pros and cons of policy options and recommendations being proposed by his cabinet and White House advisers. Instead, Truman avoided interfering in the domain of his cabinet officers and preferred to focus upon contacts within his close circle of advisers in the White House. In fact, according to Clifford, Truman looked "almost exclusively to those around him" for policy information and advice during the last few years of his administration.[30] As a result, cabinet advisers and their staffs usually determined what information reached Truman from the departments and agencies, as well as, which recommendations or policy proposals submitted by these actors should be communicated to Truman for further consideration in a formal advisory group meeting.[31] As Clifford observed, "the relationship was such that these things were talked out pretty well before the formal recommendation came over" to the president for consideration.[32] This is particularly apparent in the policy debates surrounding the decision to cross the Thirty-eighth Parallel, where Truman delegated development of policy recommendations to staffers, who eventually recommended crossing the parallel after having worked out serious disputes between themselves over the issue before presenting their recommendation to Truman and his advisers.

Thus, in terms of Truman's authority-structure and information-management preferences, a formal advisory arrangement was preferred that allowed him to retain control over the crucial decisions. However, given his inexperience, expert advisers were very influential and Truman was willing to delegate the implementation of his decisions or the formulation of policy options to staff. Truman avoided using large groups, such as the cabinet, for decision making and appeared to prefer making decisions in smaller groups composed of trusted expert advisers. Although Truman seems to have been interested in obtaining the views of cabinet members and other advisers during formal meetings and was very accessible to his staff, the advisory system was not open to outside actors. In other words, advice was normally sought only from among his immediate staff and advisers on policy issues.

Group Process

The archival record appears to support the prediction that Truman would process information at a low level of complexity, emphasize simplistic stereotypes in reaching decisions, be characterized by low self-monitoring, and use a decisive decision style. In addition, as was predicted given Truman's low need for affiliation and moderate task emphasis, evidence of interpersonal effectiveness and popularity of Truman with his advisers is prevalent in the record, as is his emphasis upon teamwork to deal with tasks confronting the group. As would be expected given his high need for power, low level of complexity, and low need for affiliation, Truman evidences low tolerance of interpersonal conflict within the group, an expectation of adviser loyalty, and a willingness to remove disruptive advisers from his inner circles. The overall pattern of interactional processes within Truman's advisory groups indicates an advisory system characterized by decisive presidential decision making, low information-processing sensitivity to the environment, low emphasis upon conformity with the political environment, effective interpersonal interactions with advisers, emphasis upon teamwork, and a low tolerance of interpersonal or group conflict.

With regard to information processing, both his associates and the archival record point to Truman's tendency to process information at a low level of complexity, often utilizing simplistic stereotypes and other heuristics in reaching his decisions. In fact, Truman often would not seek out competing views or additional information on policy proposals presented by individual advisers, would allow the emotions of the moment or the affective strength of negative stereotypes to take hold, and would make decisions without consulting the rest of his advisers. For example, during several Korean War decisions to be discussed later, Truman's simplistic information processing and the potentially rash decisions which might have been taken as a result were counteracted to some degree only by Acheson's expertise and the president's great respect for his opinions. Thus, Acheson served a critical role in Truman's foreign policy decision making by enhancing the complexity of information processing within Truman's advisory group.

However, at the same time, Truman's "black-and-white" information processing has been seen by many as playing a major role in his legendary decisiveness in decision making. For example, then Assistant Secretary of State Dean Rusk observed that one of Truman's most notable attributes was his facility for making decisions, derived in large part from his ability to "oversimplify a problem at the moment of decision," make his decision, and then go home and get a good night's sleep while never looking back (Rusk 1990, 155). As Rusk noted, the ability of Truman to reduce complex issues to their simplest level was a trait not all decision makers have (ibid., 155–56). Similarly, George Elsey remarked that Truman's less complex, "black-and-white" views of the world very likely played a major role in his decisiveness.[33] As historian Robert Donovan observed:

> It was both his strength and his weakness that he had a simple view of right and wrong. It was a source of strength that he was able to view complex problems in simple terms . . . it was partly a strong sense of what was right and what was wrong that made Truman decisive and emphatic—and, in no small measure, didactic . . . black and white came through to Truman clearly, nuances were not his cup of tea. (Donovan 1982, 25)

Richard Neustadt, who worked in the Truman administration, recalls that Truman was uncomfortable dealing with problems in the abstract, preferring instead to look at problems in concrete terms of action and be able to ask, "What am I supposed to do about this?" (ibid., 25). This emphasis upon taking action immediately upon problems and Truman's ability to view complex issues at a simple level combined to create Truman's rapid and decisive decision style. Secretary of War Stimson, for example, noted approvingly in his diary the promptness and snappiness with which Truman took up each matter and decided it during their meetings. Undersecretary of State Joseph C. Grew noted that he had presented Truman with fourteen problems requiring his attention during a private meeting and received clear directives on every one of them in less than fifteen minutes (ibid., 20)! Special Assistant to the President Averell Harriman once observed that with Truman, "you could go into his office with a question and come out with a decision from him more swiftly than from any man I have ever known" (ibid., 24).

Further, because Truman saw matters in strongly categorical terms, his decision making and positions on policy maintained a consistency for his advisers. As Elsey recently recalled:

> When Truman made a decision, you could count on it! . . . Matters would be settled. He would agree or not agree. Or say, "we'll talk about it later, but we aren't gonna decide now." That was the characteristic of Truman, . . . you always knew exactly where you stood with him on something.[34]

However, this decision style was at times a liability to Truman due to his impulsive nature and lack of immediately available staff work on a particular problem. It contributed to Truman's well-known tendency, much to the horror of his speech writers, to "shoot from the hip" during press conferences and react viscerally to policy questions in advance of detailed staff work. James Webb, who was undersecretary of state in the Truman administration, once observed that when Truman had good staff work and he understood it, he used it very effectively and integrated it into his own judgments, but when there was no staff work done, he would sometimes let his emotions rule.[35] In fact, in the early years of the Truman administration, problems would frequently arise because cabinet officers would meet with Truman privately and orally present an idea in attractive enough terms that the president would approve it on the spot without submitting it to his staff for consideration.[36] Eventually, this problem was addressed by Truman requiring all proposals presented to him orally also be sent over later in written form so that proper staff work could be done by the White House staff before its approval.[37] This helped to protect Truman from himself and his proclivity to render snap judgments on issues regardless of the available information, thereby greatly reducing contradictory or embarrassing policy decisions.

With regard to Truman's willingness to accept the input of advisers, Clifford remarked that the president was an individual who would accept suggestions from advisers and who possessed an open mind without preconceived conceptions that were frozen into place.[38] An interesting example of how advisers who disagreed with Truman would attempt to change his mind is described by Charles Murphy. He noted that while Truman was extremely tolerant of his advisers, occasionally cabinet officers and their staff, including Acheson on several occasions, felt the President really ought to change his mind on an issue, but felt they had "run out of their rope so far as they were concerned in talking to him."[39] As Murphy recalls:

> so they would ask me from time to time if I'd go back and try it one more time. I would go and occasionally I'd persuade him to change his mind, for the time being; and he would do what it was we thought he should do, but more often than not, when this happened, the same thing would crop up again in maybe a different form—maybe the same form a little bit later and we found out he really thought what he'd thought to start with; he may have taken the action, he may have signed the paper, but he really didn't agree.[40]

In terms of how Truman interacted with his advisers interpersonally, both on an individual level and within advisory groups, Clifford recalls that Truman "was a very personal, direct man, and that carried through in his contacts with other people."[41] For example, Clifford states that if Truman did not feel comfortable with or have confidence in an individual, he would not see that person very much and that particular individual would have "considerable trouble" getting his views before the president.[42] However, if Truman was comfortable with and had developed confidence in an adviser through past work, he saw that individual and continued to see him.[43] In addition, Truman tried to keep the composition of his advisory group limited to those close advisers with whom he felt comfortable and did not want to bring in a lot of additional people or have to "expand a whole lot of contacts."[44] As Clifford recalls, Truman viewed the maintenance of contact with outside departments and agencies as the job of his advisers upon whom he depended and that he "expected that we [his advisers] were in contact with a lot of the departments, that was our job to do, and that we wouldn't bring a lot of extra people in," to the advisory circle.[45]

On an interpersonal level, Truman's advisers consistently remarked about how thoughtful and considerate the president was toward his advisers. Murphy describes "an extraordinary amount of good feeling among the members of the White House staff" in the Truman administration and notes that this was mostly due to the character of Truman's personality, which was "very gentle but firm."[46] Along the same lines, Elsey recalls that Truman was never too busy to think about the members of his staff and was unfailingly thoughtful and kind in his dealings with them.[47] As Acheson observed, Truman took the blame when things went wrong, gave his lieutenants the credit when things went right, and was close enough to his aides that none had any trouble in his public or private lives that Truman was not quick to know about and try to ease (Acheson 1969, 730). Similarly, Clifford notes that although Truman often disagreed with him on policy recommendations, he was never the target of a reprimand or even a harsh word during the five years in which he worked for Truman.[48] As Elsey observed regarding his own glowing words about Truman, "These are the comments that I suppose are traditionally and tritely said about all Presidents, but, somehow I think, in Mr. Truman's case, they happen to be true and I've seen enough of some other Presidents over there to know that they're not quite so true as they are in his case."[49]

Finally, Truman also was an astute politician who considered the domestic political consequences of his policy actions. As Donovan noted, Truman always paid close attention to his politically minded staff and to influential Democrats in Congress (Donovan 1982, 109). However, although Truman attended to domestic politics, he was also not afraid to put politics aside or ignore a popular backlash if he believed the course of action he was taking was the correct one. In this sense, he demonstrated the characteristics of low self-monitors, who are driven more by their own views/beliefs than by a desire to conform to the political environment when it is at odds with those beliefs. For example, when Truman relieved General MacArthur of command in Korea in 1951, he was immediately greeted with widespread popular outrage and Republican calls from the Senate for his impeachment (ibid., 358–62). Truman ignored the political damage his decision would cause him domestically and told his staff, "You have got to decide what is right to do, and then do it, even if it is unpopular" (ibid., 358). However, from Truman's perspective, the making of good foreign policy was itself good politics, as Dean Rusk recalled the president once telling his state department advisers:

> I want to hear from you fellows on matters of foreign policy, but I don't want you to base your views upon political considerations. In the first place, good policy is good politics. In the second place, you fellows in the State Department don't know a damned thing about domestic politics. And I don't want a bunch of amateurs playing around with serious business. (Rusk 1990, 517)

In addition, Truman was willing to work with political opponents if he felt they were useful to him. For instance, when Acheson and Rusk recommended John

Foster Dulles, who was a Republican, to Truman as a special adviser on Asia policy, Truman responded to objections by his staffers to Dulles's record of running a dirty campaign against the Democrats in New York by saying, "Look! You fellows don't understand politics. Of course, John Foster Dulles is going to take time out every two years to be a Republican, but between elections we want to work with him if he's willing to work with us" (ibid., 161).

Further, Truman was intensely loyal to old friends who had stood by him over the years, and this pattern of behavior continued throughout his administration.[50] As Elsey noted, Truman "didn't have that element of cruelty" as president required to cast friends aside who were political liabilities to him.[51] As a result, the Truman administration suffered a number of political scandals and was beset by charges of "cronyism," as Truman refused to abandon friends despite the political damage they caused him, stating that "when I get behind a man, I usually stay behind him" (Donovan 1982, 182–83). Ironically, in spite of Truman's normally decisive decision style on policy matters, when he was finally brought to the point of changing his mind about an associate, his tendency was to promote the individual out of sight instead of dismissing him outright (ibid., 177). And, although Truman did eventually fire MacArthur for his insubordination, this only occurred after a long period in which Truman put up with MacArthur's behavior and seethed about it, sometimes not so quietly, to his close advisers. As noted by Donovan, like many who had been schooled in machine politics, Truman craved loyalty and personal devotion in the men surrounding him (ibid., 24).

Finally, in terms of Truman's conflictual orientation, it appears that although he was tolerant of his advisers, he disliked strong disagreements or conflict within his interpersonal environment. When there were differences of opinion among the members of the White House staff regarding policy, these disputes often were thrashed out in Truman's presence and were not resolved between the advisers beforehand. His usual response was to actively intervene and resolve such disputes by deciding the issue on the spot. As Murphy noted, these disputes were resolved "usually in his presence, and with relatively little argument and he made the decisions himself, usually rather promptly. He just didn't have much argument around him and that was all."[52] Similarly, Connelly noted that during his time in the administration, there were minor disputes between advisers, but no major clashes because Truman would never allow such disputes to get out of hand.[53] As Connelly recalls:

the President wouldn't stand for it from the beginning, because he wanted each man to run his own show, and he did not want any interference between them. If there was a question of jurisdiction, he would decide, because he wanted a ball team.[54]

Thus, the advisory group that surrounded Truman was composed of advisers who generally got along with each other, with the notable exception of Acheson and Louis Johnson, and who did not engage in heated debates over policy. Elsey later recalled that in all his years in the Truman administration, he could not recall a time when an individual adviser vehemently disagreed with the president to his face.[55] This just did not happen. And although some incidences of interpersonal conflict within Truman's advisory group, such as the Henry Wallace, James Byrnes, and Louis Johnson cases, dragged on for some time, in the end Truman did take decisive action and remove them from the group. As Elsey later observed by way of comparison, at least these cases "ended in decisive presidential action . . . In Roosevelt's case, they would have just simmered and festered on and on, getting steadily worse!"[56] Thus, where possible, Truman would resolve conflict in his advisory group immediately with a decision and demonstrated a low tolerance for such conflict in his interpersonal interactions. In cases where conflict could not be resolved and advisers became increasingly disruptive, Truman responded, despite his reluctance to fire people, by removing them from his inner circle (Preston 1996).

The Decision to Intervene in Korea (June 24-30, 1950)

The initial Korean crisis provides an excellent example of Truman's leadership style: his formal structuring of the advisory group and of advice, his willingness to delegate or defer to expert advisers, his low tolerance of intragroup conflict, his decisiveness, and low complexity of information processing. In fact, due to the condensed time period of this particular crisis, Truman actually interacted formally with his advisory group far more than in other cases where time was less urgent, such as in the decision to cross the Thirty-eighth Parallel. Still, the general patterns of advisory group structuring and use during decision making in this case is consistent with Truman's style in other cases.[57]

When Ambassador Muccio's telegram arrived in Washington late on the evening of June 24, 1950, reporting what appeared to be an "all out" North Korean offensive against the South, a state department staff led by Assistant Secretary of State Rusk immediately gathered to monitor the situation. Secretary of State Acheson, responding to Rusk's suggestion that it might be appropriate to call an emergency meeting of the U.N. Security Council to deal with the situation, phoned Truman in Independence, Missouri, to inform him of the telegram and forward this recommendation. Deferring to Acheson's expertise, Truman immediately approved this course of action and authorized the secretary of state to present a resolution on Korea in the Security Council should that be deemed necessary. Although Truman suggested returning immediately to Washington, Acheson dissuaded him, recommending that he await a more detailed, complete report of the situation the next morning. Thus, the final decision regarding approaching the United Nations was delegated by Truman to Acheson. Unable to further clarify the confused situation in Korea and recognizing that it was critically important that the decision to present the case to the Security Council appear in the morning papers simultaneously with the news of the North Korean attack, Acheson made the final decision to go to the Security Council shortly in advance of the 2 A.M. press deadline.

On Sunday, June 25, a high-level State–Defense conference met at the state department to further consider the Korean situation and determine the best course of action to recommend to the president. As Undersecretary of State James Webb recalled, "there was very real concern that the Korean invasion might be the first of several thrusts, and might be followed by one or more other actions, perhaps in other parts of the world, which would present us with multiple requirements for action that would be very difficult for us to meet."[58] State department intelligence estimates suggested that there was "no possibility that the North Koreans acted without prior instruction from Moscow" and that the United States must respond forcefully to the invasion.[59] It was further agreed that the United States could not meet the situation with half measures, but had to take a stand and stick to it or take none at all. After the meeting, Acheson phoned Truman to request he return to Washington and meet with the secretaries of state and defense, and their advisers, at Blair House that evening to deal with the situation.

When Truman arrived in Washington that evening, arrangements had been made for Acheson, Webb, and Secretary of Defense Louis Johnson to meet him at the airport and accompany him on the ride back to Blair House to answer any questions that he might have on the Korean situation. At this point, we see not only Truman's decisive decision style, but also the absolute nature of his style of information processing and his minimal desire to search for competing perspectives. As Webb recalled, as soon as the car doors were closed, Truman "immediately stated that he did not believe the action in Korea could be supported given the limitations of the Siberian Railroad and that this was a challenge that we must meet."[60] Truman then announced, "By God, I'm going to let them have it," at which point Secretary Johnson immediately turned to face the president and said, "I'm with you Mr. President."[61] Recognizing the need to avoid taking precipitate action, as well as the strained relations between Acheson and Johnson, Webb intervened, informing Truman that his staff had done a great deal of work over the previous two days and had prepared three carefully worked out, specific recommendations that he should hear before making up his mind on any action to be taken. Truman responded to this by saying, "Well O.K., of course, but you know how I feel."[62]

An excellent illustration of the informal, interpersonal interactions of

Truman's advisory group is Webb's effort to ensure that the president would give consideration to the staff work already done and not take an extreme, immediate decision. Upon arriving at Blair House, Webb followed Truman into a cloak room, closed the door, and proceeded to quickly outline the three recommendations that would be proposed by Acheson in the meeting. Further, Webb emphasized that both he and Acheson felt strongly that only two of the recommendations should be approved that night and that the third should be delayed for a few days given their determination to present the situation to the United Nations. These three recommendations were: (1) to instruct the Air Force to knock out as many North Korean tanks as possible in order to slow their advance and facilitate the evacuation of Americans from Seoul; (2) to deploy the Seventh Fleet into a ready position near Formosa; and (3) to introduce U.S. military forces into South Korea to participate in the effort to stop the North Koreans.

The circle of advisers consulted by Truman during the Korean decisions became known as the "Blair House Group" and, although some additional advisers did attend some of the subsequent meetings, the advisers who attended this first Blair House meeting on June 25 continued to be the core of Truman's advisory group dealing with Korea.[63] The first Blair House meeting is interesting because it provides an excellent example of the group dynamics within Truman's advisory group, as well as an illustration of how interpersonal conflict was dealt with by the president. The familiar pattern of Acheson opening advisory group meetings with a presentation of his recommendations for policy action, followed by some group discussion, and then Truman's approval, is clearly highlighted and continued to be the pattern in all subsequent Blair House Group meetings.[64] Beyond recommendations to authorize the Air Force to attack North Korean units interfering with the evacuation of American personnel from Seoul and to increase arms shipments to the South, Acheson suggested utilizing the U.S. Seventh Fleet to prevent a Chinese attack on Formosa. During the following discussion, Truman's advisers were unified in their support of taking immediate, forceful action in Korea along the lines suggested by Acheson. However, there also appeared to be a clear distinction between advisers who broadly favored taking action against the North Koreans with U.S. forces and those who, while favoring action by elements of the Air Force or Navy, questioned the advisability of deploying substantial U.S. ground forces in Korea. It should be noted that a debate over the use of ground forces did not materialize at this meeting. However, the statements by advisers opposing the use of U.S. ground forces in Korea is significant because this first Blair House meeting was to be the last meeting in which such concerns were voiced by these advisers. At the critical meeting on June 30, in which the decision to intervene with two divisions of U.S. ground forces was taken, these advisers remained silent regarding these concerns.

For example, although Louis Johnson had earlier expressed support for Truman's outburst on the way to Blair House, during the meeting he opposed committing ground forces to Korea and continually emphasized the importance of Formosa instead. Similarly, General Bradley, while noting that the U.S. must draw the line somewhere against the Russians, also questioned the advisability of putting in ground units, particularly if large numbers were involved. Finally, Secretary of the Army Pace, in agreement with Bradley, also expressed doubts about the advisability of putting ground forces into Korea. Even so, there was general agreement among all of Truman's advisers that the United States should take some kind of immediate action in response to the invasion and work through the United Nations in dealing with the Korean situation. During the meeting, Truman allowed Acheson to set out the initial policy recommendations and allowed his advisers to comment upon them in turn, while asking only informational questions. Finally, Truman approved all of Acheson's policy recommendations and emphasized to his staff that there should be no statements or leaks to the press until after he had spoken to Congress. This step served to centralize information management and control over policy within Truman's inner circle and minimize the input of outside actors.

In terms of interpersonal conflict, the only dispute on record was a possible disagreement between Truman's advisers over the relative importance to be placed upon Formosa during deliberations on Korea. Despite a memorandum from General MacArthur emphasizing the critical importance of Formosa, Acheson opposed pursuing policies that would link the United States too closely to Chiang Kai-shek and argued for focusing solely on the Korean situation. On the other hand, Louis Johnson, impressed by MacArthur's memorandum, wished to focus the group's discussions upon Formosa policy. Acheson, replying that Chiang was untrustworthy, insisted that the group's focus should remain fixed on the Korean question, not Formosa. As Johnson later recalled, "The only really violent discussion Secretary Acheson and myself ever had took place in that meeting."[65] At this point, Truman intervened and cut off further argument by stating that he wished to discuss the Korean situation and that Formosa would be taken up later. Thus, Truman responded to strong interpersonal conflict in this case by intervening with a decision to cut off the debate, rather than fully discuss the dispute and consider in more detail the competing policy perspectives being advocated by his advisers.

Throughout the next day, June 26, Acheson continued to take the leading role in formulating U.S. policy to deal with the rapidly deteriorating situation on the ground in Korea. For example, when the U.S. ambassador in Moscow recommended to Acheson that the U.S. refrain from approaching the Soviet government over its role in the conflict or placing on the record any comment suggesting Soviet control over the North Korean invasion forces, he was overruled by the secretary of state. Although the ambassador emphasized that this would allow the Soviets a way to withdraw from the conflict without losing face when planned American countermeasures in Korea were successful, Acheson ordered a direct approach to the Soviet government over the ambassador's objections. In justifying his position, Acheson noted that the Soviets were not prepared to risk war with the West, had to be deterred from further actions elsewhere, and that a public approach to the Soviet government provided an "excellent opportunity" to disrupt the Soviet peace offensive, which was having a certain effect on public opinion in many critical areas.[66] It should be noted that this decision was taken on Acheson's own authority, without conferring with either Truman or the Blair House advisory group.

An interesting example of Truman's perceptions of the situation and use of simplistic analogies to understand events is illustrated by an informal exchange between Truman and George Elsey, after a meeting to discuss revisions to a draft press release on Korea prepared earlier by Acheson. Elsey had remained behind to discuss the significance of Korea and expressed to the president his "very grave concern about Formosa," that it seemed to him to be "the perfect course for the Chinese communists to take."[67] Truman, walking over to a globe, commented that he was more worried about other parts of the world and that in his view, Iran would be the place where the Soviets would cause trouble if the United States was not careful.[68] As Elsey recalls, Truman went on to state:

> Korea is the Greece of the Far East. If we are tough enough now, if we stand up to them like we did in Greece three years ago, they won't take any next steps. But if we just stand by, they'll move into Iran and they'll take over the whole Middle East. There's no telling what they'll do, if we don't put up a fight now.[69]

These statements, along with many during the Blair House meetings themselves, illustrate Truman's prevalent use of enemy images, stereotypes, and simple analogies in his style of information processing (Holsti 1967; R. Hermann, 1985; Cottam 1994; Larson 1985).

By the time Acheson phoned Truman to request another meeting of the Blair House Group that evening, the fall of Seoul was imminent and the South Korean government had fled south, inquiring about the possibility of being moved to Japan to form a government-in-exile. During this second Blair House meeting, Acheson suggested that an all-out order be issued to U.S. air and naval forces to waive all restrictions on their operations in Korea, ordering them to offer the fullest possible support to the South Koreans and to give their army time to re-form by attacking North Korean military forces. Truman approved this recommendation and supported Acheson's position that no actions should be taken by U.S. forces above the Thirty-eighth Parallel. Further, Acheson also recommended that the Nationalist Chinese be told to end all operations against the Chinese mainland and that the Seventh Fleet be utilized to prevent attacks both upon and originating from Formosa. Regarding all of these recommendations, there was no debate within the group. Acheson made the recommendations and Truman approved them without discussion.

However, as the meeting was concluding, General Collins, perhaps wanting to emphasize to the group the limitations on the effectiveness of military action, stated that the situation was so bad that it was impossible to say how much good U.S. air power could do and noted that the Korean Chief of Staff had "no fight left in him."[70] Responding to this, Acheson stated that it was important for the United States to do something, even if the effort were not successful, and Johnson observed that "even if we lose Korea this action would save the situation."[71] After these comments were made, Johnson asked whether any of the military representatives had objections to the course of action outlined in the meeting and no objections were raised. Thus, despite some clear reservations by the Army Chief of Staff regarding the effectiveness of the advisory group's plans, these issues were not explored in detail or debated within the Blair House Group.

Finally, the second Blair House meeting provides an interesting example of a difference of opinion between Truman and Acheson over the president's suggestion that consideration be given to taking Formosa back as part of Japan and placing it under MacArthur's command. It illustrates Truman's consistent pattern within his decision-making style across the Korea cases of deferring to expert advisers when disputes over policy occurred, even while persistently defending and not altering his own views on the subject.

In this particular instance, Truman revealed that he had received a secret, private letter from Chiang Kai-shek a month earlier, in which the Nationalist leader had offered to "step out of the situation" if it would help.[72] Thinking that Chiang might step out if MacArthur were put in command, Truman suggested that the United States might want to proceed along those lines in order to get Nationalist Chinese forces to help in Korea. Acheson, clearly lukewarm to the idea, responded that he had considered this move, but felt it should be reserved for later and not announced at this time since it required further study. After Truman continued, Acheson argued that the Generalissimo was unpredictable, that it was possible he would resist and "throw the ball game."[73] Responding to Acheson's comment that it would perhaps be best to pursue this action later, Truman finally relented, but noted that he thought such a move was the next step. Interestingly, no other advisers joined the debate between Truman and Acheson, and the remaining policy discussions regarding Formosa were devoid of debate; Acheson's positions went un-opposed within the group. This example, as well as that of General Collins's concerns about the effectiveness of military force, reflects a consistent pattern of conflict avoidance among advisers on Truman's staff. Although debates would sometimes arise, such as between Truman and Acheson, or Johnson and Acheson, these did not evolve into free-ranging criticism of group as-sumptions by other advisers. Instead, these conflicts were resolved between the individuals involved and not explored further.

The next day, Truman, consistent with his pattern of relying upon trusted expert advisers, accepted Acheson's recommendation that Averell Harriman be brought into the Blair House Group to serve as an adviser on the Korean situation. Both Truman and Acheson felt that because of the uncertainty regarding the long-range intentions of the Soviet Union, it would be "ex-tremely useful" to have Harriman close to hand since he had "more firsthand experience and a better knowledge of the Soviet leadership" than anyone else available to Truman.[74]

Truman also met with congressional leaders to inform them of the deci-sions taken by the administration regarding Korea since the beginning of the crisis. As would be expected from a low self-monitor who has centralized decision making over policy into a tight, inner circle in the White House, Truman came to the meeting to inform them of his actions, get a sense of congressional opinion, and give the congressmen a sense of being consulted. However, he had made his decisions already and did not use the meeting to make policy. Again highlighting his use of stereotypes and simplistic analo-gies to understand events, Truman told the congressmen that he could not let the invasion pass unnoticed because it was obviously inspired by the Soviets, who would swallow one piece of Asia after another, then the Near East, and then perhaps Europe if they were not stopped in Korea.

Later that evening, James Webb came to the White House to inform Truman that Johnson had been the source of "leaks" to reporters about the Blair House meetings of June 25 and 26, and that he was feeding stories to reporters that Acheson had been "soft" on Formosa and that Johnson himself was actually responsible for Truman's order that Formosa be neutralized.[75] However, despite this report, Truman avoided conflict and did not imme-diately call Johnson on the carpet.

The next day, June 28, Truman awoke to news that Seoul had fallen and that the U.N. Security Council had passed a resolution authorizing its mem-bers to "furnish such assistance to the Republic of Korea as may be necessary to repel the armed attack and to restore international peace and security in the area."[76] Although Republican governor Thomas Dewey of New York had issued a statement supporting the administration's actions in Korea, Senate Republican Leader Robert Taft soon followed with a speech blaming the administration for the loss of China to the Communists, the division of Korea, the failure to sufficiently arm the South, and for Acheson's January speech which had been an "invitation to attack" (Acheson 1969, 410). In the face of growing right-wing attacks upon the administration's policy in the Far East, the political climate was growing more insistent upon Truman ordering a strong U.S. response to the Korean situation. However, as demonstrated by the archival record, the president and his advisers were already in this mindset before these partisan attacks and Truman, consistent with low self-monitoring, opposed focusing upon domestic policy considerations during advisory group discussions in an area where he felt they were doing the right thing.

For example, in the National Security Council meeting that afternoon, Acheson, commenting on domestic political considerations, noted that the administration could not count on the continued enthusiastic support of the public for their staunch stand on Korea, especially if such actions were to result in "casualties and taxes" (ibid., 411). As Acheson later recalled, Truman, "mistaking my purpose, which was to prepare for criticism and hard sledding, insisted that we could not back out of the course upon which we had started" (ibid.). The president stated bluntly that he did not intend to back out unless another military situation developed that had to be met by the United States elsewhere.[77] Quickly backtracking, Acheson then recommended that the military should review U.S. forces available in the Far East in the event that the president decided he must act more forcefully in Korea, which Truman immediately approved. Thus, when Truman was convinced as to the correctness of policy, he was not willing to defer to even expert advisers' concerns regarding domestic political considerations.

Similarly, Truman resisted pressure from his military advisers to alter policy positions adopted by himself and Acheson, and decisively ordered further compliance. For example, Secretary of the Air Force Finletter reported to the group that the Air Force was having difficulty combating North Korean aircraft under rules of engagement allowing operations only against planes in the air over South Korean territory, and further stated that the North's air operations could not be effectively stopped unless they were allowed to strike at bases above the Thirty-eighth Parallel. Truman replied that although it might eventually be necessary to act on this problem, it needed further consideration and he did not want to decide on this question at the present time. Acheson interjected that he hoped that aircraft would not be crossing the Thirty-eighth Parallel and Truman stated bluntly that they were not to do it.

By June 29, the situation in Korea had reached a new level of crisis, as all attempts to halt the invasion had failed and North Korean forces continued their advance. Reports from the field began to reach MacArthur suggesting that without the commitment of U.S. ground forces, the status quo ante could not be restored in Korea. MacArthur, on his own initiative, launched air strikes north of the Thirty-eighth Parallel and the Joint Chiefs tentatively approved a new directive that allowed the extension of operations into North Korea if the general believed "serious risk of loss of South Korea might be obviated thereby" (Donovan 1982, 211). Although these instructions were contrary to Truman's earlier orders, the state and defense departments both approved, and in meetings with the Joint Chiefs, Johnson decided to try to persuade Truman to commit U.S. ground forces to Korea to defend the airfields and port at Pusan during the NSC meeting that afternoon (ibid.).[78] Thus, due to Truman's delegation of implementation authority to his cabinet secretaries, an actual reversal of existing policy began to occur without the president's or his advisory group's explicit approval.

The NSC meeting focused upon whether to extend military operations above the Thirty-eighth Parallel and deploy some ground forces in Korea to defend Pusan. Secretary Johnson began by noting the state department's concurrence with a new directive to MacArthur that would authorize action above the Thirty-eighth Parallel if serious risk of the loss of South Korea would be prevented. Truman immediately interrupted Johnson to state flatly that he was uncomfortable with the wording of the directive and did "not want any implication in the letter that we are going to war with Russia at this time."[79] "We must be damn careful," Truman told Johnson, "we must not say that we are anticipating a war with the Soviet Union . . . We want to take any steps we have to push the North Koreans behind the line, but I don't want to get us over-committed to a whole lot of other things that could mean war."[80] Assuring the president that he understood his position, Johnson stated that the Joint Chiefs believed it essential to establish a beachhead in Korea to support U.S. operations.

Agreeing with the Joint Chiefs's assessment, Army Secretary Pace commented that he had "considerable reservations" about the nature of the limitations placed on MacArthur and felt that they ought to be very clear and explicit.[81] In response, Truman stated his view that some reservations were necessary, since he did not want to do anything north of the Thirty-eighth Parallel except destroy air bases, gasoline supplies, and ammunition dumps. Reiterating his own position, Truman told Pace that he could give MacArthur all the authority he needed to restore order to the Thirty-eighth Parallel, but that he was not to go north of it. However, Acheson now expressed support for Finletter's position during the last NSC meeting and began arguing in favor of allowing the Air Force to take whatever steps were necessary north of the parallel to attack North Korean airfields and army units. Acheson still continued to insist "that American planes *not* go outside of South Korea," but observed that he was now willing to support the deployment of whatever U.S. ground forces MacArthur might need in Korea to prevent what would be a "great disaster if we were to lose now."[82] However, the secretary emphasized that he felt the present proposal was still quite different from an unlimited commitment to supply all the ground forces required in Korea. Truman ended the meeting by telling his advisers that he had no quarrel with anybody and did not intend to have any, but that he wanted to know what the facts were and did not want "any leaks" by those present to the press about this meeting.[83] This last point, a clear reference to Johnson's leaking of information to the press reported to him by Webb, was a direct warning to the secretary of defense to cease his disloyalty.

Later that night, Acheson returned to the White House to discuss with Truman a communication from the Nationalist Chinese Government offering two divisions of ground forces for deployment to Korea. Truman informed Acheson that his first reaction was to accept the offer since he wanted as many members of the United Nations involved in Korea as possible (Truman 1956, 342). Acheson replied that he felt the situation of Nationalist China was different from that of other U.N. members and that Formosa was one of the areas most exposed to attack, which had been the rationale for deployment of the Seventh Fleet for its protection in the first place. Acheson noted that it would be inconsistent to spend money defending an island while its own defenders were elsewhere and questioned whether the Nationalist forces would be very useful since they would require a great deal of reequipping before being ready for combat. Truman concluded the discussion by asking Acheson to bring up the matter at a meeting with Johnson and the Joint Chiefs of Staff the next day. Thus, in this case, Truman was unwilling to simply defer to Acheson's views, but avoided further conflict with his secretary of state by instructing him to raise the issue in his absence with other advisers the next day. This allowed the president to maintain his preferred position, avoid immediate debate, and potentially obtain support for his position from other advisers before the next advisory group meeting.

Throughout the night and into the morning of June 30, the situation in Korea continued to worsen, as events propelled the Truman administration into making its final decision to intervene fully in the conflict. A telegram from MacArthur reached Acheson at 1:31 A.M. reporting that the South Korean military had entirely lost its ability to counterattack against the North Korean advance. Further, MacArthur reported that if the enemy advance were to continue, it would "seriously threaten the fall of the Republic."[84] Recommending full U.S. intervention in the conflict, MacArthur told Acheson that the only way to hold the present line or regain lost ground was to immediately introduce U.S. ground forces into the battle area, specifically, a regimental combat team and possibly two more U.S. divisions from Japan. By 3:40 A.M., MacArthur was informing Army Chief of Staff Collins that the situation had deteriorated to the point where he could no longer conduct effective operations and, requesting immediate authorization to move a U.S. regimental combat team to the area, told Collins that "time is of the essence and a clear-cut decision without delay is imperative."[85] After being contacted by Collins, Secretary of the Army Pace phoned Truman at 4:57 A.M. to inform the president of the situation and of MacArthur's request, which was immediately approved.

Later that morning, the Blair House Group met to discuss the directive that would authorize MacArthur's two-division deployment to Korea and bring about full U.S. intervention in the conflict. Having earlier phoned Pace and Johnson to inform them that he was considering giving MacArthur the two divisions from Japan, and telling them that he wanted them to consider the advisability of also accepting two Nationalist Chinese divisions for Korea, Truman proceeded to reopen the discussion with Acheson he had deferred the night before. Opening the NSC meeting, Truman informed his advisers that he had granted authority to MacArthur to deploy one regimental combat team to the battle area and now desired advice on the request that additional troops be deployed. Further, Truman formally asked his advisers whether it would be worthwhile to accept the Nationalist Chinese offer of troops, especially since Chiang Kai-shek had stated that the two divisions would be ready for sailing in five days and time was all-important.

Acheson responded by suggesting that if Nationalist Chinese troops appeared on the field in Korea, Communist China might decide to enter the conflict solely to inflict damage upon the Nationalist troops and reduce their ability to later defend Formosa. The Joint Chiefs unanimously supported Acheson's concerns and added that the Nationalist forces had little modern equipment and would be as helpless against the North Korean armor as the South Koreans had been. Instead, the Chiefs argued that U.S. transport capability would be better utilized by carrying American troops and supplies to MacArthur. Truman reiterated his concern about the U.S. ability to successfully withstand the enemy with only the small forces immediately available in Japan, but after further discussion, finally accepted the position taken by the rest of his advisers that the Nationalist offer of troops should be politely declined. Thus, Truman was eventually willing to defer to expert advice, despite his own inclination to accept the Nationalist offer. It was unanimously decided to follow up the RCT already deployed with two divisions from Japan, and Truman approved this action immediately. In addition, Admiral Sherman's proposal that a naval blockade be established around Korea was also approved without debate.

However, as the meeting concluded, Truman announced, without explanation, that he had decided to give MacArthur the authority to deploy, as needed, all the ground forces under his command in Japan, then totaling four divisions, to Korea. In this final decision, as well as in the earlier deliberations regarding the deployment of troops to Korea, there was no opposition from

Truman's advisers. Neither was there any discussion of the concerns previously expressed during the first Blair House meeting by Joint Chiefs of Staff Chairman Bradley, Pace, or Johnson about the advisability of deploying substantial U.S. ground forces in Korea. In a meeting which lasted only thirty minutes, the final decision had been taken by Truman to intervene in the Korean War, and at 11 A.M., he met with congressional leaders to inform them of his decision.

The Decision to Cross the Thirty-eighth Parallel (July–September 1950)

On July 17, Truman requested the NSC prepare a report formulating what U.S. policy should be after North Korean forces were driven back to the Thirty-eighth Parallel. At the same time, Truman also circulated a memo to his staff describing changes he intended to make in the structure and operations of his advisory group. Truman no longer wished to have policy proposals on Korea brought to him directly, but recommended only through NSC machinery.[86] Further, noting that recent NSC attendance had been so large as to discourage free discussion among his advisers, Truman limited participation in NSC meetings to the secretaries of state, defense, and treasury, the chairman of the JCS, the director of Central Intelligence, the executive secretary of the NSC, and close White House advisers Averell Harriman and Sidney Souers. Participation by any other officials was to be strictly limited, with additional members being brought in only with the president's specific approval. In addition, Truman directed the members of this select advisory group to each nominate one individual to be a member of a senior NSC staff group, which would provide the necessary staff work on policy recommendations for council meetings.

This official restructuring of Truman's advisory system shaped the way in which the decision to cross the Thirty-eighth Parallel was debated and made. As observed during the first Korean case, Truman continued his pattern of preferring inner-circle control over policy and of centralizing authority in the White House. Also apparent is Truman's preference for smaller decision groups and discomfort with groups even the size of the original Blair House gatherings. With this new advisory grouping, Truman enhanced his comfort and control over the situation. Further, his inner circle of advisers now constituted a group that Truman knew very well on an interpersonal basis and trusted to be loyal, while still providing him with expert advice he could depend upon in foreign affairs.

As a result of these changes, the critical debate over whether to cross the Thirty-eighth Parallel, and the formulation of the policy paper requested by Truman, took place not within the president's inner-circle group, but between

NSC staffers from the state and defense departments. Neither Truman nor Acheson were involved or had input into this policy debate at the lower staff level.[87] Further, serious disputes over whether to cross the parallel were settled among the staff long before the final recommendation was reported back to the president. In this regard, there was a clear difference between the NSC procedures which preserved and reported differences of opinion on policy within the Eisenhower administration and those within the Truman administration. Further, it also illustrates the degree to which Truman would delegate the formulation of policy options and recommendations to advisers and their staffs in areas of their expertise.

What was the nature of this policy debate and how was it resolved? A draft memorandum prepared by the state department's policy planning staff on July 22 took the position that the United States should restrict ground operations north of the Thirty-eighth Parallel except where essential for tactical reasons as fighting approached the parallel. In addition, noting that the danger of Soviet or Chinese involvement would greatly increase if U.N. forces crossed the Thirty-eighth Parallel, the draft concluded that the disadvantages associated with the risk of widening the conflict far outweighed the political advantages of proceeding into North Korea. However, within the state department itself, a serious dispute arose over the issue of crossing the Thirty-eighth Parallel. For example, some on the policy planning staff supported the position taken by the South Koreans that the Thirty-eighth Parallel dividing line should be eliminated, and that U.S. policy toward Korea should be geared toward the elimination of the North Korean Army and the unification of Korea. As Acheson recalled:

> The Far Eastern Division, under Dean Rusk and John Allison, strongly urged that a crossing of the 38th parallel should not be precluded . . . Paul Nitze's Policy Planning Staff, influenced by George Kennan's views, took the opposite position and argued that General MacArthur should be directed to announce, as UN Commander, that his troops would not cross the parallel in pursuit if the North Korean forces withdrew to the north of it. (Acheson 1969, 451)

The position taken by the state department immediately came under fire from John Foster Dulles, who argued that "there is every reason to go beyond the 38th Parallel except possibly one, and that is our incapacity to do so and the fact that the attempt might involve us much more deeply in a struggle on the Asiatic mainland with Soviet and Chinese Communist manpower."[88] However, state department drafts continued to resist a clear-cut recommendation to cross the parallel, although a steady drift toward this position began to emerge. The draft of August 23, for example, while recognizing growing public and congressional sentiment favoring action north of the parallel, emphasized that the United States had "no commitment to use armed force in the effort to bring about Korean independence and unity" and that decisions regarding whether to cross the Thirty-eighth Parallel should be deferred.[89]

However, from the beginning, the policy papers under discussion in the defense department took a much stronger position than the state department drafts. For instance, the July 31 department of defense draft argued that "from the point of view of military operations against North Korean forces, the 38th parallel has no more significance than any other meridian."[90] Further, noting that restoring the status quo ante would leave the Korean desire for unification unfulfilled and not result in security for South Korea, the defense department draft emphasized that "the situation in Korea now provides the United States and the free world with the first opportunity to displace part of the Soviet orbit."[91] Concluding that the unification of Korea squared with historical necessity, the draft recommended U.N. forces occupy Korea and defeat North Korean forces without regard to the parallel. This basic position of the defense department, supporting the crossing of the Thirty-eighth Parallel, remained consistent throughout a series of drafts of this policy paper over the next several months.

These differences in policy positions continued until the August 24 NSC staff assistants meeting, in which representatives from state, defense, and the armed services sought to consolidate all the agreed-upon points from the various drafts. The representatives from the other departments stated that they felt the state and defense drafts "could readily be reconciled if the State Department were willing to participate in making the essential decision now."[92] The military representatives at the meeting emphasized that the postponement of the decision recommended by the state department would delay the lengthy buildup of forces necessary if a decision to cross the parallel were taken and that, "if there was any likelihood that such operations might be called for, an immediate decision was needed."[93] The meeting ended with a recommendation that the NSC senior staff make a decision regarding whether the UN should cross the Thirty-eighth Parallel and seek to occupy Korea.

Thus, at the NSC senior staff meeting of August 25, these recommendations were taken into account and several decisions were made which altered the previous state department position. First, the state department agreed to military operations north of the Thirty-eighth Parallel, as long as UN forces kept "well clear of the Russian frontier."[94] Second, it was decided that "in the absence of Chinese Communist or Soviet participation," UN forces should not stop at the Thirty-eighth Parallel.[95] Finally, it was noted to be "politically desirable, if militarily feasible" for South Korean forces to be used primarily in actions beyond the parallel and that the participation of American forces should be minimized.[96] These new positions were subsequently adopted by the state department, which stated in revised policy drafts that halting at the Thirty-eighth Parallel made no "political or military sense unless the risk that it would provoke a major clash with the Soviet Union or Communist China were so great as to override all other considerations."[97] By September 1, these agreed-upon positions were incorporated into NSC 81, the final version of the policy paper for the president.

When NSC 81 was reviewed by Truman and his NSC advisory group on September 7, JCS Chairman Bradley expressed concerns that the paper did not clearly authorize MacArthur to take action above the Thirty-eighth Parallel. In response, Acheson emphasized that, provided MacArthur's plans could be carried out without risk of a major war with the Chinese or Soviets, the paper did provide such authorization. However, to eliminate confusion regarding MacArthur's orders, Acheson suggested the text be changed accordingly. But Acheson also insisted that the text make clear that if an actual invasion across the parallel was to occur, the final decision had to be made in Washington by the president. Truman, Johnson, and Bradley agreed with Acheson's proposal and felt there were no other problems with the paper. NSC 81 was adopted, subject to redrafting by the departments of state and defense to reflect the views expressed by Acheson and Bradley, and it was later issued as NSC 81/1 and submitted to Truman for consideration.

It should be noted that there was no serious opposition expressed within Truman's advisory group to the drastic change of U.S. policy regarding the Thirty-eighth Parallel during this last NSC meeting on the topic. Having delegated policy formulation to the NSC staff, Truman and his advisers accepted their unified recommendation to cross the parallel, without once questioning its wisdom or the flow of staff debate that had resulted in such a recommendation. Further, no discussions took place involving the potential consequences of such a policy shift, and no one except Bradley raised any concerns about the paper whatsoever. But even in this instance, Bradley was questioning the clarity of MacArthur's orders, not the wisdom of them.

In addition, Truman's low tolerance of conflict was highlighted during this case by his firing of Defense Secretary Johnson, whose self-serving leaks to the press, attacks upon Acheson, and general disloyalty had finally provoked the president into action (Ferrell 1980, 191–93). However, having reached the decision to replace Johnson by early September, Truman delayed informing him, even after he had successfully approached George Marshall about becoming secretary of defense, until being forced to on September 11 by a press leak. Truman's low tolerance of interpersonal conflict led him to delay having "to break the bad news" to Johnson until the potential of even greater outside political conflict led him to do so (ibid., 189). However, despite his reluctance, Truman clearly was moving to replace what he considered to be a disloyal and disruptive member of his advisory group prior to the leak, as demonstrated by his contacts with Marshall.

Thus, throughout the second Korean policy case, Truman's leadership style was one of delegation of policy formulation, heavy reliance upon expert recommendations, low tolerance of conflict, and extremely low-complexity information processing, characterized by limited debate and information search within his advisory group. On September 11, Truman approved the revised version of the policy paper, NSC 81/1, authorizing U.S. military action beyond the Thirty-eighth Parallel, on his own in the absence of any formal debate by his advisory group. The final draft of MacArthur's orders from the JCS, implementing NSC 81/1, was sent by Marshall to Truman on September 27. In a covering memorandum, Marshall noted that both he and Acheson had agreed to the contents of the directive written by the Joint Chiefs and that Truman's approval would permit MacArthur to conduct the necessary military operations north of the Thirty-eighth Parallel to destroy North Korea's forces. Truman approved the directive without further discussion and the new instructions were transmitted to MacArthur that day.

Conclusion

At the beginning of this chapter, an argument was made emphasizing the need for scholars engaged in groups research to improve their understanding of the influential role often played by leaders in shaping both the structural and interactional dynamics of advisory groups. This *"leader–group nexus"* (cf. Stern and Sundelius, this volume) was suggested to be particularly relevant in certain political contexts, such as the American presidency, where leaders have considerable freedom to structure their own advisory systems, select advisers, and set into place preferred group interaction norms. Truman's decision making and use of advisers throughout both Korean policy cases clearly illustrated that the personality characteristics and policy expertise of presidents, and their subsequent leadership style orientations, have a significant impact upon how advisory groups are structured and tend to interact during the policy-making process. Further, this relationship between leaders and groups has important practical policy implications for both improving advisory group performance and in designing presidential advisory systems to better compensate for leader weaknesses.

However, before discussing these implications, the findings of the case study examination of Truman's advisory system will be reviewed in light of the predictions outlined earlier in table 7.1. These predictions were based upon a series of hypothesized relationships between Truman's individual characteristics, the five key leadership style dimensions (i.e., his authority-structure, information-management, information-processing, interpersonal, and conflictual orientations), and the types of group structures and processes most likely to arise from them (see figure 7.2). Across both cases, the structural and interactional characteristics of Truman's advisory groups were consistent with the theoretical predictions proposed in table 7.1.

Given Truman's high need for power, low self-confidence, and low foreign policy expertise, several effects were anticipated on his authority-structure and information-management orientations that would affect advisory *group structure*. First, it was predicted that Truman would prefer more formal or hierarchical advisory arrangements that would ensure his direct involvement and control over the policy process. This would involve the centralization of policy formulation and decision making within the White House among trusted, inner-circle advisers, with little involvement by outside actors. In addition, Truman's advisory system was expected to emphasize managing information through the use of expert advisers to formulate policy and generate recommendations. As was illustrated throughout both cases, Truman's advisory groups were, in fact, consistently characterized by two clear patterns: one of centralization of policy-making and advice within a small inner circle in the White House; and another of leader delegation of policy formulation and advice to expert advisers.

On the other hand, given Truman's low scores on complexity and need for affiliation, several effects were anticipated in the information-processing, interpersonal, and conflictual orientations that would affect the group process of his advisory circle. For example, it was predicted that Truman would be a low self-monitor, generally process information in simple, black-and-white terms, utilize stereotypes and enemy images frequently, and not actively seek out alternative perspectives or disconfirming information. Further, a decisive decision-making style was anticipated, since seeing the world and processing information in absolute terms makes decisions much clearer and easier to formulate. Finally, a low tolerance of conflict within the group was expected given his high power needs combined with his low complexity and affiliation.

Again, across both cases, Truman's advisory groups were characterized by consistent patterns of interaction and group processes in line with these predictions. First, a clear pattern of decisiveness is apparent in Truman's interactions with advisers, especially when policy recommendations were proposed. Decisions were seldom postponed and usually proposals were adopted by Truman without any discussion of alternative viewpoints. In addition, Truman also demonstrated a consistent pattern of utilizing simplistic stereotypes and enemy images to frame policy problems, as well as one of un-critically accepting adviser recommendations. This was especially the case when they fit into his own preconceived policy ideas and stereotypes, such as the attribution of Soviet Cold War "grand strategy" to events in Korea. Such patterns are consistent with the predicted black-and-white, closed information-processing style expected of Truman. Further, a pattern of low tolerance of intragroup conflict was observed in both cases, illustrated by the firing of Johnson and the shift of policy debate away from the Formosa issue. In addition, most controversial issues tended to be resolved immediately by Truman, or "papered-over" by staffers, as in the Thirty-eighth Parallel case, without the development of strong advocacy between competing advisers within the group. However, given Truman's willingness to press his own policy views on Acheson (consistent with high power and low complexity traits), this pattern was not nearly as strong as the others previously mentioned.

Another interesting finding is that although Truman's individual characteristics and leadership style did affect advisory group structures and interactions along predicted lines, the cases also served to emphasize how important key advisers were in shaping policy outcomes. Given his tendency to rely heavily upon expert advisers to provide policy advice, who Truman's advisers were and what they were like significantly affected policy decisions. The clear implication here is that for analysts seeking to understand Truman's decision making, an awareness of his individual characteristics should lead to a recognition of the importance of focusing not just upon Truman, but also upon the views and roles of expert advisers within his advisory group. (cf. Metselaar and Verbeek; Hoyt and Garrison, this volume) Had Truman possessed greater policy expertise and self-confidence, like George Bush during the Gulf War case, this pattern of delegation to expert advisers would not be expected to exist. Instead, analysts would then be better advised to focus more upon the role of the president's own policy views and preferences in shaping advisory group interactions and decision making, and less upon the views of his advisers (cf. Preston and Young 1992; Hermann and Preston 1994b). Understanding what the leader is like is predictive of the role advisers are likely to play in the policy process and how significant their impact is likely to be on the final decisions.

For example, in the first Korean case, Acheson clearly played a key role in determining what policy options would be considered by the Blair House Group and, given Truman's high regard for his expertise, which ones were implemented. In fact, with few exceptions, Acheson's recommendations on Korea and his characterizations of the situation were adopted without significant debate by Truman. It was Acheson's influence that prevented the administration's Korea policy from becoming linked to the Formosa issue, and despite pressure from Johnson and MacArthur, succeeded in keeping the issues separate throughout the crisis. Further, Acheson's foreign policy expertise served to compensate for Truman's own weaknesses in that area and often prevented the president from embarking on rash or impulsive courses of action. Fortunately for Truman, this was an example of a very complementary fit between leader and adviser. However, it is easy to imagine that without Acheson's steadying influence on Truman, the administration's policy could have been swept down the path initially preferred by Truman, one that would not only have linked American policy in Korea inextricably with Formosa, but likely have precipitated a serious military confrontation with the Soviets.

In the second Korean case, Truman delegated the formulation of policy to a select group of expert staff rather than to Acheson. This was still consistent with his overall pattern of delegating to experts while retaining fairly centralized control over policy within the White House. However, in this case, the delegation of policy debate to staffers had the serious consequence of confining the disagreements between experts to a forum outside the view of Truman's inner circle. As a result, when Truman and his advisers accepted the recommendation of NSC 81/1 to cross the Thirty-eighth Parallel, there was no serious discussion of arguments against this action since they had been resolved earlier between staffers.

For policymakers, these two cases illustrate the dangers that exist for presidents who tend to delegate policy formulation to experts, especially if debate over alternate courses of action occurs outside the main advisory group, is "papered-over" by staffers, or is not fully discussed by the president's inner circle before a decision is taken. For such presidents, the adoption of Eisenhower's NSC procedures, requiring points of disagreement between staffers to be fully outlined in all policy papers sent to the main advisory group, could help to avoid the serious advisory group malfunction found in the second Korean case. This example from the Truman administration provides an excellent illustration of one of the many possible advisory group malfunctions that a more thorough understanding of the individual characteristics of leaders might help to avoid. Through improved knowledge of a leader's style orientations, it should be possible not only to foresee potential problems, but to provide policymakers with recommendations regarding group structures and processes geared toward preventing their occurrence. In this sense, prescriptions based upon an improved understanding of the leader–group nexus moves us closer toward policy-relevant research for practitioners (cf. George 1993b).

In addition, the Korean cases also provide an interesting illustration of how the complexity of information processing within advisory groups reacts to crisis and noncrisis situations. Numerous studies have suggested that situational factors, such as crisis, reduce the complexity of information processing within decision groups and by individuals (cf. Holsti et al. 1969; Suedfeld and Tetlock 1977; Suedfeld, Tetlock, and Ramirez 1977; Hermann 1979). Even under the best of circumstances, in groups composed entirely of highly complex individuals, the characteristics of crises described by Hermann (1969), that is, high threat, uncertainty, and time constraints, would be expected to reduce the complexity of decision making by placing constraints upon policymakers (Hermann 1969, 409–21). Given this, one would expect a greater deterioration in the information processing and quality of decision making during crises among leaders or groups of policymakers who are less cognitively complex than in groups composed of more complex individuals. This is because leaders characterized by greater complexity are more likely to bring at least some elements of their normal mode of information processing to a crisis situation than are individuals who lacked sophisticated modes of information processing in the first place.

What evidence of this dynamic do we see within the Truman cases, with a low complexity leader who would be predicted to have a closed information-processing system? Interestingly, although his advisory groups consistently demonstrated a closed pattern of information processing across both cases, there were important differences in process. For example, although the policy outcomes did not reflect it, the more thorough debate over policy options occurred in the second Korean case, not the first. In the first Korean case, Truman was limited due to time constraints and forced to avoid a lengthy process of policy formulation by a staff of advisers. As a result, he relied upon the most trusted, expert adviser within his inner circle, Acheson, to formulate policy options and recommendations, often adopting them with minimal debate.

On the other hand, the second Korean case was a noncrisis situation where Truman was not under the same kind of time constraints he had been under in the first case. And, as he had done in other noncrisis cases during his administration (such as aid to Greece and the development of the Marshall Plan), Truman delegated the formulation of policy to a small staff of expert advisers outside his inner circle (cf. Janis 1972; Donovan 1982). Thus, the Thirty-eighth Parallel debate took place over several months between strong advocates of both positions and provided the opportunity for multiple perspectives to be heard. Due to Truman's information-processing orientation, NSC 81/1's recommendations were not critically challenged before adoption by the main advisory group. In other words, Truman's style served to "short-circuit" a slightly improved process. This is consistent with the expectation that across policy contexts, Truman's advisory system would be characterized by a closed information-processing style.

Finally, it should be noted that the leader–group nexus explored in this chapter represents only one set of potential relationships between actors that are relevant to building a greater understanding of intergroup interactions affecting the behavior of decision groups (see figure 7.1). Future research should not only examine additional presidents and advisory groups, but also how the characteristics of individual advisers, or "factions" of advisers within particular groups, influence group dynamics and decisions as well. In addition, the role of outside actors and their impact upon leaders and advisory groups would be a productive area of exploration. The implications of this study are that the individual characteristics of leaders do often have an effect upon the structure and internal dynamics of advisory groups. Further, given certain leader characteristics and style orientations, the roles of individual advisers, factions, or outside actors become either more or less relevant to understanding group behavior. In other words, leader characteristics and style represent one key unlocking specific contingencies affecting groups in various ways.

NOTES

This paper was written with support from a National Science Foundation Grant (DIR-9113599) to the Research Training Group on the Role of Cognition in Collective Political Decisionmaking at the Mershon Center, Ohio State University. Additional support was provided by a research grant from the Harry S. Truman Library Institute.

1. For a similar phenomenon in the Dutch foreign policy-making setting, see Metselaar and Verbeek this volume.

2. However, these four patterns should not be viewed as mutually exclusive and pure types. Clearly, some presidents emphasize one or the other of the two dimensions that make up this typology—either authority or coordination—and move across the other dimension depending upon the situation in which they find themselves. This distinction is related to a leader's sensitivity to context or prior managerial/policy experience. For a more detailed discussion of this point, cf. Hermann and Preston 1994a, 1994b.

3. Interview conducted with George Christian, July 1993.

4. A similar distinction is the organizational literature's emphasis upon organizational survival and policy achievement as the twin goals of leadership (Hargrove 1989; Meier 1989; Miller 1987).

5. In another study, Fodor and Farrow (1979) found that high power-motivated individuals demonstrated a greater partiality toward ingratiating, "yes-men" followers than did those with a low need for power.

6. House also has suggested that the greater an individual's task expertise in a policy area, the more frequently that individual will attempt to assert power and the more likely he or she will be successful in asserting control.

7. In addition, House (1990, 204) has argued that the greater the self-confidence, the more frequently individuals will attempt to assert power.

8. Based upon ongoing personality research and measurement of leader complexity being conducted by Thomas Preston and Margaret Hermann.

9. Winter (1991, 222) observes that social-emotional leaders tend to be more

attuned to the subtle nuances of interpersonal structures and their shifting alignments in the political process.

10. As George (1980, 139) once observed, the "personal orientation to conflict" of leaders is a major factor in determining their preferences for structuring their decision-making or advisory organizations in office.

11. The personality scores referred to are based upon detailed content analysis of both spontaneous interview responses and personal diary entries made by President Truman. The distinctions made regarding the high or low nature of the scores, are based upon the range of scores occurring within a general population of over one hundred world leaders of these characteristics. This research will be presented in Hermann, Preston and Young (forthcoming). In addition, the individual characteristics of Presidents Truman, Eisenhower, Kennedy, and Johnson, and their subsequent impact upon these leaders' advisory arrangements, are presented in more detail in Preston (1996).

12. Coding manuals for Margaret Hermann's "personality assessment-at-a-distance" profiling technique are available from the author at: Washington State University, Department of Political Science, Pullman, WA.

13. Other good accounts of Truman's decision making during the Korean War are found in Janis 1972; Paige 1968: De Riviera 1968; and Whelan 1990.

14. Interview conducted with George Elsey, March 28, 1994.

15. Oral history interview, George M. Elsey, July 17, 1969, 212, Truman Library.

16. Oral history interview, Matthew J. Connelly, November 28, 1967, 133, Truman Library.

17. Oral history interview, Connelly, 132.

18. Oral history interview, George M. Elsey, February 17, 1964, 50, Truman Library.

19. Ibid., 51.

20. Ibid., 51–52.

21. Oral history interview, George M. Elsey, March 17, 1976, 24, Truman Library.

22. Ibid., 24.

23. Ibid., 26–27.

24. Ibid., 27.

25. Oral history interview, Clark M. Clifford, February 14, 1973, 424–26, Truman Library.

26. Oral history interview, Charles S. Murphy, July 24, 1963, 111, Truman Library.

27. Oral history interview, George M. Elsey, July 7, 1970, 325, Truman Library (cf. oral history interview, State Department press officer, Roger Tubby, February 10, 1970, 76–78)

28. Oral history interview, George M. Elsey, March 17, 1976, 25–26, Truman Library.

29. Interview conducted with George Elsey, March 28, 1994.

30. Oral history interview, Clark M. Clifford, February 14, 1973, 442–44, Truman Library.

31. Oral history interview, Clark M. Clifford, October 4, 1973, 14–15, Truman Library.

32. Oral history interview, Clark M. Clifford, April 13, 1971, 95, Truman Library.

33. Interview conducted with George Elsey, March 28, 1994.

34. Interview conducted with George Elsey, March 28, 1994.

35. Joint Oral History Interview: The Truman White House, Charles Murphy, Richard Neustadt, David Stowe, and James Webb, February 20, 1980, 71, Truman Library.

36. Oral history interview, Clark M. Clifford, March 16, 1972, 394, Truman Library.

37. Ibid., 395.

38. Ibid., 393.

39. Oral history interview, Charles S. Murphy, July 24, 1963, 109, Truman Library.

40. Ibid., 110.

41. Oral history interview, Clark M. Clifford, October 4, 1973, 12, Truman Library.

42. Ibid., 12.

43. Ibid., 12.

44. Ibid., 13.

45. Ibid., 13.

46. Oral history interview, Charles S. Murphy, July 24, 1963, 106, Truman Library.

47. Oral history interview, George M. Elsey, February 10, 1964, 32, Truman Library.

48. Oral history interview, Clark M. Clifford, February 14, 1973, 460, Truman Library.

49. Oral history interview, George M. Elsey, February 10, 1964, 32–33, Truman Library.

50. Ibid., 34–35.

51. Ibid., 35.

52. Oral history interview, Charles S. Murphy, July 24, 1963, 106, Truman Library.

53. Oral history interview, Matthew J. Connelly, November 30, 1967, 215, Truman Library.

54. Ibid., 214.

55. Interview conducted with George Elsey, March 28, 1994.

56. Ibid.

57. Ibid.

58. James E. Webb to John W. Snyder, April 25, 1975, General Correspondence File, 1973–75, folder 2, Box 456, Papers of James E. Webb, Truman Library.

59. Intelligence Estimate Prepared by the Estimates Group, Office of Intelligence Research, Department of State, June 25, 1950, *FRUS, 1950,* 7:148–54.

60. James E. Webb to John W. Snyder, April 25, 1975, General Correspondence File, 1973–75, folder 2, Box 456, Papers of James E. Webb, Truman Library.

61. Ibid.

62. Ibid.

63. In attendance that evening were Dean Acheson (secretary of state), Louis Johnson (secretary of defense), Dean Rusk (assistant secretary of state), Frank Pace (secretary of the army), James Webb (undersecretary of state), Philip Jessup (ambassador-at-large), John Hickerson (assistant secretary of state for U.N. affairs), Gen. Omar Bradley (chairman, JCS), Gen. J. Lawton Collins (Army Chief of Staff), Gen. Hoyt

Vandenberg (Air Force Chief of Staff), Adm. Forrest Sherman (Chief of Naval Operations), Thomas Finletter (Secretary of the Air Force), and Francis P. Matthews (Secretary of the Navy).

64. Memorandum of Conversation, June 25, 1950, "Memoranda of Conversation, May–June 1950, Acheson" folder, Box 65, Papers of Dean Acheson, Truman Library.

65. Washington Post, June 15, 1951, 2.

66. The Secretary of State to the Embassy in the Soviet Union, June 26, 1950, *FRUS, 1950,* 7:176–77.

67. "President Truman's conversations with George M. Elsey", "Korea—June 26, 1950" folder, Box 71, Papers of George M. Elsey, Truman Library.

68. Ibid.

69. Ibid.

70. Memoranda of Conversation, by the Ambassador at Large (Jessup), June 26, 1950, *FRUS, 1950,* 7:178–83.

71. Ibid., 178–83.

72. Ibid., 178–83.

73. Ibid., 178–83.

74. Oral history interview, George M. Elsey, July 10, 1970, 440, Truman Library.

75. "Blair House Meeting—June 27, 1950," June 30, 1951, "Korea, June 27, 1950" folder, Box 71, Papers of George M. Elsey, Truman Library.

76. Resolution Adopted by the United Nations Security Council, June 27, 1950, *FRUS, 1950,* 7:211.

77. "Meeting of the NSC in the Cabinet Room at the White House," June 28, 1950; "Korea—June 28, 1950" folder; Box 71; Papers of George M. Elsey; Truman Library.

78. Donovan, 211; "Phone Call from Secretary Johnson," June 29, 1950; "Korea—June 29, 1950" folder; Box 71; Papers of George M. Elsey; Truman Library.

79. "Draft, June 29, 1950"; "Korea—June 29, 1950—W.H.-State-Defense Mtg., 5 pm." folder; Subject File; Box 71; Papers of George M. Elsey; Truman Library.

80. Ibid.

81. Ibid.

82. "Draft, June 29, 1950"; "Korea—June 29, 1950—W.H.-State-Defense Mtg., 5 PM." folder; Subject File; Box 71; Papers of George M. Elsey; Truman Library; "Memorandum for the President," June 30, 1950; "Memo's for President (1950)" folder; Box 220; NSC Meetings File; President's Secretary's Files; Papers of Harry S. Truman; Truman Library.

83. "Draft, June 29, 1950"; "Korea—June 29, 1950—W.H.-State-Defense Mtg., 5 PM." folder; Subject File; Box 71; Papers of George M. Elsey; Truman Library.

84. The Commander in Chief, Far East (MacArthur) to the Secretary of State, June 30, 1950, *FRUS, 1950,* 7:248–50.

85. "Teleconference with MacArthur, 300740Z (3:40 A.M., E.D.T.)," June 30, 1950; "Korea—June 30, 1950" folder; Box 71; Subject File; Papers of George M. Elsey; Truman Library.

86. Harry S. Truman to Alben N. Barkley, July 19, 1950; President's Secretary's File; General File; Box 113; Papers of Harry S. Truman; Truman Library.

87. Interview conducted with George Elsey, March 28, 1994.

88. Memorandum by Mr. John Foster Dulles, Consultant to the Secretary of State, to the Director of the Policy Planning Staff (Nitze), August 1, 1950, *FRUS, 1950,* 7:514.

89. Draft Memorandum Prepared in the Department of State for National Security Council Staff Consideration Only, August 23, 1950, *FRUS, 1950,* 7:635–39.

90. Draft Memorandum Prepared in the Department of Defense, July 31, 1950, *FRUS, 1950,* 7:502–10.

91. Ibid., 502–10.

92. Memorandum by Mr. Walter P. McConaughy to the Ambassador at Large (Jessup), August 24, 1950, *FRUS, 1950,* 7:641–43.

93. Memorandum by Mr. Walter P. McConaughy to the Ambassador at Large (Jessup), August 24, 1950, *FRUS, 1950,* 7:641–43.

94. Memorandum of Conversation, by Mr. James W. Barco, Special Assistant to the Ambassador at Large (Jessup), August 25, 1950, *FRUS, 1950,* 7:646–48.

95. Ibid., 646–48.

96. Ibid., 646–48.

97. Draft Memorandum Prepared in the Department of State for National Security Council Staff Consideration Only, August 30, 1950, *FRUS, 1950,* 7:660–66.

CHAPTER 8

Political Manipulation within the Small Group: Foreign Policy Advisers in the Carter Administration

Paul D. Hoyt and Jean A. Garrison

Introduction

Individuals operating in a group context are often driven to alter the group's structure and processes in an effort to enhance the strength of a preferred policy option. Such political manipulation has been defined as "an attempt by one or more individuals to structure a group choice situation in a manner that maximizes the chances of a favorable outcome or minimizes the chances of an unfavorable one" (Maoz 1990, 77). This definition limits manipulation to efforts at procedural manipulation during the deliberative stage of decision making. In this chapter we argue that this conception of political manipulation is too narrow. Instead we argue that manipulation takes place in multiple ways and at different phases of the decision-making process.

This focus on political manipulation is beneficial in that it also highlights certain aspects of the decision-making process that too often are downplayed or even ignored. The first is that decision making is an inherently *political* process often characterized by competition among the participants. Second, the role of the adviser(s) in the process is emphasized. The small group is here metaphorically seen as an arena for struggles, but also as a sorter, prestructuring policy outcomes. It is because of that second function that the small group invites attempts at political manipulation.

This elaborated conception of political manipulation will be developed in this chapter by focusing on the different strategies and tactics of manipulation available to political actors at different stages of decision making. These points will be illustrated with examples taken from two foreign policy episodes within the Carter administration; the debate over the 1978 U.S. response to the escalating Iranian Revolution and the Soviet Brigade in Cuba Crisis of 1979.[1]

Group Structure, Advisers, and the Decision-making Process under Carter

The advisory structure of any particular president will reflect the decision-making style of that president as well as his concerns over the mistakes of his predecessors (see Preston, this volume). President Carter was no exception to this rule. He was determined to diverge markedly from the Nixon/Kissinger White House–centered system that produced a closed and secretive foreign policy process (cf. Haney 1995). As a result, President Carter designed a collegial and open environment in which he promoted multiple advocacy as a means of allowing divergent views on key issues from his foreign policy advisers. In this process he meant to act as the hub of the wheel in the information structure (Moens 1990, 21; George 1980). In his memoirs, Carter says, he "found through experience that a collegial approach—with a group discussing the issue as equals—is good provided the gathering includes primarily those who would be directly involved in carrying out the decisions or explaining it to the public" (Carter 1982, 59).

In reality the Carter advisory process did not approximate a collegial system for long. Despite the president's best intentions, by his second year in office collegiality between the advisers had broken down and the system became increasingly White House–centered (Moens 1990). Bureaucratic rivals such as National Security Adviser Zbigniew Brzezinski and Secretary of State Cyrus Vance, strengthened by different motives and views of the world, openly maneuvered for influence in the group processes. As the competition escalated, advisers bent on "winning" the political game engaged in a destructive and highly public bureaucratic "war."

The change over time in the Carter administration from a system of managed competition to all-out warfare raises important questions about the conditions within the administration that led to this situation. The competition for scarce political resources, or influence among political advisers, provides us with a puzzle about how and why individuals manipulate the foreign policy process. Essentially, political manipulation of the decision-making process is undertaken by actors within the group (in this case foreign policy advisers) because decision making is a time for rewards to be earned and favored positions to be advocated. The desire to gain the ear of the president leads advisers to value access to the decision-making body and to covert influence within the group and over the process of group decision making.

Advisers, therefore, play a more active role than that of a collection processor or simple interpreters of information (Cronin and Greenberg 1969). They actively attempt to maintain their status or influence within the group as well as to manipulate to see their policy positions become government policy (Hilsman 1971; George 1980). To be effective, advisers must be able to cope with the maneuvers of others as well as with complex political constraints and high levels of uncertainty (Farnham 1993, 1990; Meltsner 1990). In other words, those decision makers are strategic actors, not cognitive misers or consistency seekers, who are able and motivated to adapt in the complex operating environment of foreign policy-making.

Fiske and Taylor (1991) describe the "motivated tactician" who is "a fully engaged thinker who has multiple cognitive strategies available and chooses among them based on goals, motives and needs." Sometimes the motivated tactician "chooses wisely, in the interest of adaptability and accuracy, and sometimes the motivated tactician chooses defensively, in the interest of speed or self-esteem" (Fiske and Taylor 1991, 13). Policy advisers such as the national security adviser could be motivated by strong beliefs, personality variables, ideological commitment, or emotions, such as fear, generated by a particular situation, but overall they are policy advocates with an interest in seeing their position prevail. National Security Adviser Brzezinski exemplified this attitude of the policy advocate. He said "I am very achievement oriented and I have this peculiarity in my personality that I have come to accept: By a very large margin, I prefer winning over losing—and, although I do not say this immodestly, I'm pretty good at winning. I win a great deal. I seldom lose, very seldom" (as quoted in Wooten 1979, 2–3).

It is this notion of the group process as a political enterprise, subject to manipulative acts, that we wish to emphasize in this chapter. An empirical focus on political manipulation requires that one more closely identifies those "tools" that advisers have at hand to influence the political process. Therefore, we examine various mechanisms through which actors can seek to enter the process and enhance their position within the decision-making group.

Strategies for Small Group Manipulation in Decision Making

In the U.S. political system, foreign policy decision making is commonly a group activity, consisting of the president and a circle of advisers (Hilsman 1971).[2] As George (1980), Hess (1988), and others have noted, while the relationship between the president and his advisers can vary across administrations and even across issues, the core notion of a president and a retinue of advisers is constant. What does change are the characteristics of the group and its process.

Within a group populated by policy advisers, often acting as policy advocates, questions of access to the decision-making group, status and influence within the group (especially vis-à-vis the president), and influence over the decision-making process are central to moving the group toward a favored position. Policy actors, aware of the necessity of access and influence, make

efforts to manipulate the composition of the group during the group construction stage and to manipulate the interpersonal relations and processes of the
group during the deliberative stage.

The assumption is that the actor is seeking an advantage in the decision-
making process and feels that certain manipulations of the group would be
beneficial to their preferred position. Manipulation can be advantageous in
that it can alter the relative weight of the contending positions; it can limit the
number, nature, and sequence of options under consideration; and it can limit
the breadth and depth of information available. Thereby one may increase
what Maoz (1990) has termed the "information asymmetry" among the positions.[3]

In the world of political maneuvering and gamesmanship there are a
variety of actions that the astute political manipulator can undertake. These
can be categorized as three broad strategies with numerous specific tactics
within two stages of the decision-making process: first, the group construction
stage, and second, the group deliberation and choice stage.[4] The first strategy
is to manipulate the group's structure, that is, to take actions that alter the
group's physical make-up in self-serving ways. A second strategy is procedural in nature and entails efforts by the actor(s) to manipulate the group's
operating procedures in ways that increase the relative strength of a favored
position. Finally, there is the strategy of interpersonal manipulation that entails efforts to alter the ways in which the group's members interact and
perceive one another. An actor who is able to manipulate the decision-making
group through one or more of these strategies gains an advantage, though not
necessarily a decisive one, in the decision-making enterprise.

The identification of the various strategies and tactics was done deduc-
tively through an extensive review of the literature. Illustrations of each strategy and tactic are provided by the two cases from the Carter administration,
each of which focuses on a different aspect of the manipulation process. The
case on the U.S. response to the Iranian Revolution focuses upon structural
manipulation in the group construction stage, while the case on the Soviet
brigade in Cuba focuses on procedural and interpersonal manipulation during
the deliberative stage. The evidence for the cases was drawn from pertinent
documents, archives, memoirs, oral histories, and interviews.

Manipulation of Group Construction

Strategy I. Structural Manipulation

Structural manipulation represents an effort by actors to alter the physical
composition of a group so that favored positions are well-represented while
contrary positions are either weakened or removed. Implementation of this

strategy requires that a group's membership is not fixed or static but instead is flexible or dynamic. While flexible membership is not likely to always to be the case—it may not even be the norm—when possible, it does represent an opportunity for political manipulation.

The notion of political manipulation of a group's structure, or construction, has not been deeply researched by either political scientists or social psychologists. Social psychologists, who have long studied the group construction stage as an integral aspect of the group decision-making enterprise, have not incorporated the potential for deliberate political manipulation of this stage of the process by the actors.[5] Political scientists, on the other hand, while particularly aware of the potential for politically motivated behavior within groups, have not tended to consider the group construction stage as a possible arena for such political manipulations, with policy advocates seeking to manipulate the group's composition as part of a self-serving effort to influence the course of the subsequent policy process (Hilsman 1971; Destler 1972; Allison 1971). Combining the insights from both disciplines, it is plausible that structural manipulation can take place during the group construction stage and needs to be considered as a form of political manipulation.[6]

Attempts to strategically alter or manipulate the formation of the group in terms of who participates is unlikely to determine the final decision output. However, it is easy to see where such actions could be influential through follow-on effects. Who participates is likely to influence the course of the decision-making process, affecting the number and nature of proposed solutions, the definition of the situation, and the relative strength of factions (Destler, Gelb, and Lake 1984; Hilsman 1971). Clever political players, aware that they can use structural manipulations to influence the course of the policy debate within the group, have at their disposal a number of tactics.

For actors committed to a particular policy position, the (potential) presence of contrary views within the decision-making group can make the adoption of their preferred position difficult. In response, the actor may seek to manipulate the construction of the group in self-serving ways. With structural manipulation, it is the physical makeup of the group that is manipulated. What is key in these situations is control over who is allowed to attend the meeting(s) that will decide policy. When this control systematically overrepresents some views and underrepresents others, the final decision will likely be skewed toward certain policy preferences.

The 1978 Iranian Revolution Case

Specific tactics of structural manipulation will be illustrated with examples taken from the Carter decision-making process regarding the Iranian Revolution. Let us briefly introduce the case. In the latter months of 1978, the domestic political and religious opposition to the Shah was growing stronger. The proposition, once considered unthinkable, that the Shah might not be able to survive as the absolute ruler of Iran now began to surface among some American policymakers. As the violence continued and escalated, the Carter administration came face to face with the question of how to respond, policywise, to the turmoil in Iran.[7]

Among Carter's foreign policy advisers, three broad policy positions developed. The question became which of these positions would win out, get Carter's endorsement, and set American policy for this provocative situation. The majority view was that there must be some way of salvaging the Shah's position but it acknowledged that he would not survive as an absolute monarch. This group pressed for strong support of the Shah but was uncomfortable with the idea of urging a military solution, the so-called iron fist approach, or of taking overt American action to preserve the Shah. This group included President Carter, Secretary of State Cyrus Vance and Special Counselor George Ball.[8]

A second set of actors had difficulty accepting that the Shah had been weakened by the unrest, and believed that there must be some way of salvaging the Shah. The advocates of this position argued that the main problem was that the Shah had simply lost his confidence. In terms of policy, this group pressed for strong support of the Shah and actively considered various forms of American intervention in Iran to preserve the Shah. Key proponents of this position were National Security Adviser Zbigniew Brzezinski, Secretary of Defense Brown, and General Robert Huyser.[9]

A third group believed that the Shah was lost. Their sense of the revolution's popularity and the complete lack of support and legitimacy felt toward the Shah by the population made further support for the Shah foolhardy. In terms of policy, they argued that it was now time for the United States to cut its losses and try to create links to the opposition in Iran as means of perhaps salvaging some of its position in a post-Shah Iran. This was the view, especially as the crisis wore on, of the Ambassador to Iran William Sullivan, and State Department Country Director for Iran Henry Precht.[10] As the crisis wore on advocates from the various positions worked hard to gain the ear of Carter in order to sway official policy. Carter's own ill-defined policy preference opened up the possibility for the advocates to influence the president. As part of this policy competition, access to the inner sanctum became contested, mainly as Brzezinski and those around him worked to stack the deck against Sullivan and Precht. Structural manipulation was one strategy employed in this contest.

Overall, there are two broad categories of such construction manipulations designed to influence the decision-making process; exclusion of contrary actors from the deliberative process and inclusion of supportive actors. We shall discuss both, first in general terms and then in the context of the case.

Exclusion

This strategy entails altering the composition of the group so that only those members with a sympathetic viewpoint are included. This is what Halperin calls "reducing the circle" (Halperin 1974, 124–127). This is accomplished most readily by arranging for particular participants to simply not be invited to crucial meeting(s) (Janis 1989). The goal is to construct a group so that those present can agree on a policy decision in the absence of potentially obstructing individuals. Tactics may include holding meetings while an opponent is out of town, simply not telling an opponent of upcoming meetings, or holding secret, informal meetings outside of the official group process.

Over time, a primary schism developed between Brzezinski and Precht, the Country Director for Iran. This disagreement led Brzezinski to seek to exclude Precht from further input on Iran policy. As George Ball noted, "Brzezinski was systematically excluding the State Department [Precht] from the shaping or conduct of our Iranian policy" even to the point of warning Ball to not talk to Precht because he "leaked" (Ball 1982, 458). Several participants also noted that Precht was regularly excluded from meetings on Iran in order to remove his viewpoint from consideration.[11]

Precht was aware of these efforts. In an "Official-Informal/Secret/Eyes Only" letter to Sullivan, Precht wrote, "I presume you are aware of the Top Secret list of questions that was sent out over the weekend for the Shah. I have not been shown the list, such is the level of distrust that exists in the White House [Brzezinski] towards the State Department (and egoistically, I feel, towards myself)."[12]

Ambassador Sullivan being in Tehran was not susceptible to physical exclusion. However, his position was not given full consideration as there was a strong discounting of Sullivan's cables in Washington. For example, after a private emissary was sent to Tehran, Sullivan complained to Brzezinski. In response, "Brzezinski sent back a sharp, tart report suggesting that what the administration chose to do was none of my business. I was aware from the tenor of this reply that my views were no longer held in much regard at the White House" (Sullivan 1981, 194).

This view of Sullivan led directly to the Huyser mission. Sullivan's status in Washington continued to fall during Huyser's stay. Carter later admitted that "I relied primarily on General Huyser, who remained cool and competent. He sought to maintain as wide a range of contacts as possible around Tehran during these last days of the Shah's reign, and as far as I could tell, he always sent back balanced views" (Carter 1982, 446). Huyser later confirmed Carter's feelings about Sullivan. He reported years later that when he was briefed by Carter in January (predeparture) Carter stated that he believed that Sullivan was "deranged and disloyal" (interview with Huyser, June 25, 1993). Sullivan was aware of his declining influence. In his memoirs, he summed up this facet of American decision making with the statement that "what was new was my inability to exert any constructive influence over Washington policy decisions" (Sullivan 1981, 8).

Inclusion

The opposite strategy of "widening the circle" is also viable (Halperin 1974, 127–131). This is an attempt to diffuse the influence of opponents by packing the group with additional like-minded participants. In such an enlarged group, policy opponents, though still present, would be seen as constituting a smaller, perhaps even minority, position. As a result the contrary position looks weaker. The appearance of being outnumbered may also have some effect upon the opponents themselves. Seeing their minority position, they may decide it is better to give in. A second form of inclusion occurs when actors, upon encountering resistance to a favored position, go outside the original group to develop alternative sources of information. In this manner, it is possible to bypass, or counter, contentious members of the group.

In the Iran case, to offset the potential influence of embassy and state department reports describing the Shah's likely collapse, Brzezinski sought to manipulate the group through inclusion as well. One specific mechanism was the "Brzezinski-Zahedi channel" between the national security adviser and the Iranian ambassador in Washington.

Brzezinski has described the channel as "a useful source of information, though I was aware that his [Zahedi's] perspectives were skewed and one-sided" (Brzezinski 1983, 360). More telling is the comment of Gary Sick, Brzezinski's aide responsible for Iran, who acknowledged that this "independent pipeline to Brzezinski was evidence that the White House had begun to have serious doubts about the completeness and accuracy of the ambassador's reporting" (Sick 1985, 99).

In mid-December Ball discussed with Secretary of State Vance the

shockingly unhealthy situation in the National Security Council, with Brzezinski doing everything possible to exclude the State Department from participation in, or even knowledge of, our developing relations with Iran, communicating directly with Zahedi to the exclusion of our embassy, and using so-called back channel (CIA channel) telegrams of which the State Department was unaware. (Ball 1982, 462; see also Vance 1983, 328).[13]

Convinced of Sullivan's opposition to his preferred policy option, Brzezinski sought to lessen Sullivan's influence in Washington by sending to Iran a number of actors to act as private emissaries and agents for those in Washington. Foremost among these visits was the mission of General Robert Huyser to Iran.[14] His assignment was to interact with the Iranian military leadership and convince them to support the Shah and if this was not possible to launch a coup in order to restore order (Bill 1988; Cottam 1988). Neither Ambassador Sullivan nor the department of state were aware of the visit until it was under way. As Sullivan saw it, "basically, it [the Huyser mission] was to short-circuit the normal policy procedural system that had been set up over the years for getting the input from all the concerned agencies" (interview with William Sullivan, May 24, 1993). Others in the embassy "saw it, definitely, as a mark of a lack of confidence in the embassy" (interview with Deputy Chief of Mission Charles Naas June 7 1993).

Group Construction Manipulation under Carter: Review

Over the course of the crisis, Brzezinski sought to reduce the influence of Precht and Sullivan. As Precht became more and more convinced of the vulnerability of the Shah and the need for the United States to begin to consider an Iran without him, he also found it increasingly difficult to find forums in which he could express this view. With Carter increasingly preoccupied by the Camp David Peace Accord, Brzezinski found himself with even greater control over the policy-making structures. Using his ability to control the agenda and the guest list, Precht was simply excluded from meetings on Iran, despite being the state department officer given the task of monitoring events in that country.

Ambassador Sullivan, stationed in Iran, was not susceptible to physical exclusion. However, there were other means of limiting his influence in decision-making circles. Two primary strategies were employed. The first was to mount a campaign aimed at destroying Sullivan's credibility with Carter. Sullivan was portrayed as a renegade, unwilling to follow policy, and contemptuous of Washington.

Once labeled as insubordinate, Sullivan was further removed from the decision making through the use of alternate sources of information. This meant that Sullivan's views were given less weight as other information channels promoted by Brzezinski were utilized. This form of inclusion, specifically, the use of the "back channel" communications between Brzezinski and the Iranian ambassador to Washington, Zahedi, and the Huyser mission, was designed to bypass Sullivan in the decision-making process.

The group of actors, centered around Brzezinski, appears to have been particularly active in seeking to reduce the presence and influence of others with whom they disagreed. While the members of this group were ultimately unsuccessful in getting their policy preference to prevail, they were successful in discrediting the Precht–Sullivan position such that this policy prescription never received a full hearing in Washington.

Manipulation during Group Deliberations

Once the composition of the group is determined, there also exists another set of procedural and interpersonal options available to actors within the group process. At this stage advocates are no longer merely trying to shape who is involved in the process, but also concerned with those aspects of decision making that control the process or procedures and efforts to gain compliance through the manipulations of interpersonal relationships. As a result, the discussion of how an individual influences a target (be it bureaucratic rivals or the president) becomes relevant. To be most successful in the deliberative stage an actor must engage in "the exercise of influence unobtrusively, the legitimation of decisions and actions, and the building of additional support and power behind a favored position" (Pfeffer 1981, 138).

The fluid decision-making environment between the members of the group within the deliberative stage is similar to a bargaining process in that give-and-take over policy options occurs over time. However, we emphasize a competitive environment in which not all parties can necessarily be satisfied with what they attain.[15] As actors manipulate the way others are perceived and the procedures of the process, some lose out so that others might win (cf. Barner-Barry and Rosenwein 1985, 210).[16] In the partially structured conflictual relationships emphasized in bureaucratic politics, manipulative tactics flourish. Each party sees their competitors "rationally" pursuing their own self-interest and therefore they engage in similar tactics. When there is room to maneuver, participants room to utilize "tactics such as threats, lies, deception, promises, rewards, and bribes" (Barner-Barry and Rosenwein 1985, 214; cf. Brickman 1974; Lewicki 1983). In this environment, individuals with differing objectives or worldviews can maneuver to attain their particular objectives.

The policymaker will be more successful in influencing other members of the group (or the target) to the extent that they like him, accept the authority of his role, perceive him as an expert, and recognize the efficacy of his influence strategies and tactics (Kipnis and Schmidt 1983; cf. Wrong 1983; Cialdini 1988; Raven, 1990).[17] This literature has been influenced in particular by French and Raven's (1959) landmark study and subsequent political applications (such as Raven 1990), in which they posit that several different bases of power help explain how individuals manipulate others. The promise of reward, the threat of punishment (coercion), legitimacy, expertise, reference (or identification), and information (persuasion) shape the use of various manipulative tactics. Concepts such as authority and status within the group based on these forms of power are critical because they begin to explain how others besides the president become central decision makers. The mere perception of authority can often explain the compliance of individuals in a particular situation. In complex situations, these experts may be accorded undue deference that makes them immune to challenges (George 1980). The decision maker with influence quite often is the one who controls scarce resources of which access and information are two of the most important.[18]

These manipulative and interpersonal maneuvers can be illustrated by looking at the relationship between advisers during another foreign policy decision-making episode in the Carter administration, the case of the Soviet brigade on Cuba. The main course of events was as follows: The "discovery" of a 2000–3000-man Soviet brigade in Cuba in 1979 created new problems for the Carter administration. According to press sources, in the spring of that year, Zbigniew Brzezinski ordered CIA director Stansfield Turner to assess the "age, location, capabilities and purposes of Soviet ground forces in Cuba" (Oberdorfer 1979, A18). Subsequently, much confusion was generated over the information provided by the intelligence analysis about the nature of the Soviet unit in Cuba. While the National Security Agency felt it was not necessarily an active combat brigade, other sources felt that there were firm indications of combat troops in Cuba.

On August 22, the CIA National Foreign Assessment Center finally issued its finding that a separate Soviet "combat" brigade existed. Before a clear policy response could be formulated, however, the issue became public. First, Senator Stone of Florida got information about the brigade and in mid-July alluded to its presence in Cuba in a public hearing on the Strategic Arms Limitation Treaty (SALT II). Senator Frank Church, chairman of the Senate Foreign Relations Committee, however, was the one who formally announced the presence of the brigade in Cuba to the press just before Labor Day. Running for reelection in Idaho, Senator Church saw an opportunity to meet some of the conservative attacks on his liberal voting record. He called on the president to demand that the brigade be withdrawn immediately from Cuba and eventually added that the SALT treaty probably could not be ratified unless the Soviets agreed to remove the brigade (Carter 1982, 262; Vance 1983, 360–361). These activities led to the creation of a pseudocrisis that severely threatened the passage of the SALT II treaty and hurt the president's overall credibility in foreign policy. In short, the labeling of the troops as a "combat brigade" made the matter a red-flag issue to the public and helped it become a media item. These words also made it a U.S./Soviet problem more than a U.S./Cuban problem. Therefore, defining the brigade as a "combat" unit was of semantic and political significance.

The crisis engaged the two main competing factions in foreign policy in the Carter administration in yet another political battle.[19] Some supported Brzezinski's more hard-line position that the troops must leave and that the Soviets had aggressive intentions in North America. Others supported Vance's position to not only preserve relations with the Soviets but also to limit the crisis to Cuba. Both Secretary Vance and Brzezinski employed several manipulative strategies to shape the foreign policy process during the Soviet Brigade in Cuba Crisis (Newsom 1987, 20–23; Brzezinski 1983, Vance 1983).

The conflict between competing worldviews came to a head as the two major foreign policy advisers shaped the agenda, framed the issue differently, and in their own way attempted to shape the policy response. The particular influence strategy becomes important because the decision maker must either manipulate the conditions around the target, or at the very least, seek the compliance of the target, in this case the president. The use of particular tactics shifted over time as well as with who held the advantage within the group. The administration started out relatively hard-line (along Brzezinski's policy line) and then gradually shifted to a softer stance (closer to Vance's understanding) regarding the presence of Soviet troops in Cuba.

For conceptual purposes, the maneuvers in the influence process have been broken down into two major strategies. Procedural manipulations control the policy process of group decision making. Interpersonal tactics are utilized, on the other hand, when the process is less open and decision-making rules have been formalized, by an individual attempting to maintain a certain level of status within the group or to gain compliance.[20]

Strategy II. Procedural Manipulation

Manipulation attempts are related to the degree of control an actor has over the situation as well as people's knowledge that they are being influenced, and hence the degree to which they will attempt to influence others. It is a process-oriented focus that is distinct from group construction at least in the timing of the manipulation and the scope of the strategy. The first criterion for influence is membership in the appropriate group or "inner circle." At this point, political manipulation involves the deliberate structuring of the process or the substantive information base (to suit one's purposes) for those people involved (Maoz 1990, 90–91).

Manipulation tactics are used not only to push one's own policy options, but also to mitigate the influence of contrary positions or rivals. Scholars such as Zeev Maoz describe manipulation as a device to shape formal rules for making decisions that affect who is involved and the feasibility of agenda manipulation. Although policy groups may have well-established choice rules that cannot be changed at will, members of a group can manipulate the decisions by choosing the "right" decision rule. Sequencing alternatives is more feasible when some decision makers can control the order of proposals on the floor in a manner that suits their preferences. Manipulation also includes cases where the power holder does not interact at all with the target, but arranges the latter's environment in such a way to elicit a desired response (Wrong 1983, 28, 67; cf. Pfeffer 1981). In addition to agenda-setting and framing discussed in more detail below, manipulation may include such tactics as the "salami tactic" in which major policy choices are enacted through small, incremental steps so that each policy decision only deviates from the previous policy marginally. Cumulatively, however, this has the same effect as the single "innovative," drastic alternative (Maoz 1990, 90–91; George 1980, 40; cf. Riker 1986). The following procedural tactics illustrate how policy options get on the table and focus upon the sequencing of discussion.

Agenda-Setting

Agenda setting is a manipulation scheme that involves defining the choice rule and defining the sequence by which options are introduced into the group. In action the decision maker who determines the procedure of group decision can affect the outcome without inducing preference change and has a structural advantage to shape the process. The "rigging rule" or agenda-setting refers to engineering an apparent consensus and legitimacy for a policy that may not be acceptable for some. The decision maker decides what he/she wants in advance and then "rigs" the meeting to muffle opposition. This can include distributing intelligence reports and experts' positions that support one's position, arranging meetings when dissenters are not present, and chairing meetings with an iron hand (Janis 1989, 56; Pfeffer 1981, 146–154; cf. Maoz 1990).

In order to keep the Soviet brigade as a nonissue, Cyrus Vance attempted to set the agenda to fit his policy position. When Brzezinski (and in fact most key decision makers) was out of town over the Labor Day holiday, Vance returned on August 28 and then seized control of the issue to localize the discussion rather than letting it go out of control into the broader focus on Soviet aggressiveness or Soviet support for Cuban revolutionary activity. He also set up channels of discussion with the Soviets. In his memoirs, Vance explains that he wanted to defuse the brigade issue before it became public (Vance 1983, 360).

In particular, in the August 29 Special Coordinating Committee (SCC) meeting, chaired by David Aaron (Brzezinski's aide), in a move that appears out of character, Vance proposed a "démarche" to the Soviets on the alleged Soviet brigade in Cuba. The group decided that Vance should wait to discuss the issue with Brzezinski and then Acting Secretary of Defense Graham Claytor before any more policy steps were taken. Rather than doing that, however, Vance moved quickly on his plan to "get to work" before the presence of the brigade was leaked. Vance and his team clearly took the initiative and for one of the few times during the Carter administration Vance become a strong public advocate for a policy position.[21] Vance further had gotten the unprecedented authority to manage the crisis through the Policy Review Committee, rather than the usual channel for crisis management, Brzezinski's Special Coordinating Committee. Before this, all crises had been handled by Brzezinski (Brzezinski 1983, 347–48).[22]

Also on August 29, Undersecretary of State Newsom met with Soviet officials and over a period of several days Vance also had four "exploratory" talks in which the Soviets made it clear that they would not accommodate the Americans (Newsom 1987, 33). Brzezinski concluded in an October 12, 1979 weekly report on NSC activities to the president that "The formal machinery (SCC) was used sporadically, and the issue was left to State with the Policy Review Committee. The SCC was not convened because Cy wanted to retain control over process as well as U.S.-Soviet negotiations. You should insist if similar crises arise that the SCC manage them" (Brzezinski 1983, 566). By taking the initiative on the policy away from the National Security Advisor, Vance was able to control the process for quite some time.

Brzezinski also used his position to set the agenda in ways that would advance his preferred options to the president during the brigade crisis. On one such occasion, finding a Policy Review Committee meeting filled with Secretary Vance's "dovish State Department associates," Brzezinski urged the president to participate in the discussion. This meant that the meeting was automatically transformed into a NSC session and that the lower-level officials had to depart. As director of the NSC, Brzezinski had the responsibility to summarize the previous discussion, and he got to set the agenda to his advantage for the rest of the meeting (Brzezinski 1983, 349). His actions early in the spring of 1979 also had shaped the agenda for the administration. By repeatedly raising questions about Soviet activities in the Western Hemisphere and by ordering the intelligence review and surveillance of Cuba in the first place, he brought this issue before the administration.

Framing the Issue

By framing the issue in a particular way, the desired policy choice can also be produced. Framing involves the definition of the decision problem in which an individual's choice can be changed by framing a "given choice problem differently" (Maoz 1990, 88; cf. Bazerman and Neale 1983 and Vertzberger 1992). People do not recognize that they are being manipulated and as a result the reliability of the data or "fairness" of the choice procedures are not brought into question. Framing clearly involves the way information is presented in a group and which pieces of information are emphasized over others. In a situation where there is an asymmetrical distribution of information or a single individual in control of the information process, that decision maker is in the unique position of framing the issue in a manner that suits his or her goals. Others then find it harder to question the reality that has been created and counterframing becomes more difficult (Maoz 1990).[23]

In the competitive environment of the Carter administration, both advisers tried to frame the issue to their advantage in order to produce their desired policy choice. One administration official, Robert Beckel, described the ideological split between the two advisers and the tremendous pressure the president was under at this point in time. As Beckel explains:

> Nobody's going to agree on all things about any particular issue. This happened with how to deal with the Russian brigade. Vance wanted to say "let's just put this thing in proper perspective," Brzezinski said "no, no, no, we've got to be tough on this" and then somehow in the course of the conversation Brzezinski thought this was the opportunity to be tough on the Russians. (Beckel 1981, 35)

Vance attempted to keep the issue narrowly focused on the brigade. He felt that it was "highly unlikely that the Soviets would agree to withdraw the brigade, if this became a public issue" and wanted to defuse the issue. Vance felt he should buy time until he could talk to Anatoly Dobrynin directly to restore SALT and stability to U.S.–Soviet relations. It was an important issue but it did not warrant a "crisis" atmosphere (Newsom 1987, 38–40; Vance 1983, 360).

The decision-making context in this situation was wider than just the group focus. Vance's early actions to diffuse the issue clearly illustrated that he was attempting to keep it separate from SALT II and out of public debate. Vance worked out his plan to brief key members of Congress by telephone on August 28 in an attempt to cut off congressional opposition by saying that he had already lodged a strong protest with the Soviets. Undersecretary of State

Newsom's contacting of Senator Church, the chairman of the Senate Foreign Relations Committee, and emphasis that there was "no threat" posed by the brigade could arguably be an attempt to frame the issue in order to stop panic. Vance felt that Church "would say nothing and that there would be no public discussion" (Vance 1983, 361). Unfortunately for Vance, Senator Church did hold a news conference.

Secretary Vance's attempts to defuse the issue backfired. In that news conference Senator Church linked the combat brigade to SALT II and set up the framework by which the issue would be discussed within the media that changed the nature of the game. In his attempts to define the debate of the issue, Vance further contributed to the public crisis in his September 5 press conference when he said "I will not be satisfied with the maintenance of the status quo" (Vance 1983, 362). In reply to a posed question, he sounded tougher than he intended and sparked speculation that the U.S. would demand the removal of the brigade from Cuba. He had emphasized that the status quo was unacceptable in an attempt to limit debate to Cuba and not involve American–Soviet relations. The press grabbed hold of the phrase and took it to mean that the U.S. would force the removal of the troops. The use of the words *combat* and *status quo* caught the eye of the press and made it hard for the United States to accept the Soviet presence in Cuba (Newsom 1987, 41–44). The press also focused on whether the troops constituted a base and why the administration had not asked for their removal. The questions asked linked the issue to SALT (Newsom 1987, 35; Vance 1983, 362; Brzezinski 1983, 422; cf. Gwertzman 1979, A4; Duffy 1983).

The National Security Adviser was also busy framing the issue to suit his needs. On August 14, before the issue became public, Brzezinski alerted the president that the scheduled firing exercises of the brigade in Cuba were a serious development that could adversely affect SALT (Brzezinski 1983, 346–47). Brzezinski's strategy after the issue became public was to continue to use this episode to win support for a broader anti-Soviet strategy that reflected his belief that the Soviet Union was a threat to the interests of the United States. He pressed for "a policy decision that would put primary emphasis on the world-wide thrust of Soviet assertiveness and thus de-emphasize the Cuban issue itself" (Brzezinski 1983, 349). Brzezinski had the advantage because he only had to step up his rhetoric on the "aggressive" nature of the Soviet Union. The public nature of the crisis made the "brigade" a political issue ripe for exploitation.[24]

Repeatedly, he bolstered his position by publicly emphasizing the dangerous nature of the Soviet brigade in Cuba. As he stated, "it involves the stationing of Soviet combat forces in the Western Hemisphere in a country that at the same time is pursuing an internationally active revolutionary role. It is more, therefore a political problem" (Pincus and Wilson 1979, A19). In late

September, Brzezinski verbally attacked Cuba and said the force had "a definite combat character and capability" but left open that it could perform other functions (Gwertzman 1979b, A1). He emphasized that there was something "new" in Cuba that would make it more of a threat to the United States (Pincus and Wilson 1979, A19). Brzezinski also described Cuba and Fidel Castro as a "Soviet puppet" publicly although it strained U.S. credibility.

Brzezinski even hinted at retaliatory action publicly. He took the position that "we should stress Cuban activism world-wide on behalf of Soviet interests as the main problem . . . [and] hint to the Soviets that we will intensify our relationship with the Chinese if the Soviets are not co-operative" (Brzezinski 1983, 348). Administration officials accused Brzezinski of opening the administration to unnecessary charges that its analysis of the information could be faulty. In a memo to Brzezinski, Robert Pastor said "Soviet satellite, collaborator, ally, or partner" would be better terms to describe the Soviet–Cuban link rather than continually describing them as "Soviet Puppets" (Pastor 1979, 1).

The department of state's mishaps presented an opportunity for Brzezinski to take control of the issue once more and directly influence the president. His public and private posturing reflected his attempt to again "consolidate his ascendancy over Vance and the State Department while turning the president toward a harder line" (Smith 1986, 215). In a memo entitled "Acquiescence vs. Assertiveness" Brzezinski stated, "I think that the increasingly pervasive perception here and abroad is that in U.S.–Soviet relations, the Soviets are increasingly assertive and the U.S. more acquiescent. State's handling of the Soviet brigade negotiations is a case in point. I recommend that in the future we will have to work for greater White House control" (Brzezinski 1983, 365). The president commented "good" in the margin.

Attempts to shape the agenda and frame the issue can be helped by leaking information that can define the way that an issue is debated. In fact, just the threat of a leak may be enough to block a policy from being discussed or implemented. Leaking not only gets policies noticed, but brings the policy discussion to the attention of the public and the domestic political arena. Leaks, therefore, can be used to undermine a rival, to get a proposal through, to catch the attention of the president, to build support, to insure implementation of a policy, or to alert foreign governments (Halperin 1974, 176–181; cf. George 1980).[25]

The agenda-setting and framing tactics help explain the overt procedural tactics of decision makers to influence the decision-making process by changing the structure of the decision or shaping the way an issue is defined. In this way, the debate within the administration shifted from a debate over the presence of the Soviet brigade to the implications of the data—whether the brigade represented a threat to U.S. security or not. These strategies do not, however, fully illustrate the options available to the adviser to influence his target. The utilization of interpersonal manipulative tactics, in particular by Cyrus Vance, helps explain the final shift in the dominance of players in the process and the eventual softening of the administration's hard-line stance.

Strategy III. Interpersonal Manipulation in the Small Group

Interpersonal manipulation is characterized by attempts to shape formal and informal relationships between members of the group in order to attain one's preferred option. Decision makers engage in tactics that strengthen their own position or status within the group or shape the way other political actors are perceived. An individual can attempt to maintain his/her status within the group, for example, through the use of coercion (pressure and threats) when they perceive themselves in a strong position in the decision-making group. The use of expertise and the formation of formal or informal coalitions (or other exchanges) also illustrates some of the other ways in which individuals can alter their status within the group and therefore manipulate the process. Empirical studies of persuasion tactics in social psychology identify several potential interpersonal tactics open to a decision maker in different contexts and interdependent relationships (cf. Yukl and Tracey 1992; Yukl and Falbe 1990; Kipnis and Schmidt 1986; Cialdini 1988; Forsyth 1990, 187–210). The following tactics are a sample of those available to the decision maker. Maneuvers will vary depending on the status, commitment, capabilities and motives of the individual.

Pressure and the Use of Threats

Interpersonal tactics utilized by individuals depend partially upon structural role relationships and the sources of influence available to particular advisers. The ability to use more assertive tactics such as "pressure" successfully comes from an individual's position of strength. Pressure involves the use of more directive means of influence (or coercion) such as demands, threats, or persistent reminders to influence the target to do what the agent wants (Yukl and Tracey 1992, 525–35; cf. Kipnis and Schmidt 1986). In the political game, threatening tactics and personal attacks such as discrediting become legitimate behavior and uses of information. The personalized blame game (for example attacks are made on a rival's abilities) is but one example. Deceptive tactics such as bluffing, falsification, misrepresentation, and lying become commonplace (Lewicki 1983). The deliberate leak of information (or threat of a leak) that attacks the character of a bureaucratic rival could also be placed in this category. As illustrated, Vance and Brzezinski both placed pressure on the president and Brzezinski went so far as to blame administration mishaps and miscalculations on Vance directly.

Brzezinski tried to discredit the department of state and Cyrus Vance personally with the president and the American public. He publicly blamed the department of state for any mismanagement since they had taken over control of the issue. He felt that they precipitated the crisis by premature briefings, large discussion sessions, and a disregard of established procedures for crisis management (Brzezinski 1983, 352; Vance 1983; Newsom 1987). In a broad public blame game (or an attempt at one-upmanship), Brzezinski blamed Vance for the initial leak as well as the media's reaction to the department of state's mishandling of the brigade issue. He concluded, "there were too many participants in the decision-making process, some made unsustainable statements and there was a lack of precision in goals" (Brzezinski 1983, 566). In addition, Brzezinski threatened to resign after the resolution of the crisis if the control of such crises did not revert to the domain of the National Security Adviser.

Expertise and Coalition Building

Individuals in a weaker bargaining position may seek out allies who concur with their perspective to strengthen their bureaucratic position.[26] Building a coalition not only refers to the utilization of allies for the purpose of "social proof" to press your case in a decision making but also can serve the purpose to bring in outside expertise. Consultation with colleagues is an internal and less elaborate search for support and advice and most importantly represents an effort to continue to limit influence to those within the inner circle (Yukl and Tracey 1992, 525–35; cf. Barner-Barry 1985). Schattschneider (1975, 15) notes that "if one side is too hard-pressed, the impulse to redress the balance by inviting in outsiders is almost irresistible." In other words, private power relations can be modified by enlarging the scope of the conflict by bringing in outside help. This results in a more public strategy.[27]

In the end, Brzezinski did not prevail in his attempts to shift Carter to a harder line and Vance's utilization of coalition building in the decision-making process partially accounts for this. In his meetings with Gromyko, over time Vance became convinced that "the Soviets would not do more" (Vance 1983, 363). Further search of intelligence data had already revealed that the training unit in Cuba was permissible under the 1962 agreement between John Kennedy and Nikita Khrushchev.

Vance, therefore, broadened the number of behind-the-scenes players despite Brzezinski's disapproval in order to provide the president with outside expert advice. First, he encouraged the president to discuss the brigade issue with Senator Byrd, who had just returned from consulting with Anatoly

Dobrynin. Concerned about SALT, Byrd told the president to cool the rhetoric. Vance, also, organized a group of outside experts or senior statesmen called the "wise men" to meet with the president.[28] These men were meant to verify or question the initial conclusions of the intelligence community and Brzezinski's hard-line position that the brigade was a recent strengthening of Soviet forces in Cuba. The group gave the president wider consultation (widening the circle) and in by doing so Vance hoped that Carter would decide to take a softer stance on Cuba. In that meeting, the "wise men" concluded it was a rediscovery of an existing brigade and accused Brzezinski of deliberately trying to revive the Cold War with his hard-line rhetoric. After the meeting, Vance encouraged the president to treat the brigade issue "as a serious but isolated incident" and "not aimed at the overall U.S./Soviet relationship." It was certainly a move to take into account domestic political considerations and to move on to SALT (Brzezinski 1983, 347–50; Vance, 1983, 364). It also reflected Vance's realization that his initial attempts to frame the issue had not been successful.

Brzezinski, also, in a more limited fashion, tried to include bureaucratic allies in the process to push Carter for a tough reaction to the Cuban situation. When Vance relied upon support from Lloyd Cutler, Brzezinski balanced that by inviting presidential adviser Hedley Donovan into the Situation Room. While Brzezinski stayed opposed to the president soliciting outside advice from Senator Byrd and the "wise men," he, himself, collaborated with Secretary of Defense Brown in order to obtain a policy decision with an emphasis on the worldwide thrust of Soviet assertiveness and the de-emphasis of Cuba as an isolated case (Brzezinski 1983, 346–49). His tactics reflected his one-time dominance of the process. He needed bureaucratic allies, but at this stage of the game sought them only from within the administration.

Group Deliberation Manipulation: Review

In the long run, it was President Carter's concern for SALT II that made him take a moderate line on the Cuban brigade issue. In his memoirs, Carter indicates his tough response was formed before he knew the brigade was a remnant of a larger force from the 1960s. His October speech to the nation further reflected his ambiguous thoughts on the situation in Cuba (Carter 1982, 264; Carter 1980, 1757). The situation also reflects conditions under which these influence maneuvers can flourish.

Beyond the infighting between the advisers found in the brigade case, the utilization of these manipulation strategies by two foreign policy advisers illustrates the central role political advisers play in the policy "game." Both advisers manipulated the group situation and each was successful to a certain extent during different times in the process. Along the way, routine intelligence data was turned into a pseudocrisis. Since President Carter was unable to come up with an integrated view of what he wanted and unable to rein in the members of his inner circle, manipulation was prevalent and obvious. The public nature of the "combat brigade" debate and the scarcely concealed internal debate within the administration made Carter appear indecisive.[29] He seemed far from the active policy coordinator that he had been during the formulation of the administration's SALT stance. His credibility suffered as a result.

Conclusions

The reality, and complexity, of the U.S. foreign policy decision-making process, as discussed and subsequently illustrated in the two cases presented, calls attention to five aspects of political manipulation in group decision making. First, we need to expand our notion of what is considered to be political manipulation. In this chapter we have proposed that manipulation be considered as occurring as a structural, procedural, and/or interpersonal activity. Second, manipulation is not temporally bounded but can occur at different points, or stages, in the decision-making process. We have noted that manipulation is possible in the group's construction and deliberation stages.[30] Third, to account for the pervasiveness and perceived utility of political manipulation, we have emphasized the notion of a political motive (the adoption of a preferred policy option) among the group members. This stands in contrast to some other views of group process, including groupthink, which emphasize more social motives such as group affiliation and cohesion. Fourthly, inherent in this discussion is the underlying premise that in the decision process, advisers are political actors whose semi-independent role needs to be considered and incorporated. Conceptions of the single leader surrounded by passive assistants is simply not adequate in describing the reality of the process. Finally, there appears to be no immediate reason why our perspective on the group process cannot be applied to a broader range of cases and contexts. Research into the decision-making process in other countries, on non–national security matters, and perhaps even in the corporate world all may be advised to consider the notion of political manipulation as a dynamic element in the process.

In conclusion, it has been our contention that group decision making is a dynamic, not static, process in which actors are motivated to act strategically. Focusing on the group in this manner provides a view of decision making emphasizing the symbiotic relationship between the members of the inner circle, in the U.S. setting, and particularly between the president and his foreign policy advisers. A separate focus on only the individual or group level of analysis would miss this complex interdependent relationship between the actors. Synthesizing various bodies of literature in a more interdisciplinary and holistic approach contributes to our understanding of the totality of the decision-making process.

NOTES

1. The Carter presidency is a particularly rich context for a study of political manipulation given the combination of a relatively indecisive president (by the second half of the administration) surrounded by strong, and often divided, advisers. As President Carter came to question his own view of the world, he became particularly susceptible to the maneuvers of his advisers (see, for example, Rosati 1987). This by no means indicates that the president was unaware of the manipulations of those around him.

2. It has been noted by many scholars of foreign policy that there appear to be certain circumstances under which a focus on decision making in small groups is most appropriate. For example, Destler, Gelb, and Lake (1984) point to those factors, such as the formation of the NSC and the subsequent rise of the Special Assistant for National Security Affairs, which have led to the centralization of policy-making within the White House. Others have noted that during crisis periods, in particular, when decision-making time is short and important values and goals are threatened, that small group processes are critical because of the tendency to constrict decision making to the top levels of authority. Rosati (1981) has described crises as a time of presidential preeminence when the president and his advisers are highly interested and involved in the decision-making process.

3. Manipulation can also be a beneficial strategy in that it allows for a preferred position to be given a greater likelihood of adoption without the actor having to go through the overt, and difficult, process of persuasion. Advantage can be gained more subtly without having to attempt to alter other group members' beliefs (Maoz 1990). Persuasion tactics, however, often accompany and bolster manipulative tactics and therefore should also be considered an integral part of the influence process.

4. Of course, these strategies are simply conceptual categories and thus not mutually exclusive in the real world. For an example of the concept of stages in group decision making, see Mintzberg et al. 1976.

5. While the formation of a group is considered to be a central aspect of small groups, with a large potential impact on subsequent group operations and processes, this stage of a group's life cycle is relatively under-studied (Levine 1987). Levine also notes that most of the social psychology literature on how groups are formed can be placed into one of four perspectives: environmental, behavioral, affective, and cognitive (1987). The political perspective is conspicuously absent from this review of the literature. Some early work by Festinger and Schachter (Festinger 1950; Festinger et al. 1952; Schachter 1951, 1954) and others did show that opinion deviants are often rejected by majoritarian group members who sometimes would seek to restructure the group so that deviants were excluded. This research, while informative, paints only part of the possible story because it fails to consider that structural manipulation is not of

necessity the sole province of the majority faction in a group and that this manipulation may take place for more political than social reasons.

6. The literature on small group decision making within political science has tended to accept the existence of the group as a given, not to consider it a separate stage in the group decision-making process with potential effects on the group's output. Instead attention has focused on certain aspects of the group or its relations to other actors. One aspect of groups that has been examined is its formal structure. For example, authors have looked at the structure of the National Security Council as a decision-making institution (Prados 1991; Nathan and Oliver 1987; Lord 1988); the formal relationship between the Congress and the Executive in foreign policy-making (Crabb and Holt 1992; Spanier and Nogee 1981); the operant decision rule within the group (Hermann 1979), and the shape and style of the foreign policy advisory system (George 1980; Hess 1988). Another line of research has been to examine the nature of the relationship between the group's members. The main division here is between a more competitive view of the process, the so-called bureaucratic politics perspective (Allison 1971; Halperin 1974; Destler 1972), and those who focus more on cooperative aspects of intragroup relations, the "groupthink" perspective (Janis 1982; 't Hart 1990/1994). While neither of these perspectives focuses on how groups are formed, they do appear to share an implicit conviction that the structure of the group matters, with effects upon both the policy process and policy output. Where the foreign policy small group literature has been deficient has been in examining just how groups evolve in terms of their structure and composition.

7. For a full discussion of the Iranian Revolution and American decision making, see Cottam 1988; Bill 1988; Sick 1985; and Stempel 1981.

8. In general, they believed that the Shah could survive the current upheaval, but they felt that dramatic reforms were probably necessary. Their specific proposals varied within this general framework. Some, like Carter, urged continued support of the Shah without drastic changes, while others, for example Ball, favored the creation of alternative opposition-based governments that then may or may not be able to salvage some role for the Shah. For evidence of this position see Ball 1982; Vance 1983; and Carter 1982.

9. For evidence of this position see Brzezinski 1983; Sick 1985; Brown 1983; and Huyser 1986. Additional information was obtained through interviews conducted by the second author with Robert Huyser (June 25, 1993) and Gary Sick (May 28, 1993).

10. For evidence of this position see Sullivan 1981, 1984, and 1987. See also the following documents: "Looking Ahead: Shifting Iranian Public Attitudes," October 30, 1978, *Asnad-i* vol. 12, part 3, 166–74; "Iran and the Shah: A Rocky Road Ahead," September 21, 1978, *Asnad-i*, vol. 12, part 3, 65–71; "Thinking the Unthinkable," November 9, 1978, NSA #1711; "Attitudes and Troubles in the Iranian Military," December 21, 1978, NSA #1950; "Seeking Stability in Iran," memo from Precht to Saunders, December 19, 1978, NSA #1939; and letter from Precht to Sullivan, December 19, 1978, NSA # 1938. Additional information was obtained through interviews conducted by the second author with Henry Precht, May 18, 1993; and William Sullivan, May 24, 1993.

11. Interviews with David Newsom, June 8, 1993, and William Sullivan, May 24, 1993.

12. Letter from Precht to Sullivan, December 19, 1978, NSA #1938.

13. The very presence of Ball in the decision-making process is a good example of inclusion that failed. Brzezinski later admitted that "in selecting Ball I violated a basic rule of bureaucratic tactics: one should never obtain the services of an 'impartial' outside consultant regarding an issue that one feels strongly about without first making certain in advance that one knows the likely contents of his advice" (Brzezinski 1983, 370–71).

14. The idea of sending an emissary on this task was Brzezinski's. His original plan was to go himself because he doubted Sullivan would take any actions to save the Shah. General Huyser was given the mission after George Ball told Carter that sending Brzezinski was the "the worst idea I have ever heard" (Ball 1982, 461). Upon saying so, Ball remembers Brzezinski glared at him "with daggers in his eyes" (interview with George Ball May 27, 1993).

15. Vertzberger (1990) describes the nay-saying situation in which bureaucratic rivals are unable to resolve their differences and the policy process is stymied. Policy gridlock and certainly manipulation result (see also Stern and Sundelius, this volume).

16. It should be remembered that the amount of influence attempted within the group in the deliberative stage is determined by a process of interaction in which the behavior of people within the group is highly interdependent. This emphasis is very similar to the symbiotic relationship between the leader and the follower that is described in the literature on political leadership (see, for example, Bass 1990, 1985, and Burns 1978).

17. Stricter hierarchies provide latitude in fixing decision procedures and agendas, opportunities to get information about preferences and data, and the freedom to frame issues (Maoz 1990, 94). It follows, therefore, that in more open structures such as the Carter system, there would be room for more diverse decision makers to try to manipulate the process and also that group manipulation could be effectively countered.

18. Informational conditions, however, are arguably the most important determinants of the feasibility and success of procedural and interpersonal manipulation within the group. Asymmetrical information and expertise enable members of the group to apply various tactics successfully during the bargaining stage of group decision making. The decision maker who provides the most information is in a unique (or best) position to frame the issue. Information management becomes a means of safeguarding autonomy (Maoz 1990).

19. Once again Brzezinski and Vance showed tendencies to rely on prior beliefs or commitments to interpret new "threats" posed by the Soviet Union (see, for example, Rosati 1987). Their reactions can be understood as "a strong tendency for people to see what they expect to see and to assimilate incoming information to pre-existing images" (Jervis 1976, 117). Confirming evidence is quickly and accurately noted to support current beliefs.

20. The literature in social psychology makes a distinction between public compliance which leads to behavior change and private acceptance which most closely resembles attitude change. Levine and Russo (1987, 36) found that majorities are more

likely to produce compliance while minorities tend to produce conversion. Compliance in this literature most closely approximates the procedural and interpersonal manipulation we describe. On the other hand, private acceptance connotes a conversion or lasting preference change.

21. Vance's actions seem out of character because for most of the administration, Vance demonstrated an aversion to public advocacy that left Brzezinski to step forward. Carter describes that once it became a contest Brzezinski became very competitive. Carter describes Brzezinski as the advocate, not Vance (Carter 1982, 42–43).

22. The NSC was served by two competing committees that created two centers for foreign policy. The Special Coordinating Committee (SCC), chaired by Brzezinski, was designed to deal with specific issues which cross-cut foreign policy bureaucracies. These included issues such as crisis management and arms control. The Policy Review Committee (PRC), chaired by the relevant department secretary (quite often Cyrus Vance) was designed to develop policies that overlapped departments.

23. Prospect theory demonstrates the importance of the framing effect. They show that individuals treat the prospect of gain differently than the prospect of loss. Different policy options are chosen depending upon how the issue is framed (Tversky and Kahneman 1981).

24. The continued attempts by Brzezinski and Vance to define the debate of the issue could simultaneously be interpreted as a means for them to persuade the president to their policy position. By bolstering and legitimating their position, by persistently playing up the advantages of an option and downplaying the disadvantages, advisers make their preferred option look good and others bad. Alternately, one can solicit supportive information and refute unwelcome information about the drawbacks to a particular option (Janis 1989, 57). By legitimating his position in such a way, the decision maker can attempt to authenticate a policy given its consistency with current policy objectives and with earlier beliefs and information. In the conflictual environment, each adviser simply points out different evidence to lend credence to his/her policy preference (Cialdini 1988; Yukl and Tracey 1992; Yukl and Falbe 1990; Pfeffer 1981).

25. There is also evidence that well-timed leaks brought the issue up in the first place and also helped particular bureaucratic sides. Gloria Duffy (1983, 76) speculates that "motivation for leaking the document would have been dissatisfaction with Soviet behavior, SALT II, and the Carter State Department's approach to dealing with the Soviets. Among those who had access . . . were anti-SALT Senators' staffs or the NSC." Army Intelligence or the National Security Agency were also possibilities.

26. In a decision-making situation in which levels of status and authority are more equitable, other maneuvers become useful. In a bargaining situation, the individual can offer an exchange of favors, indicate a willingness to reciprocate later on, or promise a share of the benefits if a particular task is accomplished. Such bargaining assumes that those involved group members are willing to compromise to reach closure in the decision-making process (see, for example, Yukl and Tracey 1992; French and Raven 1959). This does not seem to be the case in these illustrations from the Carter administration.

27. The literature on the influence of minorities within the group confirms this. A

high status minority can successfully draw more attention to a particular policy option and even change the preferences of others especially if the size of the minority is enlarged (for example, see Maass, West, and Cialdini 1987, 1986; and Moscovici and Doise 1994).

28. The "wise men" were a broad cross-section made up from former Republican and Democratic officials from State, Defense, CIA, and White House officials. The "wise men" consisted of George W. Ball, McGeorge Bundy, Clark Clifford, Roswell L. Gilpatric, W. Averell Harriman, Nicholas deB. Katzenbach, Henry Kissinger, Sol Linowitz, John J. McCloy, John A. McCone, David Packard, William Rogers, Dean Rusk, James R. Schlesinger, Brent Scowcroft, and William Scranton (Vance 1983, 363).

29. Jerry Rafshoon wrote to Carter, you do not "want people to be angry with you so you too often try to soft pedal those decisions. That's a big mistake . . . In addition to not waffling or trying to please everyone you should present everything firmly . . . People want to know that once you've decided something, its decided. You're sure. You're firm. You're tough" (Rafshoon 1979, 3).

30. There is also, of course, the well-documented area of manipulation during the implementation stage as well. We have not dealt with that aspect here as it is seen as outside of the small group decision-making scope of the chapter.

CHAPTER 9

Collective Risk Taking:
The Decision-making Group

Yaacov Y. I. Vertzberger

1. Introduction

Some decisions are made by individuals, but more often decision making is a collective enterprise that involves a small group and is carried out by organizations. In nonroutine, convention-breaking risky cases, such as foreign military intervention decisions, it is unlikely that final decisions will be made through organizational SOPs. Organizational inputs are, however, crucial in this process. Organizations collect data, interpret it, and disseminate it through a highly politicized process to individual decision makers. They may also define the problem and the relevant risk dimensions as seen from each organization's perspective and thus create a pluralistic, competitive, complex, possibly enlightened—but still confusing—decision-making environment. Eventually the aggregation of these inputs and the resulting decisions take place, often in small groups composed of representatives of all or some of the relevant organizations (although the group is not necessarily composed exclusively of organizational representatives). It is therefore critical to understand whether and how risk aggregation affects the direction of risk-taking dispositions in collective decision-making contexts. For reasons related to the main emphasis of this volume, as well as space constraints, this chapter does not discuss in detail the role of organizations but focuses on the small decision-making group.

The chapter aims for a balanced view of how group risk judgments evolve and risk preferences are shaped. Such a view takes into account a broad range of causes and processes, is not dominated exclusively by social interaction variables, but is contingent upon a set of group attributes. It is important to avoid overemphasis on social interaction at the expense of other driving forces that affect group information processing and choice outcomes. This posture reflects better the essence of real-life situations in natural groups.

275

Expectations that social interaction within a group will be the main driving force for shaping individual group members' views, perceptions, and preferences are often unrealistic, especially in political decision-making groups. This view neglects to take into account that group membership is not necessarily a matter of free choice. It is usually the result of constitutional requirements, institutional arrangements, and the force of circumstances (for example, election outcomes imposing a coalition government), which allow a particular group composition to emerge as the legitimate decision-making body. That being the case, social interaction is not necessarily sought after nor will individuals readily abandon their views for commonly shared group beliefs. It is mostly in the faction, as shall be explained in some detail later on, that social interactions are more likely to play the dominant role in shaping judgments and preferences. The reason for this is that faction membership is voluntary, a product of choice. Faction membership results from explicit or implicit commonalties that are intellectual (common beliefs), functional (common goals), or emotional (mutual respect between members or shared admiration for a leadership figure). Faction members choose to share physical and social space with other members and are therefore open to influence from other faction members.

Furthermore, policy groups do not always meet frequently enough or long enough to result in the preponderance of social interaction over all other influences. Members of policy groups are subject to and exposed to the pull of contradicting social interaction influences because they are simultaneously members of more than one peer group and are often attuned to persuasion by different reference groups. This may substantially reduce the influence of the interactive process in any single group. Also, not all members are equally influenced, due to differences in personality attributes that make some group members more amenable to persuasion. Therefore, group membership composition and the consequent distribution of personality attributes in the group will be a factor in determining how important the social interaction process is likely to be in shaping risk preferences.[1] Finally, group members are not required to reach a meeting of minds to act (see George, this volume). Circumstances often impose a need for stopgap, short-term agreed-upon decisions that do not reflect an underlying commonality of beliefs and assessments, but are merely the most practical response to the situation at hand. This operational consensus is sometimes incorrectly interpreted as evidence of consensus reached through the effect of social interaction.

The following analysis, therefore, assumes that the underlying motivations for collective behavior are found neither in the simple aggregation of the attributes of the individual members of the group, nor in the group as an autonomous entity, but rather in the confluence of the two. Both views represent part of the truth; individuals matter even when they are part of a group, and the group is in itself a force that can shape individual preferences. This interactive phenomenon reflects a nexus more generally known as the agent-structure relationship.

Two sets of variables offer contingent nuanced explanations for risk-taking behavior. One set concerns group dynamics in various forms. The other set is related to group attributes. The article begins with a definition of the key terms and a disaggregation of the general concept of risk into three distinctive types. It then proceeds with a discussion of the sources of group risk judgment and risk preference formation. Arguments are illustrated by examples from American, Indian, Soviet, and Israeli foreign policy decisions that involved the use of military force in one form or another, or other high-stakes policy choices.

2. The Nature of Risk

Foreign policy risks, looked at from a decision maker's vantage point, can be defined by the answers to the following three questions in this order of presentation: (1) What are the gains or losses associated with each known outcome? (2) What is the probability of each outcome? (3) How valid are the gain or loss and probability estimates for each outcome? *Risk,* then, is the likelihood of the materialization of validly predictable direct and indirect consequences with potentially adverse values, arising from exogenous events, self-behavior, environmental constraints, or the reaction of an opponent or third party. Accordingly, risk estimates have three dimensions: outcome values (positive or negative), the probability of these outcomes, and the confidence with which the estimates of outcome values and probabilities are held by the decision maker.[2]

To be analytically useful, the generic term *risk* has to be clearly defined, its components identified and classified into three discriminated types: real (actual) risk, perceived risk, and acceptable risk. *Real risk* is the actual risk resulting from a situation or behavior, whether decision makers are aware or unaware of it. *Perceived risk* is the level of risk attributed to a situation or behavior by the decision makers. It need not be, and often is not, congruent with real risk.[3] This incongruence may be caused by unavailable information, misperception, and misinterpretation. Thus, the responses of different individuals and groups facing the same type and level of actual risk may vary because of dissimilar risk perceptions. The third type of risk is *acceptable risk,* which is the level of risk representing the net costs that decision makers perceive as sustainable and are willing to bear, in pursuit of their goals. Acceptable risk does not have to be congruent with either perceived or objective risk.

It is important to note the relative and comparative nature of risk assessments and acceptability. Decision-makers' judgments of a policy's riskiness is not only in relation to the actual content of the policy in and by itself, but also in relation to competing policies offered by others. This comparative judgment of riskiness is embedded in an important defining characteristic of the political context within which foreign policy decisions are made, that is, acceptability by their constituency (cf. Farnham 1995). To convince relevant constituencies of the merits of a particular policy its supporters have to address the manner in which others perceive and compare it to alternative policy options in order to place it within the acceptability domain. In the context of policy acceptability, longer-term future outcomes usually seem more abstract and less tangible compared with the more vivid immediate costs of a policy. Hence, the perception of a policy's riskiness is first and foremost based on its immediately observable costs, although future costs may also be taken into account.

The following sections discuss the determinants of risk judgment and risk acceptability in group decision making. More specifically, small group variables are discussed in terms of their effects on one or more elements of risk judgment and risk acceptability. These elements can be identified as: the assessment of outcome utilities: the assessment of outcome probabilities; the perceived validity of outcomes and/or probabilities assessment; the risk preferences distribution (avoidance versus acceptability) among group members; and, finally, the manner in which the focal risk option is compared with other policy options (that may be more or less hazardous) in the process that determines which policy will be acceptable to the decision makers. The small group variables affect more than one of the above-mentioned issues, and these multiple effects are sometimes causally related.

3. Group Dynamics and Causes of Risk-taking Behavior

The three types of risk (real, perceived, and acceptable) are significantly related to group performance. Faced with an opportunity for decision, the real risks for decision makers in the group vary across group members with the potential personal and political implications that result from the policy's consequences. That is, the implications of policy consequences could, for example, mean demotion, loss of status and prestige for one member, or promotion and increase in influence for another. They could have important impacts on the distribution of power in the group.

Perceived risk may or may not vary across decision makers depending on how they interpret the situation. The extent to which group members share perceptions of risk could affect the incentives for cooperation among group members and the sense of shared responsibility for outcomes. As shall be elaborated later, the extent to which risk perceptions are shared affects group dynamics and collective risk preferences. But even when risks are identically perceived, the level of acceptable risk could still be dissimilar across decision makers in the group, making it difficult to reach agreement over policy. Identifying collective attitudes toward risk requires the aggregation of individual risk attitudes into a single, collective, coherent judgment of risk, and a single collective preference toward risk-taking.[4] The difficulty of identifying aggregate group risk assessments and risk-taking preferences stems from the facts that group members' attitudes toward risk are not always expressed in similar terms, but more important these attitudes are not a simple average of the attitudes of all group members, nor do they necessarily reflect the majority's dominant position. Group preferences may be shaped by a minority in the group resulting in a position quite different from that of either the average position or the majority position in the group (cf. Kitayama and Burnstein 1994; Levine and Russo 1987; Maass et al. 1987).

How can differences between aggregate group risk dispositions and average individual risk dispositions be accounted for? One explanation must be sought in the dissimilarity between individual and collective decision making, that is, the strong impact of social influences that are grounded in both motivated and unmotivated reasoning. Essentially, decision makers are particularly likely to be receptive to social pressures when they are faced by problems with potentially serious adverse consequences. These influences will increase as ambiguity, complexity, and uncertainty of the situation increase. Individuals operating under these conditions will need to validate their judgments and choice preferences by comparing them with those of other group members (Forgas 1981; Wehman et al. 1977; Zajonc et al. 1972).

The need for security and reassurance, when the costs of error can be high, will be satisfied by conforming and adapting preferences to those predominant in the group. Conforming with other group members becomes even more tempting when, in addition to external uncertainty, people face internal doubts about their capabilities that reflect low self-esteem, the risk and complexity of decisions, or moral dilemmas raised by the issues considered (Moscovici 1976, 25–31; Steiner 1989).

The Iran-Contra affair in 1985–86 provides an illuminating illustration. The members of the policy group that was involved in the decision to supply Iran with American weapons and intelligence, in order to obtain the release of American hostages that were held by supposedly pro-Iran terrorist groups in Lebanon, faced a complex, uncertain, risky situation, with multiple stakes. At stake were not only the lives of the hostages. It was uncertain whether Iran could deliver the hostages. It was unclear with whom one was dealing in Iran, and whether any U.S. initiative might not be used by the extremists in Teheran, rather than serve to strengthen the moderates in the regime. There was also the risk that the supplied weapons would tilt the stalemated Iran–Iraq war in favor of Iran. Furthermore, the U.S. group was constantly operating in fear that the deal would leak and a premature disclosure would endanger the lives of the hostages. Moreover, the initiative posed a number of moral dilemmas. It stood in stark contrast to the U.S. principled position of not negotiating with terrorists; the weapons could be used to kill many more people than they would save; and the diversion of funds to the Contras violated U.S. law.

In this highly adversarial context, members of the policy group were intensely motivated toward self-censorship, isolation from dissonant views through strict secrecy, and the elimination of dissidents from the group. Reliability became a criterion for being allowed access to the decision-making process. The insiders came to share a view of a strategic justification well beyond the mere release of the hostages. They argued for a political dialogue with the moderates in Iran that would potentially affect the domestic power struggle in Iran in a direction favorable to U.S. interests ('t Hart 1990/1994).

Conventional wisdom on group risk taking long held that groups make riskier decisions than individuals. The so-called risky shift phenomenon was explained in terms of motivation, cognition, social interaction, and statistical aggregation of risk preferences. More specifically, it was attributed to responsibility diffusion, persuasiveness of more risk-prone group members, familiarization with the problem, and the cultural salience of the risk value (Davis 1992; Dion et al. 1970; Vinokur 1971). In spite of its widespread acceptance, the risky-shift argument is neither convincing nor supported by real-life observations, at least not in the realm of foreign policy. Many cases show that groups can be both risk-averse (e.g., Kennedy's cabinet and advisors in the Cuban missile crisis) and risk-prone (e.g., Johnson's cabinet during the early Vietnam intervention years). These examples suggest that groups as such are not consistently and automatically risk-prone. Rather, group choice is influenced by the content of the problem and the initial distribution of individual preferences within the group (Cartwright 1971), as well as other factors that shall be discussed later in detail. It should also be noted that not all significant decisions are perceived as risk dominated; some important decisions are perceived to be opportunity dominated and thus induce less cautious and more risk-acceptant preferences.

According to later findings on group behavior, the general process that takes place in groups is one of polarization, which may result in either risky or cautious shifts. Polarization indicates that social interaction within a small group tends to accentuate individual predispositions (Minix 1982; Myers 1982; Myers and Lamm 1976). In other words, group decision-making contexts produce a pull toward extremity, whether risk or caution, and not exclusively toward risk itself.[5] More specifically, there is a tendency of group discussions to amplify the initially dominant point of view in the group.

This finding implies a more extreme risk-averse (cautious shift) or risk-acceptant (risky shift) preference for a group than under similar circumstances for an individual. Where the small group is inclined toward a risky shift, this could be preceded by judgments that deemphasize warning information and/or emphasize coping and risk management skills. Where the small group produces a cautious shift, this could be associated with judgments that emphasize warning information and/or de-emphasize coping and risk management capabilities. Some of the determinants of polarization and its direction can be found in a modified version of any one or a combination of the explanations found in the risky-shift literature.

Social interaction affects both risk judgment and risk-taking preference. The influence of social interaction on risk preference occurs either directly or through the mediating role of risk judgment, where risk-taking preferences are determined by preceding evaluations of the risks involved. But how is the impact of social interaction generated? And what makes it effective? In brief, social influence works through four processes: responsibility diffusion, persuasion, familiarization, and value illumination and amplification (Dion et al. 1970). These processes affect the judgment of risk and shape the preferences toward risk acceptance or risk avoidance by satisfying some basic human social and psychological needs.

Diffusion of Responsibility

According to the responsibility diffusion explanation, in group decision-making contexts responsibility and accountability for consequences is diffused among group members. This reduces fear of failure, and thereby decision makers have incentives to make riskier decisions. Faced with a need to share responsibility, group discussions will be a source of intelligence for each member of a group in finding out whether others are willing to commit themselves to share responsibility. This information will eventually help each decision maker to make up his or her mind as to how much risk should be taken. It must be remembered, however, that judgment of whether others are willing to share responsibility can be biased. People tend to see their own judgments as common and as most appropriate for the existing circumstances (Alicke and Largo 1995; Ross et al. 1977). The false-consensus bias can generate a misleading sense of confidence stemming from misplaced perceptions of social support in group decision-making contexts.[6] This may encourage risky or cautious shifts that are based on false assumptions of shared views and responsibility. This phenomenon is particularly robust when information about other group members' views is ambiguous or when they are reluctant to reveal their true positions, a phenomenon that is common in new groups.

To the extent that responsibility sharing within the group is such that a decision cannot be attributed to any single member but only to the group as an integrated entity, this anonymity will encourage the sense of group-shared responsibility, as opposed to individual accountability, and enhance the incentive to take risk. It is not the actual probability of adversarial consequences of the decision (policy risk) that is reduced, but the anticipated adversarial personal consequences to the decision maker (political risk). When personal accountability is unevenly distributed, those members of the group who do not feel strongly about the problem (i.e., are less responsible) become subject to persuasion by those members who feel strongly about the issue (i.e., are more responsible for outcomes). The latter members' preferences set the direction of polarization toward either risk taking or risk aversion.

Similarly, in cases where some decision makers prefer a cautious but unpopular option, one that is not in line with the prevailing mood in the society at large, a group context where others have a similar preference could encourage the cautious decision maker not to give in to the prevailing mood among the public. This is not only because of the moral support from other similar-minded individuals, important as that support may be, but mainly because holding onto a deviating preference that could have very unpleasant personal consequences, especially in case it proves to be an error of judgment, is less risky when responsibility is shared with other group members.

Foreign policy decisions are particularly susceptible to the consequences of risk sharing because they are decisions made for others (the nation, or a particular group within it). When choosing for others, people tend to prefer more cautious decisions than when they make decisions for themselves. Failure in the first case would be accompanied by self-blame and a resultant need to justify the choice to others. However, when decisions for others are made by a group, the tendency toward risk avoidance is less pronounced because failure can be shared with others so that anticipated personal responsibility would be reduced (Zaleska and Kogan 1971). Furthermore, because postdecisional dissonance depends on perception of responsibility for the outcomes, the diffusion of responsibility in group contexts encourages risk acceptance because postdecisional dissonance is anticipated to be low. That is only the case, however, when individuals are convinced that other group members are either willing to share responsibility or that responsibility sharing can be somehow imposed on them.

In 1968 the supposedly powerful Soviet leader, Secretary General of the Communist Party of the Soviet Union Leonid Brezhnev, faced continued intransigence of the Czechoslovak leadership to comply with demands to slow down reforms, rein in the intellectuals and the media's criticism of the communist system, and reimpose some censorship measures. The Czechoslovak crisis was increasingly perceived as posing both a strategic threat to the integrity and security of the Warsaw Pact, because of Czechoslovakia's geostrategic position, as well as a political source of destabilization of communist parties' rule in Soviet bloc countries, especially East Germany, Poland, and the Soviet Union. Yet, in spite of pressure from the hard-liners in Czechoslovakia's Communist Party, the Soviet military, and some members of the inner circle of the Soviet Politburo—including Ukraine Communist Party leader Petr Shelest and Nikolay Podgorny, chairman of the Presidium of the Supreme Soviet—Brezhnev refused to take the risk of military intervention. He continued to hold back until August 1968, when he became sure that the other two members of the inner group who opposed intervention—Prime Minister Alexei Kosygin and Mikahail Suslov, secretary of the Central Committee—had shifted their positions. A consensus within the Politburo inner group now reassured Brezhnev of shared responsibility for the policy (Dawisha 1984; Kramer 1993; Valenta 1991).

For the purpose of responsibility-sharing causation, the formal institutional context in which decisions are made is often less important than the actual diffusion of responsibility within the group. When the members of a small group (e.g., cabinet) are known to share power and influence, group decisions may indeed become an incentive for riskier decisions than individual ones. But when power and influence are not equally distributed, and that fact is transparent and is publicly known, the fact that the decision is formally made in a group setting does not by itself necessarily produce a risky shift. Specific leading members of the group then know that they will bear most of the responsibility in case of loss and carry the burden of accountability.[7] For them, to borrow the memorable slogan favored by Harry S. Truman, "The buck stops here." Hence, in analyzing group decision settings attention must be paid to the following: the formal procedures for decision making (e.g., majority rule, unanimity); the actual, rather than formal, diffusion of power and influence within the group;[8] the public's view of who is in charge (no matter what the formal or actual allocation of responsibilities); and the individual decision makers' value systems (no matter what the formal setting for responsibility sharing is, certain individuals in the group may feel themselves more responsible for losses than other members). The combined impact of these factors will decide whether decisions made in a group setting will trigger responsibility-sharing expectations and the resultant polarization effect.

Unlike the Soviet example, in a presidential political system the constitutional lines of accountability eventually lead directly to the president, no matter how many others participate in the decision making or are consulted. President Lyndon Johnson's in 1965 to commit U.S. troops to intervention in Vietnam was not the result of responsibility shared with Secretary of Defense Robert McNamara, Secretary of State Dean Rusk, and National Security Advisor McGeorge Bundy, although these men initially support troop deployment. The president's decision was clearly driven by a sense of personal responsibility for the future of South Vietnam. This is evident in Johnson's emphatic refusal to be the president who lost South Vietnam like Truman lost China, and in his personalization of the war and accompanying fear that if he lost Vietnam he would be branded as a coward and "an unmanly man. A man without a spine" (Kearns 1976, 252). The fact that his key cabinet members supported troop deployment encouraged Johnson to pursue that path, but it did not encourage risk taking through shifting responsibilities and sharing accountability.

Persuasive Arguments

The persuasion explanation argues that persuasion does not necessarily result from the logical and informative quality of the argument, but is to a large degree a social, self-presentation phenomenon. According to this explanation, group members with more radically polarized judgments and preferences invest more resources in attempts to exert influence and lead others (Rim 1964, 1966).[9] The more self-confident and assertive members of the group are very often capable of communicating expectations that eventually their position will prevail. Thus, they create anticipations among other members that in a vote the majority will support them. These expectations may act as a powerful incentive for those who are undecided and are waiting for indications concerning which way the wind is blowing. Correctly or incorrectly, these members interpret assertiveness as a cue and throw in their support. This triggers a self-fulfilling prophecy resulting in majority support for the more polarized position. It follows that the more assertive group members are most likely to produce a polarization effect in the group. Risk-prone members tend to be strongly committed to their positions, and their arguments are more forceful and influential because a risky choice requires more deliberative efforts. However, this is not always the case.

When the cautious members are the more committed ones, then a cautious shift will be more likely (Burnstein and Katz 1971). Still, it is more frequent that risky choices elicit greater confidence and commitment by their supporters than cautious choices. Risk-prone group members, because they are deeply committed, tend to ignore initial negative feedback from their decisions; they will, therefore, further increase their commitment to the risky choice making it even more difficult to back off. As these members become more influential due to the extent of their persistent commitment, they are likely to carry the whole group with them toward risk escalation and even entrapment.

An illustration of this process can be found in Israel's cabinet shift in attitude toward the risk of military intervention in Lebanon. The three most risk-acceptant members of the decision-making group—Prime Minister Menachem Begin, Defense Minister Ariel Sharon, and Chief of Staff General

Refael Eitan—were prepared to take the risks of executing operation "Big Pines" (a larger version of what became later known as operation Peace for Galilee) as early as December 20, 1981, but the cabinet turned it down. Between December 1981 and June 1982 there were at least five abortive attempts by Begin to get cabinet approval for some sort of invasion. Either there was no majority support, or the majority was too slim for Begin's comfort (Yaniv 1987, 107–9). Yet the three decision makers persisted in their attempts to persuade the cabinet, firmly believing in the necessity and efficacy of the plan.

Begin, Sharon, and Eitan felt deep-seated revulsion toward the PLO and its leadership. Begin harbored vivid Holocaust memories that became associated with the PLO threat. All three held the traditional vision of an alliance of the non-Muslim and non-Arab minorities in the Middle East against a commonly shared Arab-Muslim threat, and they perceived the Maronites as natural allies. These factors converged to focus their attention on the PLO and Syrian short- and long-term threats to Israel on the one hand and the Christians in Lebanon on the other. These actors became highly salient subjects in information processing. Furthermore, in Begin's case selective attention driven by the availability of historical memories and immediate threats was reinforced by a cognitive style that centered on generalized patterns and did not concern itself with details. In the absence of military-strategic experience, he was in no position and had no wish to question the details of a military strategy outlined by two admired and confident generals, Sharon and Eitan. Begin fully embraced their plan (Perlmutter 1987, 379–81; Sofer 1988, 100–101, 114). But the devil was in the details.

In the period between December 20, 1981, when the cabinet rejected Begin's proposal for implementing "Big Pines," and June 1982, there was an incremental process of building commitment for an extensive military operation. Each time the cabinet considered and rejected military action, it became more difficult for those opposing the operation to stick to their position. Finally, on May 16 the cabinet refused to approve immediate action, but under Sharon's pressure a resolution was passed that another violation of the cease-fire would result in a large-scale military response (Shiffer 1984, 87). After an assassination attempt on Israel's ambassador in London, most of the ministers felt that they could not continue to oppose Begin's proposal for heavy bombing of PLO targets in Beirut by the air force. They knew that the PLO was very likely to react by shelling Israel's northern settlements, which would then force them to approve a ground operation that many of them did not want. This is clearly described by one of the ministers: "We said no so many times, and now in light of such an international drama [the assassination attempt] and the prime minister's emotional outburst we could not oppose him" (Naor 1986, 44). Apparently Begin, an experienced politician with a keen comprehension of leader–follower relations, understood this behavior pattern. He was sure that given time he could get the ministers to approve his proposals, if he persisted. The result was a shift toward greater risk acceptance by the cabinet although a substantial number of its members were initially risk-averse. On June 5, 1982, the cabinet approved by an overwhelming majority (14 for, 1 against, and 2 abstentions) a large-scale military intervention in Lebanon, operation Peace for Galilee.

Often the group's leader is its most influential and assertive member. Therefore, an important dimension of the persuasion process within the group relates to leader–follower relations (see Metselaar and Verbeek; Preston, both this volume). This relationship is to a large extent shaped by the type of leadership involved. A common leadership type is transactional leadership, where leader–follower relations are driven by implicitly or explicitly anticipated valued transactions (Bass 1985; Hollander 1986). The ability of a leader to influence the risk acceptance preferences of other group members will depend on the extent of desired rewards he or she can offer to the followers in the group. However, transformational leadership works differently. Charismatic leadership is the most salient manifestation of this broad leadership type. Charismatic leaders influence their followers toward risk acceptance through two separate but interrelated processes. They inspire and arouse deep emotional attachment in their followers; they instill in them a sense of faith and trust in the leader. This translates into confidence that risks are worth taking in pursuit of superordinate goals that transcend their own interests. At the same time, they affect their followers through the lateral relationships that develop among the followers themselves (Bass 1985; Meindle 1990). The charismatic effect of a leader is sustained and enhanced by the process of collective, interactive admiration and romanticization of the leader among the followers.

We often witness in these cases anticipatory compliance in which group members try to second-guess the leaders' positions, even before they are expressed.[10] Group members may go to extremes in either direction, risk aversion or risk acceptance, depending on their judgment of their leaders' preferences. In extreme cases group members indulge in competitive anticipatory compliance, trying to outdo each other in conforming with a position that has not even been explicitly expressed. They do not only passively conform but invest special efforts to identify, locate, and bring to the leaders' attention selective information that supports the persistence of the position in question. In this process policy revision becomes less likely. In these cases, we might not witness explicit directive leadership because there is no observable attempt to direct group members' preferences. Nonetheless the latent process of influencing is very real.

The leader–followers nexus is clearly exemplified by the social relationship within the Indian foreign policy decision-making group, as it applied to India's risky China policy in 1961–62. That policy eventually resulted in China's military offensive against India in October 1962 and India's humiliating defeat. Jawaharlal Nehru, India's much admired and charismatic prime minister and minister of external affairs and Gandhi's anointed student and heir, had since 1959 increasingly been drawn toward an noncompromising and confrontational stance in the border conflict with China. In spite of an abundance of information indicating that China would respond harshly, and that the Indian army was incapable of and unprepared for a military confrontation with China, Nehru's optimism that India would eventually prevail and that there was only a very limited chance of a full military confrontation with China went unchallenged. In fact most of the key participants in the decision-making group shared and reinforced Nehru's assessments, causing him to persist in a high-risk China policy.

The unchallenged prevalence of misperceptions and the associated risky policy can substantially be attributed to the nature of social relations within the influential group of decision makers centered around Nehru. A tightly knit faction with most of the structural characteristics of a typical Indian political faction emerged. The Nehru faction was bound together mainly by the personal ties between its leader and inner-core followers; it differentiated itself by drawing clear ideological boundaries between this core and the other participants in the decision-making process. The relationship between the members and Nehru were of the *guru–chela* (teacher–disciple) type. Nehru's followers depended on him; they drew power from his power and psychological support from their association with the great man. The members of the group were also bonded together by a shared sense of a privileged relationship with India's most respected and adored leader. In that context they were strongly motivated to comply blindly with his assessments, reinforce his policy preferences, and fiercely compete for his attention (Hoffman 1990; Vertzberger 1984b). Thus a collective enhancement of Nehru's attitudes became the norm, and uncritical persistence of the risky China policy was inevitable.

Persuasion, however, is not just induced by the effect of an assertive individual's influence. No less important is the social atmosphere in the group, which results in self-imposed conformity with the dominant opinions in the group.[11] Self-imposed conformity will be most evident where there are no conformity-constraining factors, such as prior commitment to a reference group's position that is different from the dominating view in the decision-making peer group (Asch 1958; Lamm and Kogan 1970; Myers 1982; Vertzberger 1990, 236–37), or normative commitment to multiple advocacy (George 1980). Conformity takes two forms. In the predecision stage it entails accepting the position of the majority even if it conflicts with one's own judgment. In the postdecision stage conformity entails continued support for the decision even if one comes to a conclusion that it was the wrong decision and that it should be reversed. Entrapment results from the latter type of conformity. Group members often become entrapped by the justifications, especially public justifications, that they provide for their initial decisions and actions. Forceful justifications for these decisions and actions gain a life of their own and are extremely difficult to refute at an acceptable cost.[12]

These policy justifications, deemed necessary to assure the acceptability of a decision, can become substantial roadblocks to change and prevent deviation from a prevailing position in the group even when it is recognized as incorrect. This is well illustrated by McNamara's position on the Vietnam policy from late 1965 to late 1967. The secretary of defense had been skeptical as early as late 1965 of the efficacy of both "Rolling Thunder," the strategic bombing of North Vietnam, and of combat troop deployment for a U.S. victory. Yet, as American intervention escalated during the Johnson administration, he became one of the administration's main spokesmen. McNamara explained and justified to Congress and to the American public the unavoidable necessity of escalation, while having growing, private doubts. He thus became entrapped in a public commitment to a policy in which he had little confidence, until he decided in 1967 to step down from his cabinet position and accept the presidency of the World Bank (Herring 1993; McNamara with Van De Mark 1995; Shapley 1993).

The most extreme manifestation of group-induced conformity can be found in groupthink situations, where all group members think as one. The occurrence of groupthink depends on a number of antecedent conditions (see Aldag and Fuller, this volume). The defective performance of a cohesive group will be most pronounced in situations of high stress from external or internal sources where there seems to be little hope of finding a better solution than the one advocated; such a situation will increase members' dependence on the group and the likelihood of groupthink. The most potent condition comes from leadership practices that are directive-assertive and not modified by a tradition of impartiality. This may sometimes be disguised in the form of encouraging the voicing of dissonant views, but only to shoot them down, creating a false facade of openness. Thus, group members learn that deviationists pay the price of their nonconformity and stand only a slight chance of improving the accuracy of the group's consensual conceptions. This belief, combined with the perceived material and emotional benefits of not making waves, produces over time a tendency to rationalize the group consensus as accurately reflecting situational reality. The group that becomes overoptimistic lacks the motivation to search for or attend to all available information, becomes convinced of its own invincibility and morality, and thus experiences a risky shift. In other cases, groupthink may produce collective agonizing, magnify doubt by distributing it, and thus generate excessive pessimism, which may result in procrastination, inactivity, and a cautious shift.

Peer pressure to conform in group decision making may result in two broad and different kinds of conformity. One entails true conversion to the group's position and internalization of the group's attitudes. The other is mere bandwagoning and compliance with the group's pressure for conformity, while privately doubting the group's views and course of action (McCauley 1989; Vertzberger 1990, 234–41). Does the nature of conformity matter? In the short run the source of conformity does not really make a difference. The consequences are the same whether conformity stems from compliance or internalization. But it does make a difference in the long run, because the two types of conformity reflect different levels of long-term commitments to the group's attitudes and policies. If feedback information from the policy threatens the group's cohesiveness, and the policies become an issue of contention within the group, those who merely complied are most likely to be among the first to distance themselves from those policies or actually to challenge them. Those who have internalized the group's attitudes are least likely to be attentive to dissonant information and most reluctant to reform substantially the failing policies. This is because converts are usually the staunchest believers in the subject of their attitude change, due to their large investment of emotional and cognitive energy in internalizing the new attitudes.

It is quite common to find at the core of a group a faction that is a temporary alignment of individuals. Such factions generally do not have a formally structured hierarchy or a set of rules and procedures; rules are often fuzzy and tacit, although they may become formalized de facto over time. Two key group phenomena, polarization and groupthink, are more likely to occur in the faction than in the larger group. Polarization is more likely because faction members' beliefs and attitudes are closer than in the group as a whole and reinforce one another, and therefore will be more extreme. Groupthink is more likely because the valence and initial proximity of beliefs and attitudes create the climate for the emergence of all the other symptoms of groupthink.[13] When faction members perceive themselves to be facing a hostile external environment of other competing factions in the group and see their membership as a common shield against it, their information processing is likely to be biased toward maintaining and accentuating the psychological distance between in-group and out-group. Those faction members who by their extreme positions best represent the in-group/out-group dichotomy are likely to become more influential and persuasive. In this process faction members move psychologically closer to the other in-group members; this further enhances the possibility of factional groupthink ('t Hart 1990/1994, 108–11; Vertzberger 1984a; Wilder and Allen 1978). Factional polarization and groupthink have a spillover effect on the group as a whole, either when the coercive power a faction wields can be translated into the ability to affect group risk preferences, or when its cohesive well-defined view, presented with persistence and confidence, carries the rest of the group with it.

Familiarization

The familiarization explanation assumes that the group is a social arena where the diversity of specialized information and opinions among the members is expressed and exchanged. It argues that group discussion is a process through which familiarization with a problem increases by making available to the members information that was unknown or unattended to before (Myers 1982; Sniezek 1992). As familiarization increases both the extremes of caution and boldness tend to increase. When people are unsure they will usually prefer to avoid an extreme position. But as individuals are exposed, through group interaction, to information and argumentation they had not been aware of before, ambiguities and inconsistencies are clarified. The participating decision makers are then assured that there are no hidden costs of which they were not aware (Marquis and Reitz 1969; Ridley et al. 1981). Familiarization, thus, will be more effective the more broad and diverse the views expressed. It will result in reduced apprehensions about making incorrect assessments of utility and probability judgments, and it will strengthen decision makers' confidence in the validity of their estimates.[14] As a result of having fewer doubts, group members will be disposed toward more polarized preferences in the direction of caution or risk acceptance than will average individual decision makers facing similar problems.

   In assessing polarization caused by familiarization, an observer needs to take into account a number of important factors affecting the actual practices and utility of information sharing. The notion that group members exchange specialized information available to some members only, and that it will make for better-informed decisions, is based on three underlying assumptions. The first is that there is a common understanding among group members regarding problem definition and preferred solution-type. Consequently, all members know which information is relevant for sharing with others. The second assumption is that group members have a common goal of solving the problem and therefore have a shared interest in a successful solution and have no hidden self-serving agenda. The third assumption is that solution of the problem will not adversely affect some members and be advantageous to others due to a redistribution of power and influence.

   These assumptions do not hold true, however, in many important real-world political–military problems. The issues at stake are often deeply contested and divisive, and information is not readily shared (Stasser 1992). In addition, in foreign policy areas where secrecy is considered critical, members of a decision-making group will be cut off from crucial sources of information by the situational context (see Metselaar and Verbeek, this volume). Lack of information on the actual level of risk increases the changes that group members will make lower risk judgments than what is actually called for. Consequently they will make risk decisions based on inaccurate risk assessments.

To illustrate, in analyzing the failed U.S. military Iran hostage rescue operation in April 1980, Smith (1985c, 22) observes that "For reasons of operation's security (OPSEC), then, planned implementation of the decision was never critically assessed outside the immediate commanders of the operation, and even then was never available in one document." Prior to the implementation stage, while the option of a military operation was considered by President Jimmy Carter and his advisers, there was one independent analysis of the military rescue options prepared for CIA Director Stansfield Turner, a member of the decision-making group. According to this assessment, the operation would have probably resulted in the loss of 60 percent of the hostages. This report was never sent to the president nor discussed in the decision-making meeting (Smith 1985c, 22–23). In the case of Israel's intervention in Lebanon, Defense Minister Sharon used his control over information to cleverly manipulate the decision-making process to expand the objectives and geographic range of the operation beyond the constrained authorization given by the cabinet. Prime Minister Begin and the cabinet repeatedly found themselves facing one fait accompli after another. "He [Sharon] would report constantly to Begin, much in a manner of a regimental duty officer—detail not substance" (Perlmutter 1987, 384). Thus the group decision-making process became an instrument for manipulating risk acceptability rather than an opportunity for genuine information dissemination and sharing (see also Stern; Hoyt and Garrison, both this volume).

Sometimes, however, information is not shared unwittingly due to the lack of understanding by the holder of its relevance for the problem discussed. In other cases group members find themselves in situations where a successful solution will reward certain members, and their organizations will gain improved status and influence in the decision-making process. This result would give those individuals, and the organizations they represent, important long-term advantages in the wider competition for access to societal resources. Those who find themselves in a position where the relative gains from a successful solution would not favor their position may have an interest in preventing a successful outcome. Therefore, they may not share essential information. Furthermore, knowledge can be viewed in power terms. Hoarding information is sometimes perceived as a wise strategy in anticipation of some yet unspecified use for this power-generating knowledge in the future.

The preceding discussion points to a potentially serious risk judgment bias that is unique to group decision making. The group context tends to produce an illusion among participants that they have canvassed the whole range of relevant information and are aware of all policy implications. The reality, however, is that there are barriers to information sharing that reduce exposure to information about policy costs that might have increased risk assessments. The combination of the illusion of comprehensive canvassing and the reality of limited information sharing results in a lower-than-appropriate risk judgment. This could lead to predispositions toward policies that are riskier than they seem, and these predispositions will be held with greater confidence than warranted.

Finally, two additional little-noted consequences of familiarization should be mentioned. In decision-making groups that are afflicted by bureau-organizational parochialism, where each member is mostly concerned with the risks affecting his or her organization, the interactive effects of multiple risks will be ignored even if the risks are familiar. Nobody will monitor and advertise these risks, although in reality the interactive effects of risks are the most difficult to control. The consequence of narrowly focused risk attention and the neglect of interactive effects will be the underestimation of risk assessment by each individual member. When this effect is shared across the group it has the cumulative effect of lowering group risk perceptions and increasing confidence in risk controllability. This may well encourage a risky shift in the group. The other consequence is that in tasks where a correct solution is not self-evident or will remain uncertain until some future time, even if information is shared to the fullest extent, the quality of group decision-making performance will be inferior to that of an individual decision maker because of error and bias aggregation. In these cases, group positions may serve to aggregate individual biases and errors, and hence "when individuals are error prone and functioning under a majority-type process, groups would be expected to make more errors (or more extreme errors) than individuals" (Tindale 1993, 111). Many important foreign policy decisions, including decisions concerning the use of military force, belong in this task category.

Cultural Values

The fourth explanation of polarization, a cultural-value illumination explanation, claims that risky decision opportunities elicit one of two core cultural values: risk-acceptance or caution. It should be noted that the adjective "cultural" is used here in a broad sense and could refer to societal political, or organizational cultures.[15] Once a particular cultural value becomes salient, a couple of mechanisms cause a shift in preference in a direction consistent with the revealed value (Brown 1965; Hong 1978). First, the salient value affects information flow so that it generates more verbal arguments that support the value in question than arguments that oppose it. Second, the group discussion reveals to each participant the distribution of risk preferences within the group and indicates to members which decisions are consistent with the prevailing value in the group. This enables each individual to determine the level of risk taking he or she must choose in order to appear to act risky or cautious in respect to others (Kogan and Wallach 1967, 20; Myers and Arenson 1972; Tullar and Johnson 1973; Wallach and Wing 1968).

In the case of India's China policy, for example, once it became clear to the members of Nehru's inner circle in 1960 that he had shifted from a cautious conciliatory policy toward China to a much harder stance, the discussions within the group reflected the dominance of arguments and information that reinforced a confrontational posture and rejected compromises. A similar phenomenon can be detected in the shaping of U.S. Vietnam policy in 1964–65. As it became evident that the new president Lyndon Johnson was a strong adherent of the "domino theory" and was deeply concerned with the possibility of losing South Vietnam, the result was an evident more extreme shift of the weight of arguments in his advisory group toward escalation.

A group is more likely to reflect cultural values than individual decision making. Generally, in a risk-oriented culture, decisions made by a group are more likely to reflect the norm favoring risk and will be riskier than decisions made by individuals on their own. A social environment that supports and encourages risk taking, and associates it with superior ability (Jellison and Riskind 1971), enhances the tendency toward risk taking. In a culture that values caution, however, group decisions are likely to be more cautious than individual decisions for similar reasons. Specifically, a political culture that emphasizes the high value of failure avoidance for the sake of political survival induces risk-averse policy preferences. This is especially the case when decision makers believe that the potential political costs of failure outweigh the possible benefits from policy success. On the other hand, when the costs of inaction are believed to be high, even moderate stakes may trigger risk taking. This has been noted in Soviet risk propensity in foreign policy since Stalin (Ross 1984).

Group Dynamics and Risk Taking:
Concluding Observations

The four explanations for polarization, which invoke different causes for the same phenomenon, are not mutually exclusive.[16] Very often more than one cause operates to produce the risky or cautious shift. The relevance and relative weight of each of these explanations will be context-dependent, for example by issue-areas or attributes of the individuals composing the group (e.g., cognitive styles, personality traits). Stated more generally, the relative importance of the two generic modes by which groups exert influence on individuals may vary by situational context and by issue. The *normative* mode is based on the desire to conform with the expectations of others (persuasion, responsibility-diffusion, cultural-value), while the *informational* mode is based on the acceptance of information from others (familiarization).[17]

In a group that develops a siege mentality due to real or imagined threats to its position, group members will find themselves more exposed to normative influences and thereby forge a consensus in order to face threats. When positions have to be stated publicly, normative influence is also more likely to be silent. However, when positions can be kept private, an informational influence mode is more likely to dominate. In intellective issues, where it is believed possible to develop correct fact-based solutions, informational influences are more likely to dominate. In judgmental issues that involve behavioral, political, or ethical judgments with no demonstrably correct answers, the group will attempt to produce a consensual best approximation to the "right" answer through persuasion. In all these instances a unanimity decision rule enhances the effect of the dominant influence mode (normative or informational) that is associated with the situation or issue-area in question (Kaplan 1987; Kaplan and Miller 1987).

The above generalization should be qualified by three observations. First, politically contested issues are not easily defined within one or another issue category. In fact, by framing an issue as intellective or judgmental some group members may acquire more influence than others in shaping the group's position. Those who have access to information supporting their position will prefer the issue to be defined as intellective. Members whose main resource is political manipulation of group dynamics would consider it most advantageous to disparage the value of information and describe the issue as judgmental in nature. This will weaken the weight of arguments based on information. Second, in a more cohesive group there is likely to be a stronger tendency toward normative influences compared with informational influences, even on intellective issues. This will, however, not be the case in a cohesive group in which norms of professional competence and epistemic validity are strongly emphasized and embedded in group culture. Third, individual differences among group members can be important. Cognitive complex individuals are mostly influenced by information sharing in the group. Extroverts, on the other hand, are more likely to be influenced by the need to be accepted and comply with majority views. Most experimental work, however, does not control for these and other important contextual sources of variability in the group environment. This is indicated by the research results regarding the relative validity of the four types of explanations for group influence on its members. The results were inconsistent in terms of support for one or another of these four explanations.

In brief, decisions involving risk will be taken or avoided based on two basic considerations regarding risk perception and risk acceptability. First, risk will be taken when it is perceived to be below a predetermined nonacceptability threshold. Second, risk-taking preferences will change in response to increases and decreases in the acceptability levels. The four causal explanations of the effect of group contexts on risk taking in fact imply one or both of these two generic situations. The responsibility-diffusion and familiarity explanations imply processes that result in changes in both risk acceptability and risk perceptions, mainly the latter. The persuasion and cultural-value explanations imply processes that result in group-induced changes in risk acceptability.

4. Group Attributes and Causes of Risk-taking Behavior

The preceding analysis indicated the multiple paths through which variable forms of group dynamics affect the risk judgments and preferences of individual group members, and their aggregation into a group judgment and preference. As important as these processes clearly are, group dynamics is not an exclusive causal factor. This section will cover four additional factors that shape risk behavior in a small group and are embedded in group attributes. Whether or not there will be synergism among all or some factors is a situation-specific condition.

Group Composition

Social interactions do not have similar effects on all individuals; certain people are more likely than others to be influenced or influential in group contexts. People with low self-esteem have a strong need for social approval and tend to be highly responsive to all forms of actual or anticipated social pressure. These individuals tend to be high on fear of failure and are keen to share the responsibility for possible failures of a risky course of action. They will therefore be disposed toward acceptance or avoidance of risk taking as a function of group discussion influence (Kogan and Wallach 1967, 265; Wood and Stagner 1994). Similarly, people with a cognitive style dominated by affect will be more influenced by the group context and the possibility of responsibility sharing (Henderson and Nutt 1980). In addition to global personality attributes, issue-bound considerations should be noted. Group members who, on the debated issue, score high on evaluative-cognitive consistency (the consistency between attitude and supporting beliefs) and know a great deal about the issue under discussion are much less susceptible to social influence than others (Wood and Stagner 1994). Thus, susceptibility to influence emerges from the confluence of the kind of person one is and the kind of situation or issue one is dealing with.

Group composition is an important variable. This is because as the number of independent-minded individuals increases, so too does the chance for diversity of opinions and the probability of moving away from a process of compliance with peer expectations. Leading decision makers recognize this aspect and do not trust the group processes to overcome disagreement and to produce a communality of views, especially views that are acceptable to them. They will attempt in many cases to make sure that the decision-making group is composed of like-minded members or individuals who are not likely to be overly independent-minded. In these cases, the direction of polarization can be predicted from a group's composition. For example, in a group where membership is decided by loyalty to the group leader, the direction of polarization will be decided by the position of the group leader. In a group where entry was decided by shared views and like-mindedness, it is predictable that discussions will be dominated by the shared views and lead to choice shift in the direction indicated by the shared views (Levine and Moreland 1990; Moreland and Levine 1992).

Changes in the balance of personalities can influence group risk preferences. This will take two forms that are quite often interrelated.[18] The obvious way in which the balance of personalities is affected is through several changes in group membership to bring in new people with different beliefs, values, and personality attributes. The other way this balance is affected is when a single individual, a new leader, joins the group, such as when a new president or prime minister comes to power. This second form can have a substantial impact on group processes even if all other members of the decision-making group remain the same. The new group leader's style—including accessibility, expressed tolerance for dissident views, preference for the advice of particular group members, extensive consultation and search for information or lack of it—can affect group preferences through its impact on the decision-making process and the balance of influence among group members. Even when a new leader does not initially change the composition of the group, over time group members who find that they cannot adjust to the change in leadership style leave and are replaced by others. This turnover extends the change in the balance of personalities that was triggered by the change in leadership.

These types of change in the balance of personalities are exemplified both in the Israeli and American cases. The change in government from left-wing Labor to right-wing Likud in 1977 represented a strategic change in approach to security policy. The actual implementation of the new Likud approach was delayed because in the first Begin government (1977–81) foreign and defense policies were influenced by Defense Minister Ezer Weizman, Foreign Minister Moshe Dayan, and Chief of Staff Lieutenant General Mordechai Gur. These three individuals had worldviews rooted in Labor party ideology and conceptions of national security. The Likud security doctrine was implemented only in the second Begin government (1981–83), with Ariel Sharon as defense minister, Yitzhak Shamir as foreign minister, and Lieutenant General Rafael Eitan as chief of staff. The Labor Party's security doctrine held that war was essentially a defensive and preemptive instrument, while the Likud view was substantially different. Its doctrinal base was Clausewitzian and perceived war as a legitimate means of achieving broader political objectives, including reshaping the regional political order. This approach, as expressed in the 1982 Lebanon War, was in essence an offensive military doctrine. It represented a greater willingness to accept higher risks when the situation offered a window of opportunity for achieving important political objectives and when the balance of military power was decisively in Israel's favor.

In the American case, the assassination of President John Kennedy brought Lyndon Johnson to the presidency. But this brought no immediate change in the three key positions of secretary of defense, secretary of state, and national security adviser held by Robert McNamara, Dean Rusk, and McGeorge Bundy, respectively. The main change was in decision-making style. Johnson's style was very different from his predecessor's. This made for differences in the nature of the advisory process and in the personal relationship between the president and his advisers. Over time Bundy and McNamara felt compelled to resign.

Decision-making Procedures and Norms

Group risk preferences can also be shaped by decision-making procedures and norms and by their purposeful manipulation (see also Hoyt and Garrison, this volume). There are obvious differences between majority and unanimity rules. Majority rules will, compared to unanimity rules, require less effort and less time in driving the group toward accepting or supporting risky policies. The quality of risky decisions produced by these rules will consequently be different. Unanimity rules will motivate the group toward more systematic processing of information (as opposed to heuristic processing), more attention to minority viewpoints, and therefore avoidance to tunnel vision. The greater investment of time and cognitive effort will contribute to the group's commitment to the decision and to the belief in its inevitable correctness.[19] This syndrome can backfire by leading to perseverance in the face of disconfirming information questioning the quality of the decision. Subsequently it may result in entrapment.

Decision procedures and norms can become subject to purposeful manipulation by individual group members with intentions to affect the group's risk-taking preference and choices. During the Czechoslovak crisis in 1968 the hard-liners in the Soviet Politburo were not averse to manipulating the decision-making process. On at least three occasions soft-liner Kosygin was excluded from the inner group because of his traveling schedule. This happened at the beginning of April when he was visiting Iran; at the end of May, while in Karlovy Vary; and in mid-July while in Sweden. Kosygin's trip to Sweden was used to exclude him from the decision of convening the July Warsaw meeting intended to formulate a bloc policy that would allow, if necessary, the use of military measures. He was also absent from the decision to convene an extraordinary plenum of the CPSU Central Committee to discuss the results of the Warsaw meeting. When it convened, this extraordinary plenum emphasized the threat to ideological control in the Soviet bloc. Those known for their more moderate views on Czechoslovakia were unable either to participate or to speak (Dawisha 1984, 199–201, 217–18). Kosygin did not have a chance to express his views on either occasion. In an authoritarian system such overt manipulations have an added political signaling effect. They tell those who waver which way the wind is blowing and what is politically correct. This results in increased incentives for conforming and taking the "correct" side in the policy debate.[20]

Distribution of Power

The distribution of power between more risk-acceptant and more risk-averse members is another factor that affects a group's risk preference. In a group composed of both risk-prone and risk-averse persons, where the balance of power between the two subgroups does not allow either side to impose its views on the other, and where both factions are equally committed to their risk preferences, the amount of risky or cautious shift will reflect the results of bargaining and compromise reached in intragroup deliberations. Over time there is an interactive relationship between the shifting balance of influence among policymakers and policy choices. The changing balance of influence allows for particular policy choices. When these choices are implemented they serve to enhance the power of those who supported these policies. This effect is demonstrated by the escalation of the war in Vietnam which in part reflected the changing balance of influence in the decision-making group.

The decision to escalate American involvement in Vietnam, by first initiating Rolling Thunder and then deploying combat troops, reflected a shift in the balance of influence in the decision-making group in favor of the secretary of defense and the joint chiefs of staff (JCS), mostly at the expense of the secretary of state. Johnson respected Rusk and felt comfortable with him because of the similarity in their backgrounds, but he was infatuated with McNamara's talents. More importantly, when the security of American forces was involved, the military represented the nonpartisan expertise appropriate for being given responsibility for the situation (Gallucci 1975, 32–33, 88–89;

Shapely 1993, 283). This balance of influence was soon to shift again. As McNamara became progressively disenchanted with the war, he was more often on a collision course with the JCS and General William Westmoreland, U.S. commander in Vietnam, who wanted faster and more extensive escalation. Johnson was by now committed to a military solution and began to distance himself from the progressively dovish McNamara. The influence of the JCS and General Wheeler, Army Chief of Staff, were on the rise (Clifford with Holbrooke 1991, 456–59).

Essentially, the composition of the decision-making group and the power distribution within the group reflect the institutional and political contexts in which it is embedded (see also 't Hart; Stern and Sundelius, this volume). After all, the group is a coalition of individuals representing government organizations or political parties. Therefore, risk-taking preferences and the behaviors of individual members within the group are not driven by social processes alone, as is convincingly argued by Lamborn (1985, 1991). Key members of the decision-making group may have different views on which among several suboptimal policy alternatives will best serve their parochial interests. As a rule, when decision makers face an optimal policy choice, risky or not, that poses a serious threat of adverse power redistribution, and a suboptimal policy choice that has fewer expected adverse power redistributive effects, they will prefer the latter. Hence, in a competitive organizational environment, organizations have vested interests in the advocacy, through their representatives in the decision-making group, of particular policies and actions that are not only derived from their repertoire (Anderson 1987; March and Olsen 1989), but also flow from their advance knowledge of what policies and actions can best serve their goals and suit their capabilities.

> One could argue that what institutions do is to provide us with a series of vivid experiences that then, through the availability heuristic, make us more likely to overestimate some risks and to underestimate others. Institutions might similarly supply stereotypes that make some cases seem more representative than others, from choices in characteristic ways, and suggest reference points. (Heimer 1988, 499)

These organizational imperatives can determine group members' risk acceptability. In turn this will determine their risk estimation, producing the backwards biasing of risk acceptability–risk estimation contamination effect.

In a decision-making group that is characterized by intense factional rivalry, usually motivated by a competitive organizational environment, risk preferences are not a manifestation of the polarization phenomenon. In these cases, coalition maintenance dominates calculations within the decision-making group. Therefore, the main interests and preferences of the participants

must be at least minimally satisfied. Fundamental policy changes are es-
chewed producing a muddling-through style of decision making. This will
frequently result in a cautious approach to decisions and to risk-averse behavior. Furthermore, members of a decision-making system who are averse to
running political risks (e.g., assaulting vested interests in their society) may
decide to run external risks only if their internal position either depends on it
or at least is not threatened by it.

   Risk preferences of group members will vary depending on the anticipated level of control over the policy choice and implementation. The smaller
the group, the more control each member perceives himself to have over
policy choices and implementation. Therefore, smaller decision-making
groups are more likely to prefer strong policies with high-risk elements. The
less control group members expect to have over a policy and its implementation, the more indifference they will feel toward accepting a risky policy
choice, as long as it does not generate any threat to their power position in the
short term. But when group members have little control over the policy choice
and anticipate adverse redistribution effects in case of a policy failure, they
will tend to be strongly risk averse.

Member Beliefs and Aspirations

Finally, group members' beliefs and aspirations about the group as a whole
and about themselves within the group will be important inputs into risk
acceptance or avoidance. A group that believes in its invulnerability to mistakes is more likely to make risky decisions than a group that believes that it is
vulnerable ('t Hart 1990/1994, 81–85; Thompson and Carsrud 1976). Groupthink is only one source of a socially reinforced belief in invulnerability (Janis
1982). Similarly, decision-making groups that have records of successful
decisions, or believe in the superior capabilities of their members due to their
past achievements ("the best and the brightest"), or have faith that they are
being guided by some divine power, will develop a sense of invulnerability
and be more prone than other decision-making groups to take risky decisions.
Arguably, this is an extreme case of the more general phenomenon of the
illusion of control.

   These shared beliefs may become over time group beliefs, that is: "convictions the group members (a) are aware that they share and (b) consider as
defining their 'groupness'" (Bar-Tal 1990, 36). When beliefs acquire the
status of group beliefs their centrality increases. They are easily available and
therefore accessed frequently when the group deals with judgment and choice
tasks. As individual members begin to share core beliefs and acquire a sense
of common identity, the group's success becomes more closely associated
with their self-identity and positive self-perception. They became more moti-

vated to favorably assess the group's past performance. The overestimation of past success then becomes the anchoring belief by which members infer their own expectations of self-efficacy, which are therefore overoptimistic (Cervone and Peake 1986; March et al. 1991). The more exaggerated the positive perceptions of past performance, the greater is the optimism about the group's ability to succeed in the future. This often baseless optimism encourages the members' tendency to take risks and reduces their propensity to pay attention to information that questions or contradicts their optimism. This further enhances overconfidence and raises the attention threshold for dissonant information through group-serving attributions.[21]

These phenomena are demonstrated by India's decision-making group in the 1959–62 border conflict with China. Belonging to this elitist group and serving under Nehru created an atmosphere of self-serving arrogance and confidence among group members. As a result, members of the group fed each other with optimistic estimations as to the quality of their organization's activity. There existed an atmosphere of self-satisfaction and mutual backslapping that raised the threshold for penetration of dissonant information and created even greater self-confidence and hence a sense of invulnerability. This feeling led to optimism and to a willingness to take risks that were expressed in the implementation of the Forward Policy that challenged China's territorial demands. It served to place exaggerated and unrealistic confidence in the ability of the concerned military organizations to execute successfully a policy containing such a high element of risk (Vertzberger 1984a).

A group-initiated risky policy results from a process that requires an investment of effort to establish shared group cognitions that trigger a collective assessment of being in the loss domain. These cognitions, of being in the loss domain that result in risk taking, are less likely to be challenged in the group context than in the individual decision-making context. This is because of the added costs entailed in establishing shared cognition of probabilities, outcomes, and relevant policy remedies.[22] These cognitions are then held with great confidence and tend to persevere even in the face of discrediting information. The likelihood of reversing the resulting policy declines in proportion to the antecedent invested efforts. Feedback from decisions that threatens the validity of these group beliefs may go unattended and this will contribute to policy entrapment.

Accountability is a possible remedy (Kroon et al. 1991; Tetlock 1985a; 't Hart 1990/1994, 84–85). By inducing cognitive complexity the quality of deliberations is improved at both the individual and group level. In the latter case it was found that collective and in particular individual accountability of group members decreases the chances of concurrence-seeking and thereby the probability that the group will display groupthink patterns and the related risk proneness. It also reduces the effect of deindividuation, a phenomenon that is associated with groupthink. This pathology reduces concern about longer-term consequences from the groups' action, including normative and ethical implications, and desensitizes members to a whole range of risks that flow from these consequences.

Yet, the remedial power of accountability is limited due to organizational imperatives that reinforce group-caused entrapment. The slow process of learning and adjustment to negative feedback by policy-implementing organizations creates a self-defeating momentum and reinforces self- and group-serving policy perseverance (Huber 1991). As time passes and the old policies lead top political decision makers to invest increasingly greater material and nonmaterial resources in persevering the agreed-upon policies and making them work, decision makers may find it preferable to ignore suggestions to adjust. The costs of admitting ultimate responsibility for expensive mistakes, especially when they are shared mistakes, have by then become too high, practically, psychologically, or both.

The Vietnam policies advocated by the defense department and the military services after 1965, and subsequently their risk preferences, were driven to a great degree by organizational imperatives and interorganizational relations. After the active militarization of the American presence in South Vietnam, the military (Army, Navy, Air Force, SAC) and the department of defense dominated the policy debate and the policy implementation. Although before 1965 the department of defense had demonstrated a healthy caution toward recommendations of direct military intervention, this changed when it became clear that the president was tilting toward a military resolution of the crisis. At this point the department of defense embraced the new and risky policy and became one of the main sources of optimistic assessments of the utilities of the use of force. Although it had disagreements with the military, which wanted faster escalation, the department of defense and the JCS agreed on the desirability of the use of force. They supported Westmoreland's troop requests, in spite of the risks involved. By conducting simultaneous, interlocked ground and air wars, all three services were conducting operations that they perceived as pertaining to the essence of their organizations. To shrink away from the risks involved or even seriously question the efficacy and chances of success was considered by the Army, Air Force, and Navy a blow to the underlying rationale of their missions. Furthermore, this reluctance was substantially reinforced by the traditional competition among the services. None of the services would, therefore, admit that their tasks could not eventually be accomplished successfully.

The increasing risk-taking behavior advocated by the U.S. military was driven not only by each service's need to prove itself capable of carrying out its mission, but also by the need to avoid the impression that it was *less capable* than the other services. The combined effect became a powerful incentive for organizational, cognitive closure within each service. This created the organizational equivalent of interservice groupthink that was reflected in the JCS collective attitude and resulted in policy entrapment. A change of this collective state of mind was particularly difficult to induce, as the organizational culture of the American military since before World War II was one that emphasized a "can do" attitude; an aggressive offensive doctrine and the extensive use of fire power. General Westmoreland, a typical product of West Point who shared the prevailing military organizational paradigm, could not be expected to deviate from this organizational culture or to innovate a strategy adjusted to a low-key conflict against a highly motivated enemy (Komer 1986, 48–60; Perry 1989, 136–37, 174–75). His attrition doctrine, the search-and-destroy strategy, and the emphasis on large-unit war were almost inevitable. Moreover, it was difficult even for Generals Wheeler and Johnson to speak up and explicitly criticize him. Even though Westmoreland was not their preferred choice for field commander in Vietnam, his strategy represented mainstream thinking in the military.

5. Conclusions

This chapter looked at the causal factors affecting group risk judgment and risk preferences. Social interaction and group discussion is a primary and important factor. It is not an exclusive source of influence over individual group members, aggregate group judgment, and choice outputs. Social interactions operate through a number of channels. Responsibility diffusion increases risk acceptability by reducing accountability. Persuasion is often dominated by the more risk-prone members and peer pressure toward compliance with higher risk acceptability or risk aversion. Familiarization increases the amount of available information and could result in polarization in either direction, caution or risk acceptance. Group discussion also reveals and makes salient the dominant cultural values. Depending on what these values require, caution or risk taking, group polarization will tend to evolve in that particular direction.

The effectiveness of social influences and their scope will depend on group composition and the resultant distribution of power and personality attributes within the decision making group. Group preferences can also be affected through manipulation of the institutional arrangements and procedures, or be shaped by political imperatives, such as coalition maintenance. Finally, the group response to risk is not only the result of aggregation of individual preferences. It relates also to the sense the group has of itself as an entity with a distinctive identity including a defined set of group goals and beliefs. Ironically, and for diametrically opposed reasons, both more self-confident and less confident groups are likely to be less cautious and more inclined toward taking risks. The former may do so because it is confident it can control process and outcomes. In contrast, desperation may drive the latter to gamble on boldness, with each individual member expecting to be sheltered from any negative consequences by the fact that the responsibility for the decision is shared. The challenge ahead for small group researchers is to develop a more refined understanding of the complex and subtle interplay of factors that determine the difference between realistic and pathological forms of group risk taking in foreign and security policy.

NOTES

I am grateful to Berndt Brehmer, Max Metselaar, Eric Stern, Bengt Sundelius, Paul 't Hart, and participants of the Stockholm workshop, for helpful suggestions. The author would also like to acknowledge the useful comments by Michael Brecher and Steve Walker on earlier versions, and to the members of the Mershon Center Research Training Group (RTG) on the Role of Cognition in Collective Political Decisionmaking at the Ohio State University (National Science Foundation grant DIR-9113599) for the opportunity to discuss aspects of this study. An earlier version of the article was prepared while the author was a fellow of the Program on International Economics and Politics (IEP), The East-West Center, Honolulu. I am indebted to the Center for its generous support and to IEP staff members Valerie Koenig and Cynthia Nakachi for their assistance. The project on which this study is based also benefited from the financial support of the Leonard David Institute of International Relations at the Hebrew University (Jerusalem), the S. A. Schonbrunn Research Endowment Fund, and the Authority for Research and Development of the Hebrew University.

1. It may well be the case that the relative impact of social interaction compared with other influences is culture dependent. In collectivist cultures the former will be much more important than in individualistic cultures (see Hofstede 1984, 148–75; Tse et al. 1988).

2. For a detailed discussion of the rationale for this definition, see Vertzberger 1995, and also Shapira 1995. The reader should note the difference between the terms *risk* and *cost,* which are sometimes confused. Riskiness is an attribute of the policy, while cost is an attribute of the outcome of a risky policy.

3. The distinction between real and perceived risks raises a number of important questions regarding the epistemological defensibility and practical value of this position. These are discussed in some detail in Vertzberger 1990 (35–41). The position taken places this study in the broader philosophical perspective that maintains that there are truths that are distinct from available present evidence and that may therefore remain unknown to the observer. These unobservable factors and structures cause observable phenomena or behaviors. Other works in international relations that take a similar position are, for example, Brecher et al. 1969; Holsti 1965; Sprout and Sprout 1956, 1962. A different view is adopted by, for example, Hollis and Smith (1990), and Onuf (1989). For psychologists' views about the capability of experimental testing to

distinguish reality from perception, see Taylor and Brown 1988. For a comprehensive philosophical treatment of this problem as it applies to technological hazards, see Shrader-Frechette 1991.

4. Group-level risk perceptions and preferences are in essence social cognitions of risk held by the group and formed through a sociocognitive process. This is an interactive process that combines, as shall be detailed later, individual cognitive operations and social interactions (the latter include communicating, information sharing, and attempting to influence other members' cognitions). See Larson and Christensen 1993; Klimoski and Mohammed 1994; Levine et al. 1993.

5. The polarization phenomenon is not altered by the presence of an official leader in the group if he or she allows free discussion (Lilienthal and Hutchinson 1979). It is the discussion among group members that is important for group-induced preference shift, rather than the nature of the affective bond among group members (Yinon and Bizman 1974).

6. The illusion of unanimity posited by Janis (1982) as part of the groupthink hypothesis may be seen as a corresponding group level effect. See also Fuller and Aldag (this volume).

7. Responsibility for outcomes is not necessarily shared. It may be unevenly distributed due to the fact that particular individuals: (1) play the leadership role, (2) hold central positions within the status hierarchy, (3) have particular task competencies, (4) are assigned responsibility for performance of a particular task (Leary and Forsyth 1987).

8. See Metselaar and Verbeek (this volume).

9. It should be noted that the term persuasion is used here in a broad sense, that is, not only as a cognitive process but also as a social motivation phenomenon. The persuasion explanation, in its present form, is congruent with the finding by Wallach et al. (1968) that there is no evidence that commitment to high risk taking in and by itself results in greater persuasiveness. Polarization theory contends that both the high-risk taker and the highly cautious decision maker have powers of persuasion depending on the context.

10. Anticipatory compliance may also occur in the contexts characterized by transactional leadership. See e.g., 't Hart 1990/94.

11. Conformity does not necessarily imply compliance with the majority. We know of many instances of the so-called minority effect. If the majority always prevailed, societies would rarely change, and we know that in history minorities were on many occasions able to change existing trends and convert the majority to their views. To be effective, the minority has to have a distinctive behavioral style that will first attract the majority's attention and then raise doubts within the majority about its own position. The minority must project consistency, certainty, confidence, and credibility; it thereby focuses attention on its position both when the majority already has a fixed, well-defined position and when it does not. A minority is able to project the above attributes because its members respond to the perceived external threat to their unpopular position with loyalty (in-group cohesiveness) and commitment, which is reinforced by self-bolstering (Gerard 1985; Moscovici 1976, 68–93). The minority's willingness to face conflict rather than avoid it is what makes it effective.

12. This process is somewhat similar to the process of self-perception, as demonstrated by Larson's (1985) observations with regard to the Truman Administration. Harry Truman's wavering and hesitation concerning the Soviet Union's intentions from 1944 to 1947 was transformed into a determined view of its aggressive intentions when he had to justify aid to Greece in Congress and realized the forthcoming need to aid Europe. Having made the Truman Doctrine speech that portrayed the situation in Greece as part of a global struggle between democracy and totalitarianism, he adopted beliefs about the Soviet Union that justified the portrayed threat perception.

13. Faction membership does not necessarily imply a similarity of views on all matters, only a congruence of some key beliefs and values shared by some members with greater intensity than by other group members. In some cases the sharing of views among a few members representing different organizations can be traced to a common interorganizational macroorganizational culture. For example, representatives from the three services (army, air force, and navy) share an organizational macroculture, even though their microcultures are quite different. This is enough to form the basis for a factional links. A similar phenomenon has been observed in industrial organizations; see Abrahamson and Fombrun (1994).

14. Explanations for greater confidence in group-based assessments are both cognitive and motivational. "Indeed, when the group agrees, knowing that each member has different information may enhance their confidence that they have identified the alternative favored by the preponderance of the information. That is, group members may use an information sampling heuristics: the more diverse the sets of information that group members have, the more confident one can be that the consensus choice is supported by the weight of the available evidence" (Stasser 1992, 62). From the motivational perspective, group decision making involves the investment of more resources (time and effort) than individual decision making. Group members feel, therefore, compelled to correlate the amount of resources with the quality of the product and therefore are likely to be more confident about their decisions (Mayseless and Kruglanski 1987; Sneizek 1992).

15. Things would be very simple if cultural values had only one source, such as the national culture. But in defining the relevant cultural values, decision makers are socialized by membership in multiple cultures with incongruent values toward risk taking (Vertzberger 1990, 194–200). For example, foreign ministers, who almost always are members of the group making politicomilitary decisions, are on the one hand members of their national society and national decision-making unit, and hence attuned to society's culture-base values of risk or caution. But they are also members of a world elite, whose view of astute statesmanship emphasizes caution. It is not unusual for decision makers to be more attuned to their subculture's values, or to adopt a compromise between the conflicting values.

16. It was shown, for example, that the explanation emphasizing the leadership role of more risk-prone members of a group cannot by itself satisfactorily account for a risky shift in group decision making (Hoyt and Stoner 1968). This further reinforces the view that polarization does not have a single explanation but is rooted in multiple causes. These are linked to the specific conditions existing in each particular group.

17. Normative and informational influence modes differ on five counts: (1) the

mechanism of influence, (2) assumptions about human nature and needs (approval vs. knowing and understanding our world), (3) assumptions about "correctness" of judgment (objective vs. subjective), (4) normative influence is socioemotional whereas informational influence is cognitive, (5) normative influence focuses on judgments (of others) whereas informational influence focuses on the component parts of judgment, i.e., the facts and argument (Kaplan 1987).

18. The statement about the importance of personalities distribution in the group should be modified by reference to the power distribution in the group, as is discussed later. The distribution of power within the group determines whose personality attributes, and therefore which attributes, will be important in determining group preferences and how important these attributes will be.

19. This list of positive consequences of the unanimity rule, that draws on Gaenslen 1993, should be treated with caution. It assumes equal access to policy-relevant information by all group members and hence the need by unanimity-seekers to invest a great deal of effort in convincing all members to support a particular policy. Frequently, some group members control the flow of information, while the others depend on them for access. By exercising their privileged position the few can exert influence to achieve their objectives with much less effort and in a shorter time, and consequently without the favorable results described above. For a systematic exploration of the pathologies associated with the unanimity and majority rules, see Hermann 1993.

20. There are also a number of other ways in which group policy preferences can be manipulated. See Stern and Sundelius (this volume) and Hoyt and Garrison (this volume) for discussions of manipulation.

21. When facing a failed policy, groups have an advantage over individual decision makers in providing self-serving attributions. Individuals indulging in self-serving attributions have to be concerned with the response of other key decision makers that may challenge their self-serving attribution and actually point out that it is self-serving. In groups that indulge in group-serving attributions, members do not have to be concerned with a challenge from other decision makers, especially in cohesive groups. A common preferred group-serving attribution for failure, if they can suggest one credibly, attributes failure to external extragroup factors and causes (Leary and Forsyth 1987, 175–76). Information sharing that characterizes groups' collective cognitive endeavors will generate multiple reasons for not attributing failure to the group, and for making group-serving attributions more convincing, and thus inhibit learning. Group-serving attribution also helps to preserve group cohesion by avoiding infighting over responsibility for failure.

22. These arguments are in line with prospect theory. For a discussion of prospect theory and its relevance to foreign policy decision making and group contexts, see Kahneman and Tversky 1979; Kameda and David 1990; Levy 1992a, 1992b; McGuire et al. 1987; Stein 1992; Vertzberger (in press); and Whyte and Levi 1994.

Part 3
Implications

CHAPTER 10

From Analysis to Reform
of Policy-making Groups

Paul 't Hart

The first impression that one gets of a ruler and of his brains is from seeing
the men that he has about him. When they are competent and faithful one
can always consider him wise, as he has been able to recognize their ability
and keep them faithful. But when they are the reverse, one can always form
an unfavorable opinion of him, because the first mistake that he makes is in
making his choice.

Niccolò Machiavelli, *The Prince*

Introduction

In his modern version of Machiavelli's classic treatise on how to run a government, Arnold Meltsner presents an important rationale for the kind of work
presented in this volume. He reminds us that "those who seek improvement in
the decision making of rulers should expand their appreciation of the social
factors of advising" (1990, 13). Both Machiavelli and Meltsner are acutely
aware that no matter how centralized the structure of authority in a political
system, major policy decisions always arise through social interaction between the holders of high office and those around them. Ultimately, research
on group decision making in government is about developing ideas for the
restructuring of this social interaction in ways that are regarded as productive
by those concerned.

In this final chapter I shall discuss what analytical challenges are involved in this effort. First, I shall present some of the key issues of group
performance in foreign policy-making that emerge from the other contributions to this volume. These can be read as items on a checklist for research-
based proposals to upgrade collegial advisory and decision practices ("Institutional Reform at the Micro Level"). Following this, I shall deal with a
question that is often overlooked in developing proposals for improving group

311

decision making: the problem of standards. What exactly is it that we want to improve when we design models for enhancing group decision quality, and which values are to be maximized in doing so? I shall show that there are not one but several sets of normative principles for evaluating and improving group performance in foreign policy. The key design problem is how to cope with this normative pluralism ("The Problem of Standard Setting"). Building upon this analysis, I shall evaluate two well-known sets of proposals to improve group decision making. It will be shown that they are likely to produce unintended effects and yield ambiguous results ("Trade-offs and Paradoxes in Evaluating Design Proposals").

Next, the problem of feasibility will be discussed. We know from the extensive literature on knowledge utilization in public policy that proposals for improvement of policy-making practices developed by analysts often have a limited impact upon policymakers (Weiss 1977; Lindblom and Cohen 1979). The field of foreign policy analysis is no exception. Specifically, the products of applied small group research seem not to have affected the day-to-day management of foreign policy-making all that much. To increase the future impact of their proposals, foreign policy and small group analysts need to adopt a more realistic view of their role in the policy process ("Proposals for Improvement").

Despite the emphasis that is placed here on the complexities and trade-offs of the design process, I strongly believe that as students of political group dynamics, we should continue to articulate the practical implications of our work. In the final section of this chapter, I shall outline some proposals on the road ahead for small group research on foreign policy-making, in its quest to produce policy-relevant theories.

Institutional Reform at the Micro Level: Lessons from This Volume

Transforming research findings into policy-relevant reform proposals and process interventions takes analysts into the realm of institutional reform. Usually, institutional reform efforts focus on macro-level issues, for example the design and protection of democracy, and the development of a proper mix between political and market-based forms of regulation (Dahl and Lindblom 1954; Williamson 1975; Lindblom 1977; Coase 1988). Reform also extends into meso-level issues like the organization of decision making and service delivery in a variety of policy domains (Dror 1986; Hesse and Bentz 1990). The vacuum lies at the micro level. There is a paradox here. On the one hand, the restructuring of interaction between high-level officials and other stakeholders operating at crucial nodes in the political and bureaucratic system is perhaps the most common and conspicuous means by which a newly incoming president or government tries to put its stamp on the policy-making process. Yet on the other hand, this type of micro-level institutional design has received little sustained attention from foreign policy analysts (see, however, George 1980; Janis 1982; Hermann 1993). This paradox is all the more striking since, as has been argued in the introductory chapter, high-level policy groups are close to the decisions and actions that lie at the heart of foreign policy.

Unfortunately, the existing void can only partially be filled by the many designs for effective group decision making put forward in social psychology and management studies.[1] These have not been designed to deal with the political and institutional constraints and complexities that are characteristic of groups in government. What can we learn from the present volume about improving group decision making in foreign policy? Although their prime intent has been analytical and explanatory, general chapters in this book do offer a number of different ways to think about reforming collegial policy-making government.

Complexity is to be accepted, not reduced.   First of all, setting the parameters, Fuller and Aldag's General Group Problem Solving model shows the complexity of developing prescriptive models of group decision making in organizations. The mere number of salient factors and relevant criteria to be taken into account should be sufficient grounds for caution among would-be reformers and consultants. Given this complexity, simple rules of thumb and quick-and-easy principles for improving collegial policy-making are likely to backfire—an argument that will be further developed below.

Moreover, in thinking about reforming policy-making groups, one should be careful not to reify any formal structure. For example, Metselaar and Verbeek alert us to the permeable and fluctuating boundaries that exist between different groups and factions in the foreign policy process. This suggests that there is only so much that can be accomplished by tailoring the composition of any one advisory or decision-making group: whatever its formal structure and boundaries, once in action such groups are likely to evolve and change in complex ways. In addition, there should be ongoing efforts at managing the process in action, anticipating and responding to informal processes of subgroup formation (factionalism; see also Vertzberger 1990) and intergroup linkages that develop when policy issues are processed.

Context is crucial.   Vertzberger emphasizes the importance of viewing groups in terms of their wider organizational, political, and cultural context. His analysis implies that we cannot be content with ad-hoc prescriptions to increase or decrease group size, or to prevent leaders from articulating their policy preferences at the outset of a group meeting. We should also suggest ways to create a benevolent organizational and cultural *milieu* in which the group operates, or—perhaps more realistically—to empower high-level groups and their members to operate effectively in less-than-benevolent institutional and situational contexts.

Focus on crucial interaction patterns as dependent variables.   Stern and Sundelius's chapter helps to focus the reform agenda by highlighting a number of key interaction patterns that may occur in policy-making groups. Each of these patterns has its own particular configuration of strengths and weaknesses that need to be considered in developing recommendations to change the structure and operating rules of policy-making groups.

Design structures that fit leaders.   Preston shows that there are good and not-so-good matches between a president's personal characteristics and style, and different structures and logics of the foreign policy advisory system. This has implications for organizational reform, since, as Meltsner (1990, 166) observes, "the advisory structure has to fit the ruler, not the other way around." Yet the maxim that "structures should follow people" is not universally applicable. For one thing, many countries have collegial instead of presidential systems. They lack a single dominant leader with the constitutional powers to shape the advisory system as he sees fit.

Reforming structures is not enough.   Hoyt and Garrison's analysis of intragroup manipulation efforts reinforces the central importance of *process management:* Somehow the integrity of the collegial structure and deliberation process needs to be guarded in the face of ongoing and persistent attempts by a variety of stakeholders (including the leaders themselves) to manipulate the decision making process. However, achieving such guardianship is extremely difficult to achieve in practice. In the end no guardian operating in the corridors of power will be able to focus only on protecting the quality of the collegial process. Inevitably he will develop certain substantive policy preferences of his own or be susceptible to lobbies and subtle influence tactics of advocates and outside stakeholders (see "Proposals for Improvement" for further discussion).

Complementing this view, Stern shows the additional importance of thinking dynamically about the requirements of group composition and group process management. Certain stages in a group's existence pose unique and intricate mixes of opportunities and constraints for collegial decision making, requiring different types of structural and procedural interventions facilitating their performance.

The diversity of ideas and directions that can be distilled from the chapters of this volume indicates how complex the move from analysis to design really is, even in the seemingly confined context of small group behavior. This complexity cannot be ignored or removed—it is something to be coped with by analysts, designers, and policy makers. One particularly baffling problem concerns the normative dimension of design, in other words, the standards that we use to develop proposals for improvement: what constitutes "high-quality" group performance or "good" collegial policy-making?

Improvement of What? The Problem of Standard Setting

In developing policy-relevant conclusions and suggestions for improving collegial decision making in foreign policy, there is always the temptation of moving boldly from conceptual frameworks or empirical studies of past policy episodes to detailed prescriptions for restructuring and process intervention. The dominant logic is that of the negative analogy: the solutions advanced mirror the problems highlighted in the case analysis. In this mode of policy prescription, the normative underpinnings of reform proposals are left unarticulated. In other words, analysts often fail to specify what they mean when they say that group decision making needs to be improved. The lack of an explicit set of standards by which the performance of foreign policy-making bodies is being appraised complicates the reform process. Proponents of different proposals may end up talking past each other, not realizing that their proposals are driven by alternative value priorities.

This omission is as understandable as it is unfortunate. Circumventing the problem of evaluation prevents analysts from getting into the messy and "unscientific" business of normative discourse. Rather than opening up that can of worms, it is tempting to simply assume a broad consensus about what constitutes good decision making and optimal group performance. Unfortunately, this presumed consensus does not exist in the practice of foreign policy-making. As shown in chapter 1, small groups pervade the policy process in a number of ways and forms, performing different types of functions. There is no single set of norms that can possibly cover this variety. Secondly, not only do groups and their functions differ, so do analysts' views about what constitutes the essence of policy-making and the critical tasks of groups within it. Normative pluralism is a fact of life in institutional design that small group analysts can ignore only at their peril. If they do, their prescriptions are likely to be regarded by some stakeholders as trivial, by others as unrealistic, and by yet others as offensive.

From a normative point of view, the most appropriate and realistic way to assess and improve group performance in government is to take into account multiple evaluation criteria (George 1980; Quinn 1988). Just looking back at the metaphoric functions of groups in the policy process, as formulated in the introductory chapter, one can immediately derive a range of ad hoc imperatives/criteria that seem to drive each of these faces of group action in foreign policy:

Think tank	Make analytically sound judgments of complex problems. For example: estimate an enemy's likely responses to a variety of own possible moves currently considered by the group in the course of an ongoing international conflict;
Command center	Achieve maximum control over implementation. For example: make sure that even the remotest military field units strictly adhere to rules of engagement in a crisis;
Sanctuary	Maintain emotional balance and self-esteem of members. For example: help prevent an embattled president or prime minister sliding into despair at a time when the government faces multiple, intractable national security crises;
Arena	Enable different stakeholders to articulate and dramatize their positions, yet ultimately reconcile conflicting interests effectively and fairly. For example: get the departments of foreign affairs, trade and commerce, environment, and agriculture to agree on a common national bargaining position in preparing for major, multi-issue international environmental negotiations;
Sorter	Achieve effective and efficient division of labor. For example: work out a satisfactory arrangement for delegating the preparation of cabinet positions on European Commission proposals regarding the future harmonization of national consumer taxes, transboundary water pollution policies, and police cooperation to combat the penetration of organized crime into the banking industry;
Ideologue (I)	Shape and enforce shared group beliefs and norms, and sustain team-like process. For example: punish group members who break (informal) rules of confidentiality of group deliberations;
Ideologue (II)	Protect organizational values and identity. For example: define and reassess strategic political and military national interests in periods of international systemic turbulence;
Smokescreen	Help increase organizational and political support for

decisions taken elsewhere. For example: provide the president or prime minister with unanimous cabinet support for a controversial decision to devaluate the national currency.

Each of these imperatives could drive an institutional reform effort. In combination they provide a formidable and potentially conflicting set of criteria for appraising any reform proposal put forward. This kind of variety is difficult to handle if the analyst seeks to produce a relatively concise and consistent set of proposals. For this reason, analysts tend to reduce normative complexity by placing themselves within particular philosophical and theoretical traditions. By buying into certain basic assumptions about the nature of policy-making, they are able to focus on a more limited set of criteria, ignoring or downplaying others (cf. Hermann 1993, 181, plus fn. 5). This in itself is no problem, it is even desirable. As argued above, the problem arises when this "buying in" occurs implicitly or inadvertently. Let me briefly review three major schools of thought that can be found, and the values embodied in their prescriptions for improving collegial policymaking (based on Bovens and 't Hart 1996).

Policy-making as Problem Solving

Perhaps the majority of analysts active in the group decision-making field share a problem-solving view of policy-making and the role of collegial bodies within it. At the core of this view lies the notion of "reality testing." Social problems are "out there," as are a number of ways of solving them, each with certain advantages and drawbacks, as well as (undefined) probabilities. The crucial task for policymakers is to arrive at sound and workable definitions of what the problems are, what can realistically be expected of government to diminish or perhaps completely solve them, what specific options (actions, measures, programs) are available, and which (combinations of) options stand the best chance of achieving the desired ends.

The problem-solving focus matches an emphasis on functional rationality with a voluntaristic outlook on policy-making. Its functional rationality manifests itself by the use of a means–ends framework to understand public policy-making, whereby government actors or agencies are assumed to have set goals or operational program objectives. These goals are taken as given; their origins and sensibility are not subject to analysis in the problem-solving mode. Its voluntarism is evident from its view that policy-making is a deliberate activity, whose ends can be accomplished by carefully constructed steps and procedures on the part of political and bureaucratic elites, and that is meticulously implemented by public bureaucracy.

The dominant standard by which these analysts judge group performance and collegial policy-making is the quality of information processing and deliberation. These in turn are held to be the crucial determinants of effective decisions (Herek, Janis and Huth 1987; Janis 1989; Vertzberger 1990). Policy-making groups are supposed to solicit, scan, and critically weigh all the relevant information about a policy issue that is available. The day-to-day practice of group decision making is full of social, organizational, and political dynamics that compromise this task. When groups are not careful, they will selectively neglect or misinterpret crucial information and will consequently make decisions based on a less-than-optimal or even grossly distorted picture of the situation. When this happens, one or several group and organizational pathologies are usually at work. Groupthink is one of these, but analysts have identified a number of others.

From a problem-solving perspective, the key purpose of proposals for improving group decision making is to eliminate these pathologies. Analysts are to offer ways of restructuring organizations and groups so that they seek out information more proactively and systematically, and assess it carefully and rigorously before making a policy decision. The specific policy prescriptions offered encompass structure-oriented changes in staffing, the routing of information and procedures for reporting and distributing information. In addition, they deal with the delicate dynamics of the group process, suggesting the empowerment of dissenting minorities, more open and democratic leadership styles, and a number of tactics to prevent groups from taking impulsive decisions. As we shall see later, much of Irving Janis's prescriptive work on how to prevent groupthink and improve high-level decision making is based on these problem-solving assumptions.

Policy-making as Value Articulation and Adjudication

One alternative to the problem-solving perspective emphasizes the value dimension of policy-making rather than the analytical one. Public policy-making is seen as a social and political process that evolves around the articulation and adjudication of multiple, culturally embedded values and ideologies. The conflict between these values and ideologies manifests itself in fundamental disagreements about the nature, ends, roles, and limits of government in society. In addition, there are likely to be competing views about the nature and form of policy interventions in particular social spheres and policy sectors, in this case, the key values and strategies underlying a country's foreign policy in domains like security, economy, ecology, and development. These fundamental differences may also filter through to the operational level of foreign policy implementation, and the actual performance of foreign policy agencies or officials. Somehow, policymakers, acting alone or in collegial groups, need to keep these conflicts from escalating, so as to permit continued dialogue, cooperation, and loyalty. Policy-making becomes an exercise in the management of competing values (Dahl 1982, and especially Dahl 1985).

Whereas the problem-solving approach get its analytical tools and policy prescriptions from decision theory, cognitive and social psychology, and certain parts of organizational analysis, the competing-values approach is rooted more in political science and political philosophy. The focus switches from problem solving to conflict management, from a concern with analysis to a concern with distribution and redistribution, and from the centrality of comprehensive information processing to the selective uses and manipulation of information, as well as the "management" of options in the policy process (Hermann 1993). In this perspective, the ends of policy-making are not given. They are the subject of a political process of articulation, mobilization, and accommodation. In this process argumentation becomes crucially important. This argumentation process is shaped by communication and debate, but above all by the wielding of power and influence. At the same time, politics is not merely about interests and the exercise of power. It is also about values and beliefs. These drive the political process, constrain it, and, in turn, are constantly being renegotiated and transformed by it.

Consequently, the competing-values focus emphasizes substantive and political rationality. It stresses the need to contemplate the origins and content of the competing claims that lie at the heart of the policy process. In particular, the justification of these claims in terms of the normative arguments offered by various participants becomes the focal point for inquiry and evaluation. Along with that comes a concern for the (democratic) quality of the processes by which these claims are subsequently traded off, integrated, or otherwise dealt with in the policy process. In practice, many of these processes will be taking place in collegial bodies, meetings, and other face-to-face interactions between policymakers. From this perspective, the question of access to these groups and the principles for group deliberation and decision making become vitally important, because these will determine whether all relevant values and interests are adequately represented, articulated, and incorporated into the decision-making process (Hermann 1993).

Policy-making as Institutionalized Action

A third view of policy-making emphasizes its organizational dimension. It depicts policy-making as a multiorganizational activity that involves actors operating at different levels of the political and bureaucratic hierarchy inside and outside government. These encounters are governed by complex rules and codes that are part of the institutional context in which the entire process is embedded. Sometimes these rules and codes are formalized, for example in constitutions or in specific interaction regimes that different stakeholders have agreed upon (such as corporatist forms of consultation and shared decision making between major social interest groups and the government). But in many cases, these rules and codes are more informal, based in tradition and subject to different interpretations.

Given the importance of these often very intricate rules and codes, policy-making processes are in part contingent upon how different actors interpret the institutional regime they are part of, and how they derive appropriate behaviors from it. This brings out the highly constructed and contextual nature of policy-making. It involves nonlinear, often loosely coordinated activities of people and organizations that are locked into complex patterns of interdependence, social exchange, and communication. Setbacks, reversals, disconnections, and miscommunications between them are frequent. It is exceedingly difficult to master and tame the very complexity of their interactions and to bridge the different meanings they attach to events and decisions (Brunsson 1989).

Whereas the problem-solving perspective maintains a strongly voluntaristic view of group decision making in government, the institutional perspective emphasizes the role of more immutable, yet ambiguous contextual factors that constrain and facilitate certain types of group perceptions and actions. What goes on in policy-making groups is much more a reflection of complex (inter)organizational processes that are only partly amenable to deliberate management and control. To understand group decision making in government, it becomes necessary to study not only the group itself, but also the organizations and environments in which they are embedded. Furthermore, one needs to study how different organizations relate to one another, and how they cooperate, bargain, and compete with others, and which institutional values and norms drive this process ('t Hart 1990/1994, 129–206).

The institutional perspective does not really generate a clear and consistent view about what constitutes "good" group decision making. It argues that what is considered "good" is determined by the actors themselves, as they develop shared meanings and values about both the appropriate goals and the best means of policy-making. When some of these meanings and values persist over time, they become institutionalized and can be used as standards to evaluate particular policy-making episodes (March and Olsen 1989). Yet the institutions themselves may also become problematic, for example after a major policy crisis (such as the United States' defeat in Vietnam or the Soviet invasion of Afghanistan), an institutional crisis (the Bretton Woods monetary system in 1971, the EU controlled exchange rate system in 1992), or a crisis at the group level (major cabinet crises and reshuffles, escalating interpersonal conflict, a reassignment of group tasks and prerogatives, the creation of new and competing groups in the organization). When this happens, policy-making groups may enter a period of normative uncertainty and role conflict, during which a search for new meanings, values, and rules begins (Brunsson and Olsen 1993). During these transitory periods, it is much more difficult to develop a set of evaluation principles.

Normative Pluralism

The debate on the quality of group decision making in foreign policy is made complex by the different philosophies of policy-making involved, which are grounded in different intellectual traditions and value systems about politics and policy. Analysts of group decision making are inevitably part of this process. Much as they might want to, they cannot stand aloof from it. The three schools of thought about the nature and preconditions for high-quality group performance in government presented constitute a reservoir for making more explicitly grounded policy recommendations. At the same time, they present us with the challenge of normative pluralism. If one accepts that all three views articulate a legitimate and important set of preoccupations and criteria, the ultimate challenge for group decision design is to find ways of combining or integrating them. This will involve an increased awareness for the paradoxes that may arise when evaluating group performance in government.

Trade-offs and Paradoxes in Evaluating Design Proposals

So far, I have argued that each proposal for improving group practices in government assumes certain criteria for assessing group performance in the foreign policy-making process. In a sense, then, each suggestion or technique to facilitate group performance, however innocuous or commonsensical, is contestable. The dilemmas of evaluating group performance noted earlier recur in evaluating designs for group improvement: a design developed in one tradition will have a rather different configuration of benefits and costs when judged from the perspective of others. Let me show in greater detail the complexities of evaluation and design by discussing two examples of group-decision designs: Janis's recommendations to prevent groupthink and pre-scriptive models of group composition.

Example 1: Preventing Groupthink

At the end of his classic study, Janis (1982) has formulated a set of ideas about how to prevent groupthink. These were derived more or less inductively from his case studies, combined with his normative perspective on "good" decision

TABLE 10.1.   Janis's Recommendations to Prevent Groupthink

• Each member must be critical evaluator of the group's course of action; an open climate of giving and accepting criticism should be encouraged by the leader.
• Leaders should be impartial and refrain from stating their personal preferences at the outset of group discussion; they should limit themselves initially to fostering open inquiry.
• Set up parallel groups working on the same policy question under different leaders.
• Each member of the group should privately discuss current issues and options with trusted associates outside the group and report back their reactions.
• Different outside experts should be brought in from time to time to challege the views of the core members.
• There should be one or more devil's advocates during every group meeting.
• In conflict situations, extra time should be devoted to interpreting warning signals from rivals and to constructing alternative scenarios of their intentions.
• Second chance meetings should be held to reconsider the decision once it has been reached and before it is made public.

Source: Janis 1982, 262, adapted.

making (see Janis and Mann 1977; Janis 1989). His prescriptions invite poli- cymakers strongly to "open up" the group deliberation process to outside and "unwelcome" information. The basic idea is that this improves the likelihood of the group making a more systematic and realistic assessment of the situation. It also ought to help widen the range of options under consideration and to assure that they are thoroughly scrutinized before a final choice is made (see table 10.1).

The problem with these recommendations is that some of the "solutions" Janis advances, which implicitly draw upon one set of assumptions about policy-making, would be defined as "problems" when looked upon from another. Janis may be right in asserting that groupthink impairs sound problem solving. From the perspective of managing competing values or achieving institutional action, however, groupthink may be judged more positively. This is because it helps in creating and maintaining a coherent winning coalition at the top of the organization that develops a clear policy preference, despite the usual cross pressures of different interest groups and protracted interagency deadlocks in the bureaucracy.

Likewise, although groupthink may be a threat to sound problem solving and procedural rationality, by fostering more diversity and dissensus within the group, Janis's recommendations to prevent groupthink may inadvertently result in its polar opposite: a breakdown of collegiality and a decision-making process paralyzed by factionalism and bureaucratic stalemate. In other words, looking at efforts to prevent groupthink from multiple perspectives, one becomes aware of the fact that proposals to break through extreme consensus may well have unintended and unwanted effects on other relevant dimensions

TABLE 10.2. Preventing Groupthink: Benefits (+) and Costs (−)

Normative Criteria	Impact of Groupthink	Impact of Janis's Recommendations
Problem solving perspective:		
Goal achievement/ problem-solving effectiveness (think tank)	− (increased chances of policy failure)	+ (increased critical scrutiny of options and decisions)
Institutional perspective:		
Acceptance and support within the group (ideologue)	+ (esprit de corps maintained)	+/− (more difficult to achieve consensus within government system)
Efficiency of coordination and limitation of decisional costs (sorter)	+ (quick and easy consensus in inner circle)	− (more participants, discussion: time consuming)
Limitation of decisional stress among group members (sanctuary)	+ (value trade-offs avoided)	− (value trade-offs faced)

of group performance. The design challenge is therefore not simply to mitigate extreme consensus, but rather to strike a balance between the need for constructive conflict and vigilant decision making on the one hand, and the maintenance of organizational cohesion, group collegiality, and political support on the other. This is no easy task, and it seems Nemeth and Staw (1989, 204, emphasis in the original) are right when they observe that "too few organizations know how to maintain both substantial diversity *and* strong selection processes" (see also Moscovici and Doise 1994).

Table 10.2 makes it clear that procedures to prevent groupthink by promoting more careful deliberation and checks and balances within the policy-making group come at a price. Most of the mechanisms to prevent groupthink involve a particular solution to this trade-off problem: analytical problem-solving criteria are allowed to prevail over other considerations. For example, they tend to be at odds with some of the core ideas embedded in the institutional interaction perspective. This makes recommendations to prevent groupthink potentially self-defeating. They also place heavy demands on decision makers and their organizations to devote elaborate analysis and discussion to a range of potentially important issues. Since we know that attention is the most precious yet scarcest resource of organizational decision makers, this insensitivity to the day-to-day realities of policy-making in complex organizations seriously compromises the utility of current prescriptions to prevent groupthink. Busy decision makers and overburdened staffs will have no time for them. Tenuous interagency groups and coalition cabinets cannot afford a more adversarial style.

Mechanisms that prevent groupthink are, in other words, not a panacea. The efficiency losses and decisional stress that accompany groupthink-prevention mechanisms need, in other words, to be accepted only when the likelihood and costs of failure from quick and easy decision making are judged to be high, or when extremely careful decision making may result in unusually large benefits (Janis 1989; Nutt 1989, 377). In all other situations, the "institutional" costs of groupthink prevention (such as longer decision time, loss of intra-group cohesion, lack of clear direction provided by group leadership, redundant channels of information and advice) are probably higher than the substantive, "problem-solving" benefits that may accrue from more carefully scrutinized decisions.[2]

Example 2: Composing a "Top Team"

One important way of influencing group performance is to carefully pick the group's membership in accordance with the requirements of the group's task. Crucial variables include the group's size, skills, experience, and personalities of members (cf. Hambrick and Mason 1984; Daboub, Rasheed, Priem, and Gay 1995). Social psychologists have provided us with fairly detailed guidelines on the optimal group composition for various types of problem-solving and decision-making tasks (Vroom and Yetton 1973; Shaw 1981). It is one of the areas where analysts are relatively confident in putting forward rather detailed recommendations.

Yet there are grounds to question this confidence, if one looks at these recommendations using different normative frames of policy-making. The problem-solving perspective tends to follow the recommendations of psychologists and stresses members' cognitive complexity, the heterogeneity of academic and experiential backgrounds, interpersonal skills, and levels of personal development. The competing values perspective, in contrast, focuses strongly on selecting players according to their political or bureaucratic constituency, or according to their expressed preferences with regard to a particular policy issue. The institutional perspective tends to lead to skepticism about group composition as a target for quality-improvement efforts. It tends to view policy-making groups as open, even volatile platforms for policy-making, whose composition is subject to changing logics of involvement and abstention (Kingdon 1984; Bryson and Crosby 1992; Moscovici and Doise 1994).

There are, in other words, numerous recruitment principles that may guide group composition. They are, however, not always compatible with one another, nor are they equally realistic. Each has its own merits as well as drawbacks. In table 10.3, some of the best-known principles are depicted as

TABLE 10.3.   Group Composition and Group Process

Recruitment Principle	Implications for Group Process
1. Uniformity vs. pluriformity	Forcefulness and confidentiality vs. Balance of viewpoints and interests but high decisional costs
2. Closure vs. openness	Confidentiality but administrative ethnocentrism vs. Broader external support
3. Expertise monopoly vs. redundant expertise	Quicker decisions but risk of biased problem framing and information processing vs. Slower decisions and risk of expert disagreement and conflict
4. Experience and seniority vs. mix of old and new group members	Historical expertise and lower process costs but risks of dominant analogies vs. Constructive conflict of multiple perspectives but higher process costs
5. Limited size vs. bigger size	Quicker decisions but suboptimal capability to process complexity vs. Slower decisions but quality gains

design dimensions with two extremes. Each extreme presents a design ideal type, with a particular set of advantages. The problem is that each ideal type tends to be at odds with important values embodied by the other extreme on the same dimension. Tables like these can be useful to derive different types of "group composition profiles," then evaluate these as packages on a number of criteria, rather than weighing the various dimensions of group composition separately on a more limited set of criteria. In this way, one can retain a more explicit view of the design trade-offs that are inevitably involved in adopting a particular philosophy of member selection.

When using schemes such as table 10.3, one has to keep in mind that in the political arena not all attempts to shape group composition are inspired by the desire to improve the quality of decision making. As Hoyt and Garrison (this volume) have argued, the size and membership of a policy-making group are also prime targets for manipulation attempts by group leaders, members, and outside forces. Manipulating the membership of the cabinet and its committees has traditionally been a key source of influence for British prime ministers, for example. The prime contemporary users of this prerogative,

Harold Wilson and Margaret Thatcher, have mostly employed it to get their way, not to arrive at more carefully considered decisions (James 1991). In politics, reaching the "best" decision can mean many different things (Stone 1987).

Proposals for Improvement: Practical Feasibility

This fundamental point about the political dimension of foreign policy-making practices leads to the second major question dealt with in this chapter: the practical feasibility of policy recommendations for better group decision making. A tension exists between the ideal of designing optimal groups and the practical problems that arise when it comes to implementing these designs. These problems derive from, among others, the open-ended, volatile character of policy-making groups, the role of emergent informal groups, and the politics of group manipulation. Each of these elements were highlighted in this volume, but in general these characteristics are insufficiently recognized in the problem-solving–oriented small group literature. Analysts may be fully aware of them, but they hardly ever address them head-on. Consequently, most of the conventional prescriptive options for improving group decision making in the political science and foreign policy literature are directly derived from work in social and organizational psychology. The voluntarism of the problem-solving framework shines through in the logic of prescription: the assumption is that much of what goes on inside the corridors of government and corporate organizations is malleable. Therefore, group pathologies can be reduced if not eradicated by reconstituting these groups and by facilitating their internal dynamics. Moreover, it is assumed that people of power like to hear this insight from people of insight.

In my view, a more cautious, even skeptical approach is in order. In our zeal to communicate what we see as the major practical lessons of small group research, we may all too easily forget that in the political-administrative arena "variables" such as group composition and leadership style are not easily amenable to deliberate, research-based interventions.

Embedded Groups: Institutional Limits on Reform

An essential contribution of this volume has been to not only assume but also document that collegial bodies and groups within government are embedded in institutionalized systems of policy-making. Inevitably, therefore, group *structures* are shaped by institutionally grounded norms, rules, and routines of recruitment and socialization, as well as by stakeholders' manipulation efforts (see Garrison and Hoyt, this volume). Institutional factors also constrain and facilitate a particular group's *position* and relative importance within the policy-making process (see Metselaar and Verbeek, this volume). Likewise, group *interaction patterns* are governed by formal and informal codes of conduct and decision (compare Vertzberger, and Stern and Sundelius, this volume). All of these combine to limit the impact that any group-oriented interventions proposed by researchers or consultants might have.

Let us take the United States case as an example. Preston (this volume) echoes an established leadership studies tradition and focuses strongly on the personal needs and preferences of the president as key factors shaping the foreign policy advisory system that is put in place during his reign. If this is so, personality profiling techniques may be developed as key prescriptive tools for matching advisory structures to individual needs and preferences. In my view, there are important limits to the practical usefulness of such an approach that need to be taken into account, however.

For one thing, one may question the conventional wisdom that the advisory structure is indeed to a large extent shaped by the president. Stern's account of the Bay of Pigs case shows, for example, that although Kennedy used many of his own men, thus creating a "newgroup situation," the most important inputs in the decision-making process leading up to the invasion were made by "old" advisers he inherited from the previous administration. In foreign affairs and national security, no incoming president can afford to make a complete break and ignore the experience of key officials in the diplomatic, military, and intelligence complex. Therefore, his control over group structure in the crucial first period of office is less than complete. In addition, Hoyt and Garrison and many others show that presidents are not the only ones trying to shape the structure and operating logic of the advisory system. The relative impact of presidential wishes and commands, versus that of less obtrusive attempts by other senior officials to manipulate the performance of the advisory system, has to be empirically established and cannot be taken for granted by assumption.

The outcomes of these multiple influence attempts derive, first, from the formal organizational setting in which the policy process is embedded. Departments and agencies are already in place as key stakeholders and sources of information and advice on foreign policy and security issues. They cannot be abolished or transformed at will and on the spot. Some of these agencies' structures and tasks are rooted in law, others are simply indispensable to any president no matter what his inclinations.

Second, there are the imperatives of politics. The president needs to muster wide support for his appointments. This has proven to be an increasingly difficult requirement. There is pressure on him to take into account a range of ideological, regional, bureaucratic, racial, gender, and other political cleavages and factions in composing his foreign policy team.

Finally, whichever formal structure the president puts in place when entering office, it is highly unlikely to operate as envisaged at its creation. Structures of responsibility, communication, and decision in complex organizations tend to be organic rather than mechanic, and dynamic rather than static. They are subject to constant adjustment and renegotiation. Presidents learn to appreciate what they really feel comfortable with only as they get on with their job. Preferences on whom to see for what and when are likely to change. The practice of the advisory process is highly dependent upon personal relationships between advisers and advisee. The ups and downs in those relationships are mirrored in the way the system works at any given time (Meltsner 1990). Moreover, knowing this, advisers, advisees, and other stakeholders will be all the more keen to target the structure of the decision-making process for their influence attempts (the continual struggle between Vance and Brzezinski for Carter's heart and mind is a marked case, as shown clearly in Garrison and Hoyt's chapter; see also Meltsner 1990; Moens 1990).

The same cautionary story could be told about proposals to reform other types of collegial groups operating under different institutional imperatives. Moreover, if there are such important limits on executive discretion in a spoils system like the United States', recommendations to "hand pick" advisers and "reshape" advisory structures may be even less relevant in many European systems, where incoming political appointees face the mandarins of the permanent civil service. Also, the very structure of the political executive may be more complex and ambiguous than in the United States. Each of these differences affects the viability of group-level designs for better policy-making. As Metselaar and Verbeek imply in chapter 4, for example, proposals to strengthen cabinet leadership in Dutch foreign policy require at a minimum an in-depth understanding of the intricacies of the Dutch tradition of cabinet government, an acute grasp of the political context faced by the incumbent government, and a feeling for the interpersonal dynamics within the cabinet, most importantly those between the prime minister and the minister for foreign affairs.

The Practice of Application: The Fate of Multiple Advocacy

One important attempt to develop a more comprehensive normative model of the foreign policy advisory process has been made by Alexander George in his widely noted multiple advocacy approach (George 1972, 1980). Multiple advocacy seeks to extend the overall institutional philosophy of the U.S. government (checks and balances) to the specific context of the executive organization of foreign policy-making, foreign policy being the one area where the president enjoys a relatively large executive discretion. Multiple advocacy is, in other words, an attempt to productively import the different viewpoints and policy priorities that usually exist in the political and bureaucratic context of U.S. foreign policy-making into the deliberations of the president and his innermost advisors.[3] Concretely, multiple advocacy is a procedure whereby, in a process carefully managed by a neutral "custodian," proponents of particular views or options ("advocates") flesh out their disagreements in a dialectic process of discussion and debate, serving to assist the "magistrate" (the chief executive, e.g., the president) to arrive at well thought-out choices.

Although it has met with considerable criticism (most recently, Farkas 1995), multiple advocacy has generally been warmly embraced in the scholarly community dealing with U.S. foreign policy. It is by far the best developed prescriptive process management model available. At the same time, even multiple advocacy has not had the pervasive impact that one might have hoped for, given its compatibility with core institutional doctrines in the U.S. system. The evidence suggests that its record is mixed. Since it was first articulated in 1972, it has never been fully operative in the U.S. foreign policy community. Some presidents actively disliked it (Nixon), others did not care enough about the details of policy-making to have strong feelings about it (Reagan). Carter favored and made attempts to institutionalize it. However, he was not able to prevent the advocacy process from gradually degenerating into bitter bureaucratic warfare between the national security adviser and the secretary of state. Perhaps the only president able to maintain a system with traits of multiple advocacy was George Bush. Surprisingly perhaps, multiple advocacy may have been more evident, at least de facto, in the structure of the advisory process in certain domestic policy domains, such as in economic policy under Ford and possibly Clinton (compare Porter 1980).

This ambiguous record is not altogether surprising. Multiple advocacy places a heavy burden on all parties. It can only work if those who practice it rigorously adhere to the logic of the system as a whole and the role requirements that come with it. This is often not the case. First, the confines of their assigned roles may be too much for some advisers, in particular the custodian (usually the assistant for national security affairs). It is his job in multiple advocacy to ensure that the broadest possible array of views and interests is represented, that relevant expertise is brought into the group discussion, and that unpopular options get a fair hearing. Yet being a major figure in the administration, operating at the heart of the decision-making process, they are the object of many pressures in favor of certain policies and against others. Also, they tend to be men of some stature, with well-developed views of their own. As a result, many NSC advisers tend to succumb to the temptations of using their position to influence and manipulate rather than to guard the advisory process. While formally often charged with process management and quality control, many of them—with Henry Kissinger and Zbigniew Brzezinski as the most conspicuous examples—evolved into advocates. Brzezinski, for example, had been determined to fulfill a process management role when he came to the NSC. Nevertheless, he gradually became more outspoken on substantive issues, and found himself taking a more hawkish line than Secretary of State Vance on many security issues. This produced considerable tension between the two senior officials. About halfway into the Carter presidency, Brzezinski went all-out fighting for his own policy preferences, to the detriment of his willingness and ability to fulfill the custodial role (Moens 1990).

Second, similar pressures are operative on the chief executive himself. First of all, he simply lacks the time to be his own custodian; he needs to be the magistrate and needs to have somebody else to control the advocacy process. Yet, whereas a magistrate makes decisions on a case-by-case basis, basing his views primarily upon the evidence and arguments presented, the president cannot always afford to do so. As the foremost political leader of his country, the president is supposed to show a more general sense of direction in foreign policy at all times. At the same time, he faces numerous crises, setbacks, and unintended problems that require careful consideration of past and future policies. Those are the instances where the magistrate role may be most called for. To accomplish the "leader" role, the president needs as little internal dissent and debate as possible. For the "magistrate" role, he cannot do without it. Yet, often pressures of media and public opinion for clarity, simplicity, and consistency in foreign policy seem to outweigh the need for finding sophisticated solutions to complex clusters of problems. Therefore, it seems only natural that some time into their tenure many presidents gravitate toward an inner circle rather than keep a multiple-advocacy type of advisory system. They want trusted and like-minded advisers that agree with them on fundamentals. They also need a shield to the hostile outside world of media and congressional opponents that seem to want to undercut a president's every move (cf. Ellis 1994). This tendency decreases their openness to the very logic of multiple advocacy. As Meltsner (1990, 82) argues,

> . . . there is a delicate balance between the need for the ruler to be strong-minded and the need for openness in presenting problems and receiving advice. What is required is a ruler who appears to the external world to be in charge but who, within the inner circle, has created norms of equality to promote discussion, dissent, and multiple perspectives of policy problems.

Third, although foreign policy is one of the few fields where a U.S. president has the power to act as a "magistrate" and be an ultimate decision maker, this is much less the case in the domestic policy arena. The institutional limits to the power of the president at home are far greater, decreasing the prospects for successful application of the multiple advocacy model. In recent years, however, the growing complexity and politicization of national security and other foreign policy domains has also eroded the special position of the foreign policy "decision regime" (cf. Putnam 1988). More and more, U.S. presidents have had to reckon with a wide array of domestic interests and parallel issues, forcing them to widen the network of stakeholders that have to be consulted even on vital foreign policy issues (Destler, Gelb, and Lake 1984).

This development militates against the adoption of the conventional multiple advocacy model. George's model is strongly oriented toward decision making on national security issues and assumes a stable hard core of advisers. One could, of course, try to develop different versions of multiple advocacy for other types of issue areas. In the current context of more "domesticized" foreign policy-making and more "internationalized" domestic policy-making, however, there are likely to be continuous attempts to question and renegotiate the rules governing access and deliberation. Also, the pressures for consensus and conformity inherent in a hierarchical system will not go away, no matter how the nature of foreign policy-making changes. It might well be, as Keohane (1993, 301) has observed, that national foreign policy establishments are not the most appropriate setting for institutionalizing multiple advocacy in the first place. It may have a better chance in the less hierarchical setting of international organizations like WTO and to some extent the European Union.

Conclusions and Prospects

Above I have argued that in moving from analysis to formulating reform proposals, small group analysts face two critical challenges. They need to come to terms with the dilemmas and paradoxes of normative pluralism in evaluating group performance in public policy-making. In addition they need to match the contents and presentation of their proposals to the institutional realities of policy-making that prevail in the setting where they seek to have an impact. Given these constraints, what scope is left for students of group decision making to formulate recommendations that may be relevant and constructive to the better conduct of foreign policy?

Feasibility: From "Expert" to "Advocate"

One could take an extreme relativist position and give up the ambition of developing research-based prescriptive designs and interventions. To this author, that would be tantamount to resignation. Another, in my view more productive, strategy is to reconsider our past practices in making policy recommendations, and to develop a new view of our role in the policy process. Too often, our proposals have been presented as ready-made solutions, as more or less comprehensive and scientifically grounded action proposals to policymakers. In a world of normative pluralism and bureaucratic politics, such an approach to being "policy relevant" is bound to fail. In fact, it only reinforces the inherent gap between the world of academia and the world of policy-making (George 1993a). Policymakers do not need academics to tell them how to conduct their business. To them, academics are just one group among a multitude of other advisers clamoring for attention.

If we accept this sobering situation as a fact of life (and I do not see any alternative), we should reconsider what we hope to achieve by making recommendations and how to go about it. I agree with Majone (1989, 77) who argues that "feasibility, rather than optimality should be the main concern of policy analysts, and . . . they should be as preoccupied with political and institutional constraints as with technical and economic constraints." The paradox of feasibility may well be that analysts who are serious about increasing the practical uses of the fruits of their scientific labor can only succeed if they understand and utilize the dynamics of governmental politics (cf. Dutton and Ashford 1993). Finding ways to deal creatively with the sometimes opposing requirements of detached reflection and political realism is what the art and craft of applied foreign policy analysis are all about (cf. Bovens and 't Hart 1996, 150–52).

There is much to be gained if we start to think of our policy recommendations as arguments in ongoing processes of reconsideration and reform of the policy-making process (cf. Hill and Besthoff 1994). As arguments, our recommendations will need to highlight rather than artificially obscure the identity and premises of their sponsors. To be heard, they will have to be injected into a policy arena along with other, partially competing arguments. They will be understood and evaluated in the context of claims made by others, both academics and other stakeholders. And they will be understood differently by actors occupying different positions in the arena (Bovens and 't Hart 1996).

Moreover, we cannot expect our claims to be given greater weight by policymakers because they are based on abstract modeling or systematic empirical research: policymakers are often acutely aware of the limits of science, particularly social science. We will have to convince them of the merit of our ideas both by the force of our argument and through a certain political astuteness in presenting it in the right way, at the right time, to the right people.

Substance: From "Proverbs" to "Trade-offs"

It should be clear by now that I do not believe in presenting one-dimensional arguments about unanimity versus majority rule, small- versus large-size groups, or "democratic" versus "directive" group leadership. Standing on its own, each of these arguments is incomplete and irrelevant. This is because the decision regime properties singled out for manipulation in practice are embedded in a broader system of policy-making. In this system, different meanings are attached to things like "consensus," "conflict," and "unanimity."

Any proponent of change in current practices of decision making in foreign policy needs somehow to cope with the trade-offs that exist between the needs and styles of the senior policymakers, the constraints of the values, customs, rules, and organizational structures embedded in the system, and the required political support for particular reform proposals. Just as our analysis of group decision making in foreign policy needs to be sensitive to the constraints and opportunities provided by the institutional context in which groups operate, so do our recommendations for reform.

Research: A Modest Agenda

This volume has sought to widen the agenda of political small group analysis and to articulate some conceptual tools for empirical research. Before we can aspire to develop persuasive recommendations for reform along the lines suggested above, we need a much deeper understanding of group activity in the foreign policy process. Let me therefore conclude by sketching a research strategy that may help to achieve this.

1. Move beyond "problem solving" preoccupations with information processing and choice in foreign policy-making groups.

We need to overcome the decisionist orientation that has dominated the, "problem-solving"–oriented, small group research in foreign policy analysis. In its place should come a more balanced, multidimensional conceptualization of the nature and functions of groups in the foreign policy process. This should incorporate insights from the "competing values" and "institutional" perspectives. The metaphoric survey of group functions presented in this volume can only be a heuristic starting point for the reconceptualization that is required. Ultimately, we need more rigid analytical taxonomies and typologies to allow for more systematic analysis and comparison of different kinds of groups (including collegial decision bodies, leader-centered advisory groups, interagency coordination committees, policy planning teams, and crisis management units). We should use these to assess their impact upon different dimensions of the foreign policy-making process. As argued extensively above, this reconceptualization should take place at both the analytical and the normative level. It should strengthen not only our tools for understanding groups but also the coherence of our evaluations of them. Furthermore, its starting point should be an awareness of the "embedded" nature of groups in the policy process, highlighting the importance of the institutional and political context in which they operate.

2. Develop a more explicit understanding of the methodological difficulties involved in studying foreign policy-making groups, and develop strategies for overcoming them.

Little attention has been paid in this volume to the major methodological
challenges that await a small group analyst interested in foreign policy-
making. This omission needs to be eradicated. Since small group analysts tend
to be interested in the intricacies of personal and interpersonal factors in the
behavior of elites operating in sensitive areas of public policy, they face
important constraints of data availability. One way around this dilemma is to
take the historian's route and wait for the archives to open up, that is, to study
only cases from the more distant past. In general, however, foreign policy
analysts also want to study more contemporary cases. Consequently, we will
have to be creative in developing methods to gain insight (if only by approximation) of what goes on in the proverbial corridors of power. Some rely on
personal networks and investigative journalism to make inferences, whereas
others prefer to accept the constraints of the public record yet apply more
rigorous analytic methods (such as content analysis: see Tetlock 1979; Esser
and Lindoerfer 1989; Walker and Watson 1987).

The chapters in this volume have all used rather "soft" methods of
historical case analysis based on public records, archival materials, and elite
interviews. Stern and Sundelius's six-step procedure provides researchers
working in this tradition with a useful scheme for conducting their analyses in
a more systematic and rigorous way. At the same time, the creative work by
Tetlock, Peterson, McGuire, Chang and Feld (1992) suggests that there are
other promising methodological strategies in analyzing political group dynamics that need to be acknowledged and assessed. Also, we should not forget
the important potential contributions to applied small group research of
(quasi-)experimental methods common in social psychology. Minix's (1982)
risk-taking experiments with different groups of military personnel stand out
as a rare example of policy-relevant populations of subjects working on realistic yet controlled foreign policy decision scenarios that merits much wider
imitation than it has received over the last ten years.

3. Conduct longitudinal studies of major foreign policy groups, covering
different periods in their life span.

One way to overcome decisionist biases in small group research is to follow
the example of George (1980) and especially Moens (1990) and study a
particular group as it evolves over time and as it deals with a range of foreign
policy issues. This allows us to gain a better understanding of the interplay
between institutional, political, interpersonal, situational, and idiosyncratic
forces. The "snapshot" view that tends to result from a decisional case study

approach is superseded in this type of study, which compares a range of different decisions taken by a group and the common context in which they were set (see also Hill 1991). This type of design would also enable a more controlled investigation of life-cycle types of theories about the group process, including the newgroup syndrome put forward by Stern in this volume. A particularly promising angle would be to study a group's performance during more or less simultaneous foreign policy episodes, holding constant many group-level and institutional-level factors, and to check the impact of situational factors on group structure and process. An example would be to compare systematically Kennedy's inner circle as it dealt with the Bay of Pigs planning and with the proposal for the Apollo project. Often meetings on both issues took place on the same day involving a stable hard core of participants. Yet unlike the Bay of Pigs invasion, the "man on the moon" project became seen as a major achievement. Another strategy would be to analyze a group's performance during a series of highly comparable decision episodes prior to and following a major policy crisis, a major change in the group's composition, or a major change in the institutional rules of the game. This type of design would allow studies of "group learning" in foreign policy-making, focusing on learning by analogy, learning by intervention, and learning as adaptation. Etheredge's (1985) longitudinal study of U.S. Latin American policies contains elements of this approach (see also Tetlock and Breslauer 1991; Stern and Sundelius 1997)

4. Conducting a comparative study of different types of foreign policy groups operating in the same political system.

George's (1980) survey of the evolution of presidential foreign policy management systems in the United States remains the key example here (see also Brecher 1972 on Israel). In his design, the interplay between personal needs and styles of leaders and the structure and process of advisory systems is the key issue. Similar types of studies need to be conducted in other countries, perhaps involving a slightly different analytical focus. In Britain, for example, the foreign policy-making process of subsequent cabinets might be investigated, focusing not only on the impact of prime ministerial leadership styles but also on the possible impact of party differences and differences in the makeup of the pivotal "foreign policy executive," that is, the tandem between prime minister and foreign secretary (Hill 1991).

5. Make an in-depth study of reform episodes as "natural experiments."

The initiation, development, and results of efforts to reform procedures for high-level, collegial policy-making that take place at times in various political systems, policy sectors, and public agencies provide small group scholars with the next best alternative to field experiments for examining the impact of certain prescriptive options for improving group decision making in government. Many of these reform efforts are initiated in the wake of major crises or government turnovers. Many of them are likely to be modified, compromised, transcended, or otherwise rendered less than fully effective. Yet if we take the feasibility problem sketched above seriously, information on how and why this happens is of crucial importance to analysts and prospective reformers. Occasionally, one may find real-world examples of "best practice" that may shed light on the conditions for achieving reform successes (Brunsson and Olsen 1993).

Each of these strands of research will give us important, comparative insights about how groups operate in the foreign policy process. Based on that knowledge, we will be in a better position to truly move from analysis to reform, and to develop persuasive arguments about how to adapt and improve current practices of foreign policy-making.

NOTES

The Prince, New York: New American Library, 1952, 114. Quote taken from A. Meltsner, *Rules for Rulers,* Philadelphia: Temple University Press, 1990, 64.

1. See, for example, Maier 1970; Nemiroff, Pasmore, and Ford 1976; Gladstein 1984; Gladstein-Ancona 1987; Schweiger, Sandberg, and Ragan 1986; Guzzo 1986; Schwenk 1988; Nutt 1989; Milliken and Volrath 1991; Neck and Manz 1994.

2. This recommendation for a contingent approach leaves us with three key dilemmas that fall beyond the scope of this chapter. First, how can we get senior policy-making groups to make an ade quate ex ante estimate for which one of the many foreign policy issues they routinely deal with is likely to have major potential costs and benefits associated with it? All too often, big decisions only appear big in retrospect. At the time of choice, their importance was often far less evident (at least to the decision makers). Second, who is to decide when an issue is crucial enough to warrant extensive consideration and multiple advocacy: just the president, prime minister, or group leader, or can ordinary group members also move to declare an issue of strategic importance? Third, how realistic is it to expect senior policy-making groups to alternate frequently between different styles (regimes) of collegial decision making, being consensus-minded and efficiency-oriented for one set of issues, and switching to a more analysis-oriented and adversarial advocacy mode for another?

3. Its "law court" terminology suggests that it may also have been inspired by elements of the American judicial system and the prestructured forms of argumentation and bargaining that may take place during court proceedings.

Bibliography

Abell, P., ed. 1975. *Organizations as Bargaining and Influence Systems: Measuring Intra-Organizational Power and Influence.* London: Heinemann.

Abelson, R., and A. Levi. 1985. "Decision Making and Decision Theory." In G. Lindzey and E. Aronson, eds., *The Handbook of Social Psychology* (3d ed.) 1:231–309. New York: Random House.

Abrahamson, E., and C. J. Fombrun. 1994. "Macrocultures: Determinants and Consequences." *Academy of Management Review* 19:728–55.

Acheson, D. 1969. *Present at the Creation: My Years in the State Department.* New York: W. W. Norton and Company.

Adorno, T. W., E. Frenkel-Brunswik, D. J. Levinson, and R. N. Sandord. 1950. *The Authoritarian Personality.* New York: Harper Books.

Aldag, R. J., and S. R. Fuller. 1993. "Beyond Fiasco: A Reappraisal of the Groupthink Phenomenon and A New Model of Group Decision Process." *Psychological Bulletin* 113:533–52.

Aldag, R. J., and T. M. Stearns. 1988. "Issues in Research Methodology." *Journal of Management* 14:253–76.

Alicke, M. D., and E. Largo. 1995. "The Role of Self in the False Consensus Effect." *Journal of Experimental Social Psychology* 31:28–47

Allison, G. T. 1971. *Essence of Decision: Explaining the Cuban Missile Crisis.* Boston: Little, Brown and Company.

Allison, G. T., and D. M. Messick. 1987. "From Individual Outputs to Group Outputs, and Back Again." In C. Hendrick, ed., *Group Processes* 144–66. London: Sage.

Ammerlaan, R. 1992. *Het Verschijnsel Schmelzer: Uit Het Dagboek Van Een Bedreven Politicus* (2d ed.). Baarn: Bosch En Keuning.

Anderson, A. 1983. "Decision Making by Objection" *Administrative Science Quarterly* 28:201–22.

Anderson, A. 1987. "What Do Foreign Policy Makers Do When They Make a Foreign Policy Decision? The Implications For the Comparative Study of Foreign Policy." In C. F. Hermann, C. W. Kegley, and J. N. Rosenau, eds., *New Directions in the Study of Foreign Policy,* 285–308. Boston: Allen and Unwin.

Andeweg, R. B. 1988. "Centrifugal Forces and Collective Decision Making: The Case of the Dutch Cabinet." *European Journal of Political Research* 10:125–51.

Andeweg, R. B. 1991. "Balanceren Tussen Consensus En Conflict: Besluitvorming in De Nederlandse Ministerraad." In 't Hart, De Jong, and A. F. A. Korsten, eds., *Groepsdenken in Het Openbaar Bestuur: Cruciale Beslissingen in Kleine Groepen,* 207–25. Alphen Aan Den Rijn: Samsom Tjeenk Willink.

Andeweg, R. B. 1993. "A Model of the Cabinet System: The Dimension of the Cabinet Decision Making Process." In J. Blondel and F. Muller-Rommel, eds., *Governing*

Together: The Extent and Limits of Joint Decision Making in West European Cabinets, 23–42. London: MacMillan.

Andeweg, R. B., and H. W. Nijzink. 1991. "De Verhouding Tussen Parlement en Regering." In J. J. A. Thomassen, M. P. C. M. Van Schendelen, and M. L. Zielonka-Goei, eds., *De Geachte Afgevaardigde: Hoe Kamerleden Denken over het Nederlandse Parlement,* 158–94. Muiderberg: Dick Coutinho.

Andrew, C. 1995. *For The President's Eyes Only: Secret Intelligence and The American Presidency From Washington to Bush.* New York: Harper Collins.

Art, R. J. 1973. "Bureaucratic Politics and American Foreign Policy: A Critique." *Policy Sciences* 4(4): 240–53.

Asch, S. E. 1958. "Effects of Group Pressure Upon the Modification and Distortion of Judgments." In E. E. McCoby, T. M. Newcomb, and E. L. Hartley, eds., *Readings in Social Psychology* 174–83. New York: Holt, Rinehart and Winston.

Axelrod, R. 1984/1990. *The Evolution of Cooperation.* New York: Penguin Books.

Bales, R. 1950. *Interaction Process Analysis.* Reading: Addison-Wesley.

Ball, G. 1982. *The Past Has Another Pattern: Memoirs.* New York: W. W. Norton.

Bar-Tal, D. 1990. *Group Beliefs: A Conception For Analyzing Group Structure, Processes, and Behavior.* New York: Springer-Verlag.

Barber, J. D. 1965. *Power in Committees: An Experiment in the Governmental Process.* Chicago: Rand McNally.

Barner-Barry C., and R. Rosenwein. 1985. *Psychological Perspectives On Politics.* Prospect Heights: Waveland Press.

Bass, B. M. 1960. *Leadership, Psychology, and Organizational Behavior.* New York: Harper Books.

Bass, B. M. 1967. "Social Behavior and the Orientation Inventory: A Review." *Psychology Bulletin* 68(4): 260–92.

Bass, B. M. 1983. *Organizational Decision Making.* Hamate: Richard D. Irwin.

Bass, B. M. 1985. *Leadership and Performance Beyond Expectations.* New York: Free Press; London: Collier MacMillan.

Bass, B. M. 1990a. *Bass and Stogdill's Handbook of Leadership: Theory, Research, and Managerial Applications.* New York: Free Press

Bass, B. M. 1990b. "From Transactional to Transformational Leadership: Learning to Share the Vision." *Organizational Dynamics* 18:19–31.

Bazerman, M. H. 1990. *Judgment in Managerial Decision Making,* 2d ed. New York: John Wiley and Sons.

Bazerman, M. H., T. Magliozzi, and M. A. Neale. 1985. "The Acquisition of An Integrative Response in A Competitive Market." *Organizational Behavior and Human Performance* 34:294–313.

Bazerman, M., and M. Neale. 1983. "Heuristics in Negotiation." In M. Bazerman and J. Lewicki, eds., *Negotiating in Organizations* 51–67. London: Sage.

Bennett, A. L. 1980. *International Organizations: Principles and Issues,* 2d ed. Englewood Cliffs, NJ: Prentice-Hall.

Bennett, J. 1975. "Foreign Policy As Maladaptive Behavior: Operationalizing Some Implications." *Papers of the Peace Science Society (International)* 25:85–104.

Berman, L. S. 1982. *Planning A Tragedy: The Americanization of the War in Vietnam.* New York: W. W. Norton and Company.

Bernstein, E., and M. Berbaum. 1983. "Stages in Group Decision Making: The Decomposition of Historical Narratives." *Political Psychology* 4:531–61.

Bernthal, P., and C. Insko. 1993. "Cohesiveness Without Groupthink: The Interactive Effects of Social and Task Cohesion." *Group and Organization Management* 18:66–87.

Beschloss, M. 1991. *The Crisis Years: Kennedy and Khruschev 1960–1963.* New York: Harper and Collins.

Bettenhausen, B., and J. Murninghan. 1985. "The Emergence of Norms in Competitive Decision-Making Groups." *Administrative Science Quarterly* 30:350–72.

Bieri, J. 1966. "Cognitive Complexity and Personality Development." In O. J. Harvey, ed., *Experience, Structure and Adaptability.* New York: Springer.

Bill, J. A. 1988. *The Eagle and the Lion: The Tragedy of American–Iranian Relations.* New Haven: Yale University Press.

Binning, J. F., and R. G. Lord. 1980. "Boundary Conditions For Performance Cue Effects On Group Process Ratings: Familiarity Versus Type of Feedback." *Organizational Behavior and Human Performance* 26:115–30.

Bion, W. R. 1961. *Experiences in Groups and Other Papers.* New York: Basic Books.

Blondel, J. 1982. *The Organization of Government: A Comparative Analysis of Governmental Structures.* London: Sage.

Blondel, J. 1988. "Decision-Making Processes, Conflicts, and Cabinet Government." *EUI Working Paper* 88 (327). Florence: European University Institute.

Blondel, J., and F. Müller-Rommel, eds. 1993. *Governing Together: The Extent and Limits of Joint Decision-Making in Western European Cabinets.* London: MacMillan

Boin, A., and M. Otten. 1996. "Crisis As Perfect Opportunity For Institutional Reform: The Case of the Penal Reform in the Dutch Prison System." *Journal of Contingencies and Crisis Management,* 4 (4): in press.

Bouchard J. 1991. *Command in Crisis.* New York: Columbia University Press.

Bovens, M. A., and P. 't Hart. 1996. *Understanding Policy Fiascoes.* New Brunswick: Transaction.

Bower, G. H., J. B. Black, and T. J. Turner. 1979. "Scripts in Memory For Text." *Cognitive Psychology* 11:177–220.

Bower, T. G. R. 1976. "Repetitive Processes in Child Development." *Scientific American* 235:38–47.

Bracken, 1983. *The Command and Control of Nuclear Forces.* New Haven: Yale University Press.

Bradford, L. P., and R. Lippitt. 1945. "Building A Democratic Work Group." *Personnel,* 22.

Brecher, M. 1972. *The Foreign Policy System of Israel.* Oxford: Oxford University Press.

Brecher, M. 1980. *Decisions in Crisis.* Berkeley and Los Angeles: University of California Press.

Brecher, M. 1993. *Crises: Theory and Reality.* New York: Pergamon.

Brecher, M., B. Steinberg, and J. Stein. 1969. "A Framework For Research On Foreign Policy Behavior." *Journal of Conflict Resolution* 13:75–101.

Brickman, 1974. *Social Conflict: Readings in Rule Structures and Conflict Relationships.* Lexington, MA: D. C. Heath.

Brown, H. 1983. *Thinking About National Security: Defense and Foreign Policy in A Dangerous World.* Boulder: Westview.

Brown, R. W. 1965. *Social Psychology.* New York: The Free Press.

Brown, R. W. 1988. *Group Processes: Dynamics Within and Between Groups.* Cambridge, MA: Basil Blackwell.

Browning, R. P., and H. Jacob. 1964. "Power Motivation and the Political Personality." *Public Opinion Quarterly.* 28:75–90.

Brunsson, N. 1989. *The Organization of Hypocrisy: Talk, Decisions, and Action in Organizations.* New York: Wiley.

Brunsson, N., and J. Olsen. 1993. *The Reforming Organization.* London: Routledge.

Bryson, J. W., and B. Crosby. 1992. *Leadership For the Common Good.* San Francisco: Jossey Bass.

Brzezinski, Z. 1983. *Power and Principle: Memoirs of A National Security Adviser.* New York: Farrar, Straus, and Giroux.

Burch, M. 1993. "Organizing the Flow of Business in Western European Cabinets." In J. Blondel and F. Müller-Rommel, eds., *Governing Together: The Extent and Limits of Joint Decision-Making in Western European Cabinets,* 99–130. London: MacMillan.

Burke, J., and F. Greenstein. 1989. *How Presidents Test Reality: Decisions On Vietnam, 1954 and 1965.* New York: Russel Sage Foundation.

Burleson, B. R., B. J. Levine, and W. Samter. 1984. "Decision-Making Procedure and Decision Quality." *Human Communication Research* 10:557–74.

Burns, J. M. 1978. *Leadership.* New York: Harper and Row.

Burnstein, E., and M. L. Berbaum. 1983. "Stages in Group Decision Making: The Decomposition of Historical Narratives." *Political Psychology* 4:531–61.

Burnstein, E., and M. L. Katz. 1971. "Individual Commitment to Risky and Conservative Choices As A Determinant of Shifts in Group Decisions." *Journal of Personality* 39:564–80.

Callaway, M. R., and J. K. Esser. 1984. "Groupthink: Effects of Cohesiveness and Problem-Solving Procedures On Group Decision-Making." *Social Behavior and Personality* 12:157–64.

Callaway, M. R., R. G. Marriott, and J. K. Esser. 1985. "Effects of Dominance On Group Decision Making: Toward A Stress-Reduction Explanation of Groupthink." *Journal of Personality and Social Psychology* 49(4): 949–52.

Campbell, C. 1986. *Managing the Presidency: Carter, Reagan, and the Search For Executive Harmony.* Pittsburgh: University of Pittsburgh Press.

Campbell, J. 1986. "Labs, Fields, and Straw Issues." In E. A. Locke, ed., *Generalizing From Laboratory to Field Settings,* 269–79. Lexington: Lexington Books.

Cannon, L. 1991. *President Reagan: The Role of a Lifetime.* New York: Touchstone/Simon and Schuster.

Carlsnaes, W. 1986. *Ideology and Foreign Policy: Problems of Comparative Conceptualization.* London: Basil Blackwell.

Carlsnaes, W. 1992. "The Agency-Structure Problem in Foreign Policy Analysis." *International Studies Quarterly* 36:245–70.

Carter, J. 1982. *Keeping Faith: Memoirs of A President.* Toronto: Bantam Books.

Cartwright, D. 1971. "Risk Taking By Individuals and Groups: An Assessment of Research Employing Choice Dilemmas." *Journal of Personality and Social Psychology* 20:361–78.

Cervone, D., and K. Peake. 1986. "Anchoring, Efficacy and Action: The Influence of Judgmental Heuristics On Self-Efficacy Judgments and Behavior." *Journal of Personality and Social Psychology* 50:492–501.

Cialdini, R. B. 1988. *Influence: Science and Practice,* 2d ed. New York: Harper Collins.

Cissna, K. 1984. "Phases in Group Development: The Negative Evidence." *Small Group Behavior* 15:3–32.

Clifford, C., with R. Holbrooke. 1991. *Counsel to the President.* New York: Random House.

Coase, R. H. 1988. *The Firm, the Market, and the Law.* Chicago: Chicago University Press.

Cohen, M. D., J. G. March, and J. Olsen. 1972. "A Garbage Can Model of Organizational Choice." *Administrative Science Quarterly* 17:1–25.

Collins, B. E., and H. Guetzkow. 1964. *A Social Psychology of Group Processes For Decision-Making.* New York: Wiley.

Cottam, R. 1977. *Foreign Policy Motivation.* Pittsburgh: University of Pittsburgh Press.

Cottam, R. 1988. *Iran and the United States: A Cold War Case Study.* Pittsburgh: University of Pittsburgh Press.

Courtright, J. A. 1978. "A Laboratory Investigation of Groupthink." *Communication Monographs* 5:229–46.

Crabb, C., Jr., and M. Holt. 1992. *Invitation to Struggle: Congress, the President, and Foreign Policy.* Washington DC: Congressional Quarterly, Inc.

Crabb, C., and K. Mulcahy. 1988. *Presidents and Foreign Policy Making.* Baton Rouge: Louisiana State University Press.

Craig, G., and A. L. George. 1990. *Force and Statecraft.* New York: Oxford University Press.

Cronin, T. E. 1980. *The State of the Presidency,* 2d ed. Boston: Little, Brown and Company.

Cronin, T. E., and E. Greenberg. 1969. *The Presidential Advisory System.* New York: Harper and Row.

Daboub, A. J., A. M. A. Rasheed, R. L. Priem, and D. A. Gray. 1995. "Top Management Team Characteristics and Corporate Illegal Activity." *Academy of Management Review* 20:138–70.

Dahl, R. A. 1982. *Dilemmas of Pluralist Democracy.* New Haven: Yale University Press.

Dahl, R. A. 1985. *Controlling Nuclear Weapons: Democracy Versus Guardianship.* Syracuse: Syracuse University Press.

Dahl, R. A., and C. E. Lindblom. 1954. *Politics, Economics and Welfare*. Chicago: Chicago University Press.

Davis, J. H. 1992. "Some Compelling Intuitions About Group Consensus Decisions, Theoretical and Empirical Research, and Interpersonal Aggregation Phenomena: Selected Examples, 1950–1990." *Organizational Behavior and Human Decision Processes* 52:3–38.

Davis, J., R. Laughlin, and S. S. Komorita. 1976. "The Social Psychology of Small Groups: Cooperative and Mixed-Motive Interaction." *Annual Review of Psychology* 27:501–41.

Davis, W. L., and E. J. Phares. 1967. "Internal-External Control As a Determinant of Information-Seeking in a Social Influence Situation." *Journal of Personality* 35:547–61.

Dawisha, K. 1984. *The Kremlin and the Prague Spring*. Berkeley and Los Angeles: University of California Press.

De Beus, J. G. 1977. *Morgen Bij het Aanbreken van de Dag: Nederland Driemaal op de Vooravond van Oorlog*. Rotterdam: Ad. Donker.

De Geus, B. R. 1984. *De Nieuw-Guinea Kwestie: Aspecten van Buitenlands Beleid en Militaire Macht*. Leiden: Martinus Nijhoff.

De Rivera, J. 1968. *The Psychological Dimension of Foreign Policy*. Columbus: Bobbs-Merrill.

Destler, I. M. 1972. *Presidents, Bureaucrats and Foreign Policy: The Politics of Organizational Reform*. Princeton, NJ: Princeton University Press.

Destler, I. M., L. Gelb, and A. Lake. 1984. *Our Own Worst Enemy: The Unmaking of American Foreign Policy*. New York: Simon and Schuster.

Deutsch, M., and H. B. Gerard. 1955. "A Study of Normative and Informational Influences Upon Individual Judgment." *Journal of Abnormal and Social Psychology* 53:100–107.

De Vries-Griever, A. H., and T. F. Meijman. 1987. "The Impact of Abnormal Hours of Work On Various Modes of Information Processing: A Process Model of Human Costs of Performance." *Ergonomics* 30:1287–99.

Diener, E. 1977. "Deindividuation: Causes and Consequences." *Social Behavior and Personality* 15:143–55.

Dion, K. L., R. S. Baron, and N. Miller. 1970. "Why Do Groups Make Riskier Decisions Than Individuals?" In L. Berkowitz, ed., *Advances in Experimental Social Psychology* 5:305–77. New York: Academic Press.

Donley, R. E., and D. Winter. 1970. "Measuring the Motives of Public Officials at a Distance: An Exploratory Study of American Presidents." *Behavioral Science* 15:227–36.

Donovan, R. J. 1974. *The Cold Warriors: A Policy Making Elite*. Lexington, MA: D. C. Heath and Co.

Donovan, R. J. 1977. *Conflict and Crisis: The Presidency of Harry S. Truman 1945–1948*. New York: W. W. Norton and Company.

Donovan, R. J. 1982. *Tumultuous Years: The Presidency of Harry S. Truman 1949–1953*. New York: W. W. Norton and Company.

Downey, H. K., T. I. Chacko, and J. McElroy. 1979. "Attribution of the 'Causes' of

Performance: A Constructive, Quasi-Longitudinal Replication of the Staw 1975 Study." *Organizational Behavior and Human Performance* 24:287–99.

Downs, A. 1967. *Inside Bureaucracy.* Boston: Little, Brown and Company.

Draper, T. 1991. *A Very Thin Line: The Iran-Contra Affairs.* New York: Hill and Wang.

Driver, M. J., K. Brousseau, and L. Hunsaker. 1990. *The Dynamic Decision Maker: Five Decision Styles for Executive and Business Success.* New York: Harper and Row.

Dror, Y. 1968/1983. *Public Policymaking Reexamined.* San Francisco: Chandler.

Dror, Y. 1986. *Policymaking Under Adversity.* New Brunswick: Transaction.

Duffy, G. 1983. "Crisis Mangling and the Cuban Brigade." *International Security* 8:67–87

Dunleavy, 1990. "Reinterpreting the Westland Affair: Theories of the State and Core Executive Decision Making." *Public Administration* 68:3–33.

Dunsire, A. 1978. *Control in a Bureaucracy.* London: Martin Robertson.

Dutton, J. E., and S. J. Ashford. 1993. "Selling Issues to Top Management." *Academy of Management Review* 18:397–428.

East, M. A., S. Salmore, and C. F. Hermann, eds. 1978. *Why Nations Act.* London: Sage.

Easton, D. 1965. *A Systems Analysis of Political Life.* Chicago: University of Chicago Press.

Edelman, M. 1988. *Constructing the Political Spectacle.* Chicago: University of Chicago Press.

Eden, D. 1988. "Creating Expectation Effects in OD: Applying Self-Fulfilling Prophecy." *Research in Organizational Change and Development* 2:235–67

Eden, D., and G. Ravid. 1982. "Pygmalion vs. Self-Expectancy: Effects of Instructor- and Self-Expectancy On Trainee Performance." *Organizational Behavior and Human Performance* 30:351–64.

Edwards, W. 1983. "Human Cognitive Capabilities, Representativeness, and Ground Rules For Research." In Humpreys, O. Svenson, and A. Vari, eds., *Analyzing and Aiding Decision Processes,* 507–13. Amsterdam: North-Holland Publishing.

Einhorn, H. J. 1980. "Overconfidence in Judgment." *New Directions For Methodology of Social and Behavioral Science* 4:1–16.

Elbing, A. 1978. *Behavioral Decisions in Organizations,* 2d ed. Glenview, IL: Scott, Foresman.

Ellis, R. 1994. *Presidential Lightning Rods: The Politics of Blame Avoidance.* Lawrence: Kansas University Press

Esser, J. K., and J. S. Lindoerfer. 1989. "Groupthink and the Space Shuttle Challenger Accident: Toward A Quantitative Case Analysis." *Journal of Behavioral Decision Making* 2:167–77.

Etheredge, L. S. 1978. *A World of Men: The Private Sources of American Foreign Policy.* Cambridge: MIT Press.

Etheredge, L. S. 1985. *Can Governments Learn?* New York: Pergamon Press.

Everts, P., and G. Walvern, eds. 1989. *The Politics of Persuasion.* Aldershot: Avebury.

Farkas, A. 1995. "Multiple Advocacy and Its Deleterious Effects on Policy Making."

Paper Presented at the International Studies Association Annual Meeting, Chicago, February.

Farnham, B. 1990. "Political Cognition and Decision-Making." *Political Psychology* 11(1): 83–111.

Farnham, B. 1993. "Why Context Matters: A Political Approach to Decision-Making." Paper presented at the Annual Meeting of the International Society of Political Psychology, Cambridge, MA. July.

Farnham, B. 1995. "The Impact of the Political Context on Foreign Policy Decision Making." Paper presented at the International Studies Association Annual Convention, Chicago, IL. February.

Feldman, M. S., and J. G. March. 1981. "Information in Organizations As Signal and Symbol." *Administrative Science Quarterly* 26:171–86.

Fenno, R. F. 1962. "The House Appropriations Committee as a Political System: The Problem of Integration." *American Political Science Review* 56:310–24.

Ferrell, R. H., ed. 1980. *Off the Record: The Private Papers of Harry S. Truman.* New York: Harper and Row.

Festinger, L. 1950. "Informal Social Communication." *Psychological Review* 57:271–282.

Festinger, L., H. B. Gerard, B. Hymovitch, H. H. Kelly, and B. Raven. 1952. "The Influence Process in the Presence of Extreme Deviants." *Human Relations* 5:327–46.

Fiedler, F. E. 1967. *A Theory of Leadership Effectiveness.* New York: McGraw-Hill Publishers.

Field, R. H. 1982. "A Test of the Vroom-Yetton Normative Model of Leadership." *Journal of Applied Psychology* 67:523–32.

Fiske, S. 1993. "Social Cognition and Social Perception." *Annual Review of Psychology* 44:155–94.

Fiske, S. T., and S. E. Taylor. 1991. *Social Cognition,* 2d ed. New York: McGraw-Hill.

Fleishman, E. A. 1982. "Systems For Describing Human Tasks." *American Psychologist* 37:821–34.

Flowers, M. L. 1977. "A Laboratory Test of Some Implications of Janis's Groupthink Hypothesis." *Journal of Personality and Social Psychology* 33:888–95.

Fodor, E. M., and D. L. Farrow. 1979. "The Power Motive as an Influence on the Use of Power." *Journal of Personality and Social Psychology* 37:2091–97.

Fodor, E. M., and T. Smith. 1982. "The Power Motive as an Influence on Group Decision Making." *Journal of Personality and Social Psychology,* 42.

Forgas, J. 1981. "Responsibility Attribution by Groups and Individuals: The Effects of the Interaction Episode." *European Journal of Social Psychology* 11:87–99.

Forsyth, D. R. 1983. *An Introduction to Group Dynamics.* Pacific Grove, CA: Brooks Cole.

Forsyth, D. R. 1990. *Group Dynamics.* Pacific Grove, CA: Brooks Cole.

Fowler, F. J., Jr. 1984. *Survey Research Methods.* Newbury Park, CA: Sage.

French, J. R. P., and B. H. Raven. 1959. "The Basis of Social Power." In D. Cartwright, ed., *Studies in Social Power,* 150–67. Ann Arbor: Institute of Social Research.

French, J. R. P., and R. Snyder. 1959. "Leadership and Interpersonal Power." In

Cartwright, D., ed., *Studies in Social Power.* Ann Arbor, MI: Institute of Social Research.

Gabriel, R. 1985. *Military Incompetence: Why the American Military Doesn't Win.* New York: Hill and Wang.

Gaenslen, F. 1980. "Democracy vs. Efficiency: Some Arguments from the Small Group." *Political Psychology* 2(1):15–29.

Gaenslen, F. 1992. "Decision-Making Groups." In E. Singer and V. Hudson, eds., *Political Psychology and Foreign Policy,* 165–93. Boulder, Colorado: Westview Press.

Gaenslen, F. 1993. "Decision Makers As Social Beings: Consensual Decision Making in Russia, China, and Japan." Paper prepared for the 89th Annual Meeting of the American Political Science Association, September, Washington, DC.

Gallucci, R. L. 1975. *Neither Peace Nor Honor.* Baltimore, MD: Johns Hopkins University Press.

Gase, R., ed. 1984. *Misleiding of Zelfbedrog: Een Analyse van het Nederlandse Nieuw Guinea-Beleid aan de Hand van Gesprekken Met Betrokken Politici en Diplomaten.* Baarn: Anthos.

George, A. L. 1969. "The 'Operational Code': A Neglected Approach to the Study of Political Leaders and Decision-Making." *International Studies Quarterly* 13:190–222.

George, A. L. 1972. "The Case for Multiple Advocacy in Making Foreign Policy." *American Political Science Review* 66:751–85.

George, A. L. 1980. *Presidential Decisionmaking in Foreign Policy: The Effective Use of Information and Advice.* Boulder: Westview Press.

George, A. L. 1988. "The President and the Management of Foreign Policy: Styles and Models." In C. Kegley and E. R. Wittkopf, eds., *The Domestic Sources of American Foreign Policy,* 107–26. New York: St. Martins.

George, A. L. 1991. "The Cuban Missile Crisis." In A. L. George, ed., *Avoiding War: Problems of Crisis Management,* 222–68. Boulder: Westview Press.

George, A. L. 1993a. "The Cuban Missile Crisis: Peaceful Resolution Through Coercive Diplomacy." In A. L. George and J. Simons, eds., *The Limits of Coercive Diplomacy,* 2d. ed., 111–32. Boulder: Westview Press.

George, A. L. 1993b. *Bridging the Gap: Theory and Practice in Foreign Policy.* Washington, DC: United States Institute of Peace Press.

George, A. L., and R. Keohane. 1980. "The Concept of National Interest: Uses and Limitations." In A. L. George, *Presidential Decision Making in Foreign Policy,* 217–37. Boulder: Westview Press.

George, A., and E. K. Stern. Forthcoming. *Presidential Decisionmaking in Foreign Policy: The Effective Use of Information and Advice,* 2d ed. Boulder: Westview Press.

Gerard, H. B. 1985. "When and How the Minority Prevails." In S. Moscovici, G. Mugny, and E. Von Avermaet, eds., *Perspective on Minority Influence,* 171–86. Cambridge: Cambridge University Press.

Gist, M. E. 1987. "Self-Efficacy: Implications For Organizational Behavior and Human Resource Management." *Academy of Management Review,* 12:472–85.

Glad, B. 1983. "Black-and-White Thinking: Ronald Reagan's Approach to Foreign Policy." *Political Psychology* 4:33–76

Glad, B., and M. W. Link. 1994. "Exploring the Psychopolitical Dynamics of Advisory Relations: The Carter Administration's 'Crisis of Confidence.'" *Political Psychology* 15(3): 461–80.

Gladstein, D. 1984. "Groups in Context; A Model of Task Group Effectiveness." *Administrative Science Quarterly* 29:499–517.

Gladstein, D. L., and N. Reilly. 1985. "Group Decision Making Under Threat: The Tycoon Game." *Academy of Management Journal* 28:613–27.

Gladstein-Ancona, D. 1987. "Groups in Organizations: Extending Laboratory Models." In C. Hendrick, ed., *Group Processes and Intergroup Relations,* 207–30. Beverly Hills: Sage.

Goldhamer, H. 1978. *The Adviser.* New York: Elsevier.

Golembiewski, R. T. 1962. *The Small Group.* Chicago: University of Chicago Press.

Graber, D. 1980. *Mass Media and American Politics.* Washington, DC: Congressional Quarterly Press.

Graesser, A. C., S. G. Gordon, and J. D. Sawyer. 1979. "Recognition Memory For Typical and Atypical Actions in Scripted Activities: Tests of A Script Pointer plus Tag Hypothesis." *Journal of Verbal Learning and Verbal Behavior* 18:319–32.

Greenstein, F. 1982. *The Hidden Hand Presidency: Eisenhower As Leader.* New York: Basic Books.

Greenstein, F., ed. 1988. *Leadership in the Modern Presidency.* Cambridge: Harvard University Press.

Greenwald, A. G., A. R. Pratkanis, M. R. Leippe, and M. H. Baumgardner. 1986. "Under What Conditions Does Theory Obstruct Research Progress?" *Psychological Review* 93(2): 216–29.

Grover, W. 1989. *The President As Prisoner.* Albany: State University of New York Press.

Guthman, E. O., and J. Shulman, eds. 1988. *Robert Kennedy in His Own Words: The Unpublished Recollections of the Kennedy Years.* New York: Bantam Books.

Guzzo, R. A. 1986. "Group Decision Making and Group Effectiveness in Organizations." In P.S. Goodman, ed., *Designing Effective Work Groups,* 34–71. San Francisco: Jossey Bass.

Guzzo, R. A., D. B. Wagner, E. Maguire, B. Herr, and C. Hawley. 1986. "Implicit Theories and the Evaluation of Group Process and Performance." *Organizational Behavior and Human Performance* 37:279–95.

Gwertzman, B. 1979. "Brzezinski Cautions Soviets On Cuba Unit." *New York Times,* September 23, 1979, A1, A4. New York: New York Times Press.

Hackman, J., and C. Morris. 1975. "Group Tasks, Group Interaction Process and Group Performance Effectiveness." In L. Berkowitz, ed., *Advances in Experimental Social Psychology* 8:1–66.

Halper, T. 1971. *Foreign Policy Crises: Appearance and Reality in Decision Making.* Columbus: Merrill.

Halperin, M. H. 1974. *Bureaucratic Politics and Foreign Policy.* Washington, DC: Brookings.

Hambrick, D. C., and A. Mason. 1984. "Upper Echelons: The Organization As a Reflection of Its Top Managers." *Academy of Management Review* 9:193–206.

Haney, J. 1995. "Structure and Process in Analysis of Foreign Policy Crises." In P. J. Haney, J. A. K. Hey, and L. Neack, eds., *Foreign Policy Analysis*, 99–115. Englewood Cliffs: Prentice Hall.

Hanf, K. I., and F. Scharpf, eds. 1978. *Interorganizational Policy Making*. London: Sage.

Hansen, H. J. A. 1967. *Luns, Drees, De Quay, Marijnen, Cals Over Luns*. Maaseik: Paul Brand Uitgeverij.

Hardy, C. 1985. "The Nature of Unobtrusive Power." *Journal of Management Studies* 22:384–399.

Hare, A. P., ed. 1976. *Handbook of Small Group Research*, 3d ed. New York: Free Press.

Hargrove, E. C. 1989. "Two Conceptions of Institutional Leadership." In B. D. Jones, ed., *Leadership and Politics*. Lawrence: University of Kansas Press.

Hart, P. 't. 1990/1994. *Groupthink in Government. A Study of Small Groups and Policy Failure*. Amsterdam: Swets and Zeitlinger; Baltimore: Johns Hopkins University Press.

Hart, P. 't. 1991. "Irving L. Janis' *Victims of Groupthink*." *Political Psychology* 12:247–78.

Hart, P. 't, and M. B. R. Kroon. 1997. "Groupthink in Government: Pathologies of Small-Group Decision Making." In J. L. Garnett, ed., *Handbook of Administrative Communication*, in press. Chicago: Marcel Dekker.

Hart, P. 't, U. Rosenthal, and A. Kouzmin. 1993. "Crisis Decision Making: The Centralization Thesis Revisited." *Administration and Society* 25:12–45.

Harvey, J. B. 1988. *The Abilene Paradox and Other Meditations On Management*. Lexington: Heath.

Heclo, H. 1977. *A Government of Strangers: Executive Politics in Washington*. Washington, DC: Brookings.

Heimer, C. A. 1988. "Social Structure, Psychology, and the Estimation of Risk." In W. R. Scott and J. Blake, eds., *Annual Review of Sociology* 14:491–519. Palo Alto, CA: Annual Reviews.

Heller, J. 1983. "The Dangers of Groupthink." *The Guardian*, January 31, 13.

Henderson, J. C., and R. S. Nutt. 1980. "The Influence of Decision Style on Decision Making Behavior." *Management Science* 26:371–86.

Henderson, W. 1973. *West New Guinea: The Dispute and Its Settlement*. South Orange, NJ: Seton Hall University Press.

Hensley, T. R., and G. W. Griffin. 1986. "Victims of Groupthink: The Kent State University Board of Trustees and the 1977 Gymnasium Controversy." *Journal of Conflict Resolution* 30:497–531.

Herek, G., I. Janis, and Huth. 1987. "Decisionmaking During International Crises: Is Process Related to Outcome." *Journal of Conflict Resolution* 31:203–26.

Herek, G., I. Janis, and Huth. 1989. "Quality of U.S. Decisionmaking During the Cuban Missile Crisis: Major Errors in Welch's Reassessment." *Journal of Conflict Resolution* 33:446–59.

Hermann, C. F. 1963. "Some Consequences of Crisis Which Limit the Viability of Organizations." *Administrative Science Quarterly* 8:61–82.

Hermann, C. F. 1969. "International Crisis As A Situational Variable." In Rosenau, J. N., ed., *International Politics and Foreign Policy*, 409–21. 2d ed. New York: Free Press.

Hermann, C. F., ed. 1972. *International Crises: Insights From Behavioral Research.* New York: Free Press.

Hermann, C. F. 1978. "Decision Structure and Process Influences on Foreign Policy." In M. East, S. Salmore, and C. F. Hermann, eds., *Why Nations Act,* 69–102. London: Sage.

Hermann, C. F. 1979. "The Effects of Decision Structures and Processes On Foreign Policy Behaviors." Paper presented at the Annual Meeting of the International Society of Political Psychology, Washington, DC.

Hermann, C. F. 1988. "The Impact of Single Group Decision Units on Foreign Policy." Paper Presented at the Annual Meeting of the International Studies Association, St. Louis, MO, March 29–April 2.

Hermann, C. F. 1989. "On International Crises and National Security." In T. Kolodziej and P. Morgan, eds., *Security and Arms Control,* 357–85. New York: Greenwood Press.

Hermann, C. F. 1993. "Avoiding Pathologies in Foreign Policy Decision Groups." In D. Caldwell and T.J. McKeown, eds., *Force, Diplomacy and Leadership: Essays in Honor of Alexander George,* 179–207. Boulder: Westview Press.

Hermann, C. F., and M. G. Hermann. 1982. "A Look Inside the 'Black Box': Building Upon A Decade of Research." In G. W. Hopple, ed., *Biopolitics, Political Psychology and International Politics,* 1–36. London: Pinter.

Hermann, M. G. 1979. "Indicators of Stress in Policymaking During Foreign Policy Crises." *Political Psychology* 1:27–46.

Hermann, M. G. 1980. "Explaining Foreign Policy Behavior Using Personal Characteristics of Political Leaders." *International Studies Quarterly* 24:7–46.

Hermann, M. G. 1983. *Handbook For Assessing Personal Characteristics and Foreign Policy Orientations of Political Leaders.* Columbus, OH: Mershon Center Occasional Papers.

Hermann, M. G. 1984. "Personality and Foreign Policy Decision Making: A Study of 53 Heads of Government." In D. A. Sylvan and S. Chan, eds., *Foreign Policy Decision-Making: Perceptions, Cognition, and Artificial Intelligence,* 53–80. New York: Praeger Press.

Hermann, M. G. 1986. "Ingredients of Leadership." In M. G. Hermann, ed., *Political Psychology: Contemporary Problems and Issues.* 167–192 San Francisco: Jossey-Bass Inc., Publishers.

Hermann, M. G. 1987. "Leaders' Foreign Policy Role Orientations and the Quality of Foreign Policy Decisions." In S. Walker, ed., *Role Theory and Foreign Policy Analysis,* 123–40. Durham: Duke University Press.

Hermann, M. G., and C. F. Hermann. 1989. "Who Makes Foreign Policy Decisions and How: An Empirical Inquiry." *International Studies Quarterly* 33(3): 361–87.

Hermann, M. G., C. F. Hermann, and J. Hagan. 1987. "How Decision Units Shape

Foreign Policy Behavior." In C. F. Hermann, C. W. Kegley, and J. N. Rosenau, eds., *New Directions in the Study of Foreign Policy,* 304–36. Boston: Allen and Unwin.

Hermann, M. G., and T. Preston. 1994a. "Presidents, Advisors, and Foreign Policy: The Effect of Leadership Style On Executive Arrangements." *Political Psychology* 15(1): 75–96.

Hermann, M. G., and T. Preston. 1994b. "Presidents and Their Advisers: Leadership Style, Advisory Systems, and Foreign Policy Making." In E. Wittkopf, ed., *Domestic Sources of American Foreign Policy,* 340–56. New York: St. Martin's Press.

Hermann, M. G., T. Preston, and M. Young. Forthcoming. *Who Leads Matters: Individuals and Foreign Policy.* Columbia: University of South Carolina Press.

Herring, G. C. 1993. "The Strange 'Dissent' of Robert McNamara." In J. S. Werner and L. D. Huynh, eds., *The Vietnam War: Vietnamese and American Perspectives,* 140–51. Armonk, NY: M. E. Sharpe.

Herrmann, R. 1985. *Perceptions and Behavior in Soviet Foreign Policy.* Pittsburgh: University of Pittsburgh Press.

Herrmann, R. 1988. "The Empirical Challenge of the Cognitive Revolution: A Strategy For Drawing Inferences About Perception." *International Studies Quarterly* 32:175–203.

Hess, S. 1988. *Organizing the Presidency.* Washington, DC: Brookings Institution.

Hesse, J. J., and A. Benz. 1990. *Die Modernisierung Der Staatsorganisation.* Baden-Baden: Nomos.

Hewitt, J. P., and M. L. Hewitt. 1986. *Introducing Sociology.* Englewood Cliffs: Prentice-Hall.

Higgins, T. 1987. *The Perfect Failure: Kennedy, Eisenhower and the CIA at the Bay of Pigs.* New York: Norton.

Hill, C. 1991. *British Cabinet Decisions On Foreign Policy.* Cambridge: Cambridge University Press.

Hill, C., and P. Besthoff, eds. 1994. *Two Worlds of International Relations.* London: Routledge.

Hilsman, R. 1967. *To Move A Nation.* Garden City: Doubleday and Company.

Hilsman, R. 1971. *The Politics of Policy Making in Defense and Foreign Affairs.* New York: Harper and Row.

Hilsman, R. 1987. *The Politics of Policymaking in Defense and Foreign Affairs.* Englewood Cliffs: Prentice-Hall.

Hirokawa, R. Y., D. S. Gouran, and A. E. Martz. 1988. "Understanding the Sources of Faulty Group Decision Making: A Lesson From the Challenger Disaster." *Small Group Behavior* 19:411–33.

Hoffmann, S. A. 1990. *India and the China Crisis.* Berkeley and Los Angeles: University of California Press.

Hofstede, G. 1984. *Culture's Consequences: International Differences in Work Related Values,* abridged ed. Beverly Hills: Sage.

Hogarth, R. M. 1980. *Judgment and Choice.* Chichester: John Wiley and Sons.

Hogg, M. A., and D. Abrams. 1988. *Social Identifications: A Social Psychology of Intergroup Relations and Group Processes.* London: Routledge.

Hollander, E. 1958. "Conformity, Status, and Idiosyncrasy Credit." *Psychological Review* 65:117–27.

Hollander, E. 1964. *Leaders, Groups, and Influence.* New York: Oxford University Press.

Hollander, E. 1978. *Leadership Dynamics.* New York: Free Press.

Hollander, E. 1986. "On the Central Role of Leadership Processes." *International Review of Applied Psychology* 35:39–52.

Hollis, M., and S. Smith. 1990. *Explaining and Understanding International Relations.* Oxford: Clarendon Press.

Holsti, O. R. 1965. "The 1914 Case." *American Political Science Review* 59:365–78.

Holsti, O. R. 1967. "Cognitive Dynamics and Images of the Enemy: Dulles and Russia." In Finlay, Holsti, Fagen, eds., *Enemies in Politics,* 25–96. Chicago: Rand McNally.

Holsti, O. R. 1969. "The Belief System and National Images: A Case Study." In J. N. Rosenau, ed., *International Politics and Foreign Policy,* 2d ed., 543–50. New York: The Free Press.

Holsti, O. R. 1971. "Crisis, Stress, and Decision-Making." *International Social Science Journal* 23(1): 53–67.

Holsti, O. R. 1972. *Crisis, Escalation, War.* Montreal: McGill-Queens University Press.

Holsti, O. R. 1989. "Crisis Decision Making." In P. Tetlock et al., eds., *Behavior, Society, and Nuclear War,* 8–84. New York: Oxford University Press.

Holsti, O. R., and A. L. George. 1975. "The Effects of Stress on the Performance of Foreign Policy Makers." In C. Cotter, ed., *Political Science Annual* 6:255–319. Columbus: Merrill.

Homans, G. 1950. *The Human Group.* New York: Harcourt, Brace.

Hong, L. K. 1978. "Risky Shift and Cautious Shift: Some Direct Evidence On the Culture-Value Theory." *Social Psychology* 41:342–46.

Horn, J. L. 1976. "Human Abilities: A Review of Research and Theory in the Early 1970s." *Annual Review of Psychology* 27:437–85.

House, J. M., and T. R. Mitchell. 1974. "Path-Goal Theory of Leadership." *Journal of Contemporary Business* 3:81–98.

House, R. J. 1990. "Power and Personality in Complex Organizations." In B. M. Staw and L. L. Cummings, eds., *Personality and Organizational Influence,* 181–233. Greenwich, CT: JAI Press Inc.

House, R. J., and M. L. Baetz. 1979. "Leadership: Some Empirical Generalizations and New Research Directions." *Research in Organizational Behavior* 1:341–423.

Houwaart, D. 1984. *De Mannenbroeders Door de Bocht: Herinneringen aan en van Dr W. Berghuis, Van 1956 tot 1968 Voorzitter van de Anti-Revolutionaire Partij.* Kampen: Kok.

Howell, J. M., and J. Frost. 1989. "A Laboratory Study of Charismatic Leadership." *Organizational Behavior and Human Decision Processes* 43:243–69.

Hoyt, D. 1994. "U.S. Foreign Policy Toward Empowerment in the Middle East: A

Cognitive and Group Process Approach." Unpublished Ph.D. dissertation, Columbus: Ohio State University.

Huber, G. 1980. *Managerial Decision Making*. Glenview, IL: Scott, Foresman.

Huber, G. 1991. "Organizational Learning: The Contributing Processes and the Literatures." *Organization Science* 2:88–115.

Huntington, S. 1961. *The Common Defense: Strategic Programs in National Politics.* New York: Columbia University Press.

Huydecoper Van Nigtevecht, J. L. R. 1990. *Nieuw-Guinea: Het Einde van een Koloniaal Tijdperk.* The Hague: Sdu.

Huyser, R. 1986. *Mission to Tehran.* London: Andre Deutsch.

Jackall, R. 1988. *Moral Mazes: The World of Corporate Managers.* New York: Oxford University Press.

James, S. 1991. *British Cabinet Government.* London: Routledge.

Janis, I. L. 1959. "Motivational Factors in the Resolution of Decisional Conflicts." In M. R. Jones, ed., *Nebraska Symposium On Motivation 1959,* Lincoln: University of Nebraska Press

Janis, I. L. 1971. "Groupthink." *Psychology Today* 5 (November):43–46, 74–76.

Janis, I. L. 1972. *Victims of Groupthink: A Psychological Study of Foreign-Policy Decisions and Fiascoes.* Boston: Houghton Mifflin.

Janis, I. L. 1982. *Groupthink: Psychological Studies of Policy Decisions and Fiascoes,* 2d ed. Boston: Houghton Mifflin.

Janis, I. L. 1985. "International Crisis Management in the Nuclear Age." *Applied Social Psychology* Annual 6:63–86.

Janis, I. L. 1989. *Crucial Decisions: Leadership in Policymaking and Crisis Management,* New York: The Free Press.

Janis, I. L., and L. Mann. 1977. *Decision Making: A Psychological Analysis of Conflict, Choice, and Commitment.* New York: Free Press.

Jansen Van Galen, J. 1984. *Ons Laatste Oorlogje. Nieuw-Guinea, de Pax Neerlandica, de Diplomatieke Kruistocht en de Vervlogen Droom van een Papoea-Natie.* Weesp: Van Holkema En Warendorf.

Jellison, J. M., and J. Riskind. 1971. "Attribution of Risk to Others As A Function of Their Ability." *Journal of Personality and Social Psychology* 20:413–15.

Jenkins, B., and A. Gray. 1983. "Bureaucratic Politics and Power: Developments in the Study of Bureaucracy." *Political Studies* 31:177–93.

Jervis, R. 1976. *Perceptions and Misperceptions in International Politics.* Princeton: Princeton University Press.

Jervis, R. 1989. "Political Psychology—Some Challenges and Opportunities." *Political Psychology* 10(2): 481–93.

Johnson, R. T. 1974. *Managing the White House: An Intimate Study of the Presidency.* New York: Harper and Row.

Jones, S. 1986. "Addressing Internal Politics: A Role For Modeling in Consultant-Client Interaction." *Small Group Behavior* 17:67–82.

Kahneman, D., and A. Tversky. 1979. "Prospect Theory: An Analysis of Decision Under Risk." *Econometrica* 47:263–91.

Kameda, T., and J. H. Davis. 1990. "The Function of the Reference Point in Individual and Group Risk Decision Making." *Organizational Behavior and Human Decision Processes* 46:55–76.

Kaplan, M. 1987. "The Influencing Process in Group Decision Making." In C. Hendrick, ed., *Group Processes,* 189–212. Newbury Park, CA: Sage.

Kaplan, M., and C. Miller. 1987. "Group Decision Making and Normative Versus Informational Influence: Effects of Type and Issue and Assigned Decision Rule." *Journal of Personality and Social Psychology* 53:306–13.

Karvonen, L., and B. Sundelius. 1987. *Internationalization and Foreign Policy Management.* Aldershot: Gower Publications.

Katzenstein, 1985. *Small States and World Markets.* Ithaca: Cornell University Press.

Kaufman, H. 1971. *The Limits of Organizational Change.* University: University of Alabama Press.

Kearns, D. 1976. *Lyndon Johnson and the American Dream.* New York: Harper and Row.

Kegley, C. W. 1987. "Decision Regimes and Comparative Study of Foreign Policy." In C. F. Herman, C. W. Kegley, and J. N. Rosenau, eds., *New Directions in the Study of Foreign Policy,* 247–68. Boston: Allen and Unwin.

Keohane, R. O. 1993. "International Multiple Advocacy in U.S. Foreign Policy." In D. Caldwell and T. J. McKeown, eds., *Diplomacy, Force, and Leadership,* 285–304. Boulder: Westview.

Khong, Y. F. 1992. *Analogies at War.* Princeton: Princeton University Press.

King, G., R. Keohane, and S. Verba. 1994. *Designing Social Inquiry.* Princeton: Princeton University Press.

Kingdon, J. W. 1984. *Agendas, Alternatives and Public Policies.* Boston: Little, Brown and Company.

Kinnard, D. 1977. *President Eisenhower and Strategy Management: A Study in Defense Politics.* Lexington: University of Kentucky Press.

Kipnis, D., and S. Schmidt. 1983. "An Influence Perspective On Bargaining Within Organizations." In M. H. Bazerman and R. J. Lewicki, eds., *Negotiating in Organizations,* 303–19. Beverly Hills: Sage Publications.

Kitayama, S., and E. Burnstein. 1994. "Social Influence, Persuasion and Group Decision Making." In S. Shavit and T. C. Brock, eds., *Persuasion: Psychological Insights and Perspectives,* 175–93. Boston: Allyn and Bacon.

Kleck, R. E., and J. Wheaton. 1967. "Dogmatism and Responses to Opinion-Consistent and Opinion-Inconsistent Information." *Journal of Personality and Social Psychology.* 5:249–52.

Kleinmuntz, B. 1990. "Why We Still Use Our Heads Instead of Formulas: Toward An Integrative Approach." *Psychological Bulletin* 107:296–310.

Klimoski, R., and S. Mohammed. 1994. "Team Mental Model: Construct Or Metaphor?" *Journal of Management* 20:403–37.

Kogan, N., and M. A. Wallach. 1967. "Risk Taking As A Function of the Situation, the Person, and the Group." In G. Mandler, Mussen, N. Kogan, and M. A. Wallach, eds., *New Directions in Psychology,* 3:111–278. New York: Holt, Rinehart and Winston.

Komer, R. W. 1986. *Bureaucracy at War: U.S. Performance in the Vietnam Conflict.* Boulder: Westview.

Kotter, J. P., and R. Lawrence. 1974. *Mayors in Action.* New York: Wiley.

Kozak, D. C., and Keagle, J. M., eds. 1988. *Bureaucratic Politics and National Security: Theory and Practice.* Boulder: Lynne Rienner.

Kramer, M. 1993. "The Prague Spring and the Soviet Invasion of Czechoslovakia." *Cold War International History Project Bulletin* 1(3): 2–13, 54–55.

Kroon, M. B. R., P. 't Hart, and D. Van Kreveld. 1991. "Managing Group Decision Making Processes: Individual Versus Collective Accountability and Groupthink." *International Journal of Conflict Management* 2:91–115.

Kruglanski, A., and D. Webster. 1991. "Group Members' Reactions to Opinion Deviates and Conformists at Varying Degrees of Proximity to Decision Deadline and of Environmental Noise." *Journal of Personality and Social Psychology* 61 (2): 212–25.

Lamborn, A. C. 1985. "Risk and Foreign Policy Choice." *International Studies Quarterly* 29:385–410.

Lamborn, A. C. 1991. *The Price of Power: Risk and Foreign Policy in Britain, France and Germany.* Boston: Unwin Hyman.

Lamm, H., and N. Kogan. 1970. "Risk Taking in the Context of Intergroup Negotiation." *Journal of Experimental Social Psychology* 6:351–63.

Larson, D. W. 1985. *Origins of Containment: A Psychological Explanation.* Princeton: Princeton University Press.

Larson, J. R., and C. Christensen. 1993. "Groups As Problem-Solving Units: Toward A New Meaning of Social Cognition." *British Journal of Social Psychology* 32:5–30.

Lauderdale, P., Smith-Cunnien, J. Parker, and J. Inverarity. 1984. "External Threat and the Definition of Deviance." *Journal of Personality and Social Psychology* 46(5): 1058–68.

Laughlin, R. 1980. "Social Combination Processes of Cooperative Problem-Solving Groups On Verbal Intellective Tasks." In M. Fishbein, ed., *Progress in Social Psychology* 1:127–55. Hillsdale, NJ: Erlbaum.

Laughlin, R., and C. Earley. 1982. "Social Combination Models, Persuasive Arguments Theory, Social Comparisons Theory, and Choice Shift." *Journal of Personality and Social Psychology* 42:273–80.

Lawler, E. J., and S. B. Bacharach. 1983. "Political Action and Alignments in Organizations." In S. B. Bacharach, ed., *Research in the Sociology of Organizations* 2:83–107. Greenwich, CT: JAI Press.

Lawrence, R., and J. W. Lorsch. 1969. *Organization and Environment: Managing Differentiation and Integration.* Homewood, IL: Irwin.

Leana, C. R. 1985. "A Partial Test of Janis' Groupthink Model: Effects of Group Cohesiveness and Leader Behavior On Defective Decision Making." *Journal of Management* 11:5–17.

Leary, M. R., and D. R. Forsyth. 1987. "The Attribution of Responsibility For Collective Endeavours." In C. Hendrick, ed., *Group Processes,* 167–88. Newbury: Sage.

Lebow, R. N. 1981. *Between Peace and War: The Nature of International Crisis.* Baltimore: John Hopkins University Press.

Lebow, R. N. 1987. *Nuclear Crisis Management: A Dangerous Illusion.* Ithaca: Cornell University Press.

Lebow, R. N., and J. Stein. 1993. "Afghanistan, Carter, and Foreign Policy Change: The Limits of Cognitive Models." In D. Caldwell and T. J. McKeown, eds., *Diplomacy, Force, and Leadership,* 95–127. Boulder: Westview Press.

Lebow, R., and J. Stein. 1994. *We All Lost the Cold War.* Princeton: Princeton University Press.

Levine, J. 1980. "Reaction to Opinion Deviance in Small Groups." In Paulus, ed., *Psychology of Group Influence.* Hillsdale, NJ: Erlbaum.

Levine, J., and R. Moreland. 1990. "Progress in Small Group Research." *Annual Review of Psychology* 41:585–634. Palo Alto, CA: Annual Reviews.

Levine, J. M., L. B. Resnick, and E. T. Higgins. 1993. "Social Foundations of Cognition." In L. W. Porter and M. R. Rosenzweig, eds., *Annual Review of Psychology* 44:585–612.

Levine, J. M., and E. M. Russo. 1987. "Majority and Minority Influence." In C. Hendrick, ed., *Group Processes,* 13–54. Newbury Park: Sage.

Levy, J. S. 1992a. "An Introduction to Prospect Theory." *Political Psychology* 13:171–86.

Levy, J. S. 1992b. "Prospect Theory and International Relations: Theoretical Applications and Analytical Problems." *Political Psychology* 13:283–310.

Lewicki, R. J. 1983. "Lying and Deception: A Behavioral Model." In M. H. Bazerman and R. J. Lewicki, eds., *Negotiating in Organizations,* 68–90. London and Beverly Hills: Sage.

Lewin, K. 1948. *Resolving Social Conflicts.* New York: Harper.

Lewis, E. 1983. *Public Entrepreneurship.* Bloomington: Indiana University Press.

Liden, R. C., and T. R. Mitchell. 1988. "Ingratiatory Behaviors in Organizational Settings." *Academy of Management Review* 13:572–87.

Lijphart, A. 1966. *The Trauma of Decolonization: The Dutch and West New Guinea.* New Haven: Yale University Press.

Lilienthal, R. A., and S. L. Hutchinson. 1979. "Group Polarization (Risky Shift) in Led and Leaderless Group Discussions." *Psychological Reports* 45:168.

Lindblom, C. E. 1977. *Politics and Markets.* New York: Basic Books.

Lindblom, C. E., and D. K. Cohen. 1979. *Usable Knowledge: Social Science and Social Problem Solving.* New Haven: Yale University Press.

Longley, J., and D. Pruitt. 1980. "Groupthink: A Critique of Janis' Theory." In L. Wheeler, ed., *Review of Personality and Social Psychology* 1:74–93. Beverly Hills: Sage.

Lord, C. 1988. *The Presidency and the Management of National Security.* New York: The Free Press.

Lord, R. G., and K. J. Maher. 1991. *Executive Leadership, Information Processing: Linking Perceptions and Performance.* Boston: Unwin Hyman.

Lowi, T. 1985. *The Personal President: Power Invested, Promise Unfulfilled.* Ithaca, NY: Cornell University Press.

Ludwig, S. 1973. "Dangers of Group Thinking." *International Management,* 285:69–70.

Luechauer, D. L. 1989. "Groupthink Revisited: A Dramaturgical Approach." Paper presented at the Meetings of the Academy of Management, Washington, DC. March.

Lynn, L. E. 1987. *Managing Public Policy.* Boston: Little, Brown and Co.

Maass A., S. G. West, and R. B. Cialdini. 1987. "Minority Influence and Conversion." In C. Hendrick, ed., *Group Processes,* 55–79. Newbury Park: Sage Publications.

Maier, N. R. F. 1970. *Problem Solving and Creativity in Individuals and Groups.* Belmont: Brooks Cole.

Majone, G. 1989. *Evidence, Argument, and Persuasion in the Policy Process.* New Haven: Yale University Press.

Manz, C. C., and H. Sims Jr. 1982. "The Potential for 'Groupthink' in Autonomous Work Groups." *Human Relations* 35:773–84.

Maoz, Z. 1990. "Framing the National Interest: The Manipulation of Foreign Policy Decisions in Group Settings." *World Politics* 43:77–111.

Maoz, Z. 1991. *National Choices and International Processes.* Cambridge: Cambridge University Press.

March, J. G. 1962. "The Business Firm As A Political Coalition." *Journal of Politics* 24:662–78.

March, J. G. 1976. "The Technology of Foolishness." In J. G. March and J. Olsen, eds., *Ambiguity and Choice in Organizations,* 69–81. Bergen, Norway: Universitetsforlaget.

March, J. G. 1994. *A Primer On Decision Making.* New York: Free Press.

March, J. G., and J. Olsen. 1989. *Rediscovering Institutions: The Organizational Basis of Politics.* New York: The Free Press.

March, J. G., L. S. Sproull, and N. Tamuz. 1991. "Learning From Samples of One or Fewer." *Organization Science* 2:1–13.

March, J. G., and R. Weissinger-Babylon, eds. 1986. *Ambiguity and Command: Organizational Perspectives On Military Decision Making.* Marshfield: Pitman.

Markus, H. R., and S. Kitayama. 1991. "Culture and the Self: Implications For Cognition, Emotion, and Motivation." *Psychological Review* 98:224–53.

Markus, H., and R. B. Zajonc. 1985. "The Cognitive Perspective in Social Psychology." In G. Lindzey and E. Aronson, eds., *The Handbook of Social Psychology,* 3d ed., 1:137–230. New York: Random House.

Marquis, D. G., and H. J. Reitz. 1969. "Effects of Uncertainty On Risk Taking in Individual and Group Decisions." *Behavioral Science* 14:281–88.

Mayseless, O., and A. W. Kruglanski. 1987. "What Makes You So Sure? Effects of Epistemic Motivation On Judgmental Confidence." *Organizational Behavior and Human Decision Processes* 39:162–83.

McCauley, C. 1989. "The Nature of Social Influence in Groupthink: Compliance and Internalization." *Journal of Personality and Social Psychology* 57:250–60.

McClelland, D. C. 1975. *Power: The Inner Experience.* New York: Irvington.

McClelland, D. C., and R. E. Boyatzis. 1982. "Leadership Motive Pattern and Long-Term Success in Management." *Journal of Applied Psychology* 67:737–43.

McClelland, D. C., and D. Burnham. 1976. "Power Is the Great Motivator." *Harvard Business Review* 54(2): 100–110.

McElroy, T. C., and H. K. Downey. 1982. "Observation in Organizational Research: Panacea to the Performance-Attribution Effect?" *Academy of Management Journal* 25:822–35.

McGrath, J. E. 1984. *Groups: Interactions and Performance*. Englewood Cliffs, NJ: Prentice-Hall.

McGrath, J., and D. Kravitz. 1982. "Group Research." *Annual Review of Psychology* 33:195–230.

McGrath, J., et al. 1993. "Groups, Tasks, and Technology." *Small Group Behavior* 24(3): 406–20.

McGuire, T. W., S. Kiesler, and J. Siegel. 1987. "Group and Computer-Mediated Discussion Effects in Risk Decision Making." *Journal of Personality and Social Psychology* 52:917–30.

McNamara, R. S. with B. Vand De Mark. 1995. *In Retrospect: The Tragedy and Lessons of Vietnam*. New York: Times Books.

Meertens, R. W., and H. Wilke. 1993. *Group Performance*. London: Routledge.

Meier, K. J. 1989. "Bureaucratic Leadership in Public Organization." In B. D. Jones, ed., *Leadership and Politics*. Lawrence: University of Kansas Press.

Meijer, H. 1994. *Den Haag-Djakarta: De Nederlands-Indonesische Betrekkingen 1950–1962*. Utrecht: Aula.

Meindle, J. R. 1990. "On Leadership: An Alternative to the Conventional Wisdom." In B. M. Staw and L. L. Cummings, eds., *Research in Organizational Behavior* 12:159–203. Greenwich, CT: JAI Press.

Meltsner, A. J. 1990. *Rules For Rulers: The Politics of Advice*. Philadelphia: Temple University Press.

Merton, R. K. 1948. "The Self-Fulfilling Prophecy." *Antioch Review* 8:193–210.

Metselaar, M. V., and B. Verbeek. 1995, "De Cognitive Dimensie Van Besluitvorming: Minister Luns En Het Nieuw-Guinea Conflict." In P. 't Hart, M. Metselaar, and B. Verbeek, eds., *Publieke Besluitvorming*, 229–60. Den Haag: Vuga.

Meyer, J. W., and B. Rowan. 1977. "Institutionalized Organizations: Formal Structure As Myth and Ceremony." *American Journal of Sociology* 83:340–63.

Miller, G. J. 1987. *Administrative Dilemmas: The Role of Political Leadership*. Political Economy Working Paper. June. St. Louis, MO: Washington University.

Milliken, F. J., and D. A. Volrath. 1991. "Strategic Decision-Making Tasks and Group Effectiveness: Insights From Theory and Research On Small Group Performance." *Human Relations* 44:1229–53

Miner, J. B. 1978. "Twenty Years of Research On Role-Motivation Theory of Managerial Effectiveness." *Personnel Psychology*, 31(4): 739–60.

Minix, D. A. 1982. *Small Groups and Foreign Policy Decision Making*. Washington: University Press of America.

Mintzberg, H., D. Raisinghani, and A. Theoret. 1976. "The Structure of 'Unstructured' Decision Processes." *Administrative Science Quarterly* 21:246–75.

Moens, A. 1990. *Foreign Policy Under Carter*. Boulder: Westview Press.

Montanari, J. R., and G. Moorhead. 1989. "Development of the Groupthink Assessment Inventory." *Educational and Psychological Measurement* 49:209–19.

Moorhead, G. 1982. "Groupthink: Hypothesis in Need of Testing." *Group and Organization Studies* 7:429–44.

Moorhead, G., and J. R. Montanari. 1982. "Groupthink: A Research Methodology." In G. White, ed., *Proceedings of the 14th Annual Meeting of the American Institute For Decision Sciences* 1:380–82. San Francisco.

Moorhead, G., and J. R. Montanari. 1986. "An Empirical Investigation of the Groupthink Phenomenon." *Human Relations* 39:399–410.

Moreland, R. 1987. "The Formation of Small Groups." In C. Hendrick, ed., *Group Processes,* 80–110. Newbury Park: Sage.

Moreland, R., and J. M. Levine. 1988. "Group Dynamics Over Time: Development and Socialization in Small Groups." In J. E. McGrath, ed., *The Social Psychology of Time: New Perspectives* 151–81. London: Sage.

Moreland, R. L., and J. M. Levine. 1992a. "The Composition of Small Groups." In E. Lawler, B. Murkovsky, C. Ridgeway, and H. Walker, eds., *Advances in Group Processes* 9:237–80. Greenwich, CT: JAI Press.

Moreland, R. L., and J. M. Levine. 1992b. "Problem Identification By Groups." In S. Worschel, W. Wood, and J. A. Simpson, eds., *Group Process and Productivity,* 17–47. London: Sage.

Morgan, G. W. 1986. *Images of Organization.* London: Sage.

Moscovici, S. 1976. *Social Influence and Social Change.* London: Academic Press.

Moscovici, S. 1985. "Social Influence and Conformity." In G. Lindzey and E. Aronson, eds., *Handbook of Social Psychology* 2:347–412. New York: Random House.

Moscovici, S., and W. Doise. 1994. *Conflict and Consensus: A General Theory of Collective Decisions.* London: Sage Publications.

Moscovici, S., A. Mucci-Faina, and A. Maas, eds. 1994. *Minority Influence.* Chicago: Nelson Hall Publishers.

Mullen, B., and C. Copper. 1994. "The Relation Between Group Cohesiveness and Performance: An Integration." *Psychological Bulletin* 115(2): 210–27.

Myers, D. G. 1982. "Polarizing Effects of Social Interaction." In H. Brandstaetter, J. H. Davis, and G. Stocker-Kreichgauer, eds., *Group Decision Making,* 125–61. London: Academic Press.

Myers, D. G., and S. J. Arenson. 1972. "Enhancement of Dominant Risk Tendencies in Group Discussion." *Psychological Reports* 30:615–23.

Myers, D. G., and H. Lamm. 1976. "The Group Polarization Phenomenon." *Psychological Bulletin* 83:602–27.

Naor, A. 1986. *Cabinet at War: The Functioning of the Israeli Cabinet During the Lebanon War (1982).* Tel Aviv: Lahav (in Hebrew).

Nathan, J., and J. Oliver. 1987. *Foreign Policy Making and the American Political System.* Boston: Little, Brown, and Company.

Neack, L., J. A. K. Hay, and J. Haney, eds. 1995. *Foreign Policy Analysis: Continuity and Change in Its Second Generation.* Englewood Cliffs: Prentice-Hall.

Neck, C. P., and C. C. Manz. 1994. "From Groupthink to Teamthink: Toward the

Creation of Constructive Thought Patterns in Self-Managing Teams." *Human Relations* 47:929–52.

Nemeth, C. J. 1986. "Differential Contributions of Majority and Minority Influence". *Psychological Review* 93:23–32.

Nemeth, C., and B. M. Staw. 1989. "The Trade Offs of Social Control and Innovation Within Groups and Organizations." In L. Berkowitz, ed., *Advances in Experimental Social Psychology* 22:175–210. New York: Academic Press.

Nemiroff, M., and W. A. Pasmore. 1975. "Lost at Sea: A Consensus-Seeking Task." In J. E. Jones and W. Pfeiffer, eds., *The 1975 Annual Handbook For Group Facilitators* 28–34. La Jolla, CA: University Associates.

Nemiroff, M., W. A. Pasmore, and D. L. Ford. 1976. "The Effects of Two Normative Structural Interventions on Established and Ad Hoc Groups: Implications For Improving Decision Making Effectiveness." *Decision Sciences* 7:841–55.

Neustadt, R. E. 1960. *Presidential Power: The Politics of Leadership.* New York: John Wiley and Sons.

Neustadt, R. E. 1980. *Presidential Power: The Politics of Leadership from FDR to Carter.* New York: John Wiley.

Neustadt, R. E., and E. R. May. 1986. *Thinking in Time: The Uses of History For Decision Makers.* New York: Free Press.

Newsom, D. 1987. *The Soviet Brigade in Cuba.* Bloomington: Indiana University Press.

Nisbett, R., and L. Ross. 1980. *Human Inference: Strategies and Shortcomings of Human Judgement.* Englewood Cliffs, NJ: Prentice Hall.

Nousiainen, J. 1993. "Decision-Making, Policy Content and Conflict Resolution in Western European Cabinets." In J. Blondel and F. Müller-Rommel, eds., *Governing Together,* 259–82. London: Sage.

Nutt, C. 1986. "Group Decision Making." *Principles of Decision Making.* Draft manuscript.

Nutt, C. 1989. *Making Tough Decisions.* San Francisco: Jossey Bass.

Nydegger, R. V. 1975. "Information Processing Complexity and Leadership Status." *Journal of Experimental Social Psychology* 11.

Oberdorfer, D. 1979. "Chapter 1: Brigada Unwelcome Site in Cuba." *The Washington Post.* Washington. September 9: A1, A18.

Olsen, J. 1983. "Governing Norway: Segmentation, Anticipation and Consensus Formation." In R. Rose and E. N. Suleiman, eds., *Presidents and Prime Ministers,* 203–55. Washington: American Enterprise Institute.

Onuf, N. G. 1989. *World of Our Making: Rules and Rule in Social Theory and International Relations.* Columbia: University of South Carolina Press.

Osborn, A. F. 1963. *Applied Imagination,* 3d ed. New York: Scribner's.

Ostrom, E. 1990. *Governing the Commons.* Cambridge: Cambridge University Press.

Paige, G. D. 1968. *The Korean Decision.* New York: Free Press.

Park, W. W. 1990. "A Review of Research On Groupthink." *Journal of Behavioral Decision Making* 3:229–45.

Perlmutter, A. 1987. *The Life and Times of Menachem Begin.* Garden City, NY: Doubleday and Company.

Perry, M. 1989. *Four Stars.* Boston: Houghton Mifflin Company.

Pfeffer, J. 1981. *Power in Organizations.* Marshfield, MA: Pitman.

Pika, J. A. 1988. "Management Style and the Organizational Matrix: Studying White House Operations." *Administration and Society* 20:3–29.

Pincus, W., and G. C. Wilson. 1979. "Chapter 3: Dilemma, Saving Salt I." *The Washington Post* September 9: A19. Washington

Pious, R. 1988. *The American Presidency.* New York: Ballantine.

Polsby, N. W. 1984. *Political Innovation in America.* New Haven: Yale University Press.

Poole, J., and R. Hirokawa, eds. 1986. *Communication and Group Decision Making.* London: Sage.

Porter, R. B. 1980. *Presidential Decision Making: The Economic Policy Board.* Cambridge: Cambridge University Press.

Posner-Weber, C. 1987. "Update On Groupthink." *Small Group Behavior* 18:118–25.

Prados, J. 1991. *Keepers of the Keys: A History of the National Security Council From Truman to Bush.* New York: William Morrow.

Preston, T. 1996. "The President and His Inner Circle: Leadership Style and the Advisory Process in Foreign Policy Making." Ph.D. dissertation. Columbus: Ohio State University.

Preston, T., and M. Young. 1992. "An Approach to Understanding Decision Making: The Bush Administration, the Gulf Crisis, Management Style, and Worldview." Paper presented at 33rd Annual Meeting of the International Studies Association.

Puchinger, G., ed. 1978. *Dr. Jelle Zijlstra. Gesprekken en Geschriften'.* Naarden: Strengholt.

Purkitt, H. 1992. "Political Decision Making in Small Groups." In E. Singer and V. Hudson, eds., *Political Psychology and Foreign Policy,* 219–45. Boulder: Westview Press.

Putnam, R. D. 1988. "Diplomacy and Domestic Politics: The Logic of Two-Level Games." *International Organization* 42:427–60.

Quinn, R. 1988. *Beyond Rational Management.* San Francisco: Jossey Bass.

Rabbie, J. M., J. C. Schot, and L. Visser. 1989. "Social Identity Theory: A Conceptual and Empirical Critique From the Perspective of A Behavioral Interaction Model." *European Journal of Social Psychology* 19:171–202.

Radley, A. 1991. "Solving A Problem Together: A Study of Thinking in Small Groups." *Journal of Phenomenological Psychology* 22(1): 39–59.

Raven, B. H. 1990. "Political Applications of the Psychology of Interpersonal Influence and Social Power." *Political Psychology* 11(3): 493–520.

Reeves, R. 1993. *President Kennedy.* New York: Simon and Schuster.

Rehwinkel, J. 1991. *De Minister-President: Eerste Onder Gelijken of Gelijke Onder Eersten?* Zwolle: Tjeenk Willink.

Richardson, J. L. 1994. *Crisis Diplomacy: The Great Powers Since the Mid-Nineteenth Century.* New York: Cambridge University Press.

Ridley, D. R., D. Young, and D. E. Johnson. 1981. "Salience As A Dimension of Individual and Group Risk Taking." *The Journal of Psychology* 109:283–91.

Riker, W. H. 1984. "The Heresthetics of Constitution-Making: The Presidency in 1787

With Comments On Determinism and Rational Choice." *American Political Science Review* 78(1): 1–16.

Riker, W. H. 1986. *The Art of Political Manipulation.* New Haven: Yale University Press.

Rim, Y. 1964. "Personality and Group Decisions Involving Risk." *Psychological Record* 14:37–45.

Rim, Y. 1966. "Machiavellianism and Decisions Involving Risk." *British Journal of Social and Clinical Psychology* 5:30–36.

Ripley, B. 1993. "Psychology, Foreign Policy and International Relations." *Political Psychology* 14:403–16.

Ripley, B. 1995. "Cognition, Culture, and Bureaucratic Politics." In L. Neack, J. Hey, and Haney, eds., *Foreign Policy Analysis: Continuity and Change in Its Second Generation,* 85–98. Englewood Cliffs: Prentice-Hall.

Roberts, J. M. 1988. *Decision Making During International Crises.* London: Mac-Millan.

Robinson, S., and Weldon, E. 1993. "Feedback Seeking in Groups: A Theoretical Perspective." *British Journal of Social Psychology* 32:71–86.

Rockman, B. A. 1978. "America's Departments of State: Irregular and Regular Syndromes of Policy Making." *American Political Science Review* 75:911–27.

Rokeach, M. 1954. "The Nature and Meaning of Dogmatism." *Psychological Review* 61:194–204.

Rosati, J. A. 1981. "Developing A Systematic Decision-Making Framework: Bureaucratic Politics in Perspective." *World Politics* 33(2): 234–52.

Rosati, J. A. 1987. *The Carter Administration's Quest For Global Community: Beliefs and Their Impact On Behavior.* Columbia: University of South Carolina Press.

Rosati, J. A. 1993. *The Politics of U.S. Foreign Policy.* Fort Worth, TX: Harcourt Brace Jovanovich.

Rosati, J. A. 1995. "A Cognitive Approach to the Study of Foreign Policy." In Neack, L., J. A. K. Hay, and J. Haney, eds., *Foreign Policy Analysis: Continuity and Change in Its Second Generation,* 49–70. Englewood Cliffs: Prentice Hall.

Rose, R., and E. N. Suleiman, eds. 1983. *Presidents and Prime Ministers.* Washington: American Enterprise Institute.

Rosenau, J. N. 1966. "Pre-theories and Theories of Foreign Policy." In R. Barry Farrell, ed., *Approaches to Comparative and International Politics,* 27–92. Evanston: Northwestern University Press.

Rosenau, J. N., ed. 1967. *Domestic Sources of Foreign Policy.* New York: Free Press.

Rosenau, J. N., ed. 1974. *Comparing Foreign Policies: Theories, Findings, Methods.* New York: Halsted.

Rosenthal, R., and Jacobson, L. 1968. *Pygmalion in the Classroom: Teacher Expectation and Student Intellectual Development.* New York: Holt, Rinehart and Winston.

Rosenthal, U. 1984. *Rampen, Rellen, Gijzelingen: Crisisbesluitvorming in Nederland.* Amsterdam/Dieren, the Netherlands: De Bataafsche Leeuw.

Rosenthal, U., and P. 't Hart. 1991. "Experts and Decisionmakers in Crisis Situations." *Knowledge* 12:350–73.

Rosenthal, U., P. 't Hart, and A. Kouzmin. 1991. "The Bureau-Politics of Crisis Management." *Public Administration* 69(2): 211–33.

Ross, D. 1984. "Risk Aversion in Soviet Decisionmaking." In J. Valenta and W. C. Potter, eds., *Soviet Decisionmaking For National Security,* 237–51. London: George Allen and Unwin.

Ross, L., D. Greene, and D. House. 1977. "The 'False Consensus' Effect: An Egocentric Bias in Social Perception and Attribution Processes." *Journal of Experimental Social Psychology* 13:279–301.

Rotter, J. B. 1966. "Generalized Expectancies For Internal Versus External Control of Reinforcement." *Psychological Monographs: General and Applied* 80.

Rusk, D. 1990. *As I Saw It.* New York: W. W. Norton and Company.

Sagan, S. 1991. *The Limits of Safety.* Princeton: Princeton University Press.

Sampson, M. 1987. "Cultural Influences On Foreign Policy." In C. F. Hermann, C. W. Kegley, and J. N. Rosenau, eds., *New Directions in The Study of Foreign Policy,* 384–405. Boston: Allen and Unwin.

Sandelands, L., and L. St. Clair. 1993. "Towards An Empirical Concept of Group." *Journal For The Theory of Social Behavior* 23(3): 423–58.

Sanders, B. D. 1980. "Avoiding the Groupthink Zoo." *Supervision,* 42:10–13.

Schachter, S. 1951. "Deviation, Rejection, and Communication." *Journal of Abnormal Psychology* 46:190–207.

Schachter, S., et al. 1954. "Cross-Cultural Experiments On Threat and Rejection." *Human Relations* 7:403–39.

Scharpf, F. 1989. "Decision Rules, Decision Styles, and Policy Choices." *Journal of Theoretical Politics* 1:149–76.

Schattschneider, E. E. 1975. *The Semisovereign People.* Hinsdale, IL: Dryden Press.

Schlesinger, A. 1965. *A Thousand Days.* Boston: Houghton-Mifflin Co.

Schriesheim, C. A., and M. A. Von Glinow. 1977. "The Path-Goal Theory of Leadership: A Theoretical and Empirical Analysis." *Academy of Management Journal* 20:398–405.

Schroder, H. M., M. J. Driver and S. Streufert. 1967. *Human Information Processing: Individuals and Groups Functioning in Complex Social Situations.* New York and London: Holt, Rinehart and Winston.

Schweiger, M., W. R. Sandberg, and J. W. Ragan. 1986. "Group Approaches For Improving Strategic Decision Making: A Comparative Analysis of Dialectical Inquiry, Devil's Advocacy, and Consensus." *Academy of Management Journal* 29:51–71.

Schwenk, C. R. 1988. *Essence of Strategic Decision Making.* Lexington: Heath.

Scott, W. A. 1963. "Cognitive Complexity and Cognitive Balance." *Sociometry.* 26:66–74.

Scriven, M. 1976. "Maximizing the Power of Causal Investigations: The Modus Operandi Method." *Evaluation Studies Review Annual,* 1:101–18.

Seashore, S. E. 1954. *Group Cohesiveness in the Industrial Work Group.* Ann Arbor: University of Michigan Press.

Seligman, M. E. 1991. *Learned Optimism.* New York: A. A. Knopf.

Senge, 1990. *The Fifth Discipline: The Art and Practice of the Learning Organization.* New York: Doubleday/Currency.

Shapira, Z. 1995. *Risk Taking: A Managerial Perspective.* New York: Russell Sage Foundation.

Shapley, D. 1993. *Promise and Power: The Life and Times of Robert McNamara.* Boston: Little, Brown and Company.

Shaw, M. E. 1973. "Scaling Group Tasks: A Method For Dimensional Analysis." JSAS: Catalog of Selected Documents in Psychology, 3, 8 (Ms. No. 294).

Shaw, M. 1981. *Group Dynamics,* 3d ed. New York: McGraw Hill.

Shepard, G. H. 1988. "Personality Effects On American Foreign Policy, 1969–84: A Second Test of Interpersonal Generalization Theory." *International Studies Quarterly* 32:91–123.

Sherif, M. 1936. *The Psychology of Social Norms.* New York: Harper and Bros.

Shiffer, S. 1984. *Snow Ball: The Story Behind the Lebanon War* (in Hebrew). Tel Aviv: Edanim.

Shrader-Frechette, K. S. 1991. *Risk and Rationality: Philosophical Foundations For Populist Reforms.* Berkeley and Los Angeles: University of California Press.

Sick, G. 1985. *All Fall Down: America's Tragic Encounter With Iran.* New York: Random House.

Smith, G. 1986. *Morality, Reason and Power—American Diplomacy in the Carter Years.* New York: Hill and Wang.

Smith, H. K. 1988. *The Power Game: How Washington Works.* New York: Ballantine Books.

Smith, S. 1985a. "Groupthink and the Hostage Rescue Mission." *British Journal of Political Science* 15:117–23.

Smith, S. 1985b. "Policy Preferences and Bureaucratic Position: The Case of the American Hostage Rescue Mission." *International Affairs* 61:9–25.

Smith, S. 1985c. "The Hostage Rescue Mission." In S. Smith and M. Clarke, eds., *Foreign Policy Implementation,* 11–32. London: George, Allen and Unwin.

Sniezek, J. A. 1992. "Group Under Uncertainty: An Examination of Confidence in Group Decision Making." *Organizational Behavior and Human Decision Processes* 52:124–55.

Snow, C. 1964. *The Corridors of Power.* Harmondsworth: Penguin.

Snyder, G., and P. Diesing. 1977. *Conflict Among Nations.* Princeton: Princeton University Press.

Snyder, M. 1987. *Public Appearances, Private Realities: The Psychology of Self-Monitoring.* New York: W. H. Freeman and Company.

Snyder, R. C., H. W. Bruck, and B. Sapin. 1954. "Decision-Making as an Approach to the Study of International Politics." *Foreign Policy Analysis Project Series,* No. 3, Princeton, NJ.

Snyder, R. C., H. W. Bruck, and D. Sapin. 1962. *Foreign Policy Decision Making.* New York: Free Press.

Snyder, R. C., and G. D. Paige. 1958. "The United States Decision to Resist Aggression in Korea: The Application of an Analytic Scheme." *Administrative Science Quarterly* 3:341–78.

Sofer, S. 1988. *Begin: An Anatomy of Leadership.* Oxford: Basil Blackwell.

Sorrels, J. P., and J. Kelley. 1984. "Conformity by Omission." *Personality and Social Psychology Bulletin* 10(2): 302–5.

Spanier, J., and J. Nogee. 1981. *Congress, the Presidency and American Foreign Policy.* New York: Pergamon Press.

Sprout, H., and M. Sprout. 1956. *Man-Milieu Relationship Hypotheses in the Context of International Politics.* Princeton: Center of International Studies, Princeton University.

Sprout, H., and M. Sprout. 1962. *Foundations of International Politics.* Princeton: Van Nostrand.

Sprout, H., and M. Sprout. 1965. *The Ecological Perspective in Human Affairs.* Princeton: Princeton University Press.

Sprout, H., and M. Sprout. 1969. *Foundations of International Politics.* Princeton, NJ: Van Nostrand.

Stasser, G. 1992. "Pooling of Unshared Information During Group Decisions." In S. Worchel, W. Wood, and J. A. Simpson, eds., *Group Process and Productivity,* 48–67. London: Sage.

Staw, B. M. 1975. "Attribution of the 'Causes' of Performance: A General Alternative Interpretation of Cross-Sectional Research On Organizations." *Organizational Behavior and Human Performance* 13:414–32.

Stein, J. G. 1992. "International Co-operation and Loss Avoidance: Framing the Problem." *International Journal* 47:202–34.

Stein, J. G., and R. Tanter. 1980. *Rational Decision Making.* Columbus: Ohio State University Press.

Steinbruner, J. 1974. *The Cybernetic Theory of Decision.* Princeton: Princeton University Press.

Steiner, I. D. 1972. *Group Process and Productivity.* New York: Academic Press.

Steiner, I. D. 1976. "Task-Performing Groups." In J. W. Thibaut, J. T. Spence, and R. C. Carson, eds., *Contemporary Topics in Social Psychology* 393–422. Morristown, NJ: General Learning Press.

Steiner, I. D. 1982. "Heuristic Models of Groupthink." In H. Brandstaetter, J. H. Davis, and G. Stocker-Kreichgauer, eds., *Group Decision Making,* 503–24. London: Academic Press.

Steiner, I. D. 1986. "Paradigms and Groups." *Advances in Experimental Social Psychology* 19:251–89.

Steiner, P. 1989. "In Collusion With the Nation: A Case Study of Group Dynamics at Strategic Nuclear Policymaking Meeting." *Political Psychology* 10(4): 647–73.

Stempel, J. D. 1981. *Inside the Iranian Revolution.* Bloomington: Indiana University Press.

Stern, E. K. 1992. "Information Management and the Whiskey On the Rocks Crisis." *Cooperation and Conflict* 27:45–96.

Stern, E. K. 1993. "Dissecting Crisis Decision: A Neo-Institutional Approach." Paper presented at the European Consortium For Political Research Joint Sessions. Leiden, the Netherlands, April.

Stern, E. K., and B. Sundelius. 1993. "Penetrating the Elusive Small Decision Group:

An Analytical Tool Set and Case Findings." Paper presented at the European Consortium for Political Research, Leiden, the Netherlands, April.

Stern, E. K., and B. Sundelius. 1994. "The Essence of Groupthink." *Mershon International Studies Review* 1:101–8.

Stern, E., and B. Sundelius. 1997. "Sweden's Twin Monetary Crises of 1992: Rigidity and Learning in Crisis Decision Making." *Journal of Contingencies and Crisis Management.* 5(1): in press.

Stern, E., and B. Sundelius. Forthcoming. *The Imperative of Decision: Sweden, U137, and the USSR.*

Sternberg, R. J. 1985. "Implicit Theories of Intelligence, Creativity, and Wisdom." *Journal of Personality and Social Psychology* 49:607–27.

Stogdill, R. M. 1974. *Handbook of Leadership.* New York: Free Press.

Stogdill, R. M., and B. M. Bass. 1981. *Stogdill's Handbook of Leadership: A Survey of Theory and Research.* New York: The Free Press.

Stone, D. A. 1987. *Policy Paradox and Political Reason.* Chicago: Scott, Foresman.

Streufert, S., and R. W. Swezey. 1986. *Complexity, Managers, and Organizations.* Orlando, New York, London: Academic Press.

Stumpf, S. A., R. D. Freedman, and D. E. Zand. 1979. "Judgmental Decisions: A Study of Interactions Among Group Membership, Group Functioning, and the Decision Situation." *Academy of Management Journal* 22:765–82.

Stumpf, S. A., D. E. Zand, and R. D. Freedman. 1979. "Designing Groups For Judgmental Decisions." *Academy of Management Review* 4:589–600.

Suedfeld, P., and A. Rank. 1976. "Revolutionary Leaders: Long-Term Success As a Function of Changes in Conceptual Complexity." *Journal of Personality and Social Psychology.* 34.

Suedfeld, P., P. Tetlock, and C. Ramirez. 1977. "Integrative Complexity of Communications in International Crisis." *Journal of Conflict Resolution* 21:169–84.

Sullivan, W. 1981. *Mission to Iran.* New York: W. W. Norton.

Sullivan, W. 1984. *Obbligato 1939–1979: Notes On A Foreign Service Career.* New York: W. W. Norton.

Sullivan, W. 1987. "Iran: A View From Iran". *World Affairs* 149(4): 215–18.

Sutton, C. D., and R. W. Woodman. 1989. "Pygmalion Goes to Work: The Effects of Supervisor Expectations in A Retail Setting." *Journal of Applied Psychology* 74:943–50.

Swap, W. C. 1984a. "Destructive Effects of Groups On Individuals." In W. C. Swap and Associates, eds., *Group Decision Making,* 69–95. Beverly Hills: Sage.

Swap, W. C. 1984b. "How Groups Make Decisions: A Social Psychological Perspective." In W. Swap, ed., *Group Decision Making,* 45–68. London: Sage.

Tajfel, H. 1982. "Social Psychology of Intergroup Relations." *Annual Review of Psychology* 33:1–39.

Talbott, S. 1984. *Deadly Gambits: The Reagan Administration and the Stalemate in Nuclear Arms Control.* New York: Vintage Books.

Tannenbaum, A. 1966/1992. "The Group in the Organization." Reprinted in V. Vroom and Deci, eds., *Management and Motivation,* 121–28. New York: Penguin Books.

Taylor, D. W., C. Berry, and C. H. Block. 1958. "Does Group Participation When

Using Brainstorming Facilitate Or Inhibit Creative Thinking?" *Administrative Science Quarterly* 3:23–47.

Taylor, S. E., and J. D. Brown. 1988. "Illusion and Well-Being: A Social-Psychological Perspective On Mental Health." *Psychological Bulletin* 103:193–210.

Tetlock, P. 1979. "Identifying Victims of Groupthink From the Public Statements of Decision Makers." *Journal of Personality and Social Psychology* 52:700–709.

Tetlock, P. 1985a. "Accountability: The Neglected Social Context of Judgement and Choice." In K. L. Cummings and B. M. Staw, eds., *Research in Organizational Behavior* 7:297–332. Greenwich, CT: JAI Press.

Tetlock, P. 1985b. "Integrative Complexity of American and Soviet Foreign Policy Rhetorics: A Time-Series Analysis." *Journal of Personality and Social Psychology* 49:565–85.

Tetlock, P., and G. W. Breslauer, eds. 1991. *Learning in US and Soviet Foreign Policy*. Boulder: Westview.

Tetlock, P., R. Peterson, C. McGuire, S. Chang, and Feld. 1992. "Assessing Political Group Dynamics: A Test of the Groupthink Model." *Journal of Personality and Social Psychology* 63(3): 403–25.

Thiebault, J.-L. 1994. "The Organisational Structure of Western European Cabinets and Its Impact On Decision-Making." In J. Blondel and F. Müller-Rommel, eds., *Governing Together*, 77–98. London: Macmillan.

Thompson, J. E., and A. L. Carsrud. 1976. "The Effects of Experimentally Induced Illusions of Invulnerability and Vulnerability On Decisional Risk Taking in Triads." *The Journal of Social Psychology* 100:263–67.

Thompson, L. et al. 1988. "Group Negotiation: Effects of Decision Rule, Agenda, and Aspiration." *Journal of Personality and Social Psychology* 54:86–95.

Thompson, V. 1961. *Modern Organization*. New York: Alfred A. Knopf.

Thomson, Jr., and C. James. 1968. "How Could Vietnam Happen? An Autopsy." *The Atlantic Monthly,* April.

Tindale, R. S. 1993. "Decision Errors Made By Individuals and Groups." In N. Castellan Jr., ed., *Individual and Group Decision Making: Current Issues,* 109–24. Hillsdale, NJ: Lawrence Erlbaum Associates.

Torrance, E. 1953. "Methods of Conducting Critiques of Group Problem-Solving Performance." *Journal of Applied Psychology,* 37.

Tower Commission Report. 1987. New York: Bantam Books.

Truman, H. S. 1953. *Years of Trial and Hope.* Garden City, NY: Doubleday and Company, Inc.

Tse, D. K., K.-H Lee, I. Vertinsky, and D. A. Wehrung. 1988. "Does Culture Matter? A Cross-Cultural Study of Executives' Choices, Decisiveness, and Risk Adjustment in International Marketing." *Journal of Marketing* 52(4): 81–95.

Tucker, D. 1973. "Some Relationships Between Individual and Group Development." *Journal of Human Development* 16:249–72.

Tuckman, B. 1965. "Developmental Sequence in Small Groups." *Psychological Bulletin* 63(6): 384–99.

Tuckman, B., and M. Jensen. 1977. "Stages of Group Development Revisited." *Group and Organization Studies* 2(4): 417–27.

Tullar, W. L., and D. F. Johnson. 1973. "Group Decision-Making and the Risky Shift: A Trans-National Perspective." *International Journal of Psychology*, 8:117–23.

Turner, B. A. 1991. "The Rise of Organisational Symbolism." In J. Hassard, ed., *The Theory and Philosophy of Organizations: Critical Issues and New Perspectives*, 83–96. London: Routledge.

Turner, J. C. 1987. *Rediscovering the Social Group: A Self-Categorization Theory.* Oxford: Blackwell.

Turner, J. C. 1991. *Social Influence.* Pacific Grove: Brooks Cole.

Tversky, A., and D. Kahneman. 1973. "Availability: A Heuristic For Judging Frequency and Probability." *Cognitive Psychology* 5:202–32.

Tversky, A., and D. Kahneman. 1981. "The Framing of Decisions and the Psychology of Choice." *Science* 211:453–58.

Tversky, A., and D. Kahneman. 1986. "Rational Choice and the Framing of Decisions." *Journal of Business* 59:251–278.

Valenta, J. 1991. *Soviet Intervention in Czechoslovakia 1968: Anatomy of a Decision.* Revised edition. Baltimore: Johns Hopkins University Press.

Van De Ven, A. H., and A. L. Delbecq. 1971. "Nominal Versus Interacting Groups For Committee Decision-Making Effectiveness." *Academy of Management Journal* 14:203–12.

Van Raalte, E. 1977. *Het Nederlandse Parlement.* 's Gravenhage: Staatsuitgeverij.

Vance, C. 1983. *Hard Choices.* New York: Simon and Schuster.

Vandenbroucke, L. 1984. "Anatomy of A Failure: The Decision to Land at the Bay of Pigs." *Political Science Quarterly* 99(3): 471–91.

Vandenbroucke, L. 1993. *Perilous Options.* New York: Oxford University Press

Veldkamp, G. M. J. 1993. *Herinneringen 1952–1987: La Carnaval Des Animaux Politiques.* 's Gravenhage: SDU.

Verba, S. 1962. *Small Groups and Political Behavior: A Study of Leadership.* Princeton: Princeton University Press.

Verbeek, B. 1992. "Anglo-American Relations 1945–1956: A Comparison of Neorealist and Cognitive Psychological Approaches to the Study of International Relations." Florence, Ph.D. thesis, European University Institute.

Verbeek, B. 1994. "Do Individual and Group Beliefs Matter? British Decision Making During the 1956 Suez Crisis." *Cooperation and Conflict*, 29(4): 307–32.

Vertzberger, Y. 1984a. "Bureaucratic-Organizational Politics and Information Processing in A Developing State." *International Studies Quarterly* 28:69–95.

Vertzberger, Y. 1984b. *Misperceptions in Foreign Policy Decisionmaking: The Sino-Indian Conflict, 1959–1962.* Boulder, CO: Westview Press.

Vertzberger, Y. 1990. *The World in Their Minds: Information Processing, Cognition, and Perception in Foreign Policy Decisionmaking,* Stanford, CA: Stanford University Press.

Vertzberger, Y. 1992. "Risk in Foreign Policy Decisionmaking: The Forgotten Dimension." Paper delivered at the 33d Annual ISA Convention, Atlanta, Georgia.

Vertzberger, Y. 1995. "Rethinking and Reconceptualizing Risk in Foreign Policy Decisionmaking: A Sociocognitive Approach." *Political Psychology* 16:347–80.

Vertzberger, Y. In press. *Risk Taking and Decisionmaking: Foreign Military Intervention.* Stanford: Stanford University Press.

Vinokur, A. 1971. "Review and Theoretical Analysis of the Effects of Group Processes Upon Individual and Group Decisions Involving Risk." *Psychological Bulletin* 76:231–50.

Von Bergen, C. W., Jr., and R. J. Kirk. 1978. "Groupthink: When Too Many Heads Spoil the Decision." *Management Review* 67:44–49.

Voss, J., and E. Dorsey. 1992. "Perception and International Relations: An Overview." In E. Singer and V. Hudson, eds., *Political Psychology and Foreign Policy,* 3–30. Boulder: Westview Press.

Vroom, V. H., L. D. Grant, and T. S. Cotton. 1969. "The Consequences of Social Interaction in Group Problem-Solving." *Organizational Behavior and Human Performance,* 4(1): 77–95.

Vroom, V. H., and P. W. Yetton. 1973. *Leadership and Decision Making.* Pittsburgh: Pittsburgh University Press.

Vroom, V. H., and A. G. Jago. 1978. "On the Validity of the Vroom-Yetton Model." *Journal of Applied Psychology* 63:151–62.

Walker, S. G. 1983. "The Motivational Foundations of Belief Systems: A Re-Analysis of the Operational Code Construct." *International Studies Quarterly* 27:179–201.

Walker, S. G. 1990. "The Evolution of Operational Code Analysis." *Political Psychology* 11(2): 403–18.

Walker, S. G., and G. Watson. 1989. "Groupthink and Integrative Complexity in British Foreign Policy-Making: The Munich Case." *Cooperation and Conflict* 24:199–213

Walker, S. G., and Watson G. 1992. "The Cognitive Maps of British Leaders, 1938–1939: The Case of Chamberlain-in-Cabinet." In V. Hudson and E. Singer, *Political Psychology and Foreign Policy,* 31–58. Boulder: Westview Press.

Wallace, M. D., and Suedfeld. 1988. "Leadership Performance in Crisis: The Longevity-Complexity Link." *International Studies Quarterly,* 32:439–52.

Wallach, M. A., and C. W. Wing. 1968. "Is Risk A Value?" *Journal of Personality and Social Psychology* 9:101–6.

Wallach, M. A., N. Kogan, and R. B. Burt. 1968. "Are Risk Takers More Persuasive Than Conservatives in Group Discussion?" *Journal of Experimental Social Psychology* 4:76–88.

Wayne, S., and G. Ferris. 1990. "Influence Tactics, Affect, and Exchange Quality in Supervisor-Subordinate Interactions: A Laboratory Experiment and Field Study." *Journal of Applied Psychology* 75(5): 487–99.

Wehman, P., M. A. Goldstein, and J. R. Williams. 1977. "Effects of Different Leadership Styles On Individual Risk-Taking in Groups." *Human Relations* 30:249–59.

Weick, K., and K. Roberts. 1993. "Collective Mind: Heedful Interrelating on Flight Decks." *Administrative Science Quarterly* 18:357–81.

Weiss, C. H. 1977. *Using Social Research in Public Policymaking.* Lexington: Heath.

Welch, D. 1989. "Crisis Decisionmaking Reconsidered." *Journal of Conflict Resolution* 33:430–45.

Welch, D. 1992. "The Organizational Process and Bureaucratic Politics Paradigms: Retrospect and Prospect." *International Security* 17(2): 112–46.

Weldon, E., and G. M. Gargano. 1985. "Cognitive Efforts in Addictive Task Groups: The Effects of Shared Responsibility on the Quality of Multiattributive Judgments." *Organizational Behavior and Human Decision Processes* 36:348–61.

Welsh, M. A., and E. A. Slusher. 1986. "Organizational Design As A Context For Political Activity." *Administrative Science Quarterly* 31:389–402.

Wendt, A. 1987. "The Agent-Structure Problem in International Relations Theory." *International Organization* 41:335–70.

Wheelan, S., and R. McKeage. 1993. "Developmental Patterns in Large and Small Groups." *Small Group Research* 24(1): 60–83.

Whelan, R. 1990. *Drawing the Line.* Boston: Little, Brown, and Company.

Whicker, M. L., J. Pfiffner, and R. A. Moore, eds. 1993. *The Presidency and the Persian Gulf War.* London: Praeger.

White, G. 1994. "The Interpersonal Dynamics of Decision Making in Canadian Provincial Cabinets." In M. Laver and K. A. Shepsle, eds., *Cabinet Ministers and Parliamentary Government,* 251–69. Cambridge: Cambridge University Press.

White, R. K., and R. Lippitt. 1960, 1977. *Autocracy and Democracy.* New York: Harper and Row.

Whyte, G. 1989. "Groupthink Reconsidered." *Academy of Management Review* 14:40–56.

Whyte, G., and A. S. Levi. 1994. "The Origins and Function of the Reference Point in Risky Group Decision Making: The Case of the Cuban Missile Crisis." *Journal of Behavioral Decision Making* 7:243–60.

Wilder, D. A., and V. L. Allen. 1978. "Group Membership and Preference For Information About Others." *Personality and Social Psychology Bulletin* 4:106–10.

Wilensky, H. 1967. *Organizational Intelligence.* New York: Free Press.

Williamson, O. E. 1975. *Markets and Hierarchies.* New York: Free Press.

Winter, D. G. 1973. *The Power Motive.* New York: Free Press.

Winter, D. G. 1987. "Leader Appeal, Leader Performance, and the Motive Profiles of Leaders and Followers: A Study of American Presidents and Elections." *Journal of Personality and Social Psychology* 52:196–202.

Winter, D. G., and A. J. Stewart. 1977. "Content Analysis as a Technique for Assessing Political Leaders." In M. G. Hermann, ed., *A Psychological Examination of Political Leaders,* 21–61. New York: Free Press.

Winter, D. G., M. G. Hermann, W. Weintraub, and S. G. Walker. 1991. "The Personalities of Bush and Gorbachev Measured at A Distance: Procedures, Portraits, and Policy." *Political Psychology* 12(2): 215–45.

Wood, W., and B. Stagner. 1994. "Why Are Some People Easier to Influence Than Others?." In S. Shavit and T. C. Brock, eds., *Persuasion: Psychological Insights and Perspectives,* 149–74. Boston: Allyn and Bacon.

Woodward, B. 1979. *The Brethren: Inside the Supreme Court.* New York: Simon and Schuster.

Woodward, B. 1991. *The Commanders.* New York: Simon and Schuster.

Woolsey-Biggart, N., and G. G. Hamilton. 1984. "The Power of Obedience." *Administrative Science Quarterly* 29:540–49.

Wooten, J. 1979. "Here Comes Zbig." *Esquire.* November.

Worchel, S., D. Coutant-Sassic, and M. Grossman. 1992. "A Developmental Approach to Group Dynamics." In S. Worchel, W. Wood, and J. A. Simpson, eds., *Group Process and Productivity,* 181–202. London: Sage.

Wrong, D. H. 1983. *Power: Its Forms, Bases and Uses.* New York: Harper and Row Publishers.

Wrong, D. H. 1988. *Power: Its Forms, Bases and Uses.* 2nd ed. Chicago: University of Chicago Press.

Wyden, 1979. *The Bay of Pigs: The Untold Story.* New York: Simon and Schuster.

Yaniv, A. 1987. *Dilemmas of Security: Politics, Strategy and the Israeli Experience in Lebanon.* New York: Oxford University Press.

Yinon, Y., and A. Bizman. 1974. "The Nature of Affective Bonds and the Degree of Personal Responsibility As Determinants of Risk Taking For 'Self and Others.'" *Bulletin of the Psychonomic Society* 4(2a): 80–82.

Young, O. 1989. *International Cooperation: Building Regimes For the Environment and Natural Resources.* Ithaca: Cornell University Press.

Yukl, G., and C. Falbe. 1990. "Influence Tactics and Objectives in Upward, Downward, and Lateral Influence Attempts." *Journal of Applied Psychology* 75(2): 132–40.

Yukl, G., and J. B. Tracey. 1992. "Consequences of Influence Tactics Used With Subordinates, Peers, and the Boss." *Journal of Applied Psychology* 77(4): 525–35.

Zajonc, R. B., R. J. Wolosin, and M. A. Wolosin. 1972. "Group Risk-Taking Under Various Group Decision Schemes." *Journal of Experimental Social Psychology* 8:16–30.

Zaleska, M., and N. Kogan. 1971. "Level of Risk Selected By Individuals and Groups When Deciding For Self and For Others." *Sociometry* 34:198–213.

Zijlstra, J. 1992. *Per Slot van Rekening: Memoires.* Amsterdam, Antwerpen: Contact.

Ziller, R. 1977. "Group Dialectics: The Dynamics of Groups Over Time." *Human Development* 20:293–308.

Ziller, R. C., W. F. Stone, R. M. Jackson, and N. J. Terbovic. 1977. "Self–Other Orientations and Political Behavior." In M. G. Hermann, ed., *A Psychological Examination of Political Leaders.* New York: Free Press.

Zimmerman, W. 1973. "Issue Area and Foreign Policy Process: A Research Note in Search of A General Theory." *American Political Science Review* 67:1204–12.

Zuber, J., H. Crott, and J. Werner. 1992. "Choice Shift and Group Polarization: An Analysis of the Status of Arguments and Social Decision Schemes." *Journal of Personality and Social Psychology* 62(1): 50–61.

Archival and Interview Sources

Chapter 4. Metselaar and Verbeek

Cals Papers, Public and Private Papers of Jo Cals, KVP-Documentatiecentrum, Nijmegen.

De Quay, J. *De Quay Papers.* Public and Private Papers of J. De Quay, Including His Diaries. Algemeen Rijksarchief at 's Hertogenbosch.

Gase, R. 1986. Interview With Dr. J. Zijlstra, *Vrij Nederland,* January 4, 1986.

Romme Papers. Public and Private Papers of Professor Carl Romme, Algemeen Rijksarchief at the Hague.

Van Roijen Papers. Public and Private Papers of J. W. Van Roijen, Algemeen Rijksarchief at the Hague.

Chapter 7. Preston

The Ambassador in Korea (Muccio) to the Secretary of State, June 25, 1950, *Foreign Relations of the United States* (FRUS), 7:125–26.

G. Bernard Noble Memorandum to George M. Elsey, June 29, 1951, "Acheson's Phone Call to the President, June 24, 1950"; in "Korea—June 24, 1950" Folder, Box 71, Papers of George M. Elsey, Truman Library.

Not Titled, June 25, 1950, Korea—June 25, 1950 Folder, Box 71, Papers of George M. Elsey, Truman Library.

Acheson's Phone Call to the President, June 25, 1950, Korea—June 25, 1950 Folder, Box 71, Papers of George M. Elsey, Truman Library.

Harry S. Truman to George M. Elsey, June 27, 1950, Korea—June 25, 1950 Folder, Box 71, Papers of George M. Elsey, Truman Library.

James E. Webb to John W. Snyder, April 25, 1975, General Correspondence File, 1973–75, Folder 2, Box 456, Papers of James E. Webb, Truman Library.

Memorandum of Conversation, June 25, 1950, "Memoranda of Conversation, May–June 1950, Acheson" Folder, Box 65, Papers of Dean Acheson, Truman Library.

Memorandum On Formosa, By General of the Army Douglas MacArthur, Commander in Chief, Far East, and Supreme Commander, Allied Powers, Japan, June 14, 1950, FRUS, 1950, 7:161–65.

"Johnson Gives Inside Story of Decision to Fight in Korea," *Washington Post,* June 15, 1951, P.2, "Korea—June 25, 1950" Folder, Box 71, Papers of George M. Elsey, Truman Library.

Albert L. Warner, "How the Korean Decision Was Made," *Harper's,* June, 1951, 102, "Korea—June 24, 1950" Folder, Box 71, Papers of George M. Elsey, Truman Library.

"Acheson, Not Joint Chiefs, Urged War, Johnson Asserts," *The New York Times,* June 15, 1951, 4, "Korea—June 25, 1950" Folder, Box 71, Papers of George M. Elsey, Truman Library.

The Ambassador in the Soviet Union (Kirk) to the Secretary of State, June 26, 1950, FRUS, 1950, 7:169–70.

The Secretary of State to the Embassy in the Soviet Union, June 26, 1950, FRUS, 1950, 7:176–77.

"Events of Monday Morning, June 26, 1950"; "Korea—June 26, 1950" Folder, Box 71, Papers of George M. Elsey, Truman Library.

Harry S. Truman to George M. Elsey, June 27, 1950, "Blair House Meeting, June 26, 1950" In "Korea—June 26, 1950" Folder, Box 71, Papers of George M. Elsey, Truman Library.

The Ambassador in Korea (Muccio) to the Secretary of State, June 27, 1950, FRUS, 1950, 7:176.

The Ambassador in Korea (Muccio) to the Secretary of State, June 27, 1950, FRUS, 1950, 7:173.

Memoranda of Conversation, By the Ambassador at Large (Jessup), June 26, 1950, Frus, 1950, 7:178–83.

"President's Phone Call to Harriman," June 27, 1950; "Korea—June 27, 1950" Folder; Box 71; Papers of George M. Elsey, Truman Library.

"Persons Present at the President's Meeting at 11:30 A.M., Tuesday, June 27, in the Cabinet Room," "July 27th, 1950—Congressional Leaders Meeting" Folder, Box 71, Papers of George M. Elsey, Truman Library.

Untitled, "July 27, 1950, Congressional Leaders Meeting" Folder, Box 71, Papers of George M. Elsey, Truman Library.

"Meeting of the NSC in the Cabinet Room at the White House," June 28, 1950; "Korea—June 28, 1950" Folder; Box 71; Papers of George M. Elsey, Truman Library.

"Memorandum For the President," June 29, 1950, "Memo's For President (1950)" Folder; Box 220; NSC Meetings File; President's Secretary's Files; Papers of Harry S. Truman, Truman Library.

"Meeting of the NSC in the Cabinet Room at the White House," June 28, 1950; "Korea—June 28, 1950" Folder; Box 71; Papers of George M. Elsey, Truman Library.

"Phone Call From Secretary Johnson," June 29, 1950; "Korea—June 29, 1950" Folder; Box 71; Papers of George M. Elsey, Truman Library.

"Minutes of the 59th Meeting of the National Security Council Held On Thursday, June 29, 1950 in the Conference Room at the White House," June 29, 1950.

"NSC Meeting No. 5" Folder; Box 208; National Security Council Meetings File; President's Secretary's Files; Papers of Harry S. Truman, Truman Library.

"Draft, June 29, 1950"; "Korea—June 29, 1950—W.H.-State-Defense Mtg., 5pm." Folder; Subject File; Box 71; Papers of George M. Elsey, Truman Library.

"Memorandum For the President," June 30, 1950; "Memo's For President (1950)" Folder; Box 220; NSC Meetings File; President's Secretary's Files; Papers of Harry S. Truman, Truman Library.

The Commander in Chief, Far East (MacArthur) to the Secretary of State, June 30, 1950, FRUS, 1950, 7:248–50.

"Call From Frank Pace," June 30, 1950; "Korea—June 30, 1950" Folder; Box 71; Subject File; Papers of George M. Elsey, Truman Library.

"9:30 A.M. Meeting With the President," June 30, 1950; "Korea—June 30, 1950" Folder; Box 71; Subject File; Papers of George M. Elsey, Truman Library.

"President's Call to Pace and Call From Louis Johnson," June 30, 1950; "Korea—June 30, 1950" Folder; Box 71; Subject File; Papers of George M. Elsey, Truman Library.

"Untitled," June 30, 1950; "Korea—June 30, 1950—Congressional Leaders Meeting, 11 A.M." Folder; Box 71; Subject File; Papers of George M. Elsey, Truman Library.

"Future United States Policy With Respect to North Korea," July 17, 1950; President's Secretary's Files: National Security Council Meetings; Box 208; Papers of Harry S. Truman, Truman Library.

Harry S. Truman to Alben N. Barkley, July 19, 1950; President's Secretary's File; General File; Box 113; Papers of Harry S. Truman, Truman Library.

Draft Memorandum Prepared By the Policy Planning Staff, July 22, 1950, FRUS, 1950, 7:449–54.

Memorandum By the Director of the Office of Northeast Asian Affairs (Allison) to the Director of the Policy Planning Staff (Nitze), July 24, 1950, FRUS, 1950, 7:458–61.

Memorandum By Mr. Walter McConaughy to the Ambassador at Large (Jessup), August 24, 1950, FRUS, 1950, 7:641–43.

Memorandum of Conversation, By Mr. James W. Barco, Special Assistant to the Ambassador at Large (Jessup), August 25, 1950, FRUS, 1950, 7:646–48.

Memorandum By Mr. Walter McConaughy, of the Staff of the Ambassador at Large (Jessup), August 25, 1950, FRUS, 1950, 7:649–52.

Memorandum By the Executive Secretary of the National Security Council (Lay), September 1, 1950, FRUS, 1950, 7:685–93.

"Memorandum For the President," September 8, 1950; "Memos For President (1950)" Folder; National Security Council Meetings File; Box 220; President's Secretary's Files; Papers of Harry S. Truman, Truman Library.

"NSC Meeting" September 7, 1950; "Memos For President (1950)" Folder; NSC Meetings File; Box 220; President's Secretary's Files; Papers of Harry S. Truman, Truman Library.

"Minutes of the 67th Meeting of the National Security Council Held On Thursday, September 7, 1950 in the Conference Room of the White House," September 7, 1950.

"NSC Meeting, No. 67, September 7, 1950" Folder; National Security Council Meetings File; Box 209; President's Secretary's Files; Papers of Harry S. Truman, Truman Library.

"Memorandum For the President," September 11, 1950; "NSC Meeting No. 67, September 7, 1950" Folder; National Security Council Meetings File; Box 209; President's Secretary's Files; Papers of Harry S. Truman, Truman Library.

George C. Marshall to Harry S. Truman, September 27, 1950; "Korea—Marshall, G. C." Folder; Korean War File; Box 243; President's Secretary's Files; Papers of Harry S. Truman, Truman Library.

Chapter 8. Hoyt and Garrison

Beckel, R. 1981. Miller Center Interviews. Carter Presidency Project, November 13, 1981. Jimmy Carter Presidential Library (cited as JCPL). 1:1–78.

Brzezinski, Z., M. Albright, L. Denend, and W. Odom. 1982. Miller Center Institute. Carter Presidency Project, XV, Feb. 18, 1982. JCPL. 1:1–91.

Carter, J. 1980. "September 25 News Conference" Public Papers of the Presidents: Jimmy Carter, 1753–58. Washington, DC: U.S. Government Printing Office.

Jordan, H. 1977. "Projecting An Image" Memoranda. "President Carter, 96/77–12/27/77" Box 39, Powells Files. JCPL. (Memo Was Unnamed But Looked Like Jordan's Style).

Pastor, Robert. 1979. Memo, From Pastor to Zbigniew Brzezinski. September 21, 1979. "Executive Co-38 7/1/79–1/20/81" White House Central File, Subject File, Box Co-21. JCPL.

Rafshoon, J. 1979. Memo From Rafshoon to the President. "Memos From Jerry Rafshoon June, July, August 1979" Box 28, Rafshoon Files. JCPL.
Interviews for Iran Case
George Ball, Princeton, NJ. May 27, 1993.
General Robert Huyser (Ret.), Washington DC. June 25, 1993.
Charles Naas, Washington DC. June 7, 1993.
David Newsom, Charlottesville, VA. June 8, 1993.
Henry Precht, Cleveland, OH. May 18, 1993.
Gary Sick, New York, NY. May 28, 1993.
William Sullivan, New York, NY. May 24, 1993.

Contributors

Ramon J. Aldag is professor of management at the Graduate School of Business Administration, University of Wisconsin, Madison. He has published widely in the field of management and organizational behavior.

Sally Riggs Fuller is assistant professor of management and organization at the University of Washington, Seattle. Her fields of study are group problem solving, the role of politics in organizational decision making, and organizational communication.

Jean A. Garrison is assistant professor at the College of General Studies, Division of Social Sciences at Boston University. Her research is on foreign policy decision making, small group decision making, bureaucratic politics, and the presidency.

Alexander L. George held the Graham H. Stuart Professorship in Political Science at Stanford University, and is a renowned expert on foreign and security policy, presidential decision making, and political psychology.

Paul 't Hart is associate professor of public administration at Leiden University, The Netherlands. His publications are on crisis management, social-psychological dimensions of public policy-making, administrative theory, and policy evaluation.

Paul D. Hoyt is assistant professor of political science at West Virginia University. His research focuses on foreign policy decision making and Middle Eastern politics.

Max V. Metselaar is assistant professor at the department of military business sciences of the Royal Military Academy in Breda, The Netherlands. His research is on international crises, decision making, and information management.

Thomas Preston is assistant professor at the department of political science, Washington State University. His work in political psychology is on presidential leadership and decision making, group dynamics, and in security policy on nuclear proliferation.

Eric K. Stern is research associate at the department of political science at Stockholm University, Sweden. His published works cover small group behavior, crisis management, security policy, and presidential decision making.

Bengt Sundelius is docent at the department of government at Uppsala University, Sweden. His published work includes research on small states in world politics, security policy, and crisis management.

Bertjan Verbeek is associate professor of political science at the Free University of Amsterdam, The Netherlands. He is interested in international political economy, foreign policy decision making, and European politics.

Yaacov Y. I. Vertzberger is professor of international relations at the Hebrew University of Jerusalem. He has published widely on international conflict and security in Asia, foreign policy decision making, and comparative foreign policy.

Index

accountability, 301–2; individual *versus* group, 282

Acheson, Dean: in Korea intervention crisis, 224, 225–27, 231, 241–42; role in foreign policy decisions, 219; on Truman leadership style, 216

advisory groups: composition of, 328; conformity in, 165; dynamics of, 128; under Eisenhower, 203–4; interactional characteristics of, 208; interpretation of information by, 195; under Johnson, 203, 204; and leadership styles, 192–93; and newgroup syndrome, 186; presidential, 171–72; role in policy-making, 7, 49, 250–51; structural characteristics of, 205; tolerance for conflict within, 211; under Truman, 212–14, 224, 240–41

advocacy, multiple, 48, 133, 328–31

agenda-setting, 265; as manipulation, 261–62

anticipation, in subgroup activity, 24

arena, policy-making group as, 316

assembly effect, 72

authority patterns, types of, 202

avoidance, defensive, 58

"back channel" tactics, in international negotiation, 23

balanced critical deliberation, as pattern of interaction, 131–33

Ball, George: in Iranian revolution crisis, 254; in Vietnam escalation crisis, 22

Bank of Sweden, and 1992 monetary crisis, 3–4

Bay of Pigs crisis: case study of, 153–88; extragroup setting for, 171–73; as foreign policy fiasco, 10; and groupthink, 57, 61; "groupthink" analysis of, 42; history of, 169–70; intragroup setting for, 173–77; and leader power, 74; lessons of for Kennedy administration, 187; and newgroup syndrome, 169–85

Begin, Menachem, 284–85, 291, 296–97

belief systems, and group dynamics, 300–301

Bissell, Richard, 172, 176, 180

Bretton Woods system collapse, 13

Brezhnev, Leonid, and Czechoslovak crisis, 282–83

Brzezinski, Zbigniew: and Cuba/Soviet brigade crisis, 260, 262, 264; in Iranian revolution crisis, 254; manipulation by, 250, 267; as policy advocate, 251, 329, 330

Bundy, McGeorge, and Bay of Pigs crisis, 173, 175

bureaucratic politics, 128–29, 142; and group manipulation, 258; manipulation in, 145

Bush, George: group norms in administration of, 163; and Gulf War crisis, 147, 241

cabinet system: in British politics, 5, 16, 325–26; culture of, 135; in Netherlands, 108–9, 111, 328; politics of, 128–29, 142; study of, 335

cabinets: changes in, and newgroup syn-

377